CODE:BREAKER

Volume 2

Akimine Kamijyo

Translation and Adaptation by
William Flanagan

Lettered by
North Market Street Graphics

DEL REY

Ballantine Books • New York

Code:Breaker, volume 2 is a work of fiction. Names, characters, places, and incidents are the products of the author's imagination or are used fictitiously. Any resemblance to actual events, locales, or persons, living or dead, is entirely coincidental.

A Del Rey Manga/Kodansha Trade Paperback Original

Published in the United States by Del Rey, an imprint of The Random House Publishing Group, a division of Random House, Inc., New York.

Publication rights arranged through Kodansha Ltd.

First published in Japan in 2008 by Kodansha Ltd., Tokyo

ISBN 978-0-345-52228-3

Printed in the United States of America

www.delreymanga.com

9 8 7 6 5 4 3 2 1

Translator/Adapter: William Flanagan
Lettering: North Market Street Graphics

CONTENTS

Honorifics Explained

Throughout the Del Rey Manga books, you will find Japanese honorifics left intact in the translations. For those not familiar with how the Japanese use honorifics and, more important, how they differ from American honorifics, we present this brief overview.

Politeness has always been a critical facet of Japanese culture. Ever since the feudal era, when Japan was a highly stratified society, use of honorifics—which can be defined as polite speech that indicates relationship or status—has played an essential role in the Japanese language. When you address someone in Japanese, an honorific usually takes the form of a suffix attached to one's name (example: "Asuna-san"), is used as a title at the end of one's name, or appears in place of the name itself (example: "Negi-sensei," or simply "Sensei!").

Honorifics can be expressions of respect or endearment. In the context of manga and anime, honorifics give insight into the nature of the relationship between characters. Many English translations leave out these important honorifics and therefore distort the feel of the original Japanese. Because Japanese honorifics contain nuances that English honorifics lack, it is our policy at Del Rey not to translate them. Here, instead, is a guide to some of the honorifics you may encounter in Del Rey Manga.

-*san*: This is the most common honorific and is equivalent to Mr., Miss, Ms., or Mrs. It is the all-purpose honorific and can be used in any situation where politeness is required.

-*sama*: This is one level higher than "-san" and is used to confer great respect.

-*dono*: This comes from the word "tono," which means "lord." It is an even higher level than "-sama" and confers utmost respect.

-*kun*: This suffix is used at the end of boys' names to express familiarity or endearment. It is also sometimes used by men among friends, or when addressing someone younger or of a lower station.

-*chan*: This is used to express endearment, mostly toward girls. It is also used for little boys, pets, and even among lovers. It gives a sense of childish cuteness.

Bozu: This is an informal way to refer to a boy, similar to the English terms "kid" and "squirt."

Sempai/
Senpai: This title suggests that the addressee is one's senior in a group or organization. It is most often used in a school setting, where underclassmen refer to their upperclassmen as "sempai." It can also be used in the workplace, such as when a newer employee addresses an employee who has seniority in the company.

Kohai: This is the opposite of "sempai" and is used toward underclassmen in school or newcomers in the workplace. It connotes that the addressee is of a lower station.

Sensei: Literally meaning "one who has come before," this title is used for teachers, doctors, or masters of any profession or art.

-[blank]: This is usually forgotten in these lists, but it is perhaps the most significant difference between Japanese and English. The lack of honorific means that the speaker has permission to address the person in a very intimate way. Usually, only family, spouses, or very close friends have this kind of permission. Known as *yobisute*, it can be gratifying when someone who has earned the intimacy starts to call one by one's name without an honorific. But when that intimacy hasn't been earned, it can be very insulting.

CODE:BREAKER

上条明峰

AKIMINE KAMIJYO

02

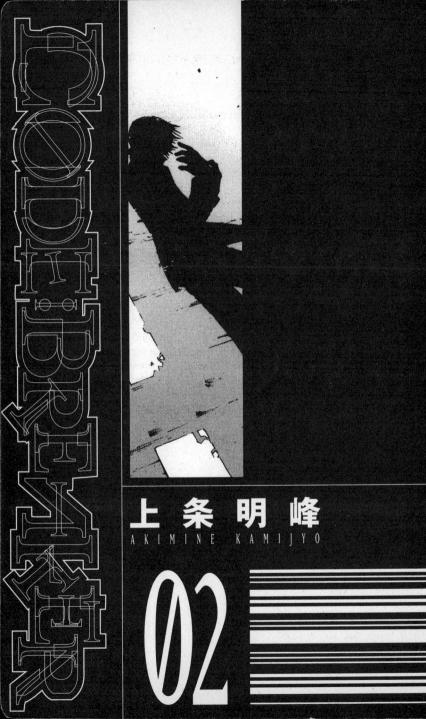

CHARACTERS ~ Introduction to the Characters Appearing in this Volume ~

CONNECT TO.....

>CØDE:BREAKER 02...

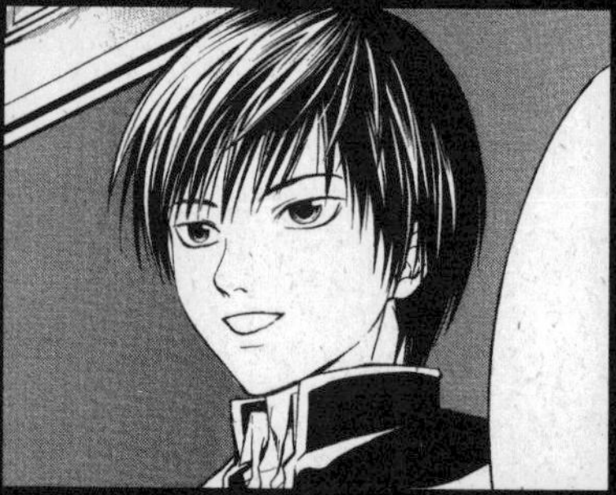

REI ÔGAMI

おおがみ れい
大神 零

A Cøde:Breaker who punishes the guilty who the law cannot touch. The blue flame that comes from his left hand burns evil criminals to ashes. His origins are completely shrouded in mystery. He calls Sakura, who he can't burn, a "Deviant Breed" and keeps a close eye on her.

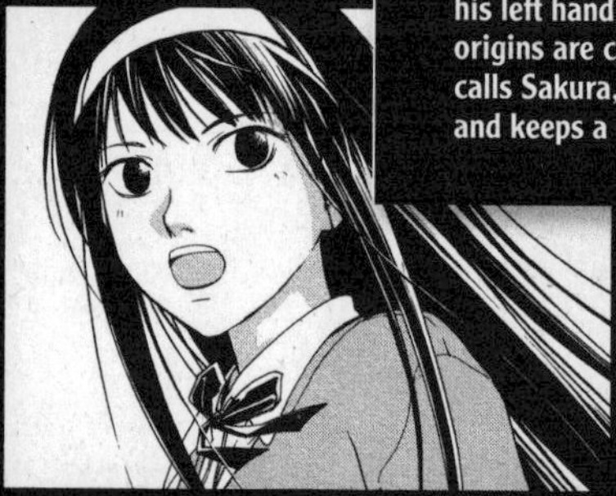

SAKURA SAKURAKOJI

さくらこうじ さくら
桜小路 桜

Although her outward appearance looks like that of a meek, fragile beauty, she is actually a high-school coed with a strong sense of justice. She also loves and possesses a high degree of skill in martial arts. She was living as a normal student until one night she witnessed Ôgami burning some gang members with his blue flame. At once her life changed, and now she often finds herself in mortal danger as she involves herself in Ôgami's missions.

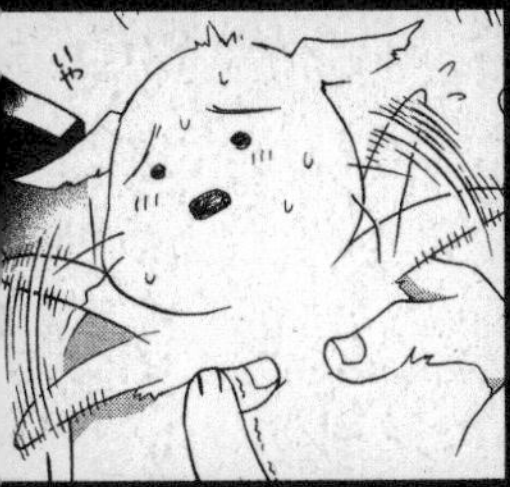

PUPPY

『子犬』

The child of Dog that Sakura is now keeping as a pet. It was named by Sakura, and despite being Sakura's pet, it warmed up to Ôgami instead. It may be able to understand Ôgami better than anyone else.

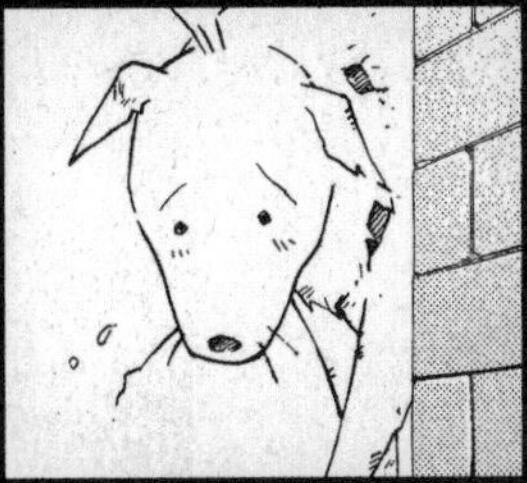

DOG

『犬』

An abandoned dog that Sakura had been feeding. At one time Dog was the pet of a homeless old man, but a gang of juvenile delinquents murdered Dog's former master. When Sakura confronted the gang, Dog tried to protect her and suffered mortal wounds. Dog's life eventually ended at Ôgami's hands.

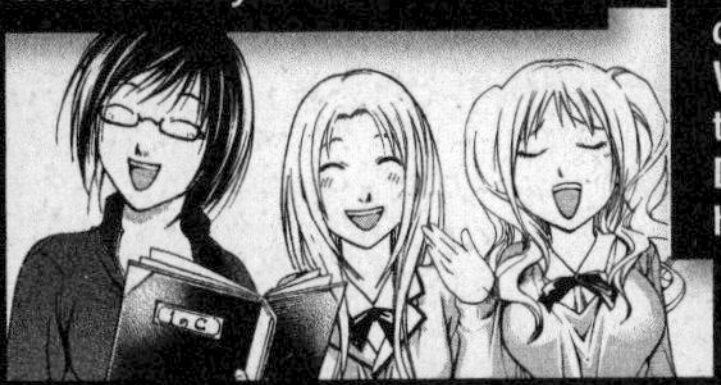

MS. KANDA and the CLASSMATES

Homeroom teacher, Ms. Kanda, and Sakura's classmates.

STORY ~

Sakura Sakurakoji is living life as a normal high-school girl when one night she witnesses a mysterious young man setting fire to a gang of criminals, burning them with a blue flame. The next day, the same boy is introduced to Sakura's class as Rei Ôgami, a new student transferring in. But in private, he admits to Sakura that he is something called a "Code:Breaker," one who punishes criminals who the law cannot touch. Since he can allow no witnesses to live, he tries to burn Sakura as well, but he finds he cannot. Ôgami starts calling Sakura a "Deviant Breed" and keeps a close watch over her. One day, Sakura follows Ôgami into an office used by the Yakuza. Ôgami, ignoring Sakura's protests, burns one criminal after the next to ashes, then he turns his flames on the police that came due

CODE:BREAKER_02_ CONTENTS

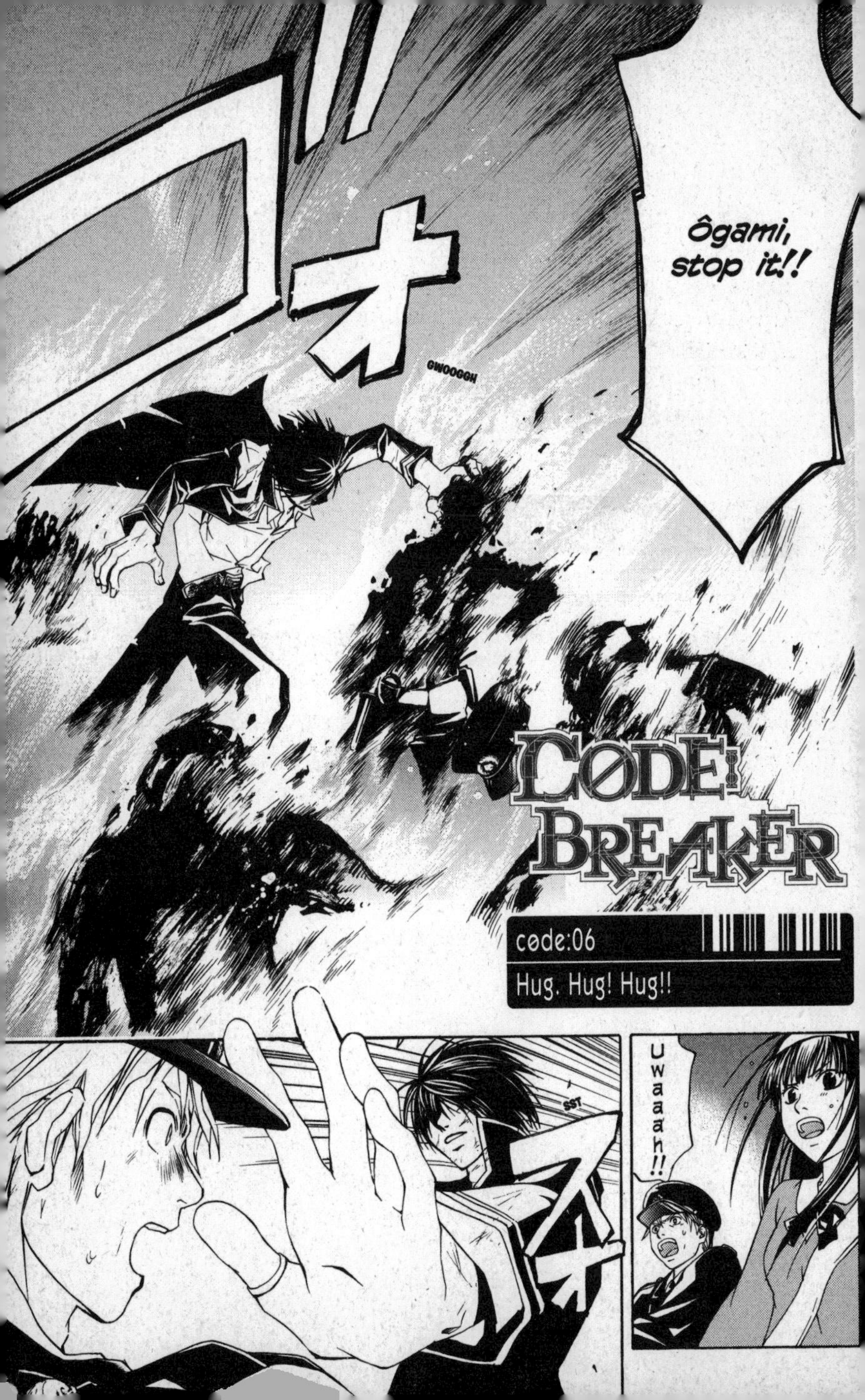
ôgami, stop it!!
GWOOGGH
CODE:BREAKER
code:06
Hug. Hug! Hug!!
Uwaaah!!
SST

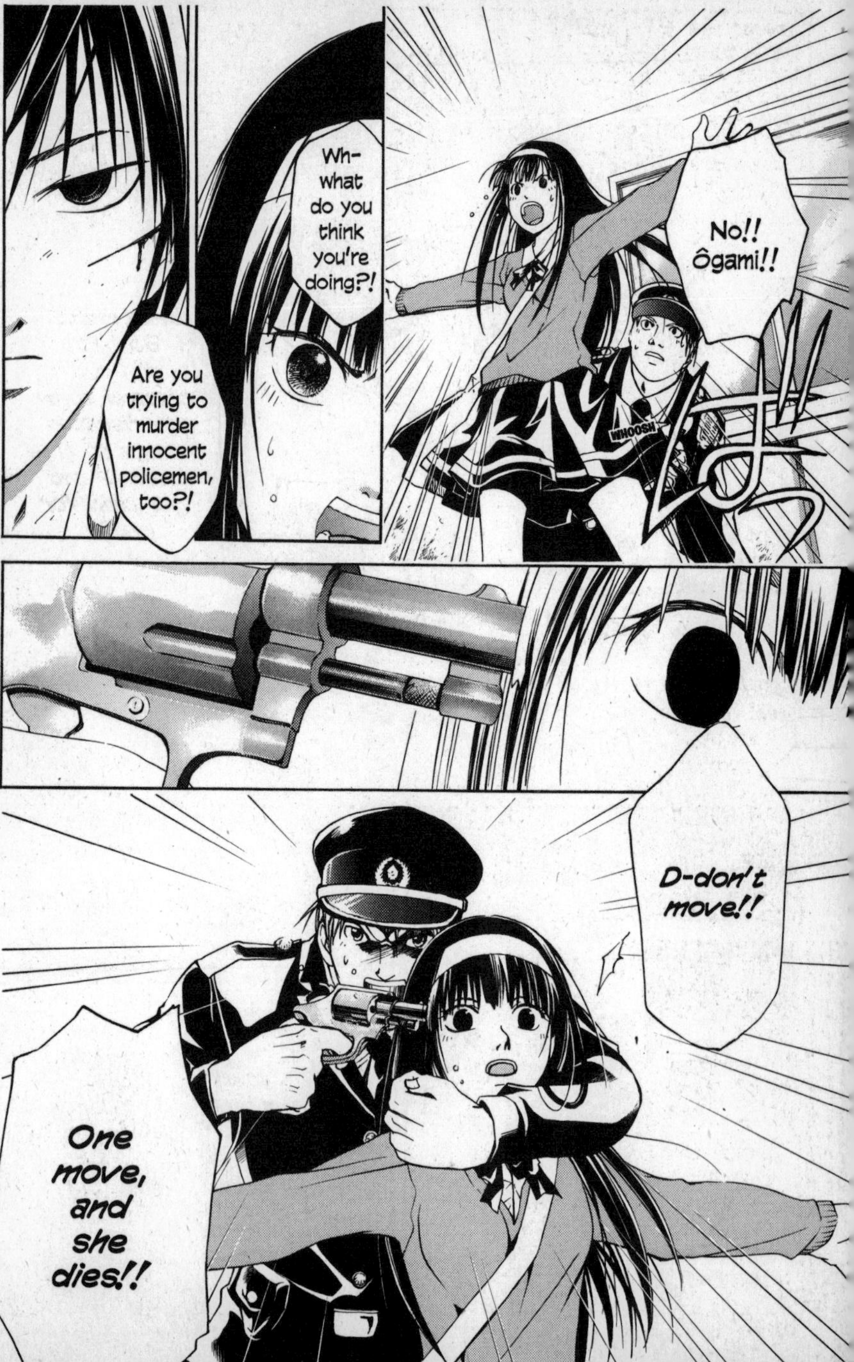
No!! Ôgami!!
WHOOSH
Wh- what do you think you're doing?!
Are you trying to murder innocent policemen, too?!
D-don't move!!
One move, and she dies!!

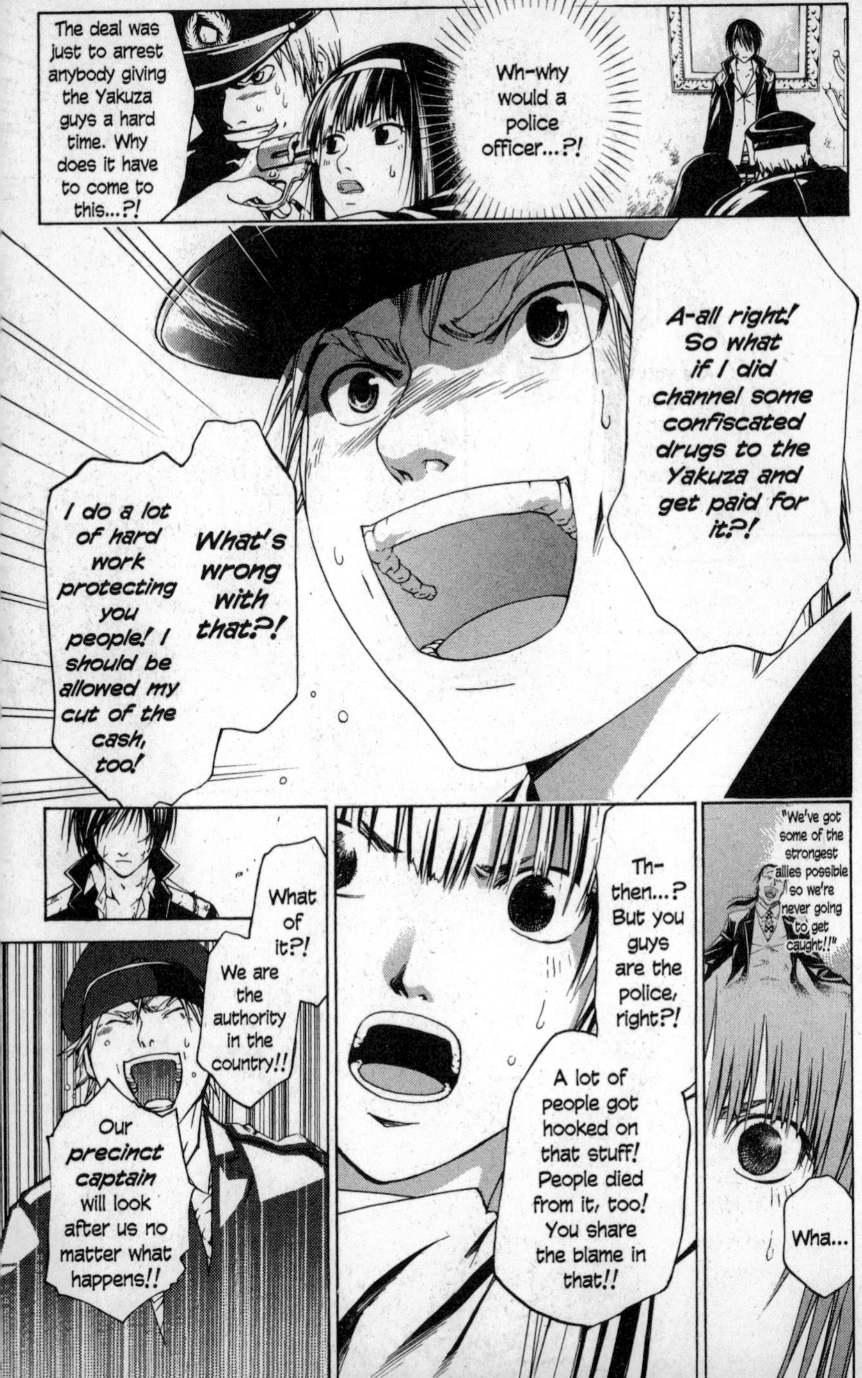
Wh-why would a police officer...?!
The deal was just to arrest anybody giving the Yakuza guys a hard time. Why does it have to come to this...?!
A-all right! So what if I did channel some confiscated drugs to the Yakuza and get paid for it?!
What's wrong with that?!
I do a lot of hard work protecting you people! I should be allowed my cut of the cash, too!
"We've got some of the strongest allies possible so we're never going to get caught!!"
Wha...
Th-then...? But you guys are the police, right?!
A lot of people got hooked on that stuff! People died from it, too! You share the blame in that!!
What of it?! We are the authority in the country!!
Our precinct captain will look after us no matter what happens!!

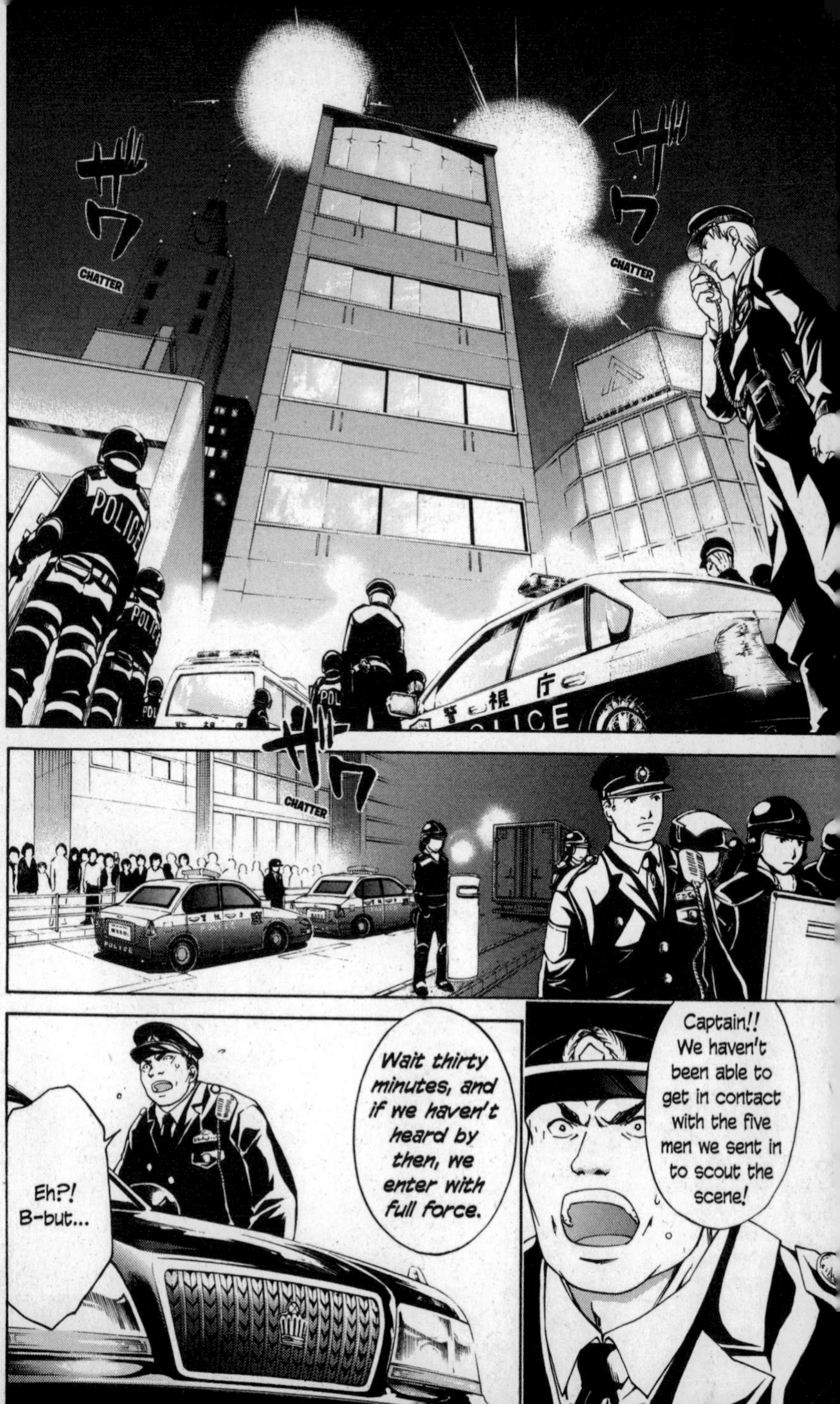
ザワ
CHATTER
ザワ
CHATTER
警視庁
POLICE
ザワ
CHATTER
Captain!! We haven't been able to get in contact with the five men we sent in to scout the scene!
Wait thirty minutes, and if we haven't heard by then, we enter with full force.
Eh?! B-but...

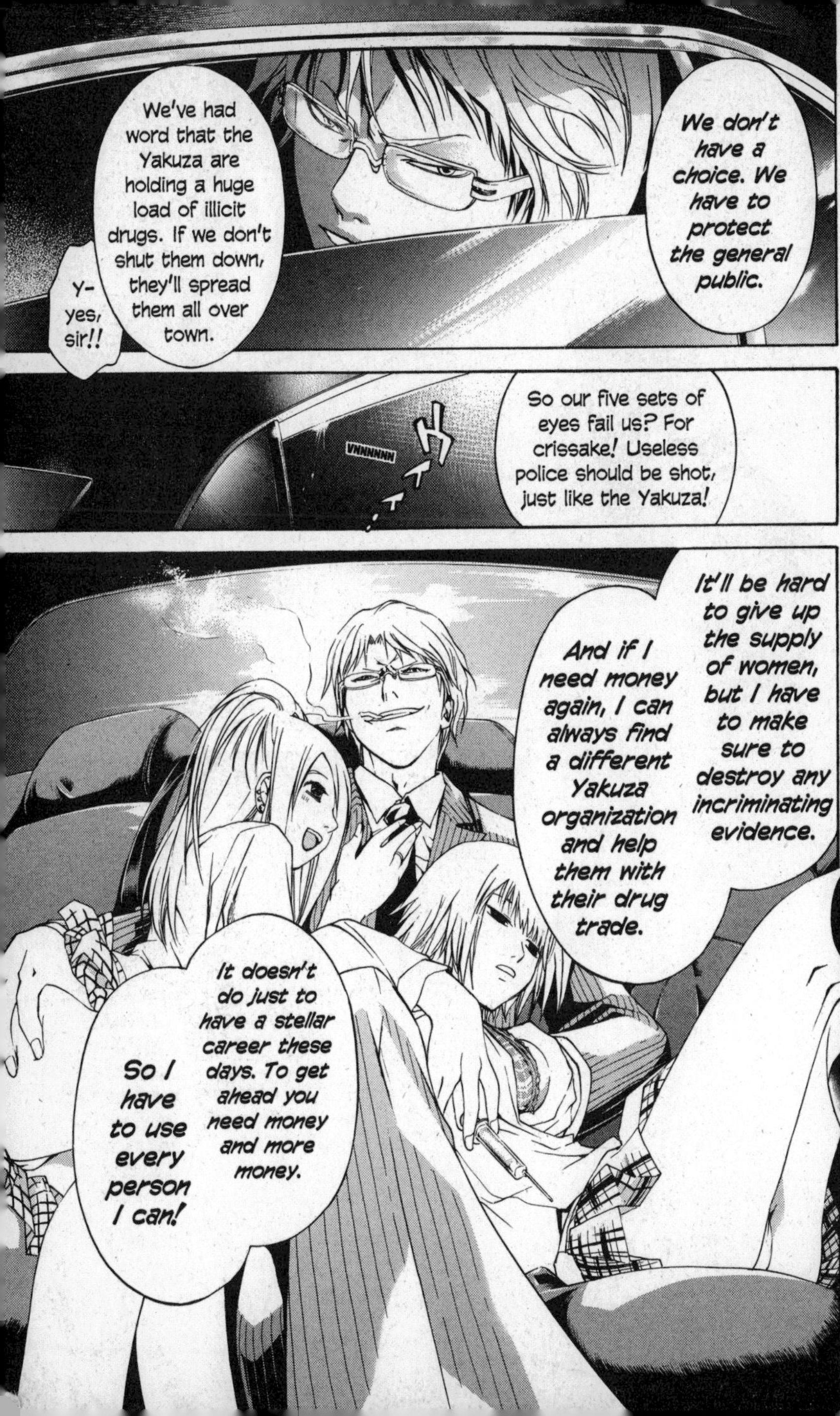
We don't have a choice. We have to protect the general public.
We've had word that the Yakuza are holding a huge load of illicit drugs. If we don't shut them down, they'll spread them all over town.
Y-yes, sir!!
VNNNNNN
So our five sets of eyes fail us? For crissake! Useless police should be shot, just like the Yakuza!
It'll be hard to give up the supply of women, but I have to make sure to destroy any incriminating evidence.
And if I need money again, I can always find a different Yakuza organization and help them with their drug trade.
It doesn't do just to have a stellar career these days. To get ahead you need money and more money.
So I have to use every person I can!

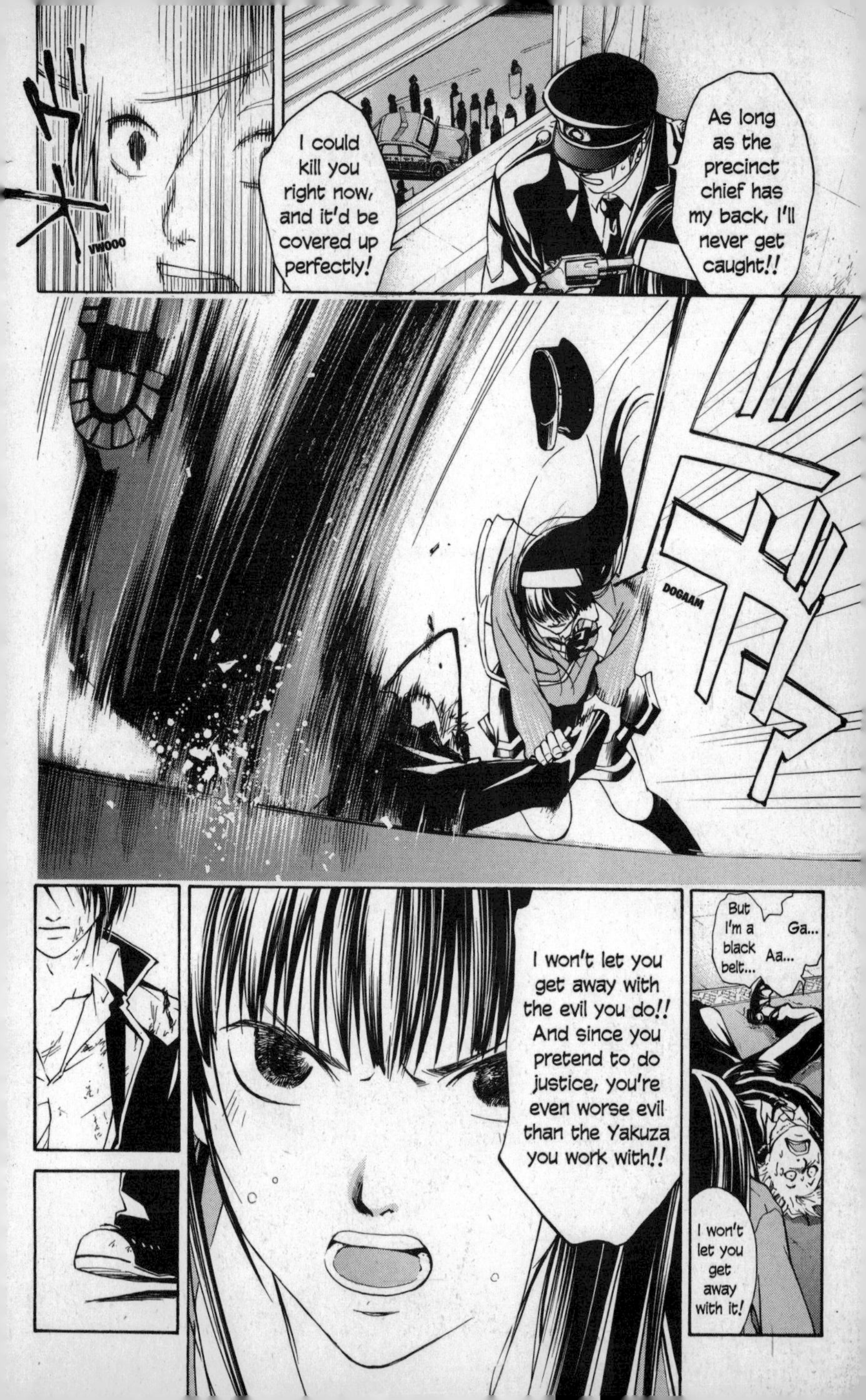
As long as the precinct chief has my back, I'll never get caught!!
I could kill you right now, and it'd be covered up perfectly!
VWOOO
DOGAAM
Ga...
Aa...
But I'm a black belt...
I won't let you get away with it!
I won't let you get away with the evil you do!! And since you pretend to do justice, you're even worse evil than the Yakuza you work with!!

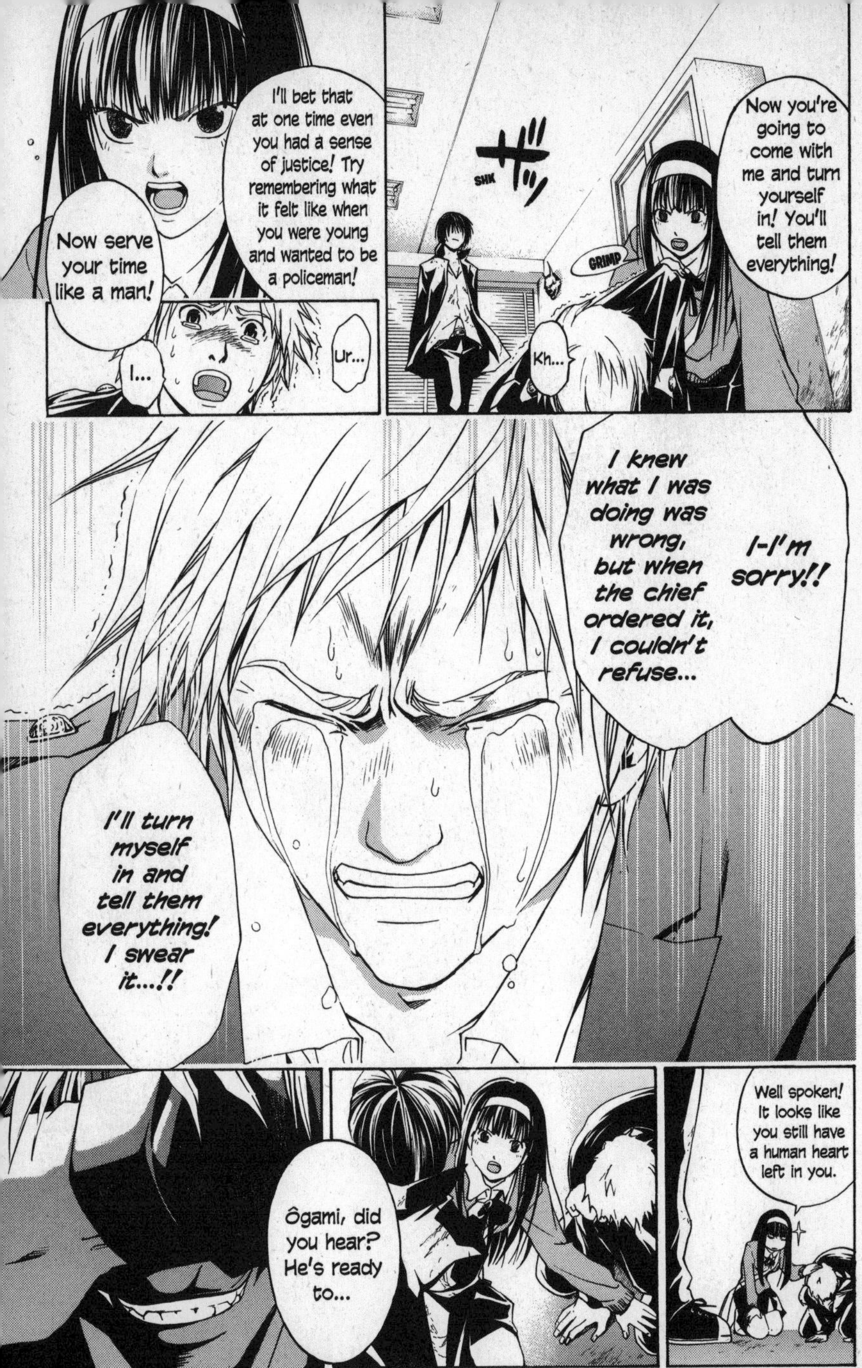
Now you're going to come with me and turn yourself in! You'll tell them everything!
ザッ
SHK
GRIMP
Kh...
I'll bet that at one time even you had a sense of justice! Try remembering what it felt like when you were young and wanted to be a policeman!
Now serve your time like a man!
Ur...
I...
I-I'm sorry!!
I knew what I was doing was wrong, but when the chief ordered it, I couldn't refuse...
I'll turn myself in and tell them everything! I swear it...!!
Well spoken! It looks like you still have a human heart left in you.
Ôgami, did you hear? He's ready to...

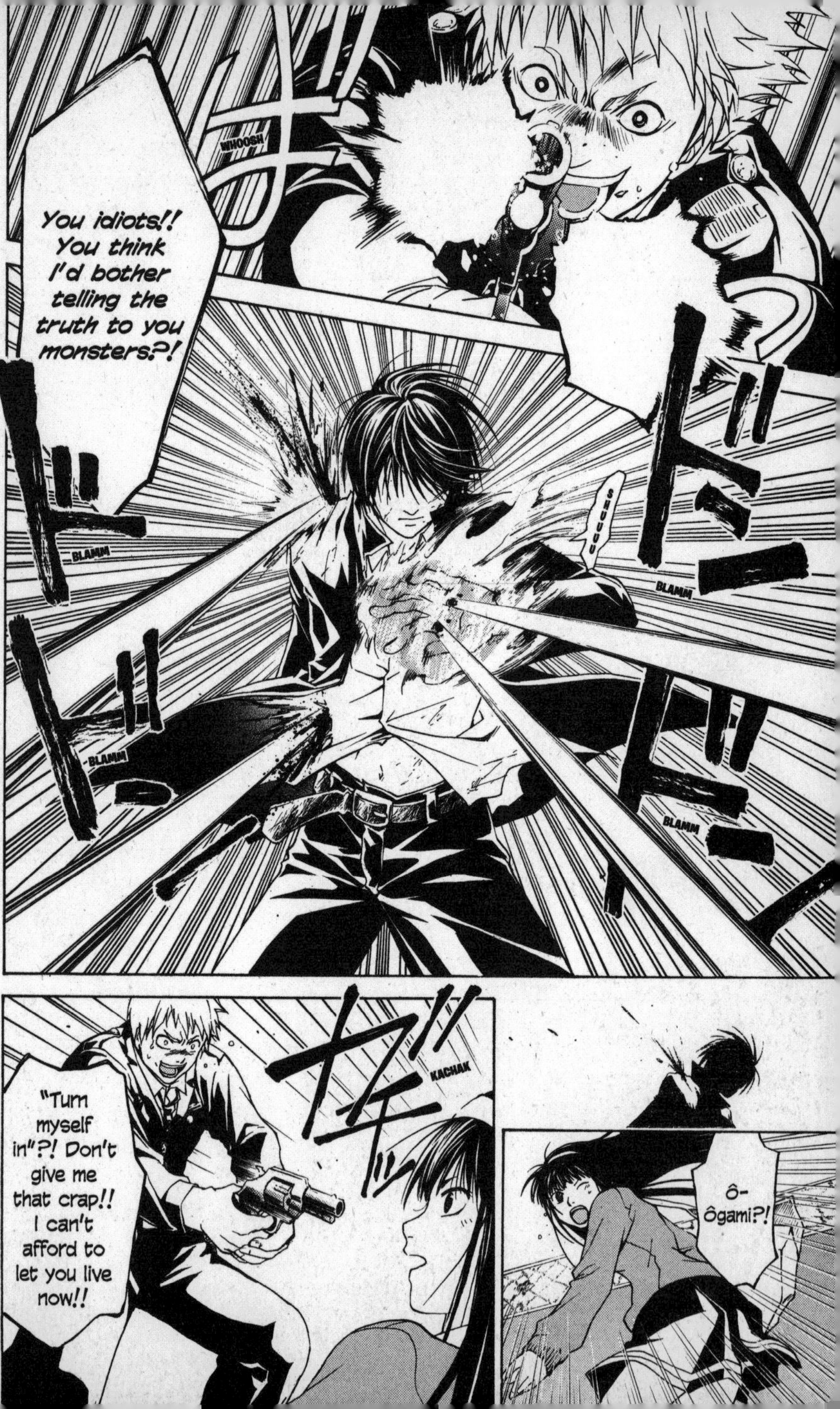
WHOOSH
You idiots!! You think I'd bother telling the truth to you monsters?!
SHUUUU
BLAMM
BLAMM
BLAMM
BLAMM
Ô-ôgami?!
KACHAK
"Turn myself in"?! Don't give me that crap!! I can't afford to let you live now!!

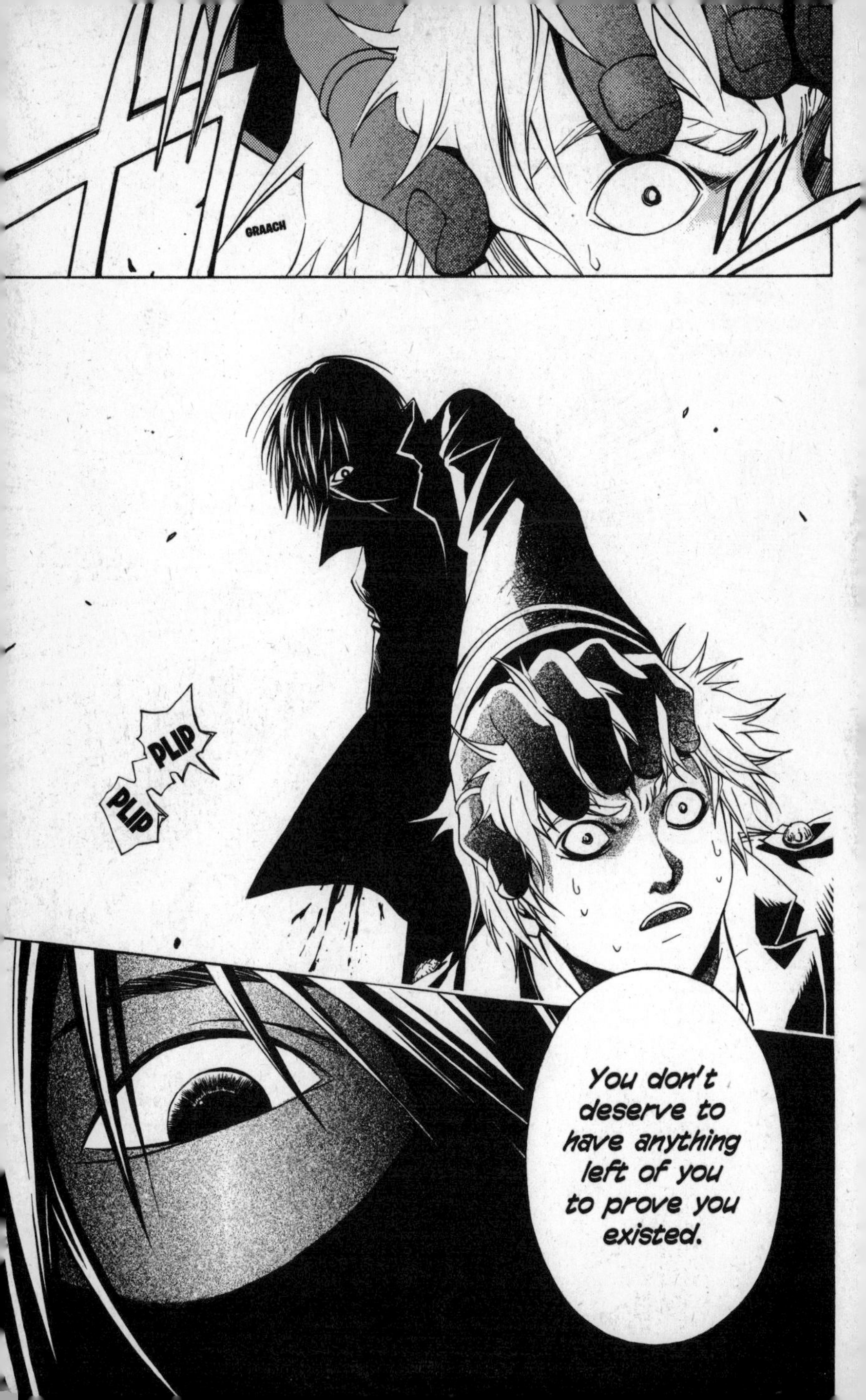
GRAACH
PLIP
PLIP
You don't deserve to have anything left of you to prove you existed.

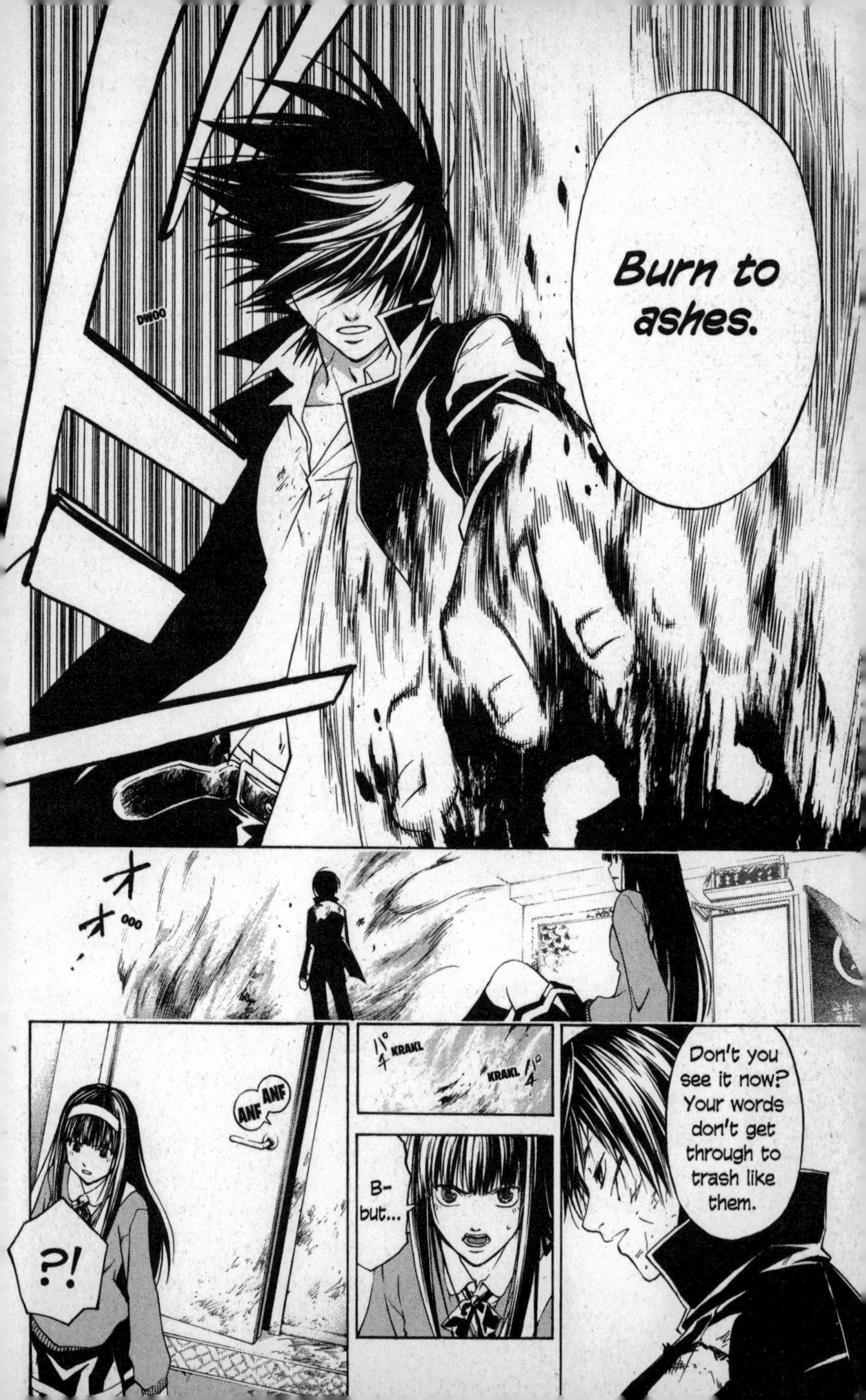
Burn to ashes.
DWOO
ooo
Don't you see it now? Your words don't get through to trash like them.
KRAKL
KRAKL
B- but...
ANF ANF
?!

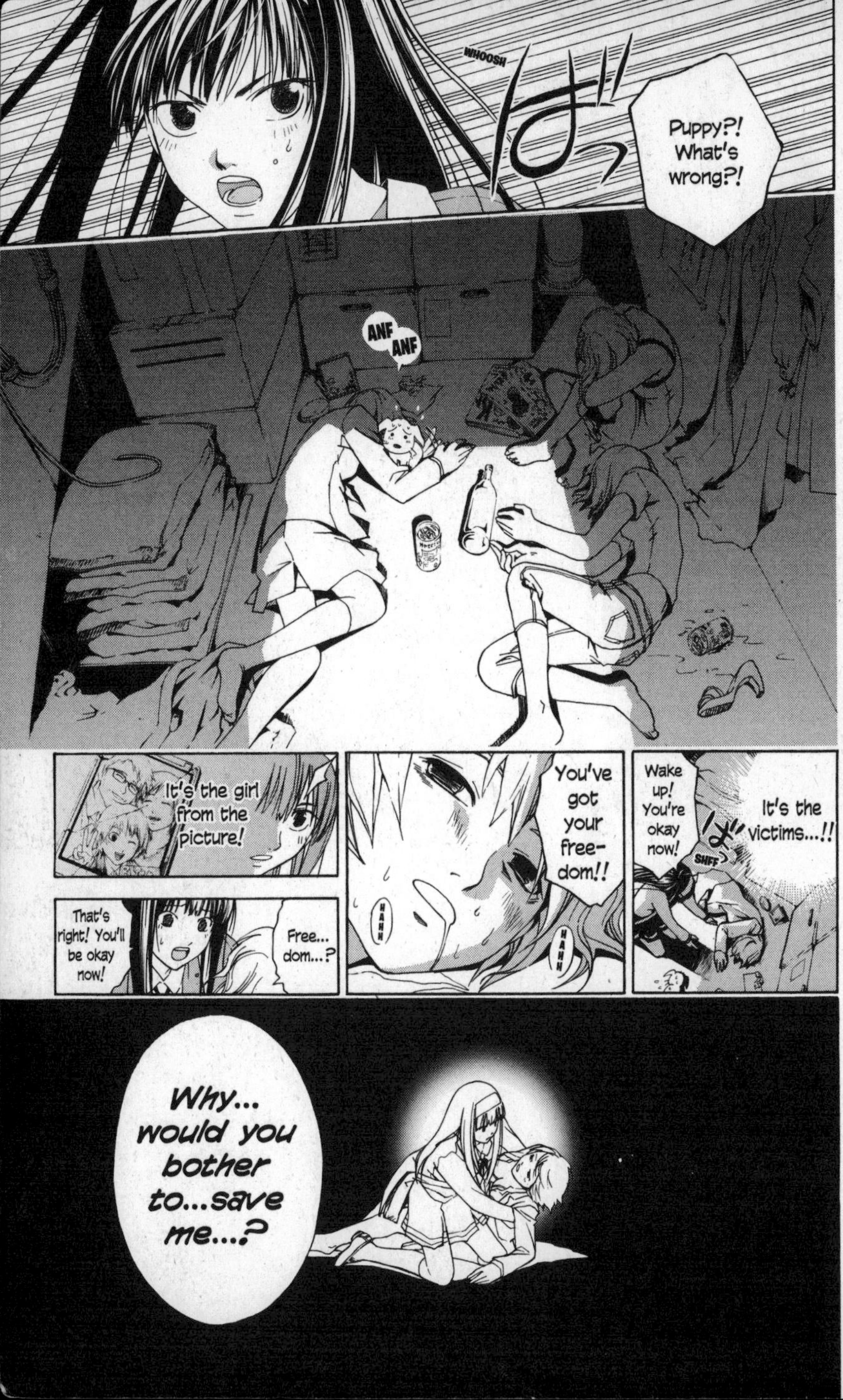
WHOOSH
Puppy?! What's wrong?!
ANF ANF
It's the victims...!!
Wake up! You're okay now!
SHFF
You've got your free-dom!!
HAHH
HAHH
It's the girl from the picture!
Free... dom...?
That's right! You'll be okay now!
Why... would you bother to...save me...?

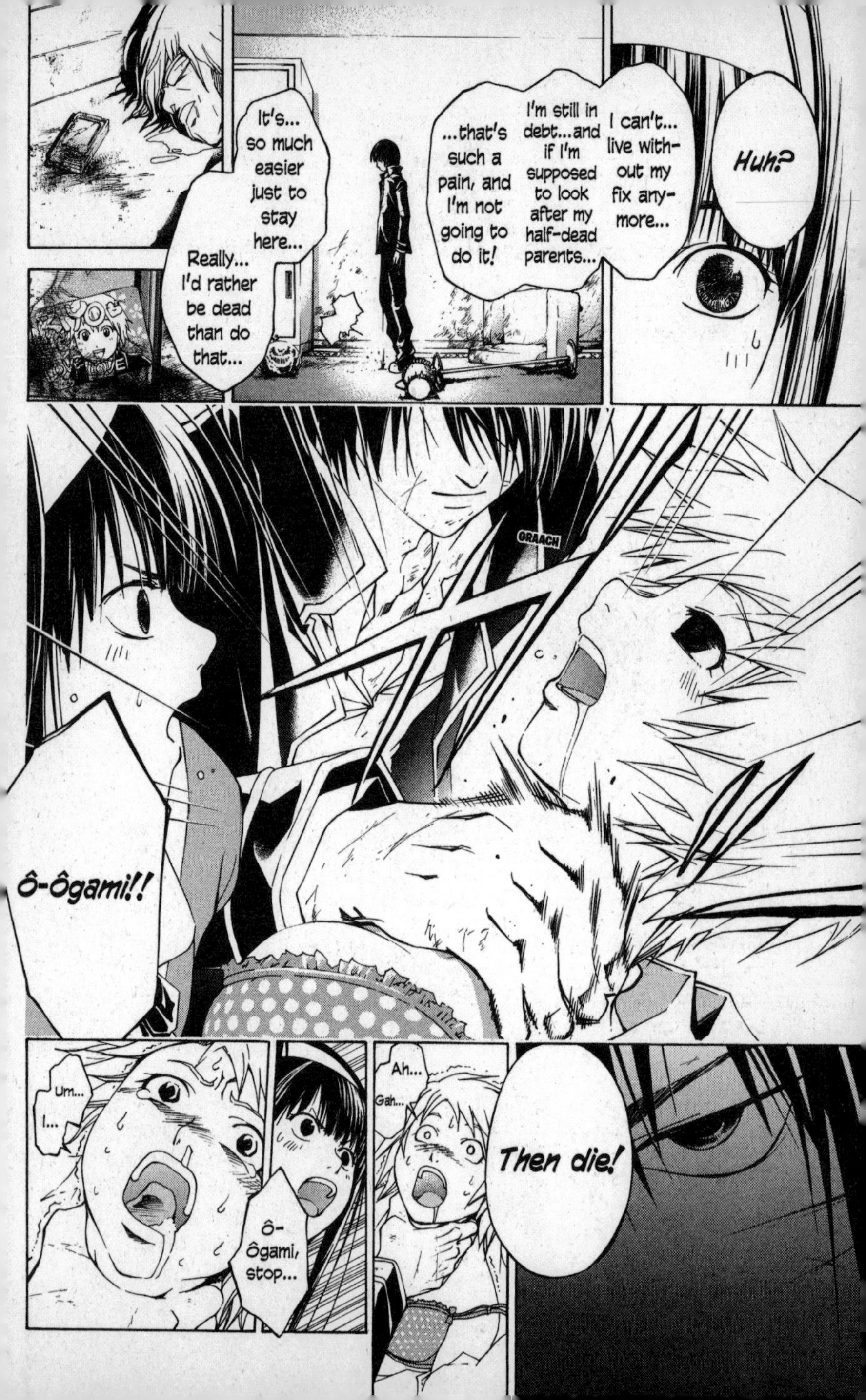
Huh?
I can't... live without my fix anymore...
I'm still in debt...and if I'm supposed to look after my half-dead parents...
...that's such a pain, and I'm not going to do it!
It's... so much easier just to stay here...
Really... I'd rather be dead than do that...
GRAACH
Ô-Ôgami!!
Then die!
Ah...
Gah...
Ô-Ôgami, stop...
Um... I...

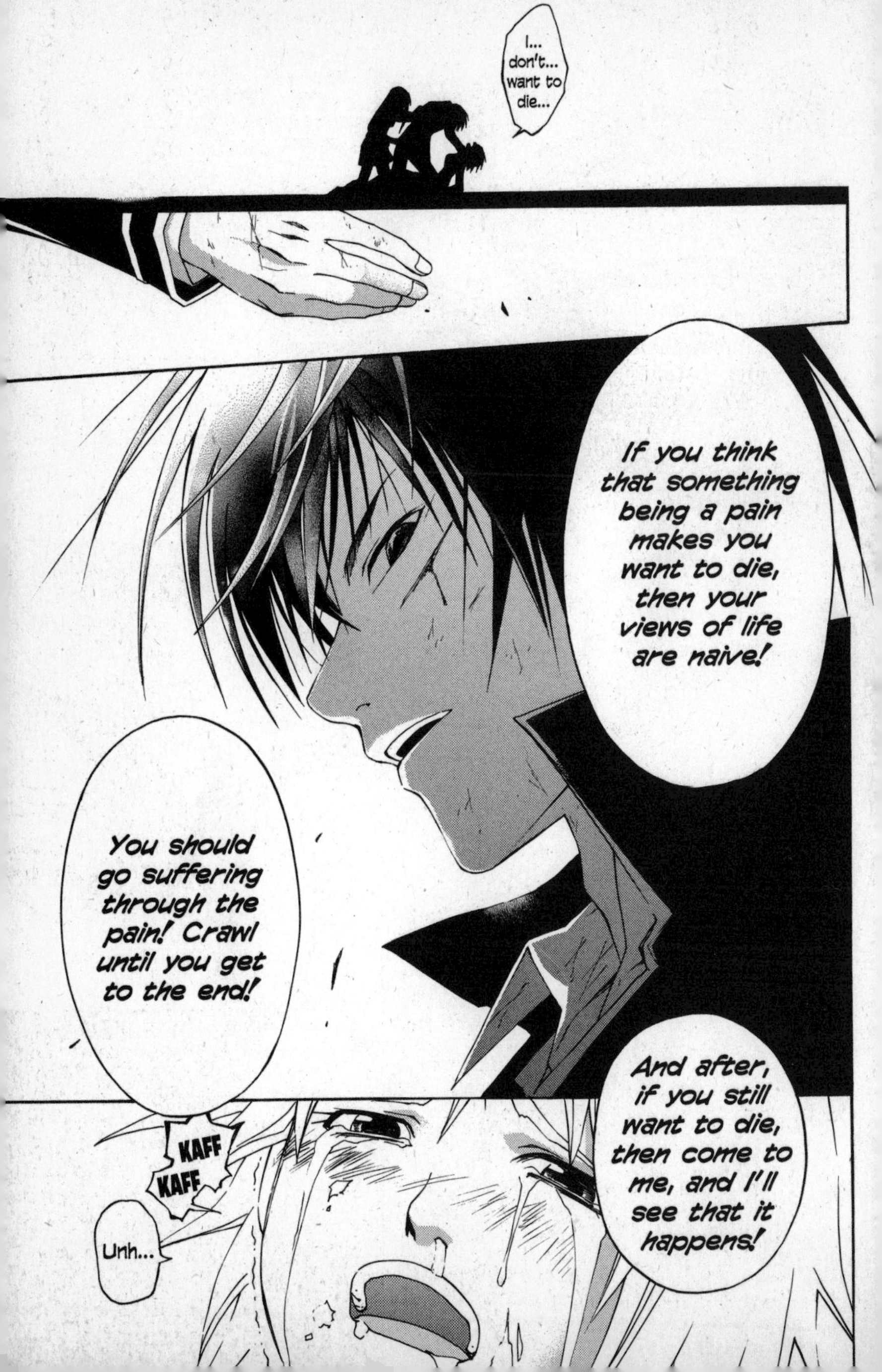
I... don't... want to die...
If you think that something being a pain makes you want to die, then your views of life are naive!
You should go suffering through the pain! Crawl until you get to the end!
And after, if you still want to die, then come to me, and I'll see that it happens!
KAFF KAFF
Unh...

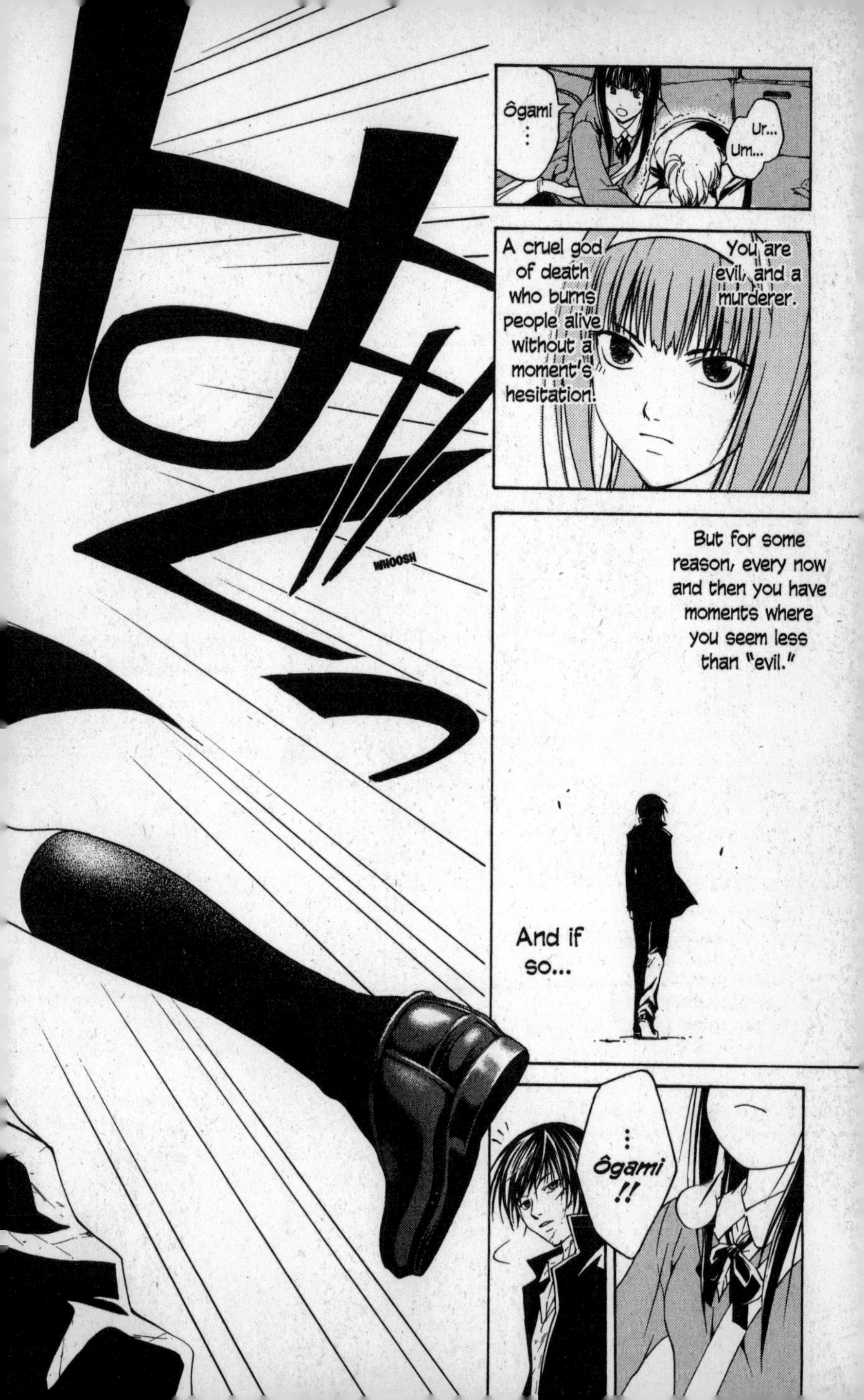
Ur... Um...
Ôgami...
You are evil, and a murderer.
A cruel god of death who burns people alive without a moment's hesitation.
But for some reason, every now and then you have moments where you seem less than "evil."
And if so...
...Ôgami!!
WHOOSH

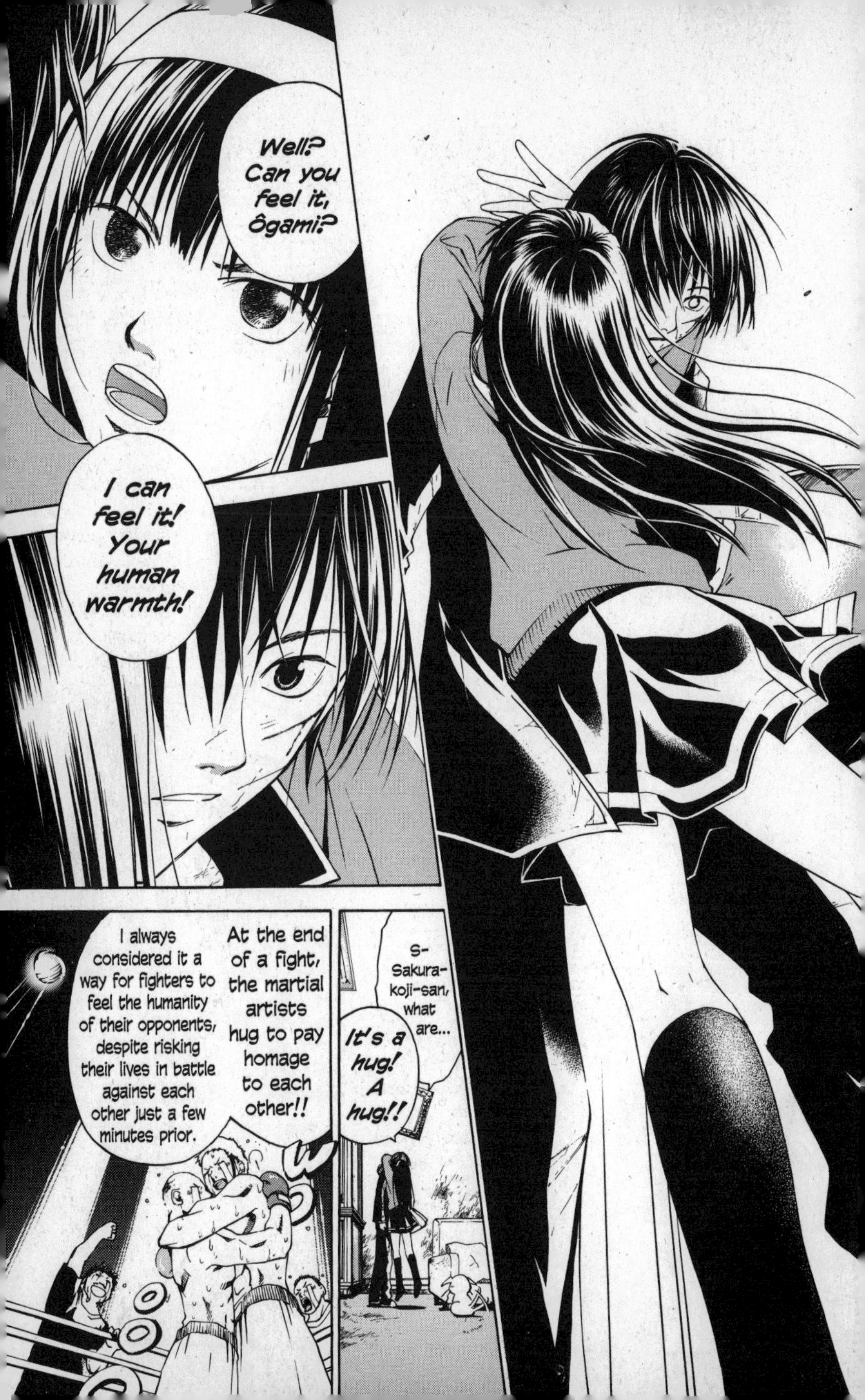
Well? Can you feel it, Ôgami?
I can feel it! Your human warmth!
S-Sakura-koji-san, what are...
It's a hug! A hug!!
At the end of a fight, the martial artists hug to pay homage to each other!!
I always considered it a way for fighters to feel the humanity of their opponents, despite risking their lives in battle against each other just a few minutes prior.

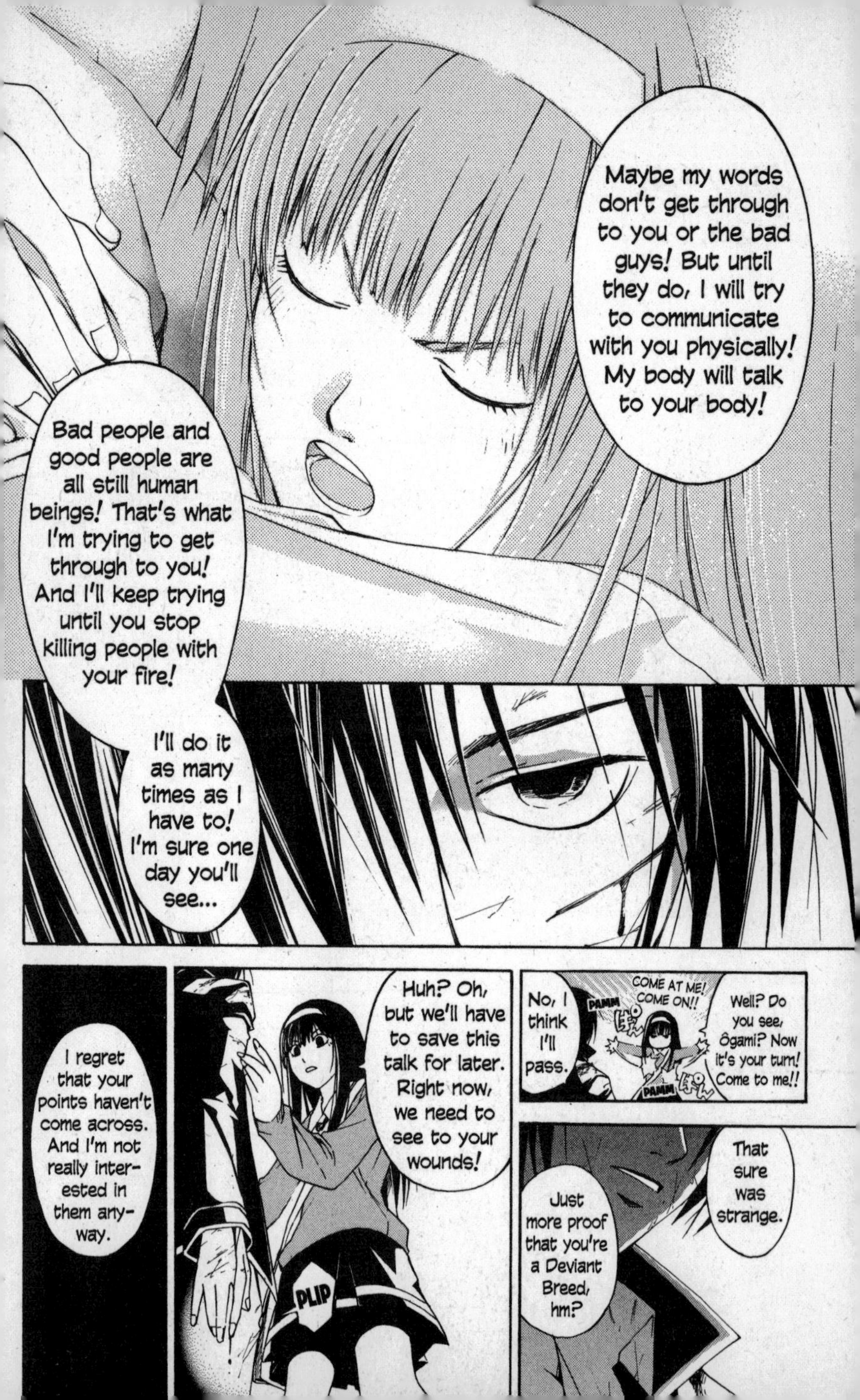
Maybe my words don't get through to you or the bad guys! But until they do, I will try to communicate with you physically! My body will talk to your body!
Bad people and good people are all still human beings! That's what I'm trying to get through to you! And I'll keep trying until you stop killing people with your fire!
I'll do it as many times as I have to! I'm sure one day you'll see...
Well? Do you see, Ôgami? Now it's your turn! Come to me!!
COME AT ME! COME ON!!
PAMM
PAMM
No, I think I'll pass.
That sure was strange.
Just more proof that you're a Deviant Breed, hm?
Huh? Oh, but we'll have to save this talk for later. Right now, we need to see to your wounds!
PLIP
I regret that your points haven't come across. And I'm not really interested in them anyway.

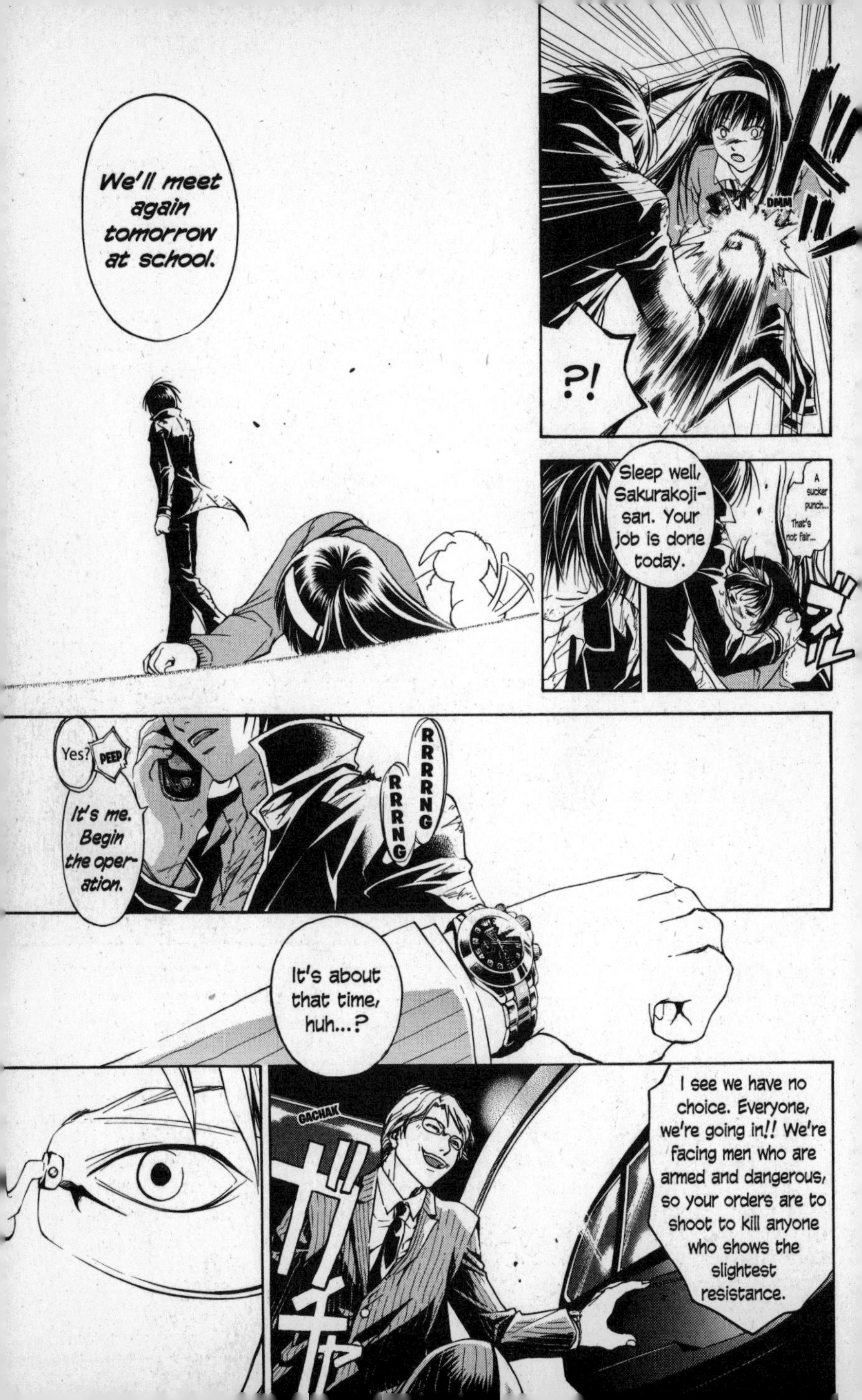
DMM
?!
Sleep well, Sakurakoji-san. Your job is done today.
A sucker punch... That's not fair...
We'll meet again tomorrow at school.
RRRRNG
RRRNG
Yes?
PEEP
It's me. Begin the operation.
It's about that time, huh...?
I see we have no choice. Everyone, we're going in!! We're facing men who are armed and dangerous, so your orders are to shoot to kill anyone who shows the slightest resistance.
GACHAK

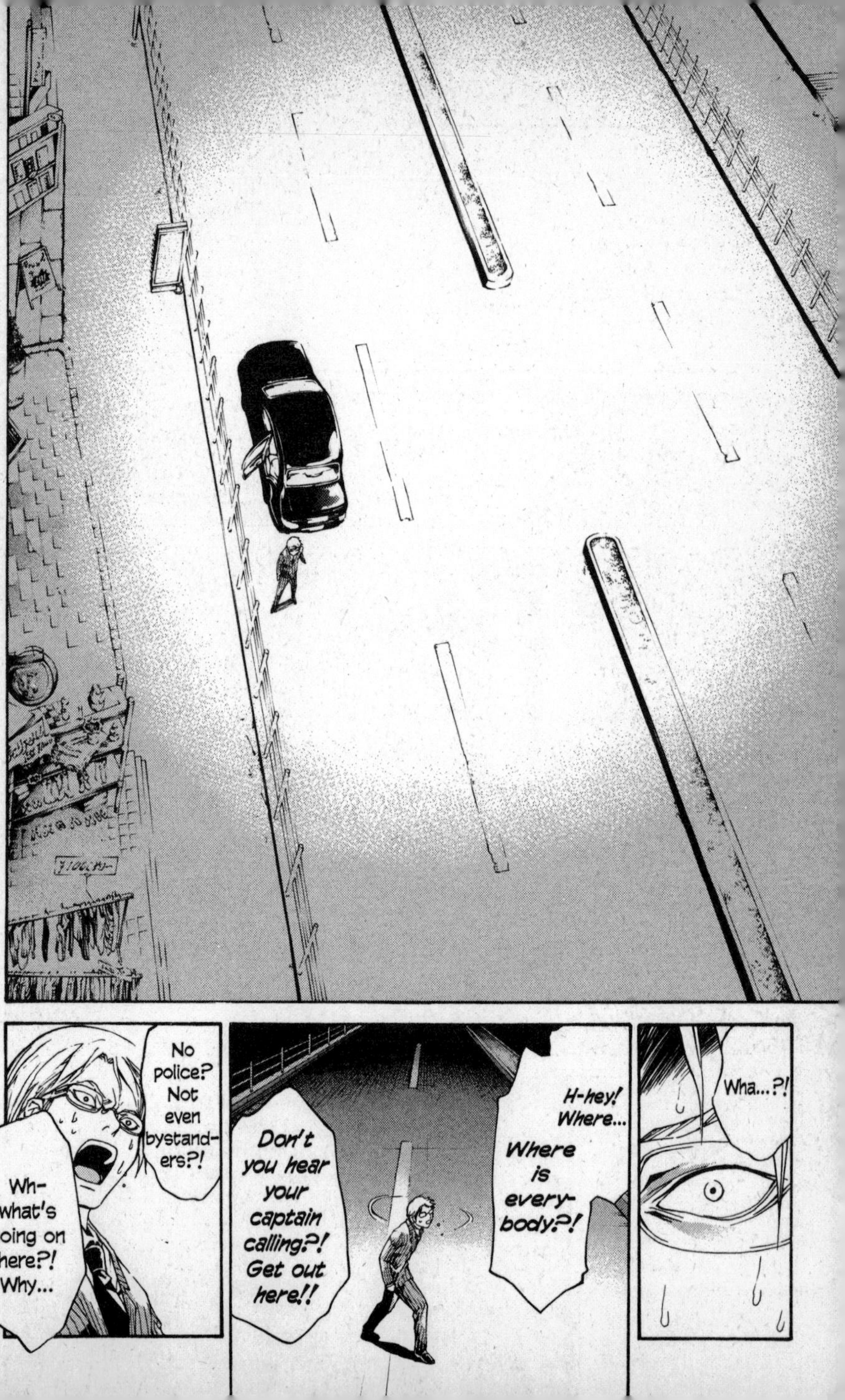
Wha...?!
H-hey! Where...
Where is every-body?!
Don't you hear your captain calling?! Get out here!!
No police? Not even bystand-ers?!
Wh-what's going on here?! Why...

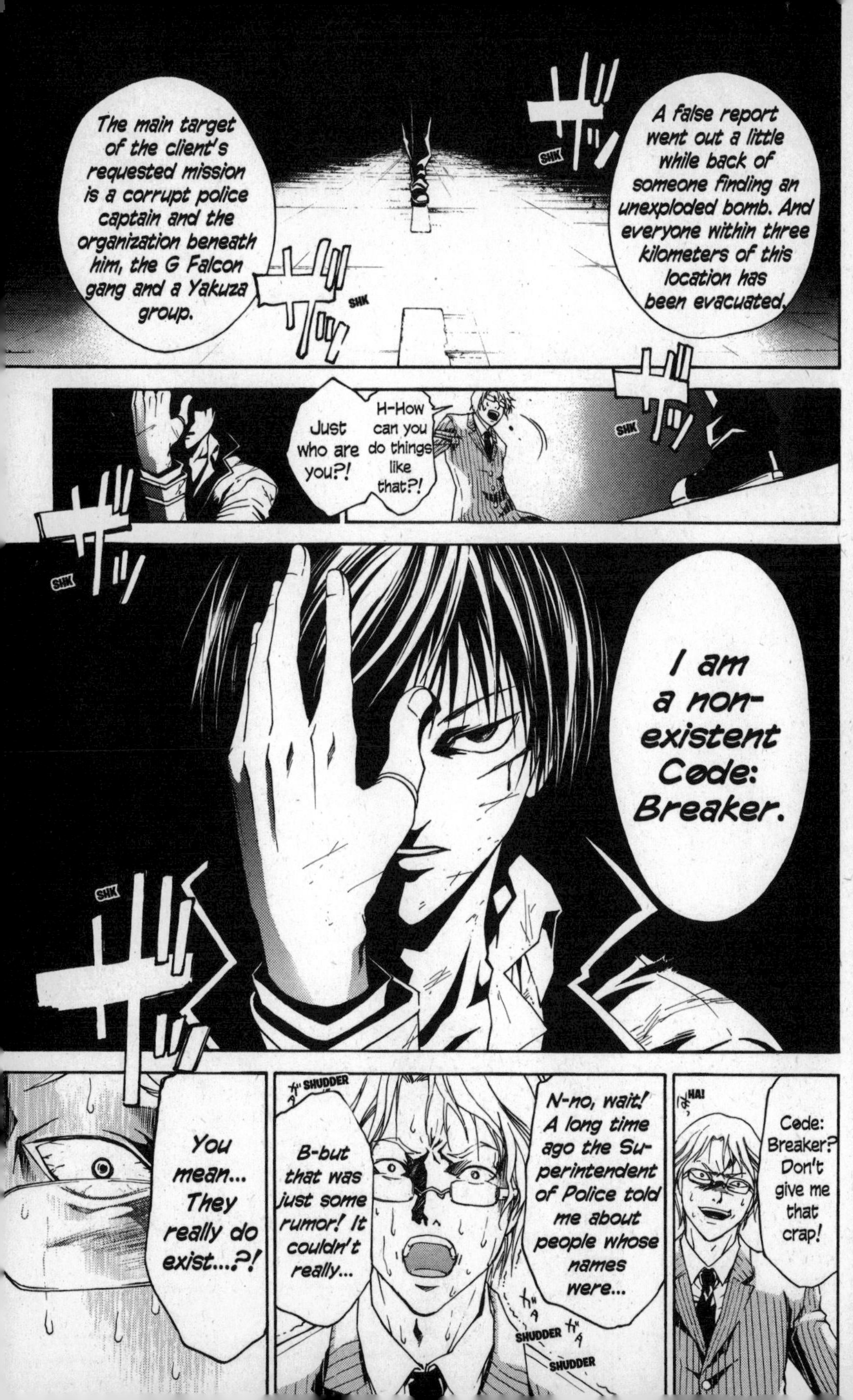
SHK
A false report went out a little while back of someone finding an unexploded bomb. And everyone within three kilometers of this location has been evacuated.
The main target of the client's requested mission is a corrupt police captain and the organization beneath him, the G Falcon gang and a Yakuza group.
SHK
SHK
H-How can you do things like that?!
Just who are you?!
SHK
I am a non-existent Code: Breaker.
SHK
SHK
HA!
Code: Breaker? Don't give me that crap!
N-no, wait! A long time ago the Superintendent of Police told me about people whose names were...
SHUDDER
B-but that was just some rumor! It couldn't really...
SHUDDER
SHUDDER
You mean... They really do exist...?!

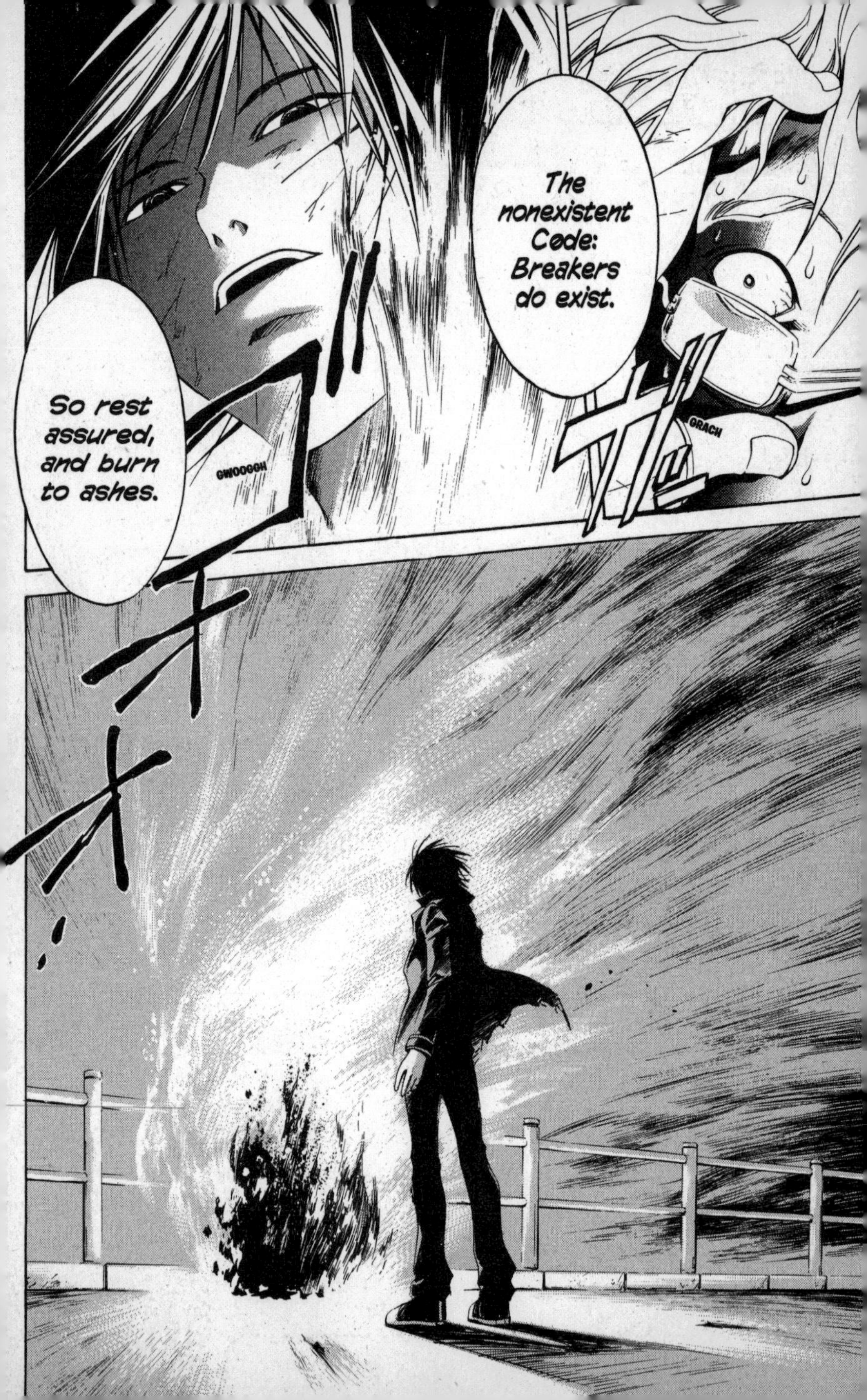
The nonexistent Code: Breakers do exist.
GRACH
So rest assured, and burn to ashes.
GWOOGGH

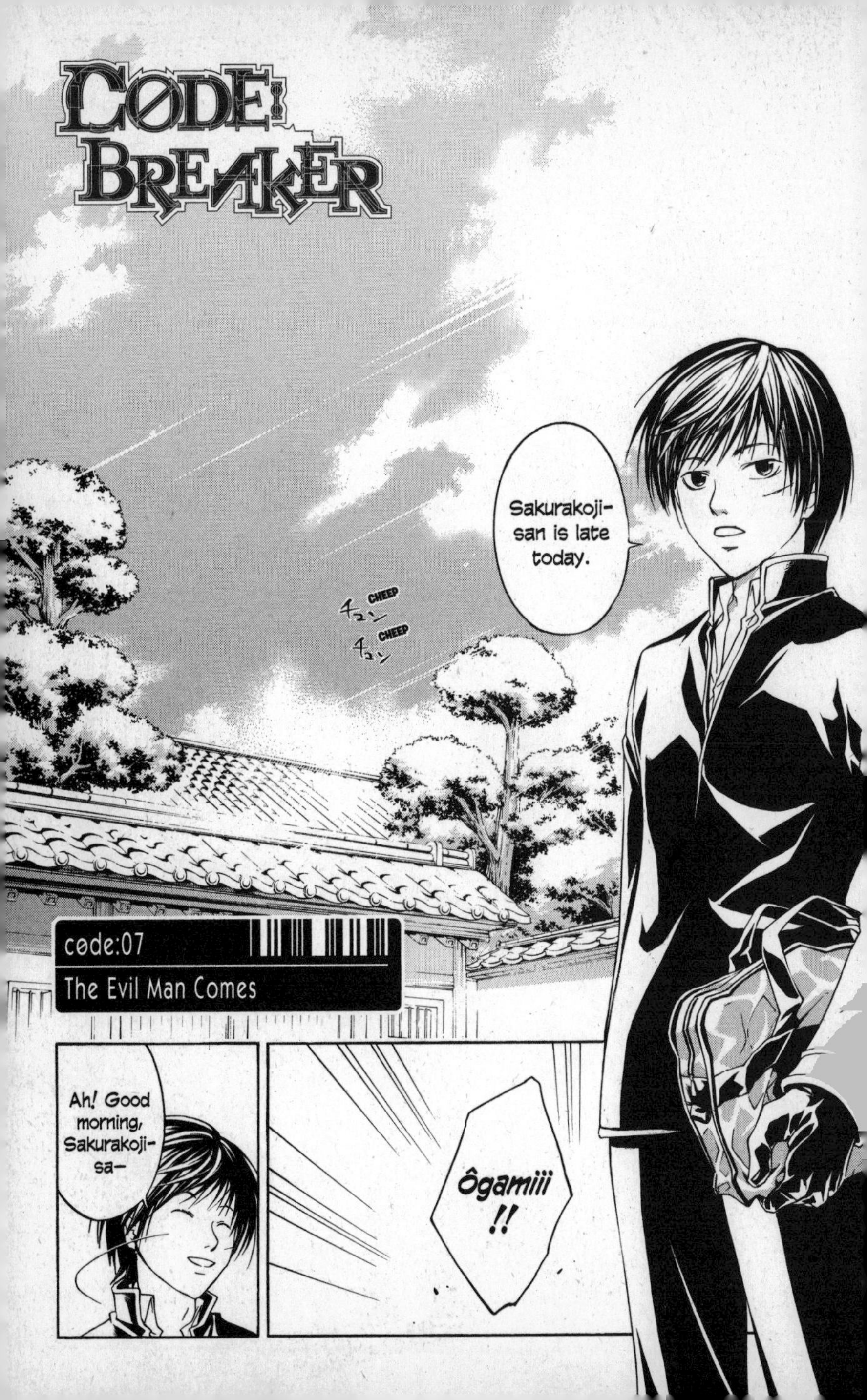
Sakurakoji-san is late today.
CHEEP
CHEEP
CODE:BREAKER
code:07
The Evil Man Comes
Ôgamiii!!
Ah! Good morning, Sakurakoji-sa—

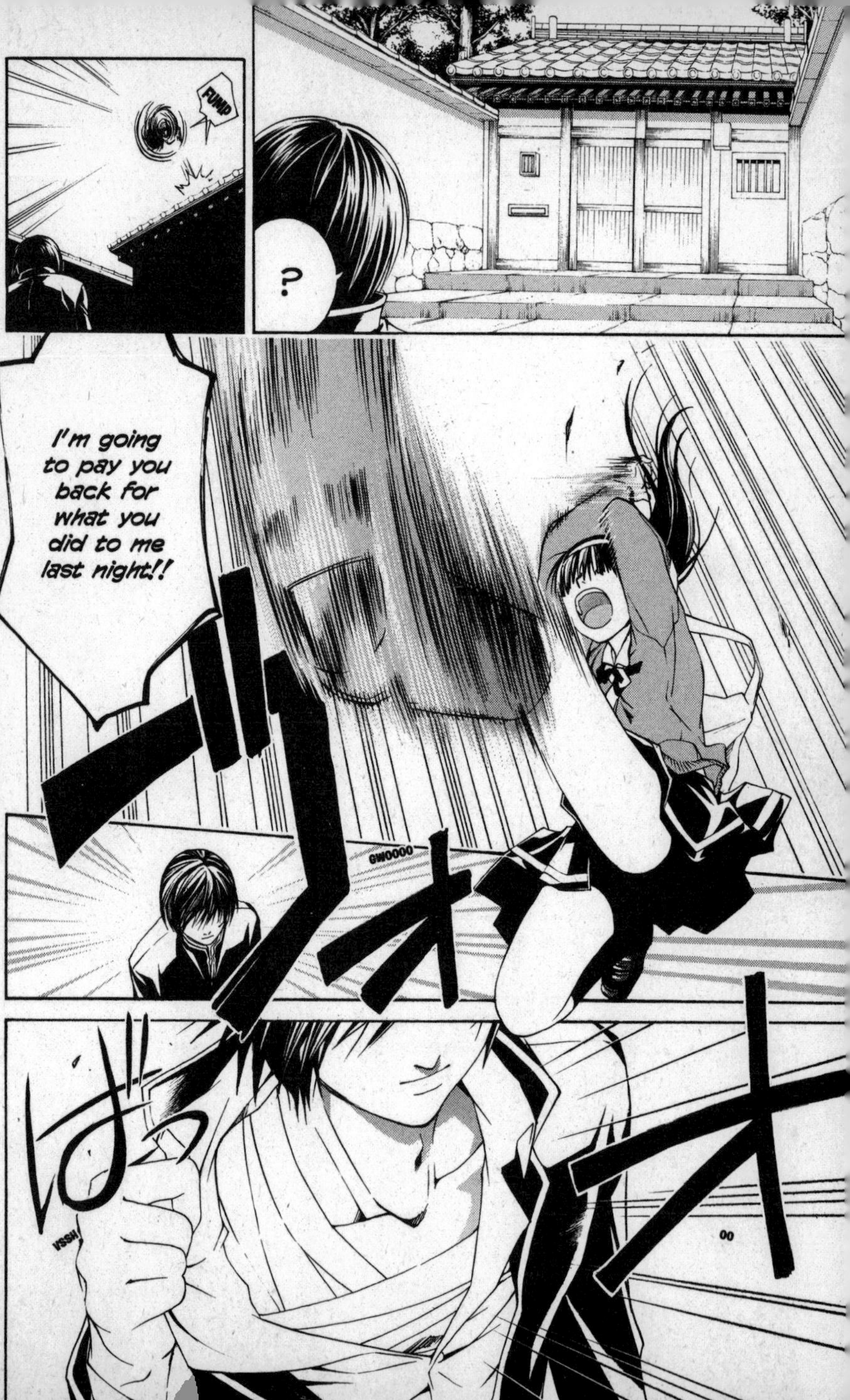
?
FUMP
I'm going to pay you back for what you did to me last night!!
GWOOOO
OO
VSSH

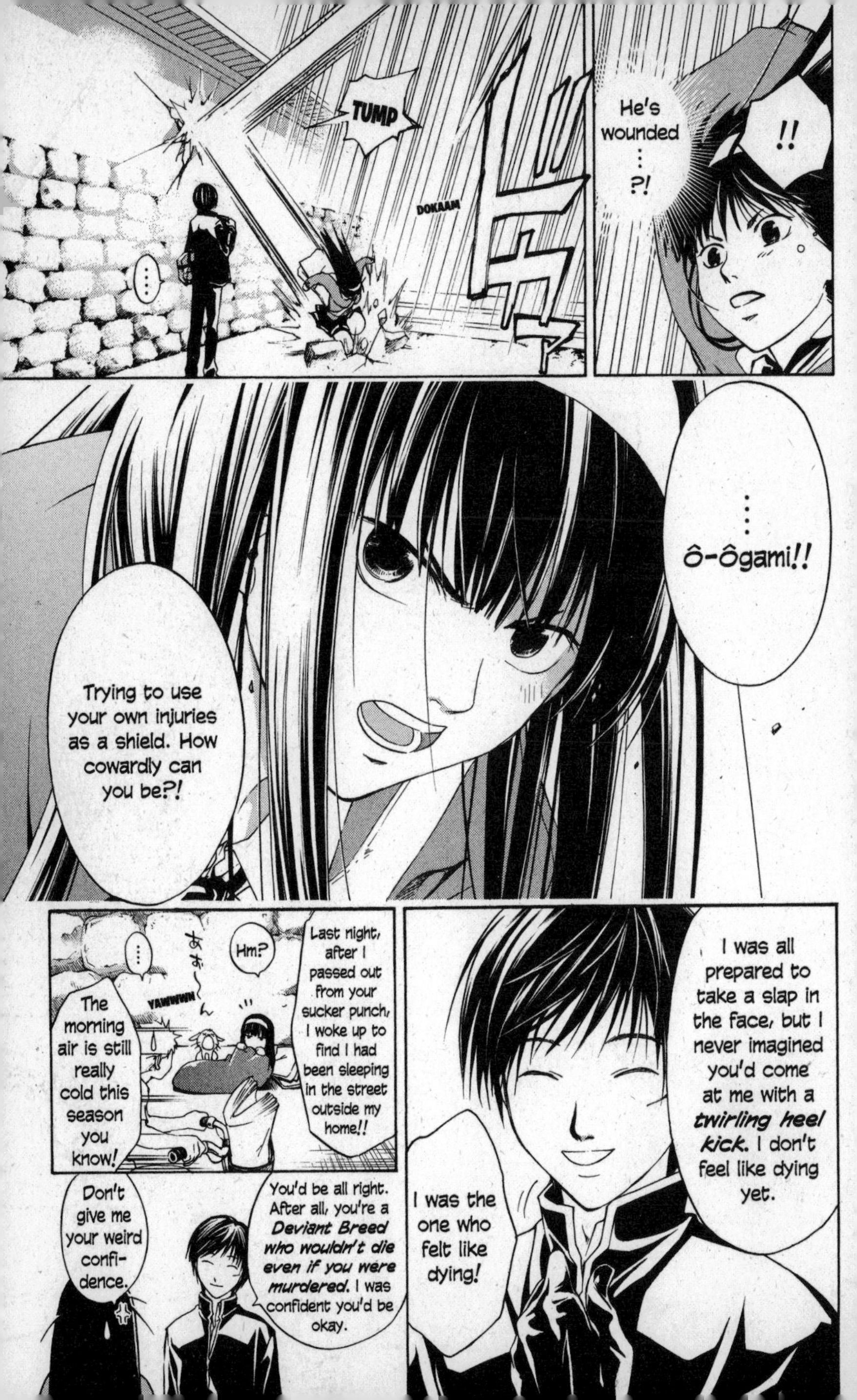
He's wounded ...?!
!!
TUMP
DOKAAM
...
...Ô-Ôgami!!
Trying to use your own injuries as a shield. How cowardly can you be?!
I was all prepared to take a slap in the face, but I never imagined you'd come at me with a *twirling heel kick*. I don't feel like dying yet.
I was the one who felt like dying!
Last night, after I passed out from your sucker punch, I woke up to find I had been sleeping in the street outside my home!!
Hm?
あお～ん
YAWWWN
...
The morning air is still really cold this season you know!
You'd be all right. After all, you're a *Deviant Breed who wouldn't die even if you were murdered*. I was confident you'd be okay.
Don't give me your weird confi-dence.

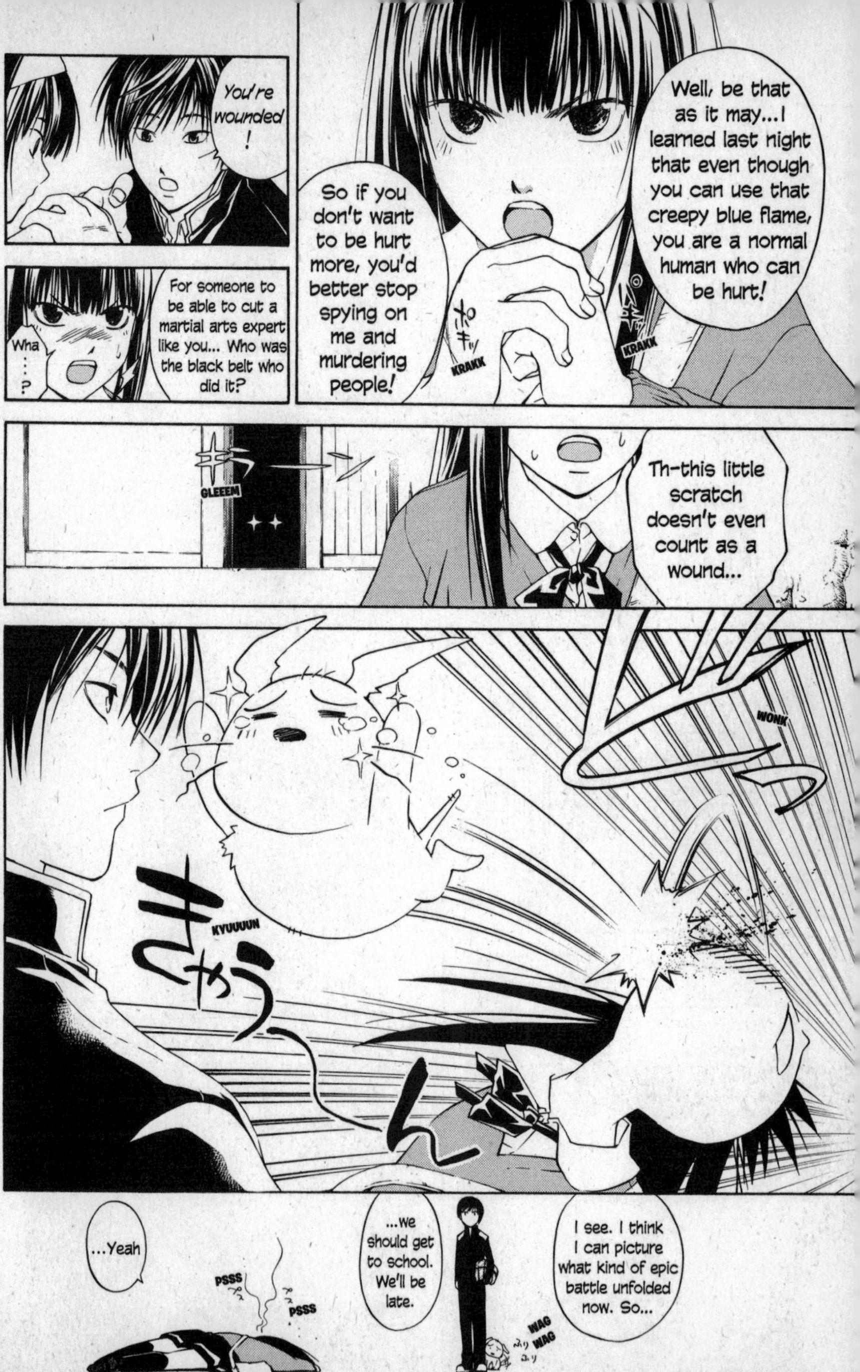
Well, be that as it may...I learned last night that even though you can use that creepy blue flame, you are a normal human who can be hurt!
KRAKK
So if you don't want to be hurt more, you'd better stop spying on me and murdering people!
KRAKK
You're wounded!
For someone to be able to cut a martial arts expert like you... Who was the black belt who did it?
Wha...?
Th-this little scratch doesn't even count as a wound...
GLEEEM
WONK
KYUUUUN
I see. I think I can picture what kind of epic battle unfolded now. So...
WAG WAG
...we should get to school. We'll be late.
...Yeah
PSSS
PSSS

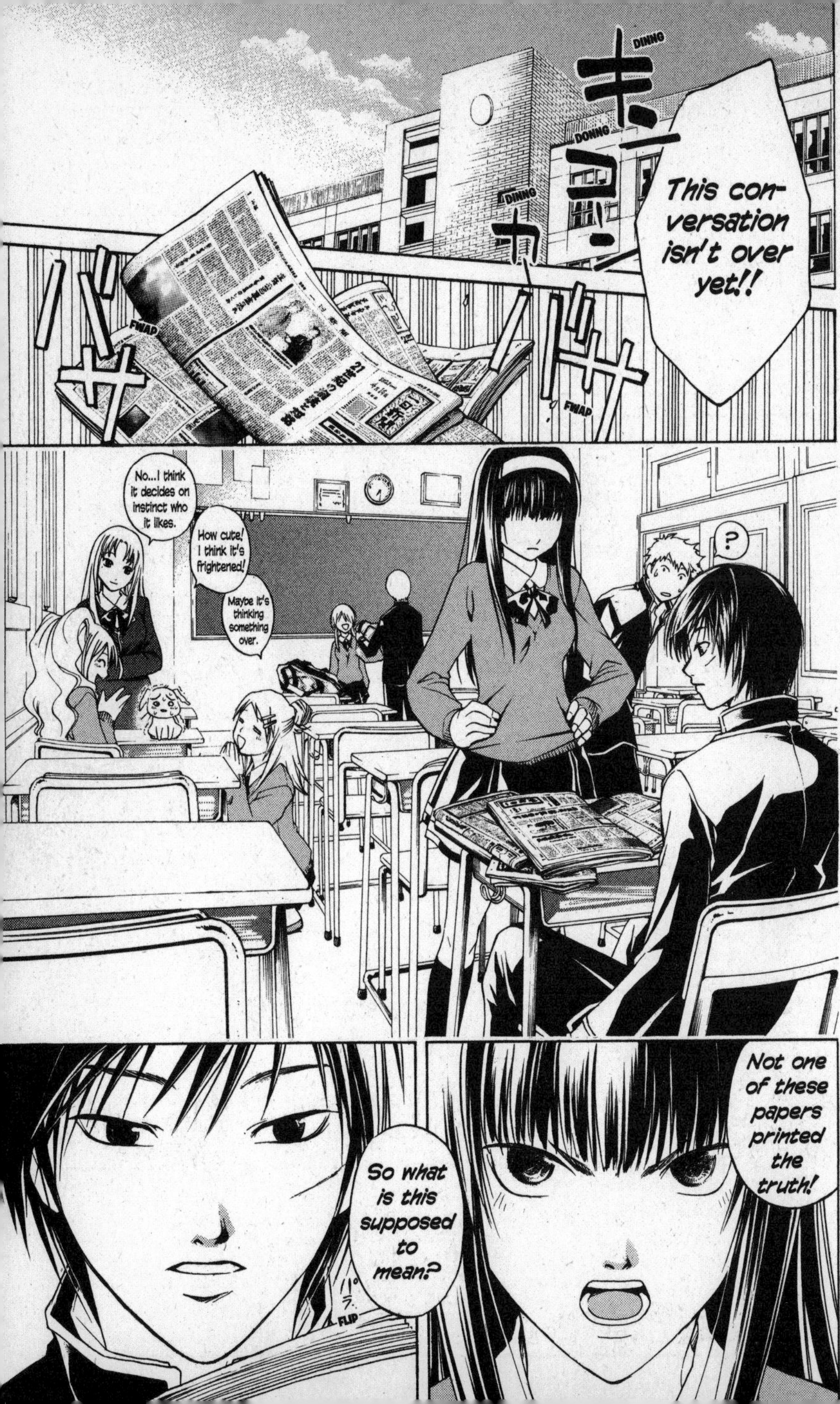
DINNG
DONNG
DINNG
This conversation isn't over yet!!
FWAP
FWAP
?
How cute! I think it's frightened!
Maybe it's thinking something over.
No...I think it decides on instinct who it likes.
Not one of these papers printed the truth!
So what is this supposed to mean?
FLIP

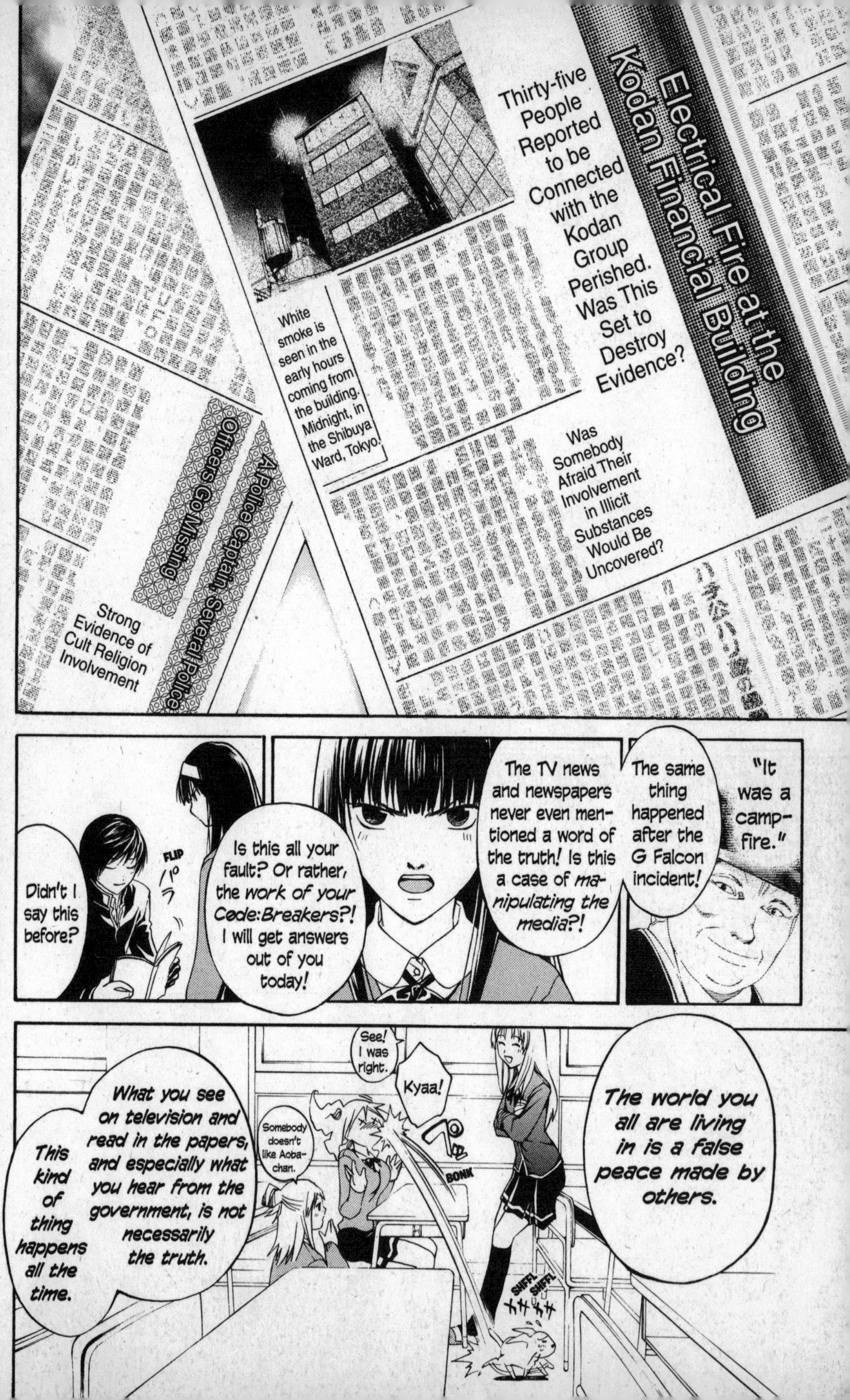
Electrical Fire at the Kodan Financial Building
Thirty-five People Reported to be Connected with the Kodan Group Perished. Was This Set to Destroy Evidence?
Was Somebody Afraid Their Involvement in Illicit Substances Would Be Uncovered?
White smoke is seen in the early hours coming from the building. Midnight, in the Shibuya Ward, Tokyo.
A Police Captain, Several Police Officers Go Missing
Strong Evidence of Cult Religion Involvement
"It was a campfire."
The same thing happened after the G Falcon incident!
The TV news and newspapers never even mentioned a word of the truth! Is this a case of manipulating the media?!
Is this all your fault? Or rather, the work of your Code:Breakers?! I will get answers out of you today!
FLIP
Didn't I say this before?
The world you all are living in is a false peace made by others.
See! I was right.
Kyaa!
What you see on television and read in the papers, and especially what you hear from the government, is not necessarily the truth.
Somebody doesn't like Aoba-chan.
BONK
This kind of thing happens all the time.
SHFFL SHFFL

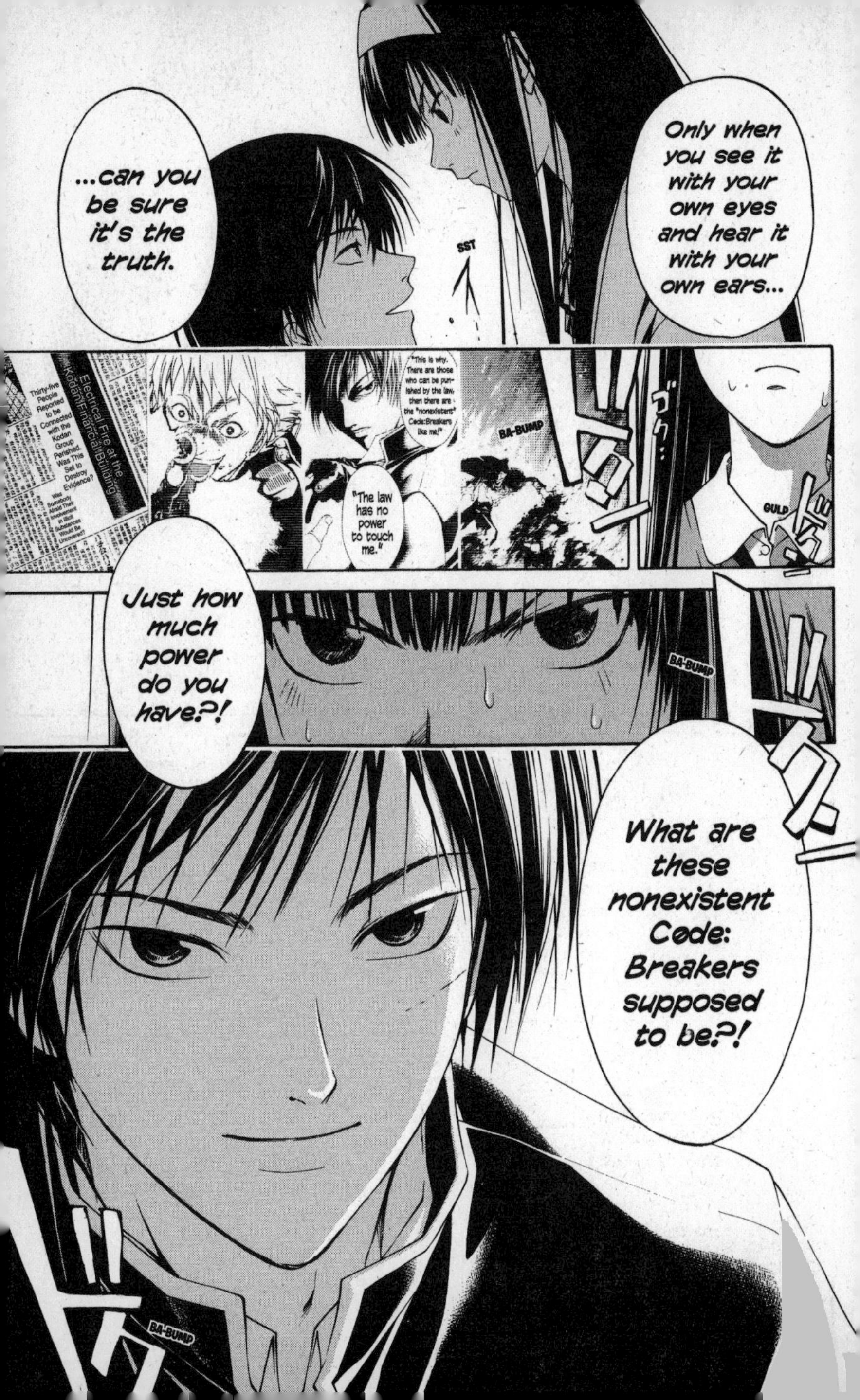
Only when you see it with your own eyes and hear it with your own ears...
SST
...can you be sure it's the truth.
GULP
BA-BUMP
"This is why. There are those who can be punished by the law, then there are the "nonexistent" Code:Breakers like me!"
"The law has no power to touch me."
Electrical Fire at the Kodan Financial Building
Thirty-five People Reported to be Connected with the Kodan Group Perished. Was This Set to Destroy Evidence?
Was Somebody Afraid Their Involvement in Illicit Substances Would Be Uncovered?
BA-BUMP
Just how much power do you have?!
What are these nonexistent Code: Breakers supposed to be?!
BA-BUMP

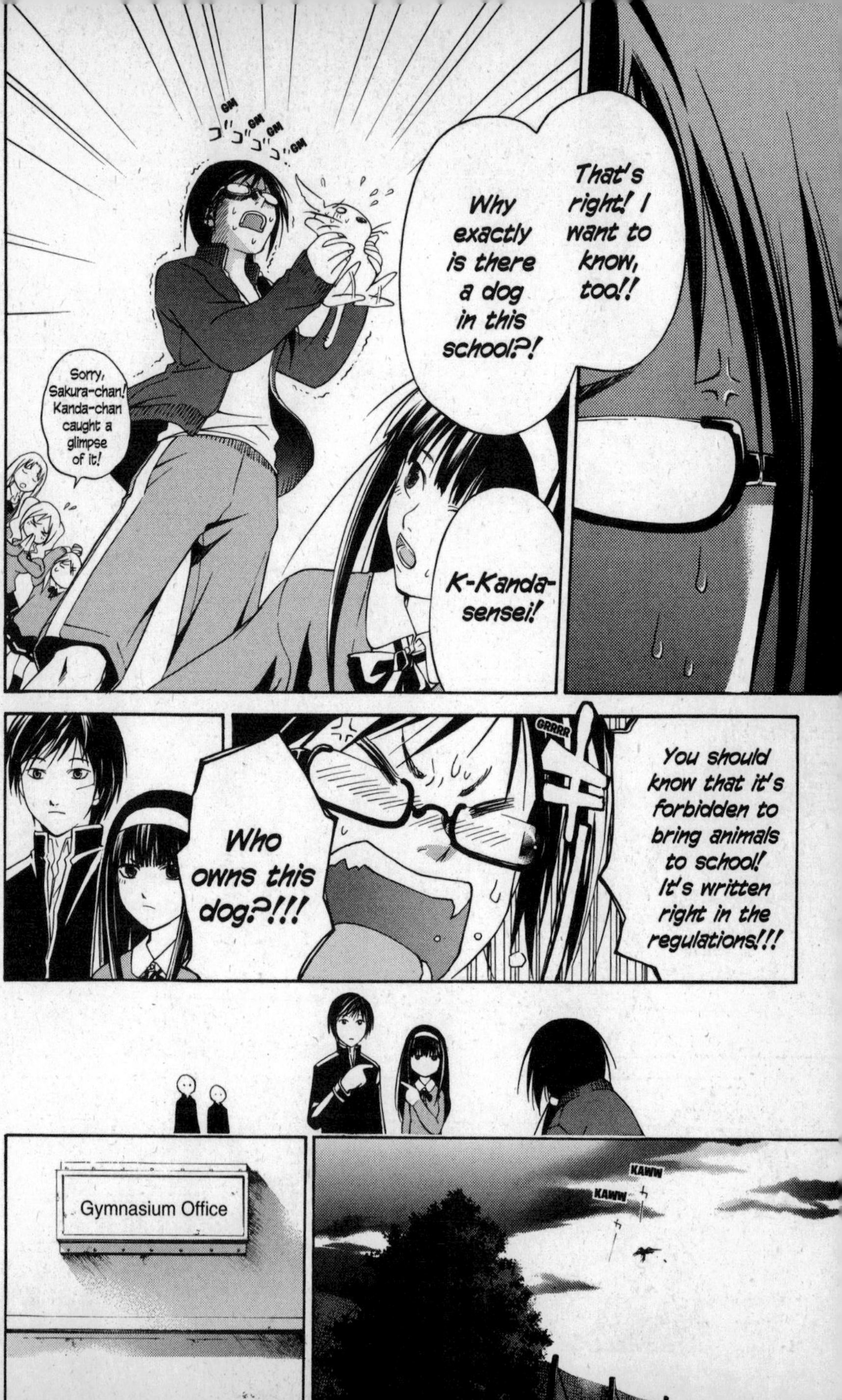
That's right! I want to know, too!!
Why exactly is there a dog in this school?!
K-Kanda-sensei!
GM GM GM GM
Sorry, Sakura-chan! Kanda-chan caught a glimpse of it!
GRRRR
You should know that it's forbidden to bring animals to school! It's written right in the regulations!!!
Who owns this dog?!!!
KAWW
KAWW
Gymnasium Office

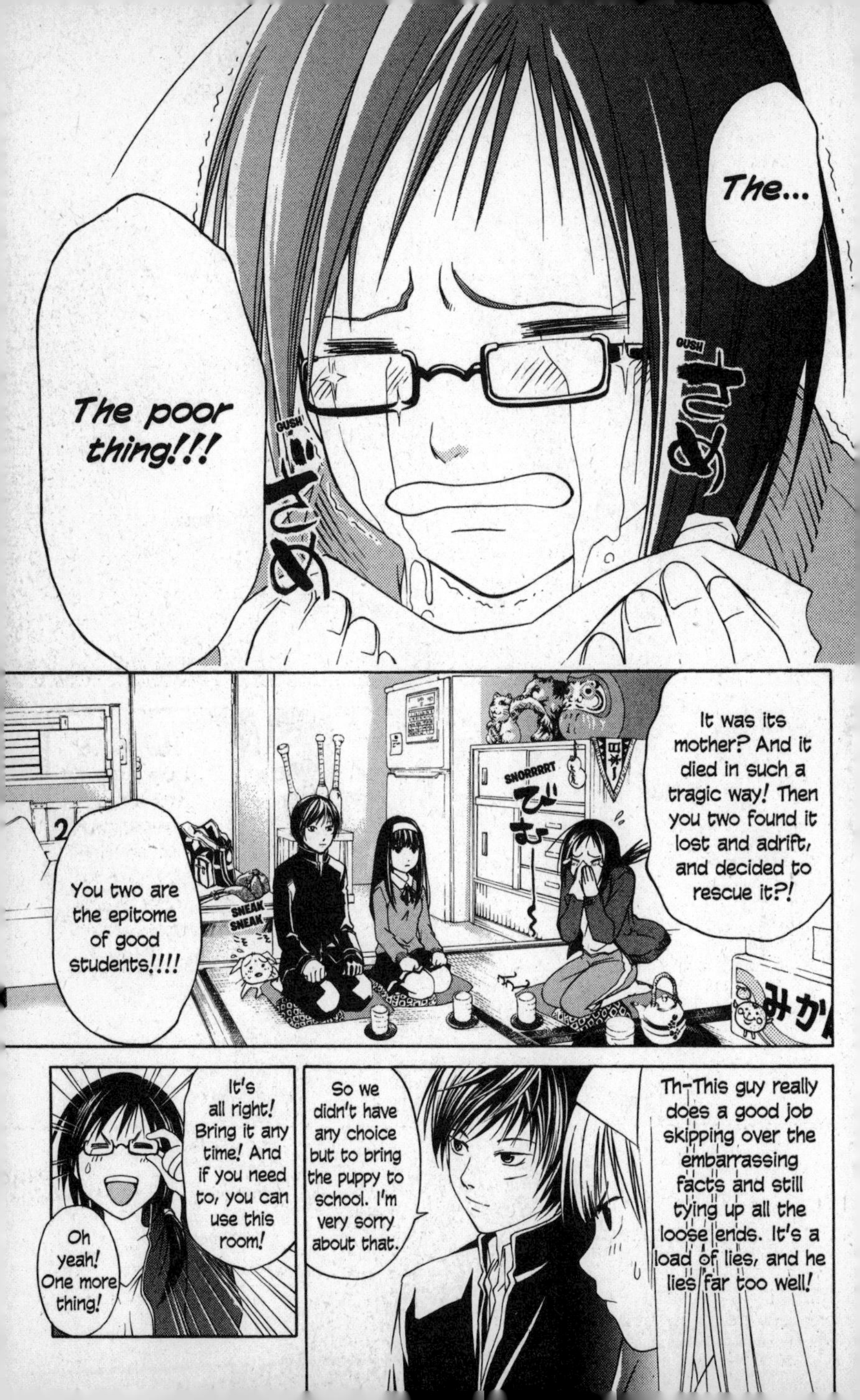
The...
GUSH
GUSH
The poor thing!!!
It was its mother? And it died in such a tragic way! Then you two found it lost and adrift, and decided to rescue it?!
SNORRRRT
SNEAK SNEAK
You two are the epitome of good students!!!!
Th-This guy really does a good job skipping over the embarrassing facts and still tying up all the loose ends. It's a load of lies, and he lies far too well!
So we didn't have any choice but to bring the puppy to school. I'm very sorry about that.
It's all right! Bring it any time! And if you need to, you can use this room!
Oh yeah! One more thing!

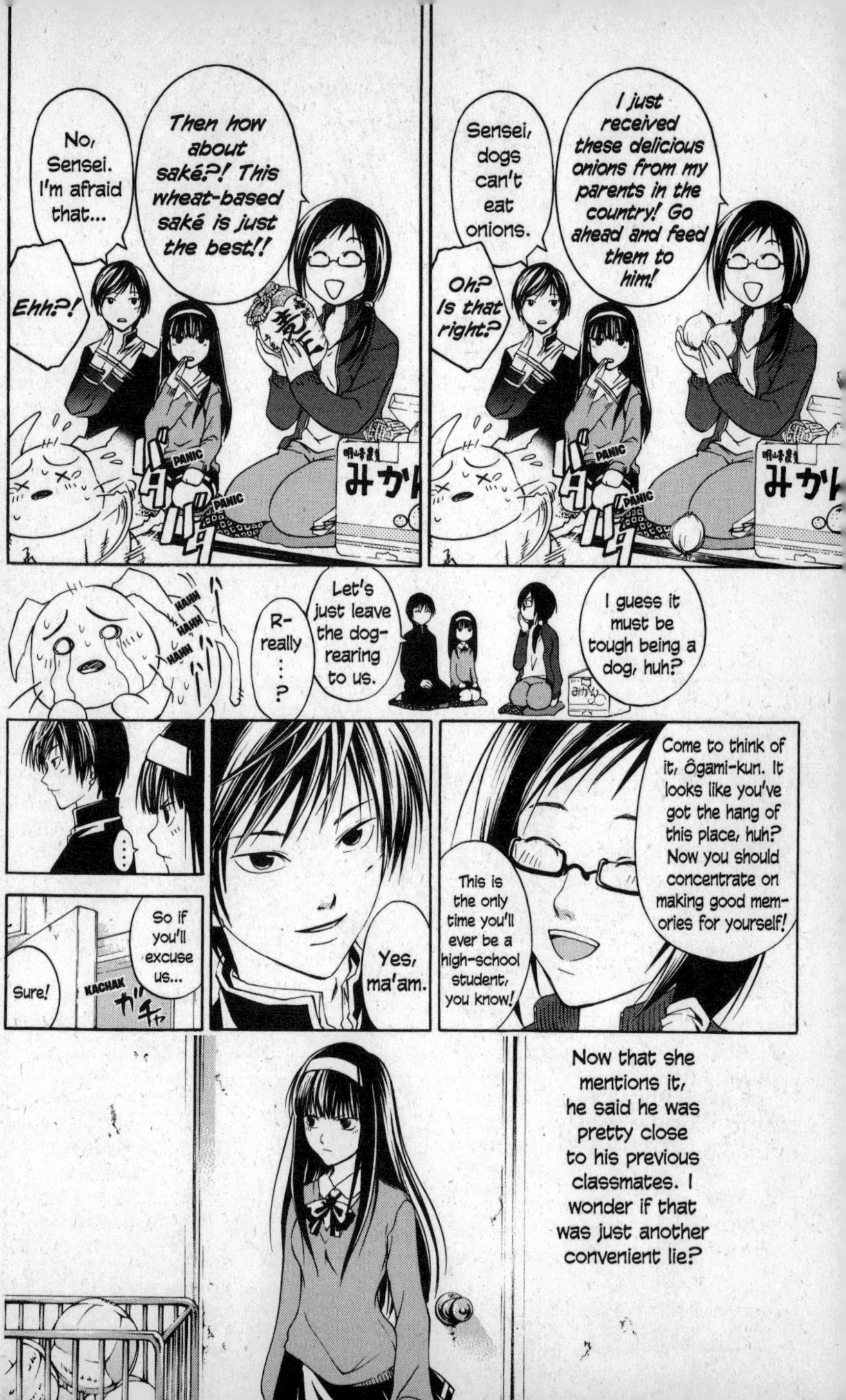
I just received these delicious onions from my parents in the country! Go ahead and feed them to him!
Sensei, dogs can't eat onions.
Oh? Is that right?
PANIC
PANIC
Then how about saké?! This wheat-based saké is just the best!!
No, Sensei. I'm afraid that...
Ehh?!
PANIC
PANIC
I guess it must be tough being a dog, huh?
Let's just leave the dog-rearing to us.
R-really...?
HAHH HAHH HAHH
Come to think of it, Ôgami-kun. It looks like you've got the hang of this place, huh? Now you should concentrate on making good memories for yourself!
This is the only time you'll ever be a high-school student, you know!
Yes, ma'am.
....
So if you'll excuse us...
KACHAK
Sure!
Now that she mentions it, he said he was pretty close to his previous classmates. I wonder if that was just another convenient lie?

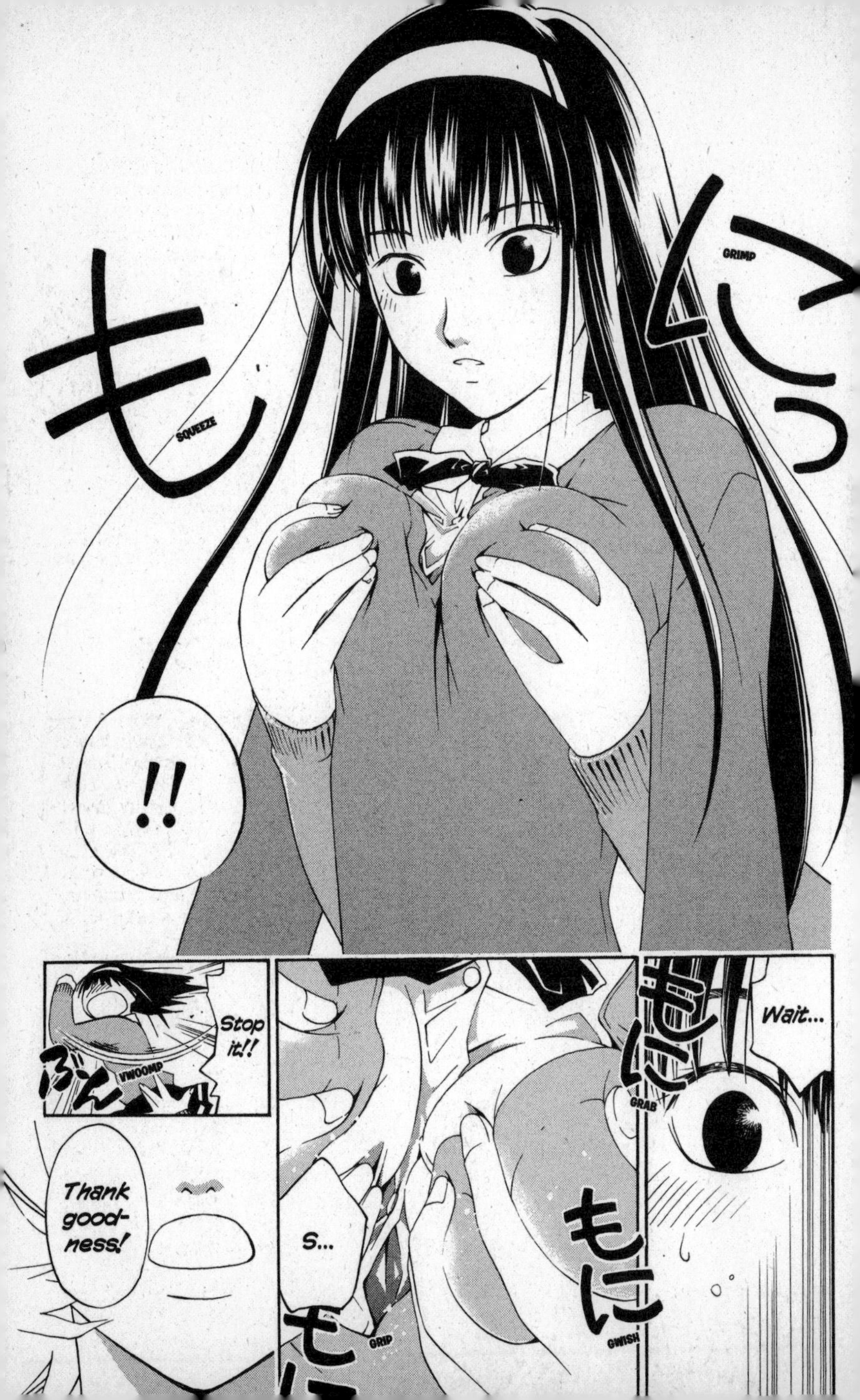
GRIMP
SQUEEZE
!!
Wait...
GRAB
GWISH
S...
GRIP
Stop it!!
VWOOMP
Thank goodness!

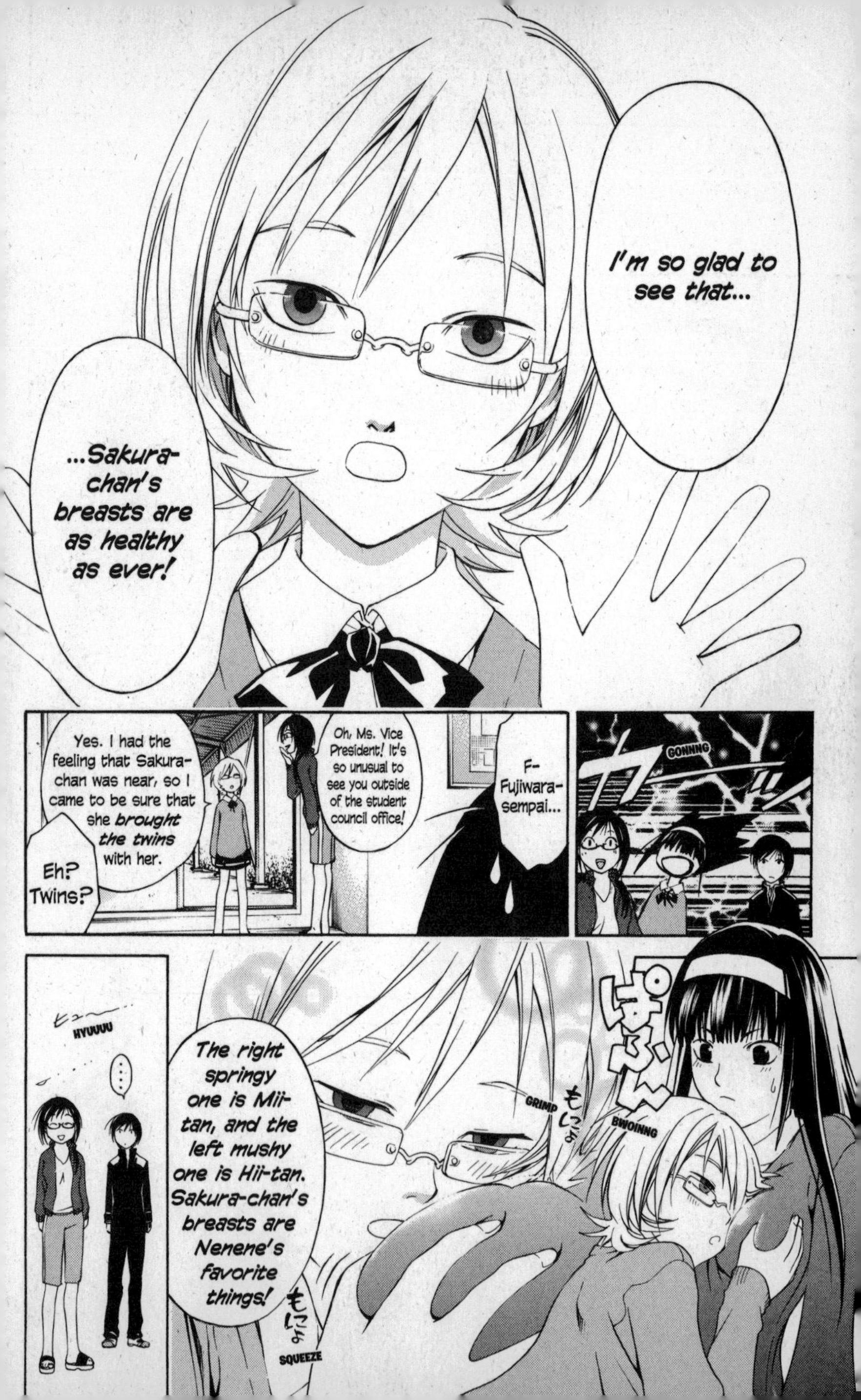
I'm so glad to see that...
...Sakura-chan's breasts are as healthy as ever!
GONNNG
F- Fujiwara-sempai...
Oh, Ms. Vice President! It's so unusual to see you outside of the student council office!
Yes. I had the feeling that Sakura-chan was near, so I came to be sure that she brought the twins with her.
Eh? Twins?
ぱふん
BWOINNG
もにょ
GRIMP
The right springy one is Mii-tan, and the left mushy one is Hii-tan. Sakura-chan's breasts are Nenene's favorite things!
もにょ
SQUEEZE
ヒュ〜〜
HYUUUU
...

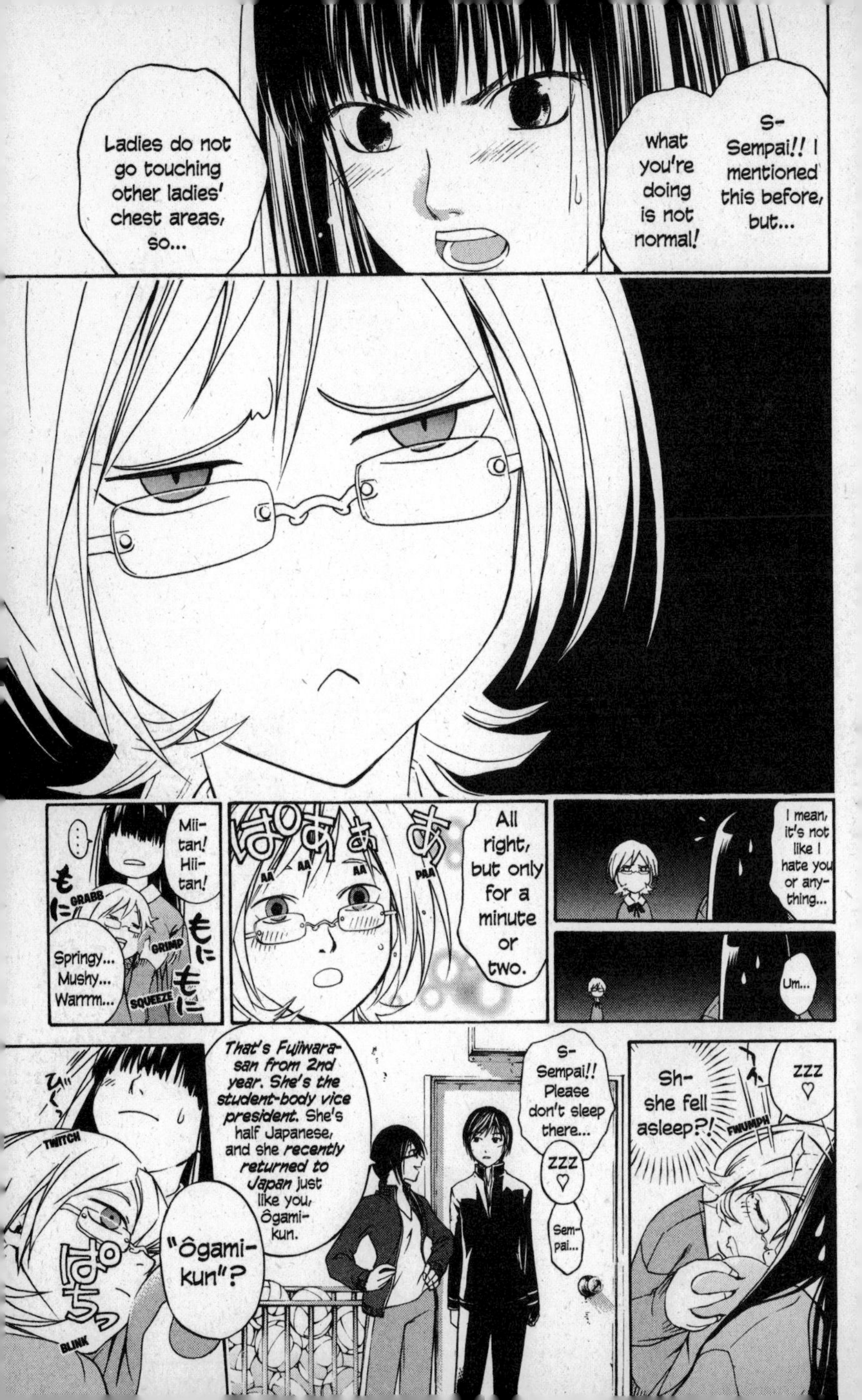
S-Sempai!! I mentioned this before, but...
what you're doing is not normal!
Ladies do not go touching other ladies' chest areas, so...
I mean, it's not like I hate you or anything...
Um...
All right, but only for a minute or two.
AA AA AA PAA
Mii-tan! Hii-tan!
...
GRABB
GRIMP
SQUEEZE
Springy... Mushy... Warmm...
ZZZ ♡
Sh-she fell asleep?!
FWUMPH
S-Sempai!! Please don't sleep there...
ZZZ ♡
Sempai...
That's Fujiwara-san from 2nd year. She's the student-body vice president. She's half Japanese, and she recently returned to Japan just like you, Ôgami-kun.
TWITCH
"Ôgami-kun"?
BLINK

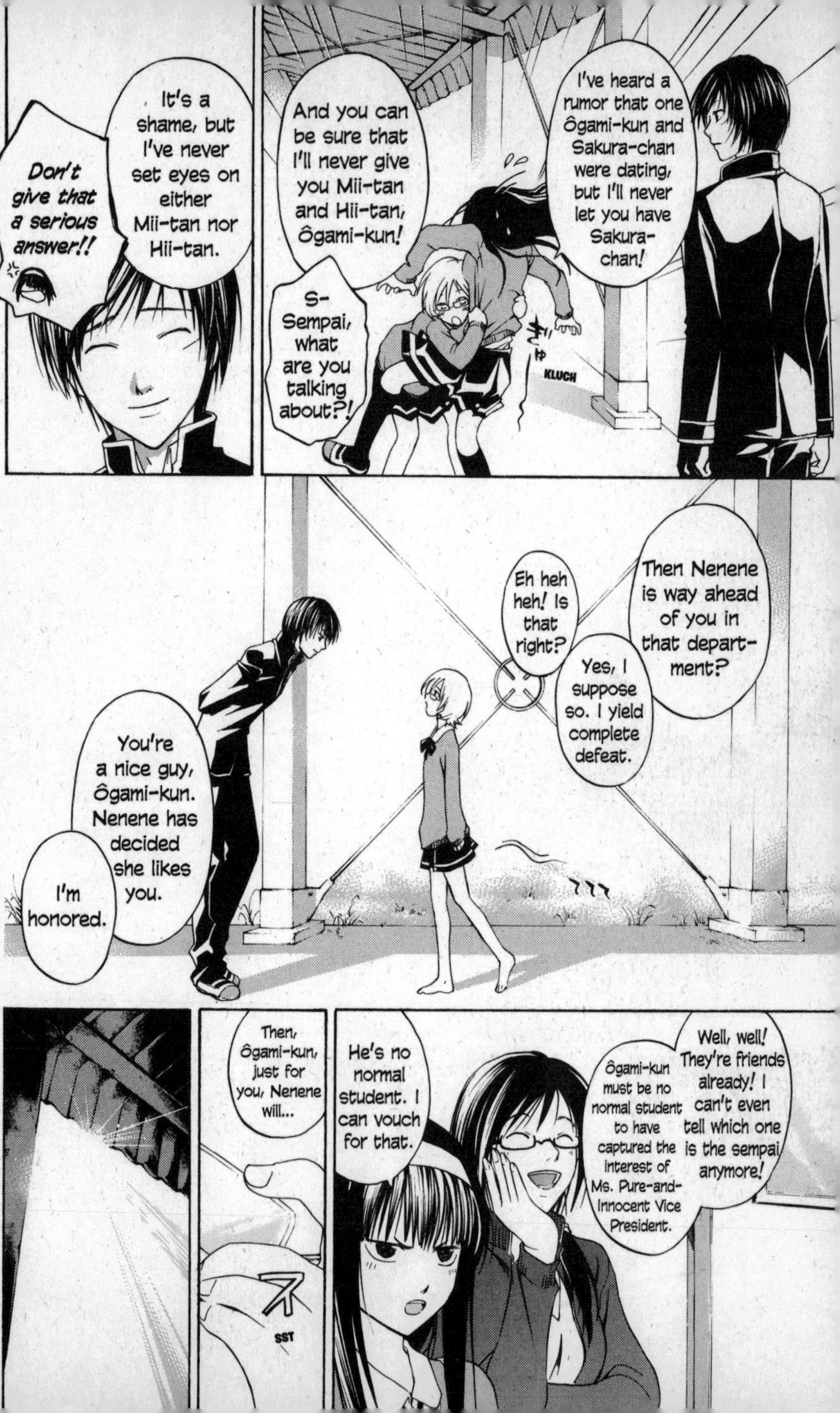

I've heard a rumor that one Ôgami-kun and Sakura-chan were dating, but I'll never let you have Sakura-chan!
And you can be sure that I'll never give you Mii-tan and Hii-tan, Ôgami-kun!
S-Sempai, what are you talking about?!
KLUCH
It's a shame, but I've never set eyes on either Mii-tan nor Hii-tan.
Don't give that a serious answer!!
Then Nenene is way ahead of you in that department?
Eh heh heh! Is that right?
Yes, I suppose so. I yield complete defeat.
You're a nice guy, Ôgami-kun. Nenene has decided she likes you.
I'm honored.
Well, well! They're friends already! I can't even tell which one is the sempai anymore!
Ôgami-kun must be no normal student to have captured the interest of Ms. Pure-and-Innocent Vice President.
He's no normal student. I can vouch for that.
Then, Ôgami-kun, just for you, Nenene will...
SST

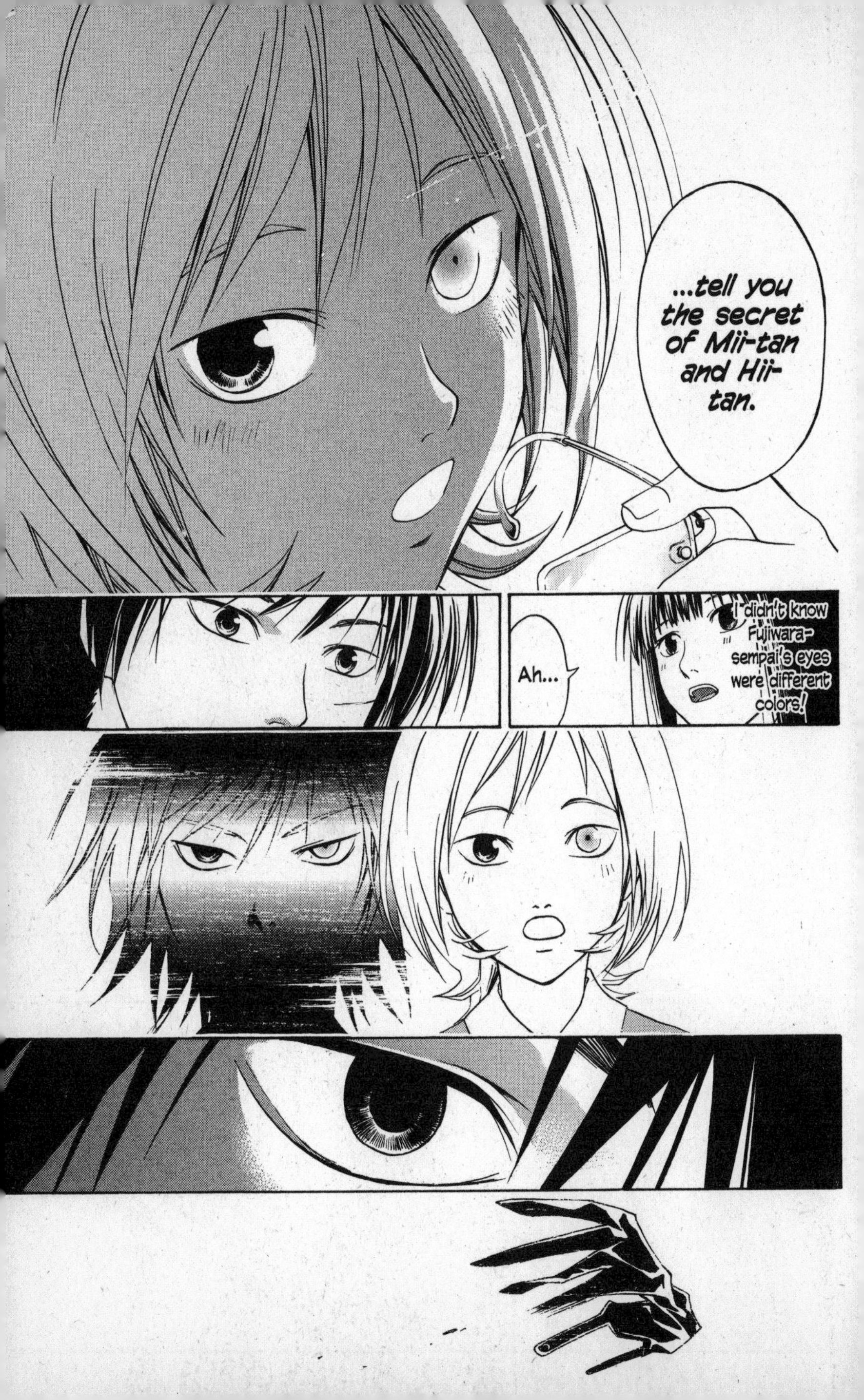
...tell you the secret of Mii-tan and Hii-tan.
I didn't know Fujiwara-sempai's eyes were different colors!
Ah...

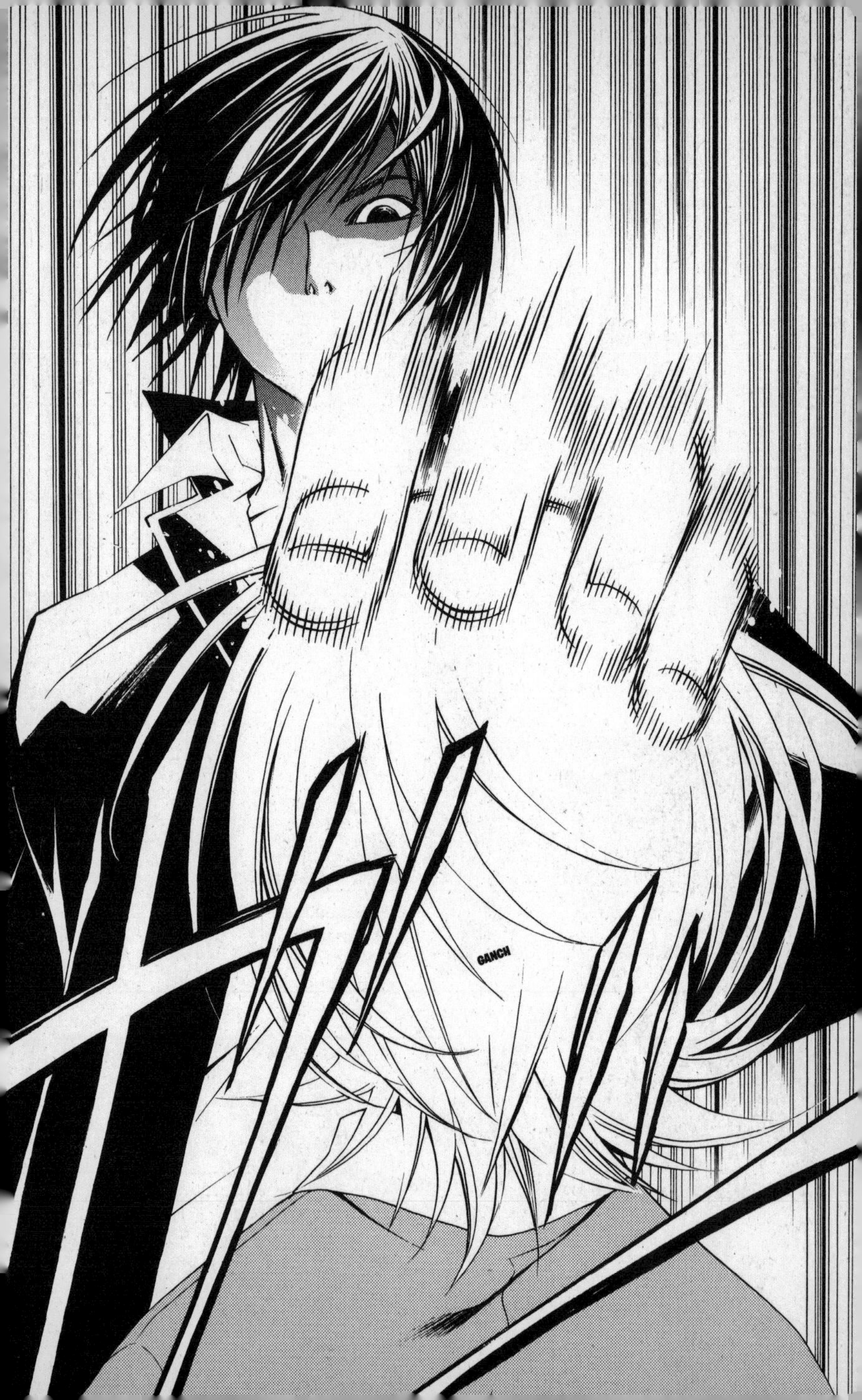
GANCH

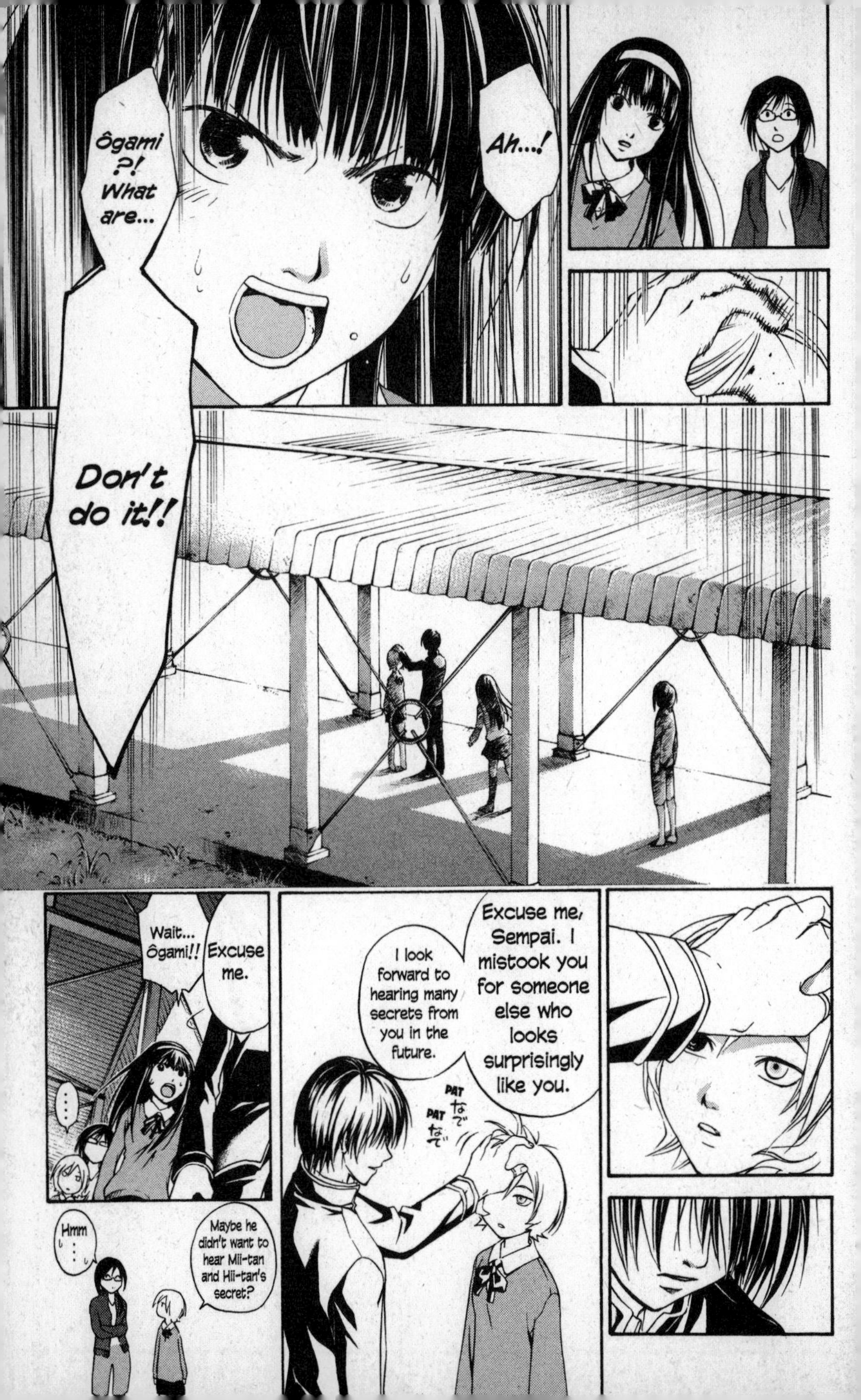
Ah...!
Ôgami?! What are...
Don't do it!!
Excuse me, Sempai. I mistook you for someone else who looks surprisingly like you.
I look forward to hearing many secrets from you in the future.
PAT なで
PAT なで
Excuse me.
Wait... Ôgami!!
...
Maybe he didn't want to hear Mii-tan and Hii-tan's secret?
Hmm

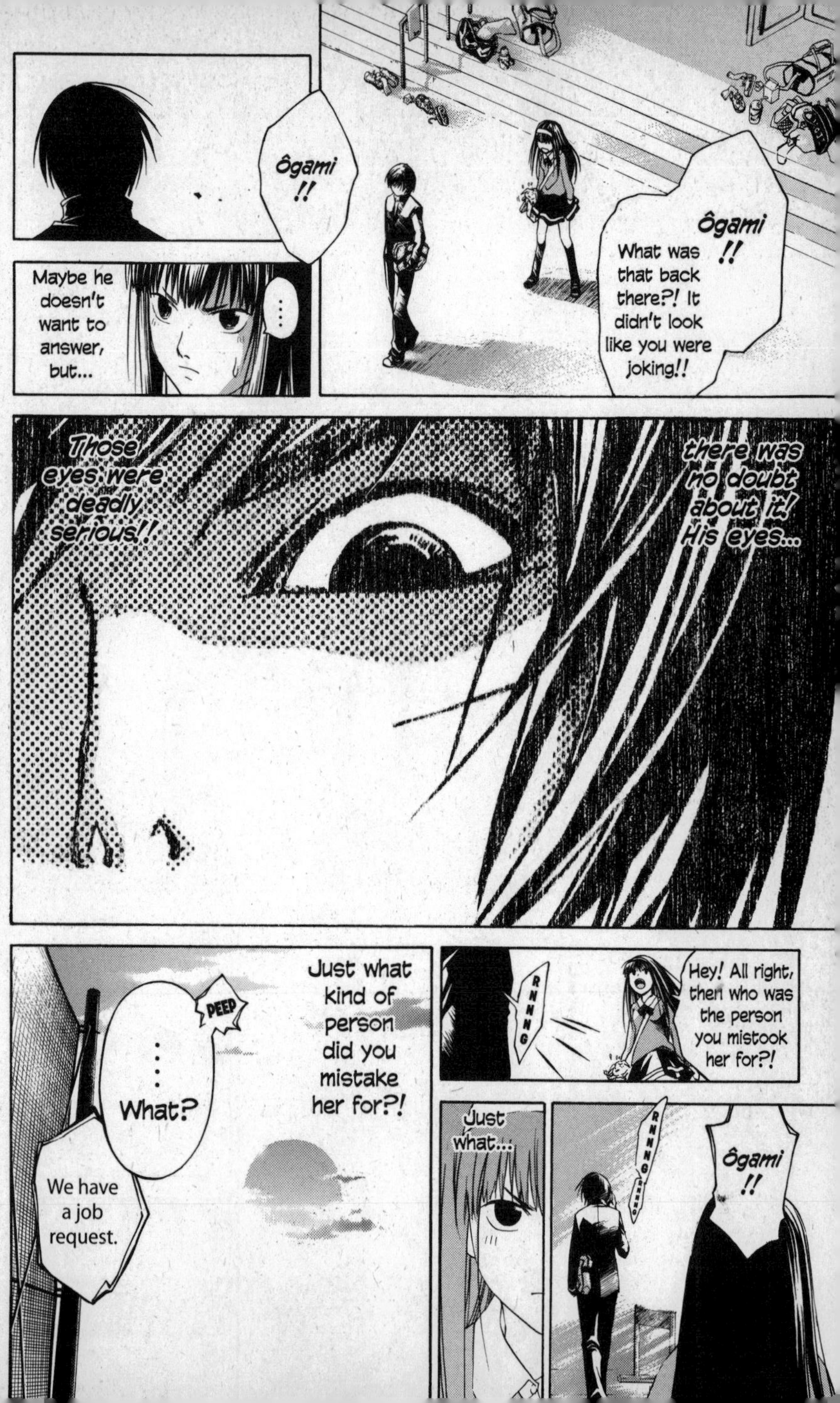
Ôgami!!
What was that back there?! It didn't look like you were joking!!
Ôgami!!
....
Maybe he doesn't want to answer, but...
there was no doubt about it! His eyes...
Those eyes were deadly serious!!
Hey! All right, then who was the person you mistook her for?!
RNNNG
Ôgami!!
RNNNG
Just what...
Just what kind of person did you mistake her for?!
PEEP
.... What?
We have a job request.

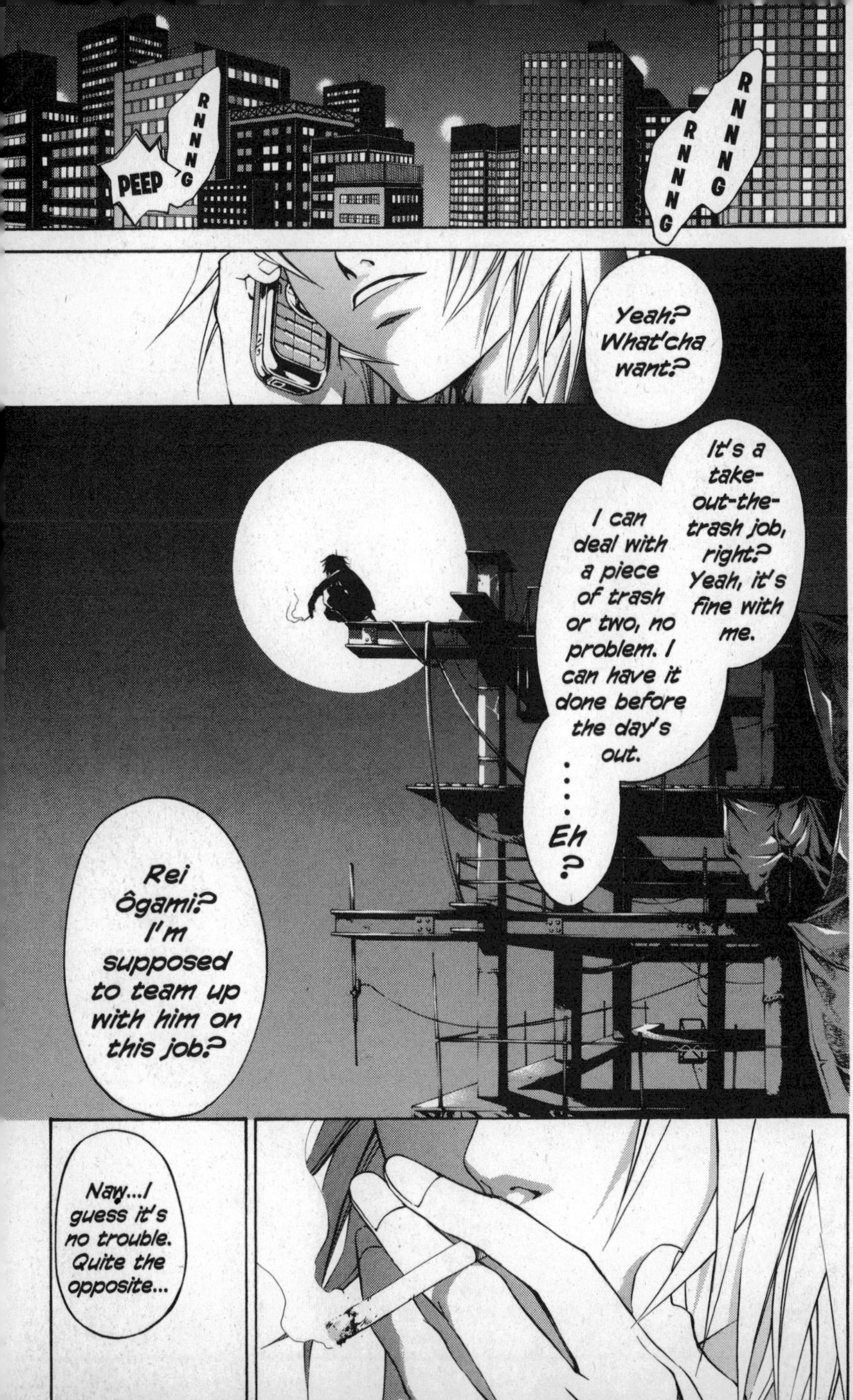
RNNNG
RNNNG
RNNNG
PEEP
Yeah? What'cha want?
It's a take-out-the-trash job, right? Yeah, it's fine with me.
I can deal with a piece of trash or two, no problem. I can have it done before the day's out.
.... Eh?
Rei Ôgami? I'm supposed to team up with him on this job?
Naw...I guess it's no trouble. Quite the opposite...

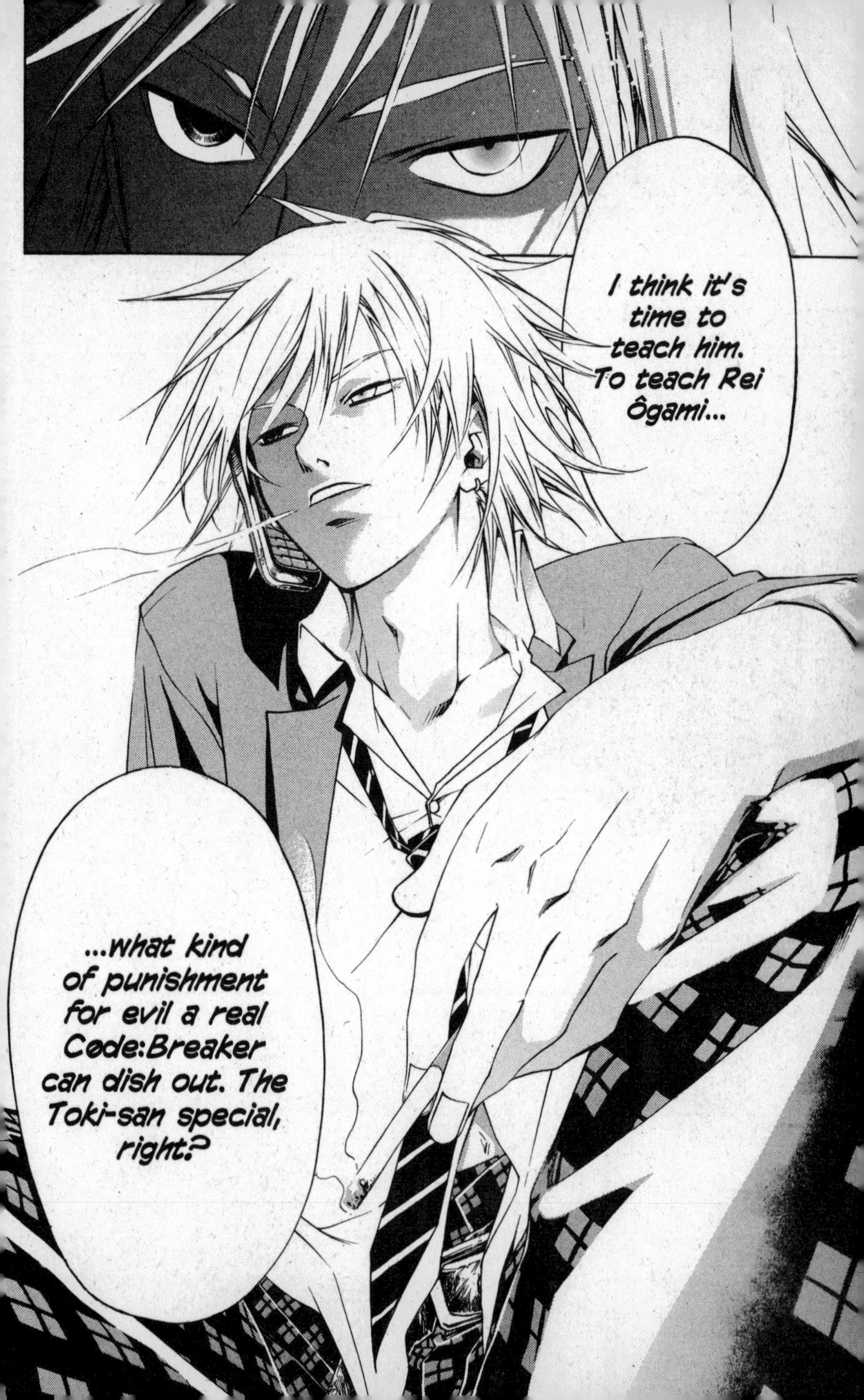
I think it's time to teach him. To teach Rei Ôgami...
...what kind of punishment for evil a real Code:Breaker can dish out. The Toki-san special, right?

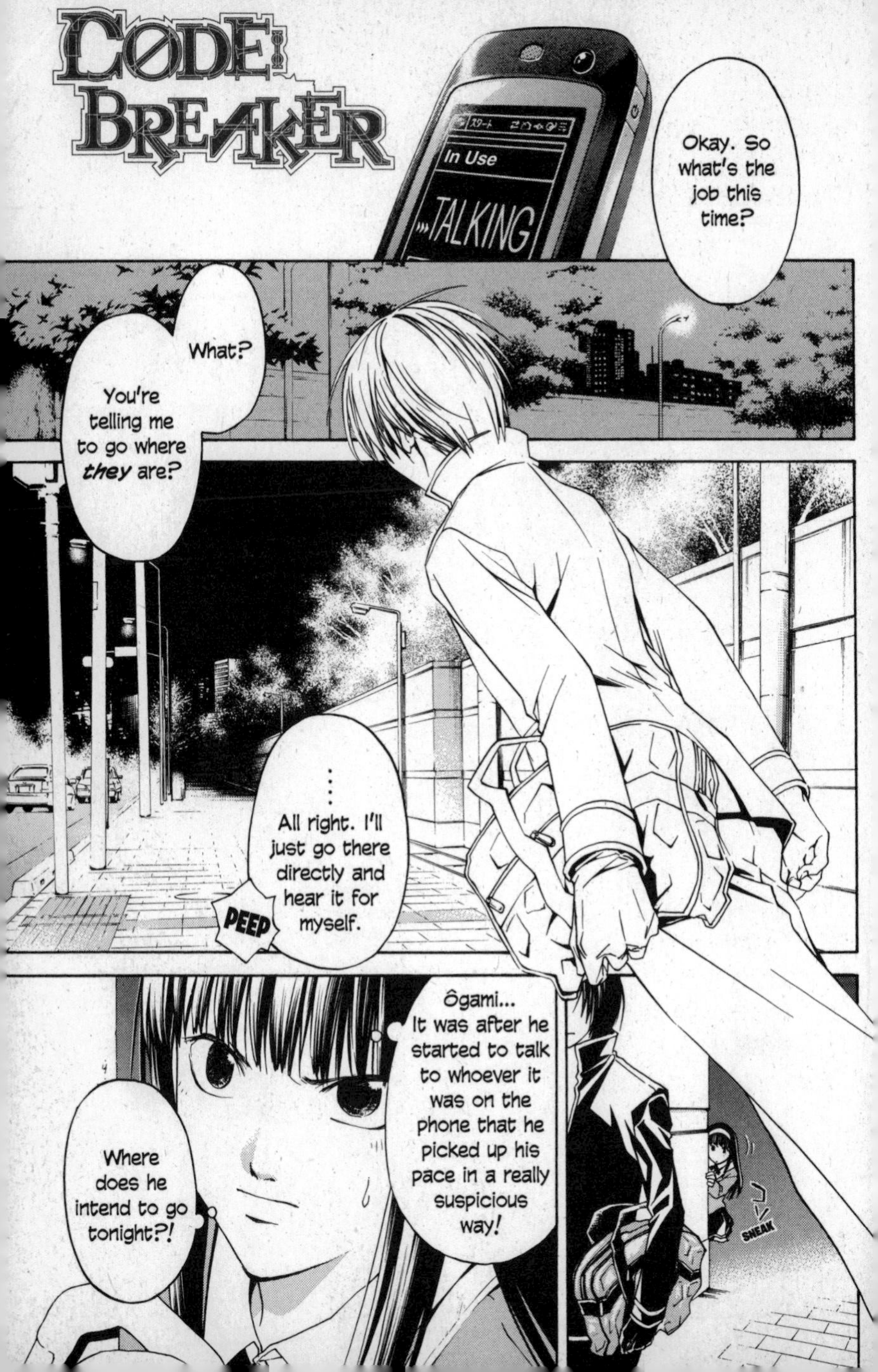
CODE:BREAKER
In Use
TALKING
Okay. So what's the job this time?
What?
You're telling me to go where *they* are?
....
All right. I'll just go there directly and hear it for myself.
PEEP
Ôgami... It was after he started to talk to whoever it was on the phone that he picked up his pace in a really suspicious way!
SNEAK
Where does he intend to go tonight?!

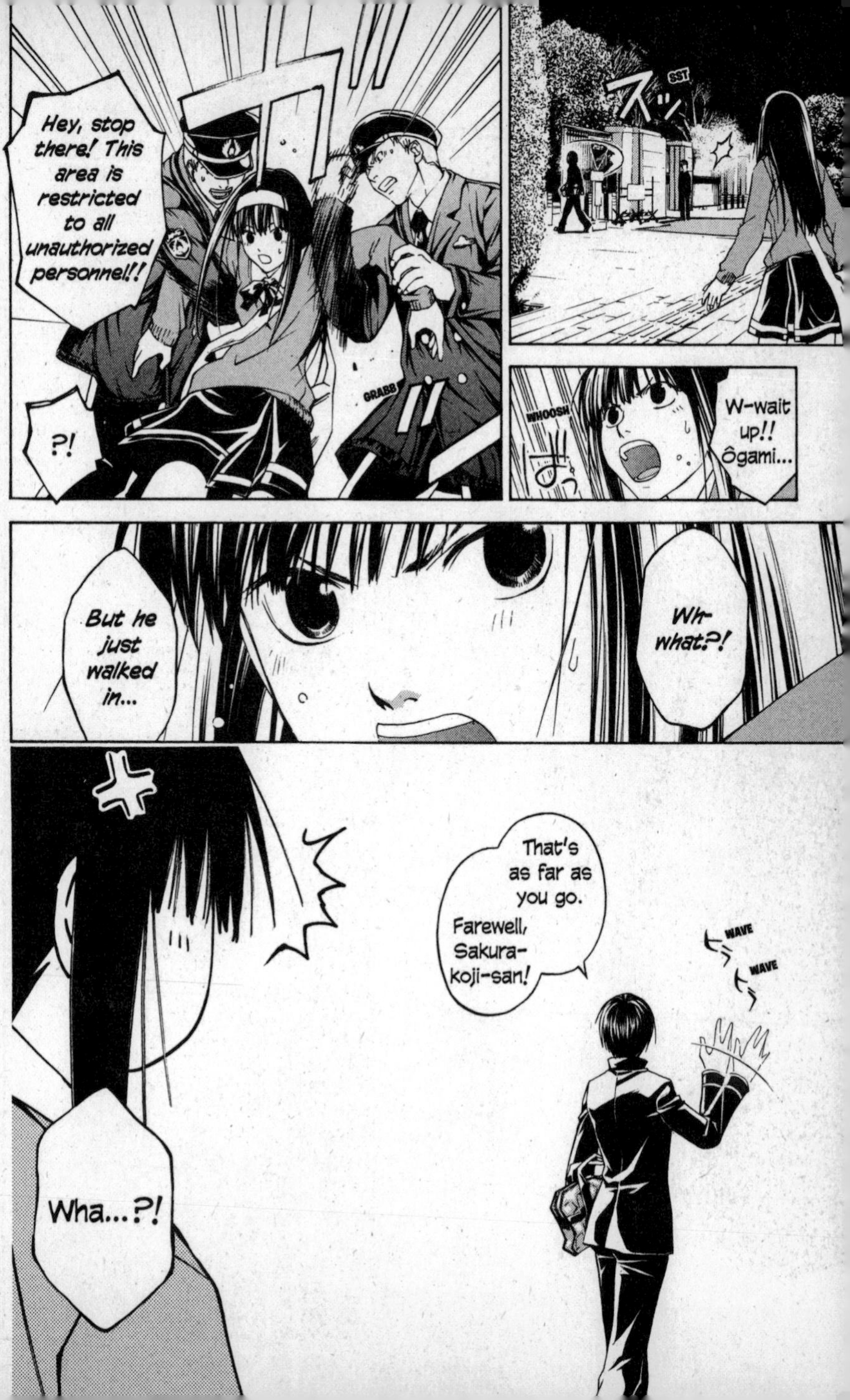
SST
WHOOSH
W-wait up!! Ôgami...
Hey, stop there! This area is restricted to all unauthorized personnel!!
?!
GRABB
Wh-what?!
But he just walked in...
That's as far as you go. Farewell, Sakura-koji-san!
WAVE
WAVE
Wha...?!

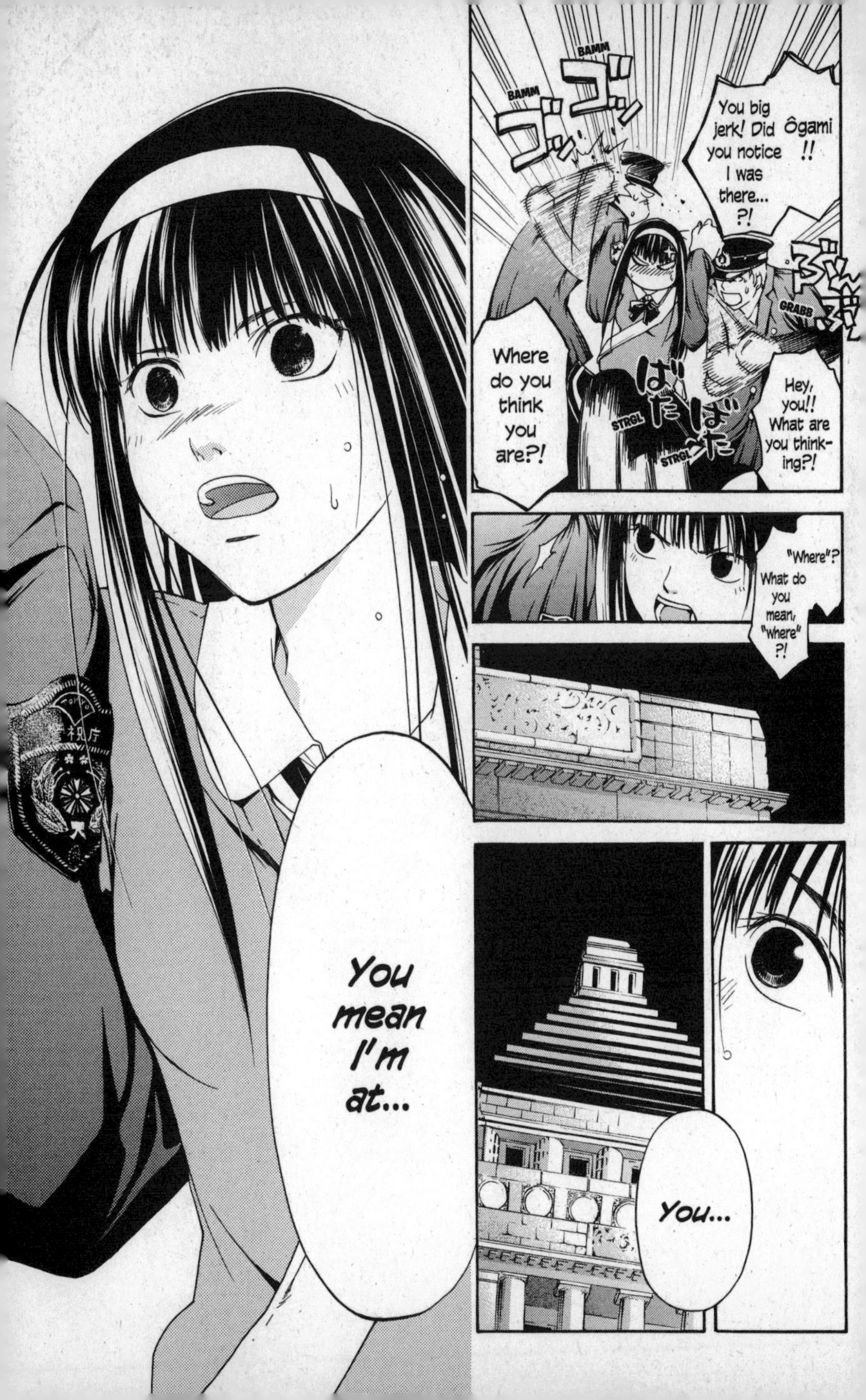

Ôgami!!
You big jerk! Did you notice I was there...?!
BAMM
BAMM
GRABB
Hey, you!! What are you thinking?!
STRGL
STRGL
Where do you think you are?!
"Where"? What do you mean, "where"?!
You...
You mean I'm at...

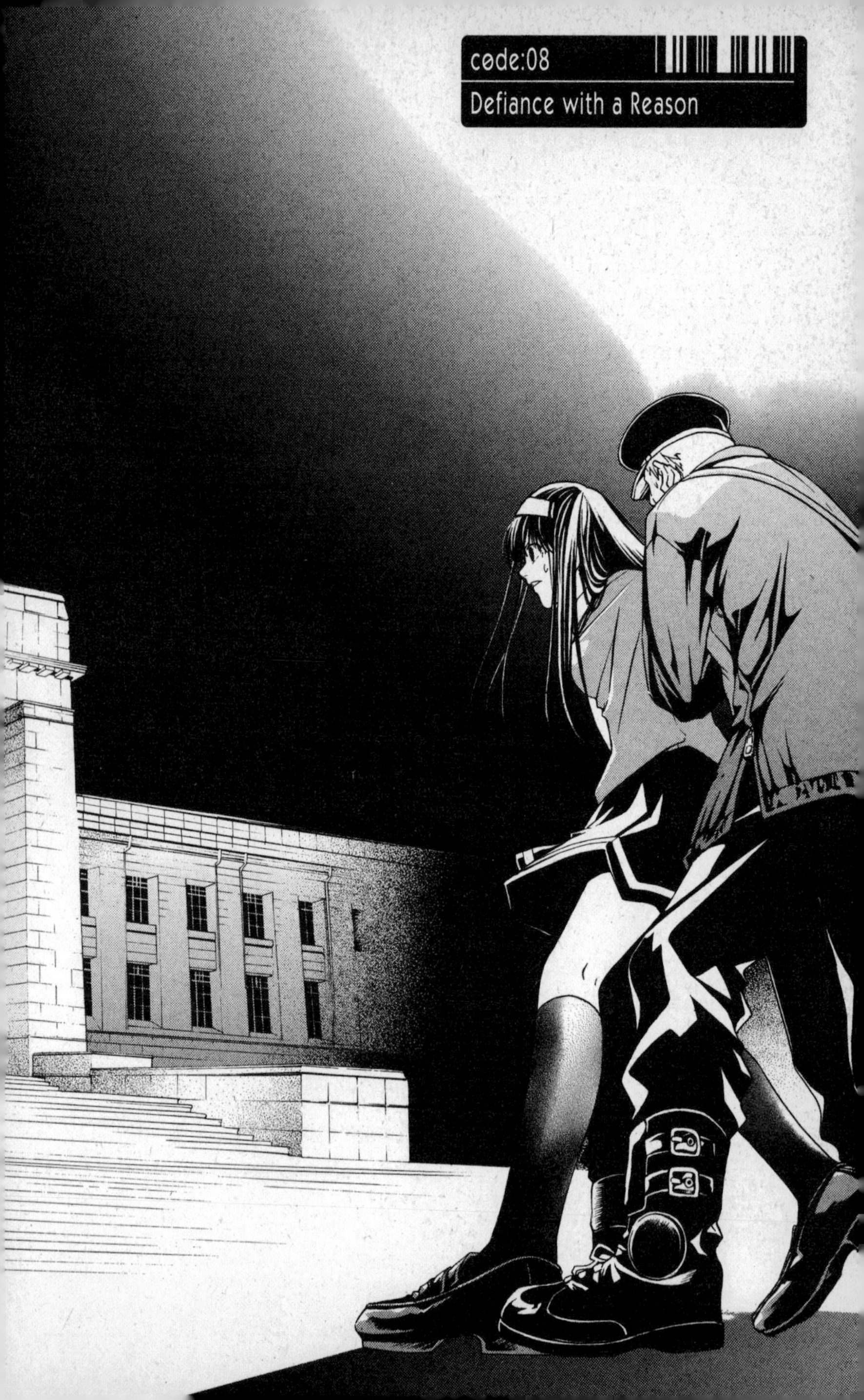
code:08
Defiance with a Reason

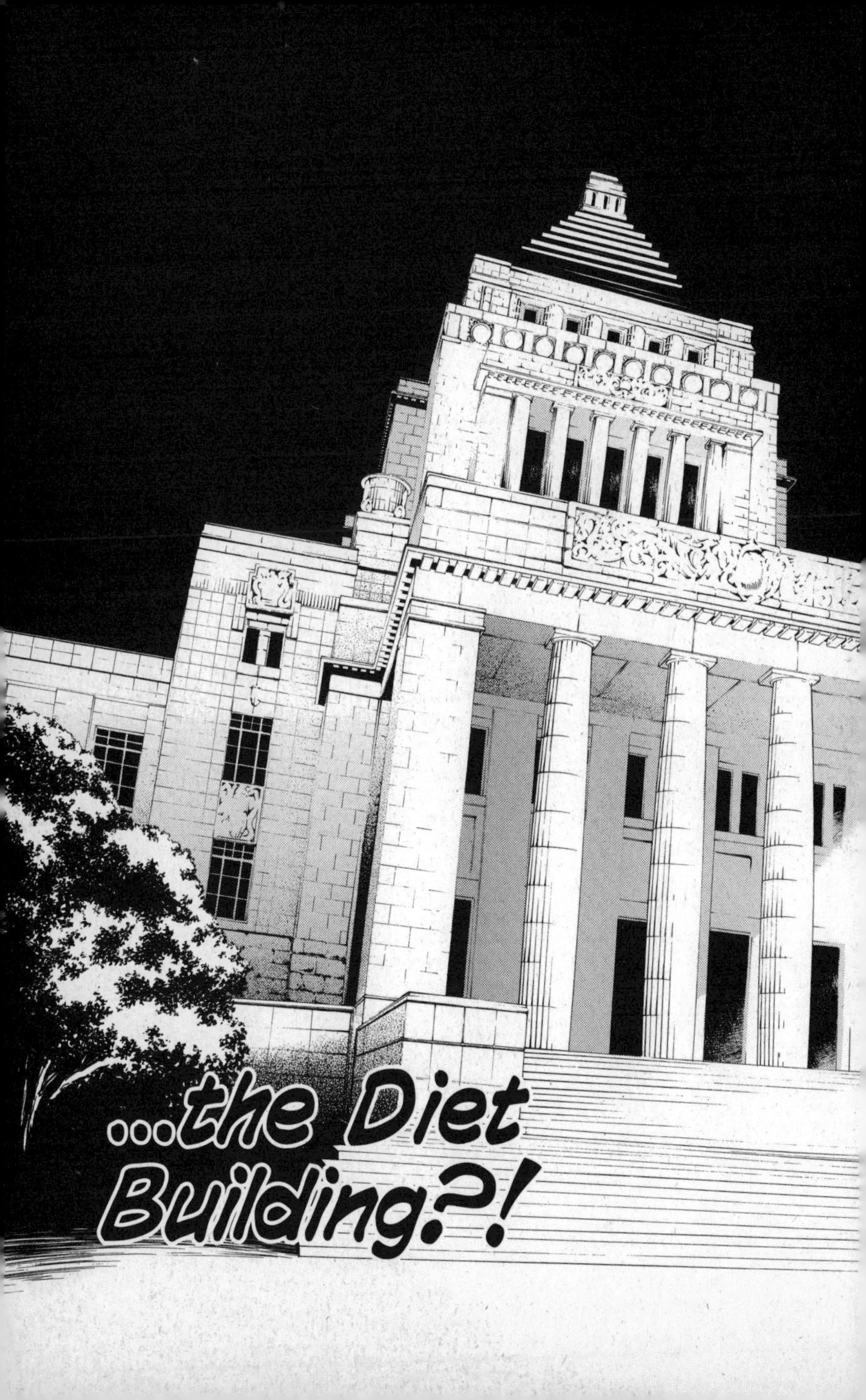
...the Diet Building?!

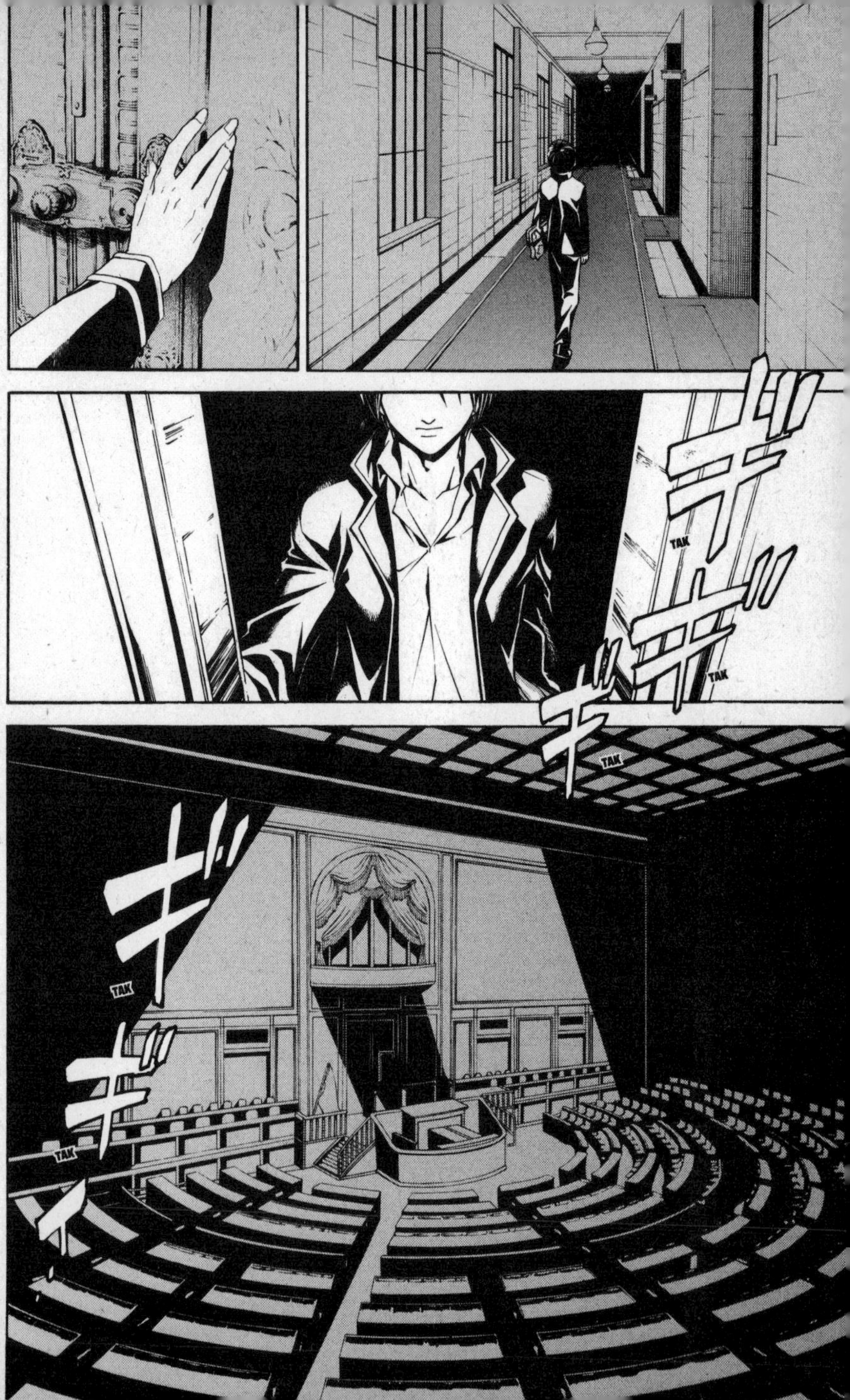
TAK
TAK
TAK
TAK
TAK

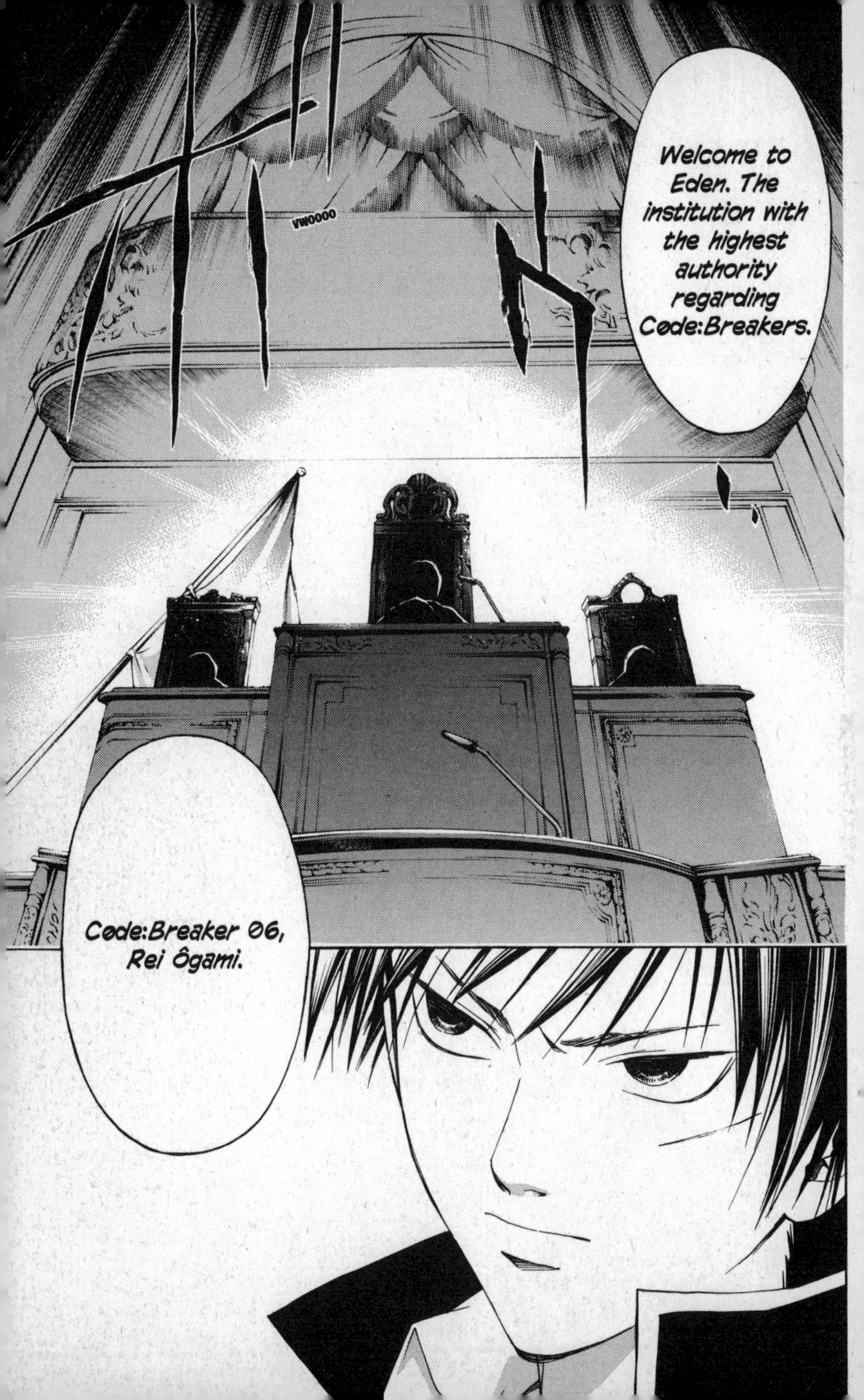
Welcome to Eden. The institution with the highest authority regarding Code:Breakers.
VWOOO
Code:Breaker 06, Rei Ôgami.

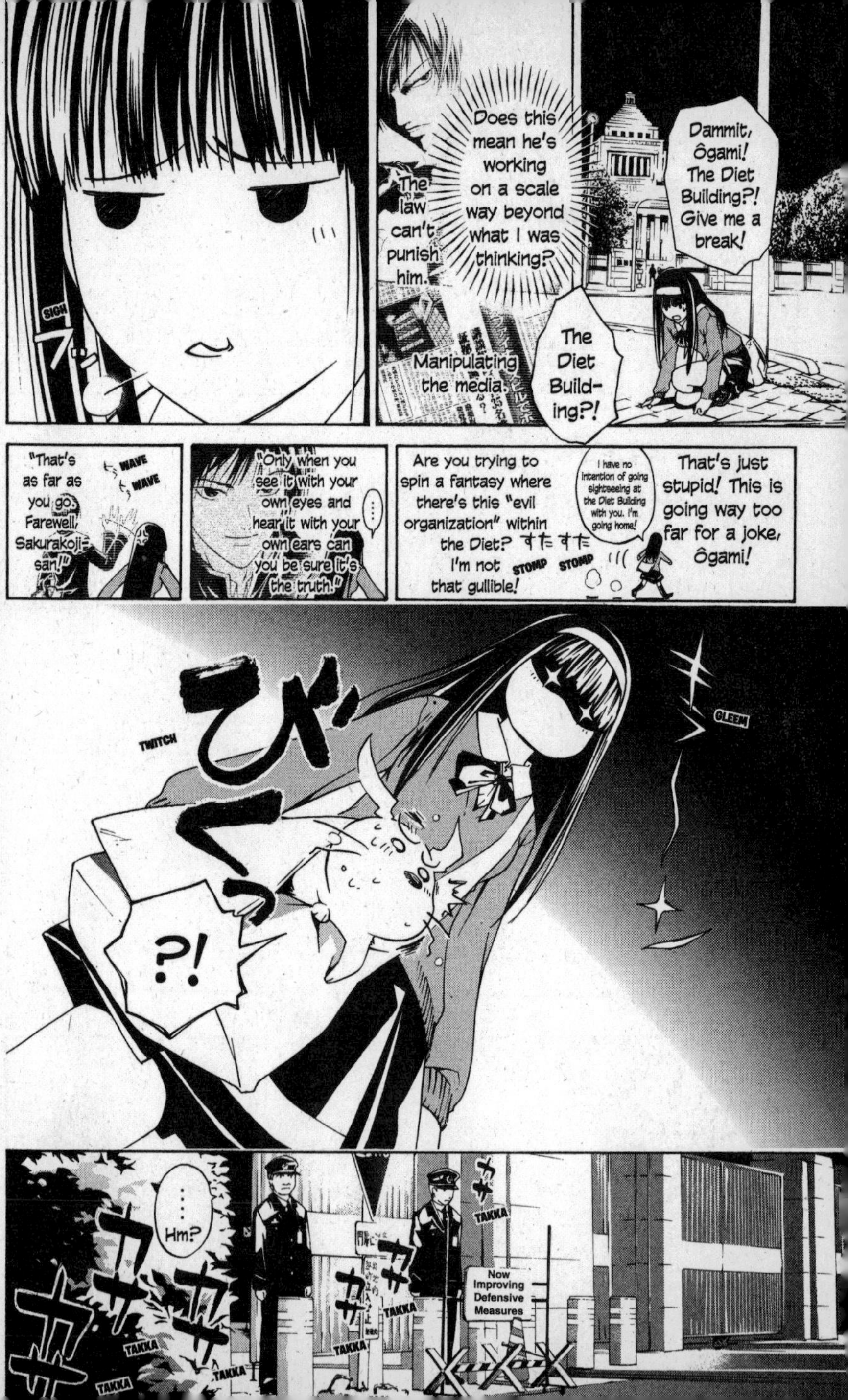
Dammit, Ôgami! The Diet Building?! Give me a break!
The Diet Build-ing?!
Does this mean he's working on a scale way beyond what I was thinking?
The law can't punish him.
Manipulating the media.
SIGH
That's just stupid! This is going way too far for a joke, Ôgami!
I have no intention of going sightseeing at the Diet Building with you. I'm going home!
Are you trying to spin a fantasy where there's this "evil organization" within the Diet?
すたすた
STOMP STOMP
I'm not that gullible!
...
"Only when you see it with your own eyes and hear it with your own ears can you be sure it's the truth."
WAVE WAVE
"That's as far as you go. Farewell, Sakurakoji-san!"
GLEEM
TWITCH
びくっ
?!
...
Hm?
TAKKA
Now Improving Defensive Measures
TAKKA
TAKKA
TAKKA
TAKKA
TAKKA

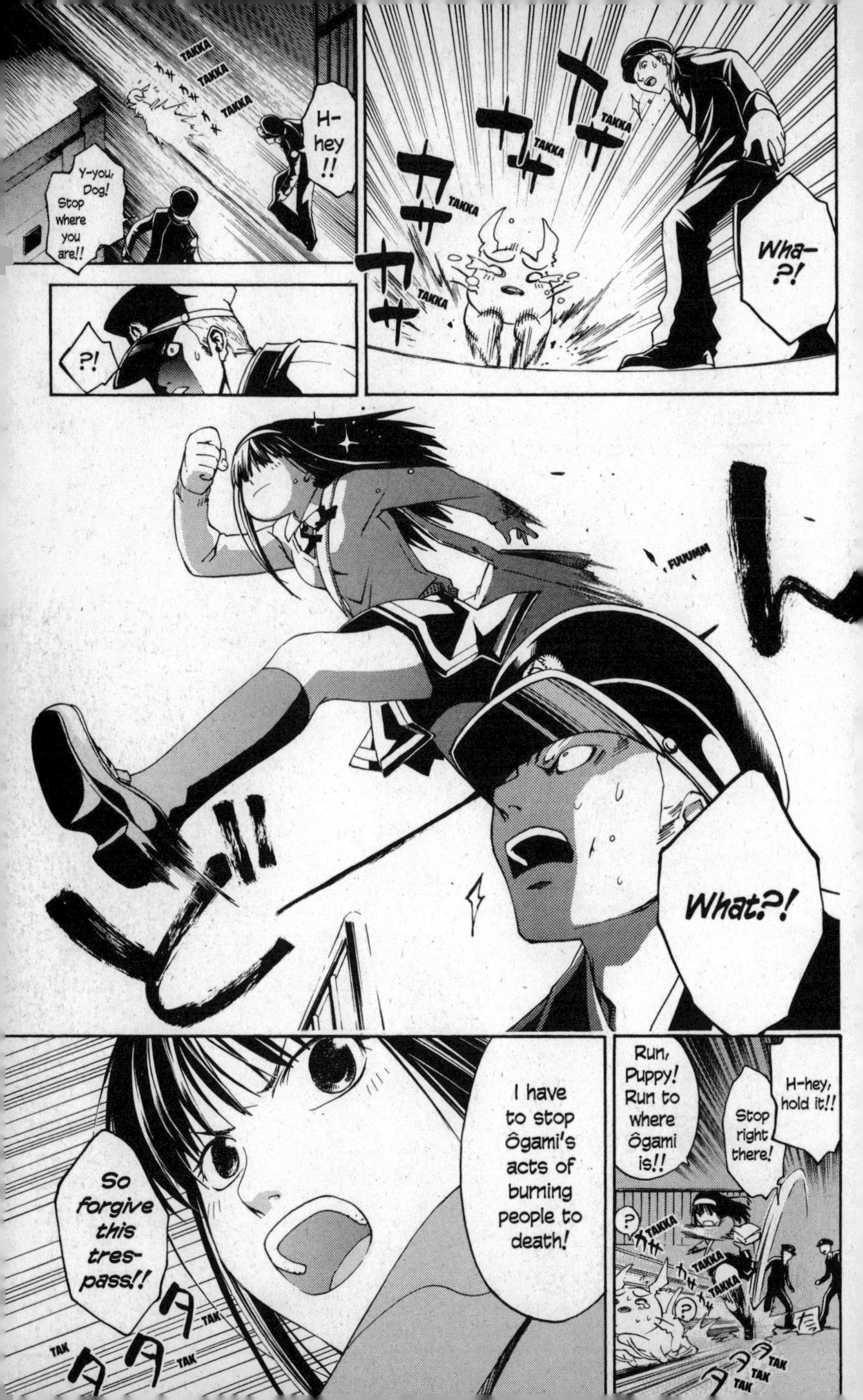

TAKKA
TAKKA
TAKKA
TAKKA
Wha— ?!
TAKKA
TAKKA
TAKKA
H-hey!!
Y-you, Dog! Stop where you are!!
?!
FUUUMM
What?!
H-hey, hold it!!
Stop right there!
Run, Puppy! Run to where Ôgami is!!
?
TAKKA
TAKKA
TAKKA
?
TAK
TAK
TAK
I have to stop Ôgami's acts of burning people to death!
So forgive this tres-pass!!
TAK
TAK
TAK

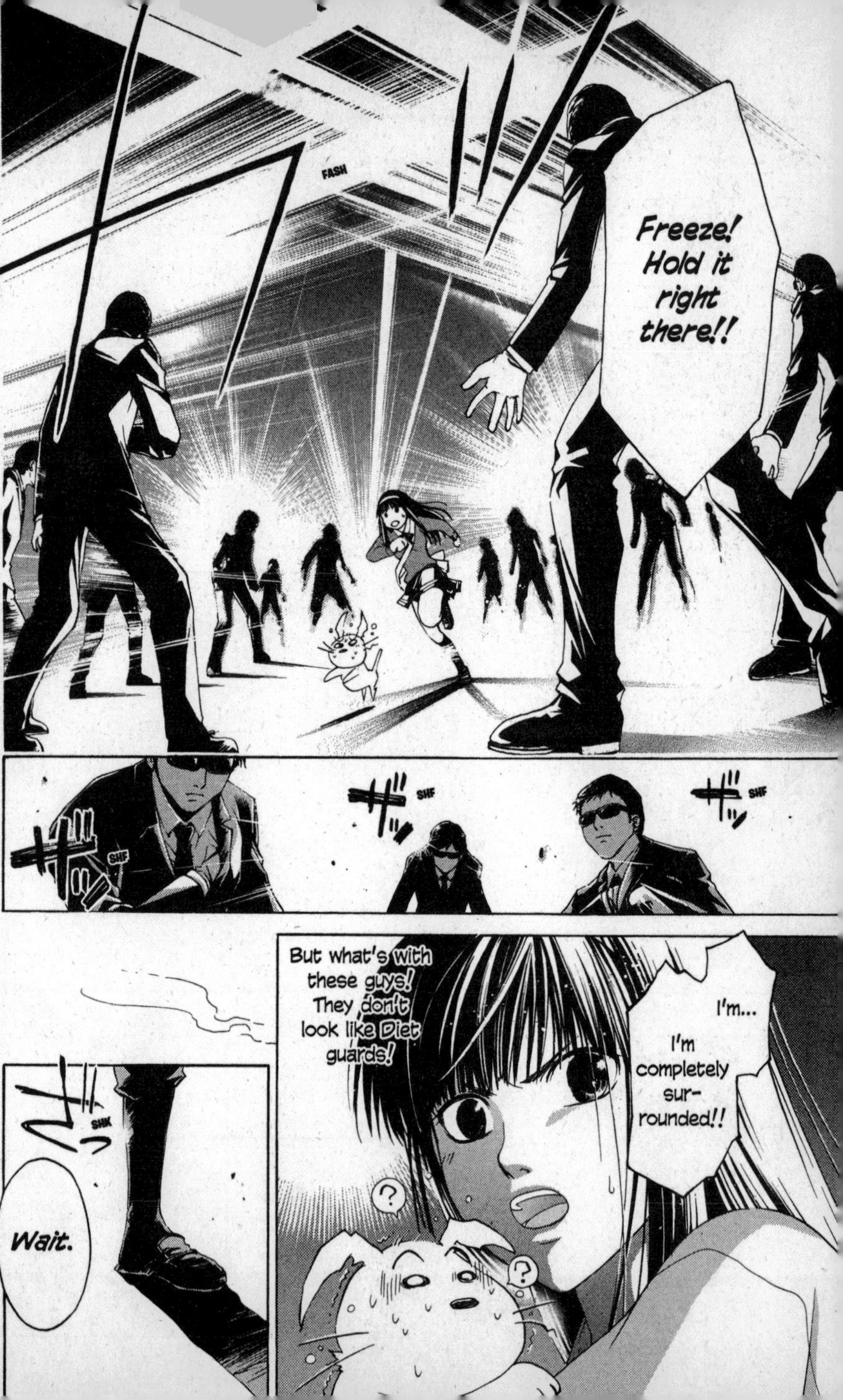
Freeze! Hold it right there!!
FASH
SHF
SHF
SHF
I'm...
I'm completely sur-rounded!!
But what's with these guys! They don't look like Diet guards!
SHK
Wait.

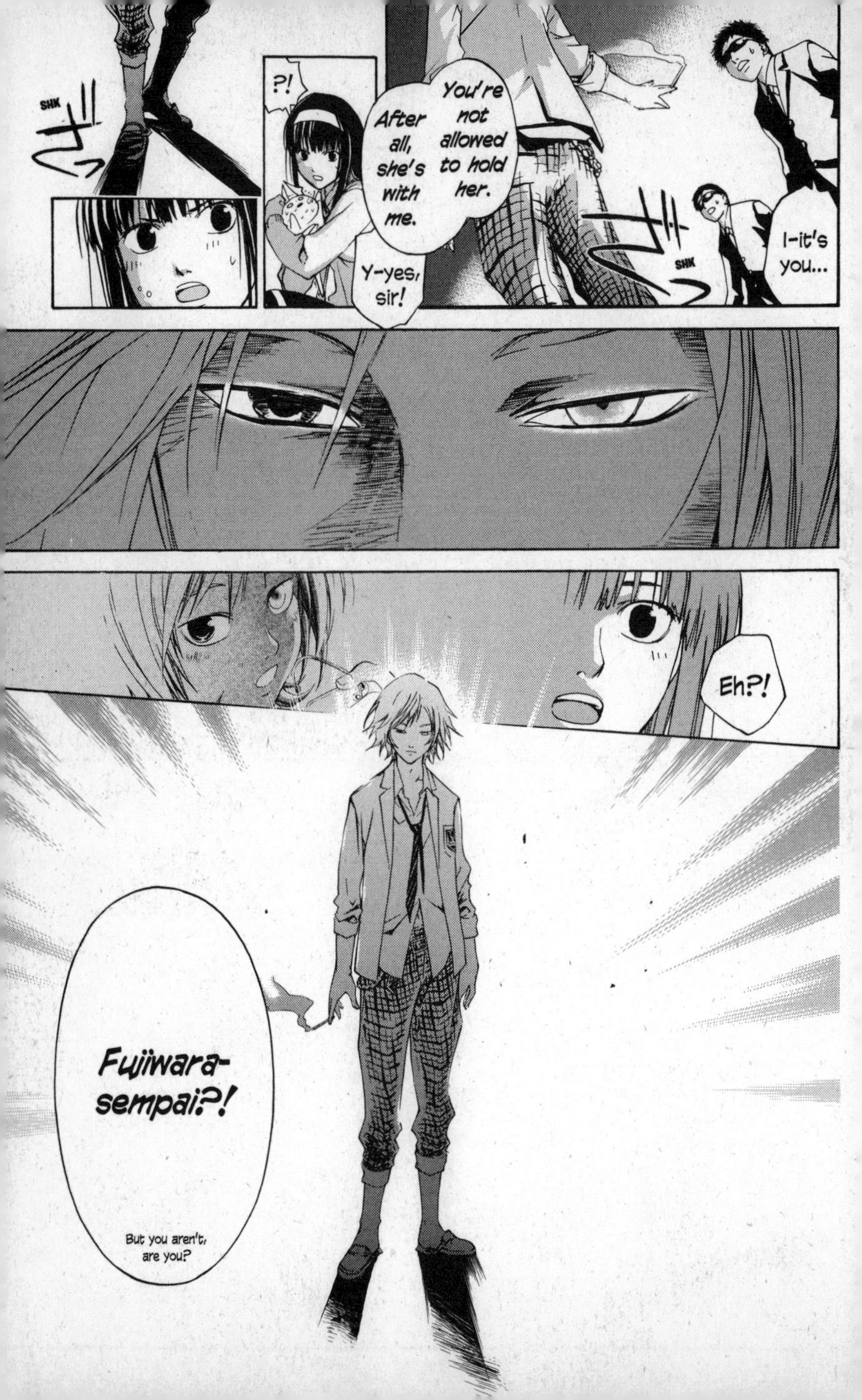
SHK
I-it's you...
You're not allowed to hold her.
After all, she's with me.
?!
Y-yes, sir!
SHK
Eh?!
Fujiwara-sempai?!
But you aren't, are you?

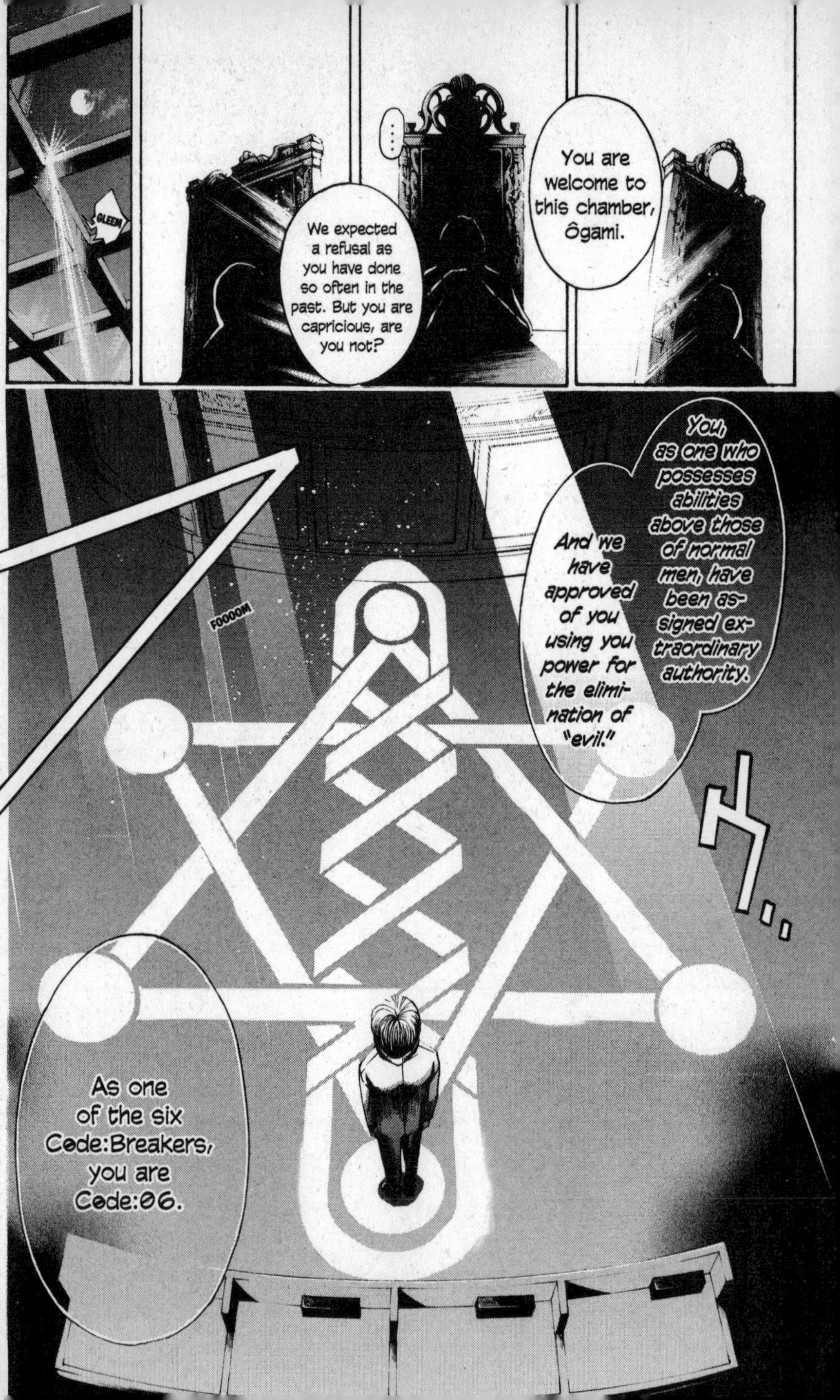
You are welcome to this chamber, Ôgami.
...
We expected a refusal as you have done so often in the past. But you are capricious, are you not?
GLEEM
You, as one who possesses abilities above those of normal men, have been assigned extraordinary authority.
And we have approved of you using you power for the elimination of "evil."
FOOOOM
As one of the six Code:Breakers, you are Code:06.

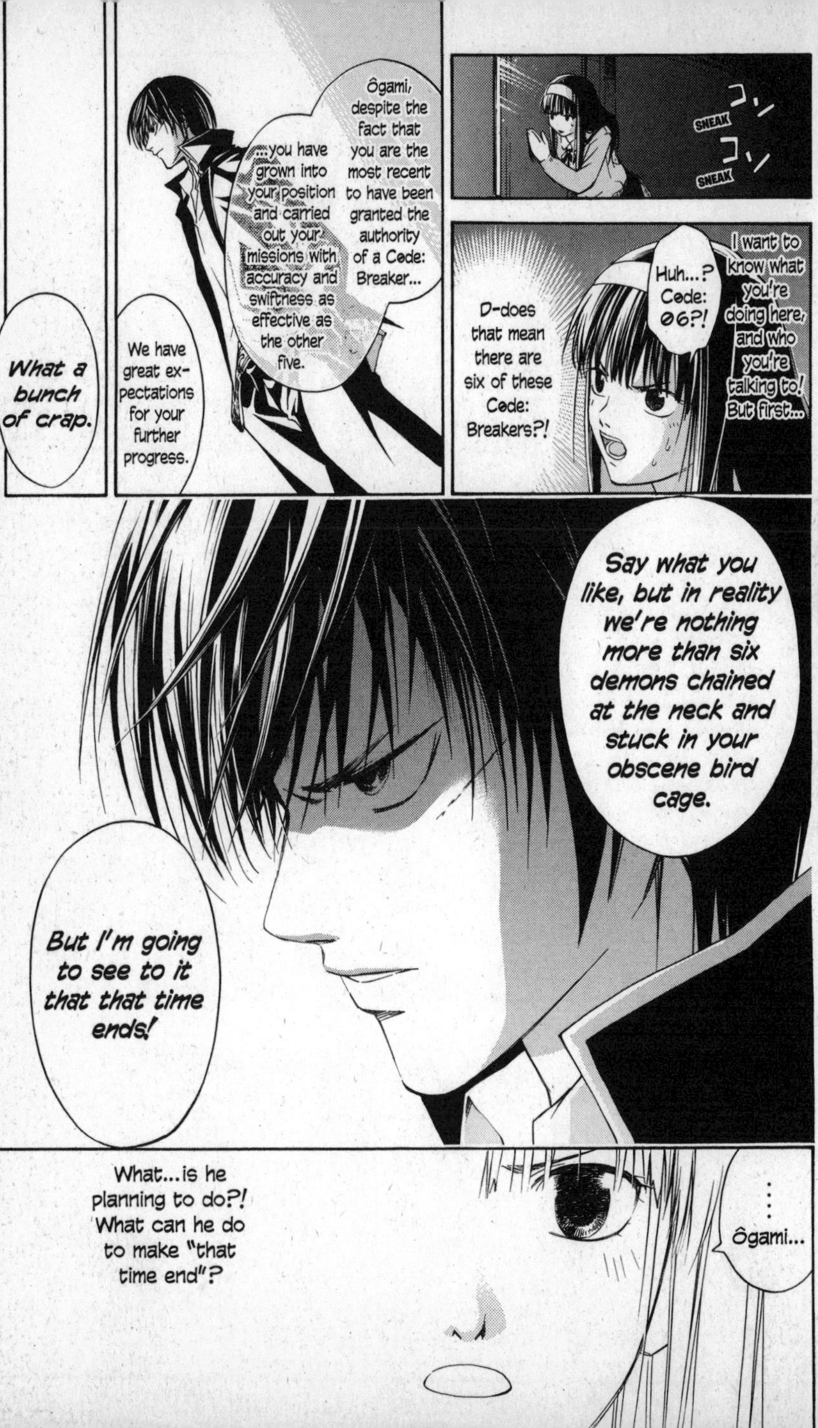
SNEAK
SNEAK
I want to know what you're doing here, and who you're talking to! But first...
Huh...? Code: 06?!
D-does that mean there are six of these Code: Breakers?!
Ôgami, despite the fact that you are the most recent to have been granted the authority of a Code: Breaker...
...you have grown into your position and carried out your missions with accuracy and swiftness as effective as the other five.
We have great expectations for your further progress.
What a bunch of crap.
Say what you like, but in reality we're nothing more than six demons chained at the neck and stuck in your obscene bird cage.
But I'm going to see to it that that time ends!
...Ôgami...
What...is he planning to do?! What can he do to make "that time end"?

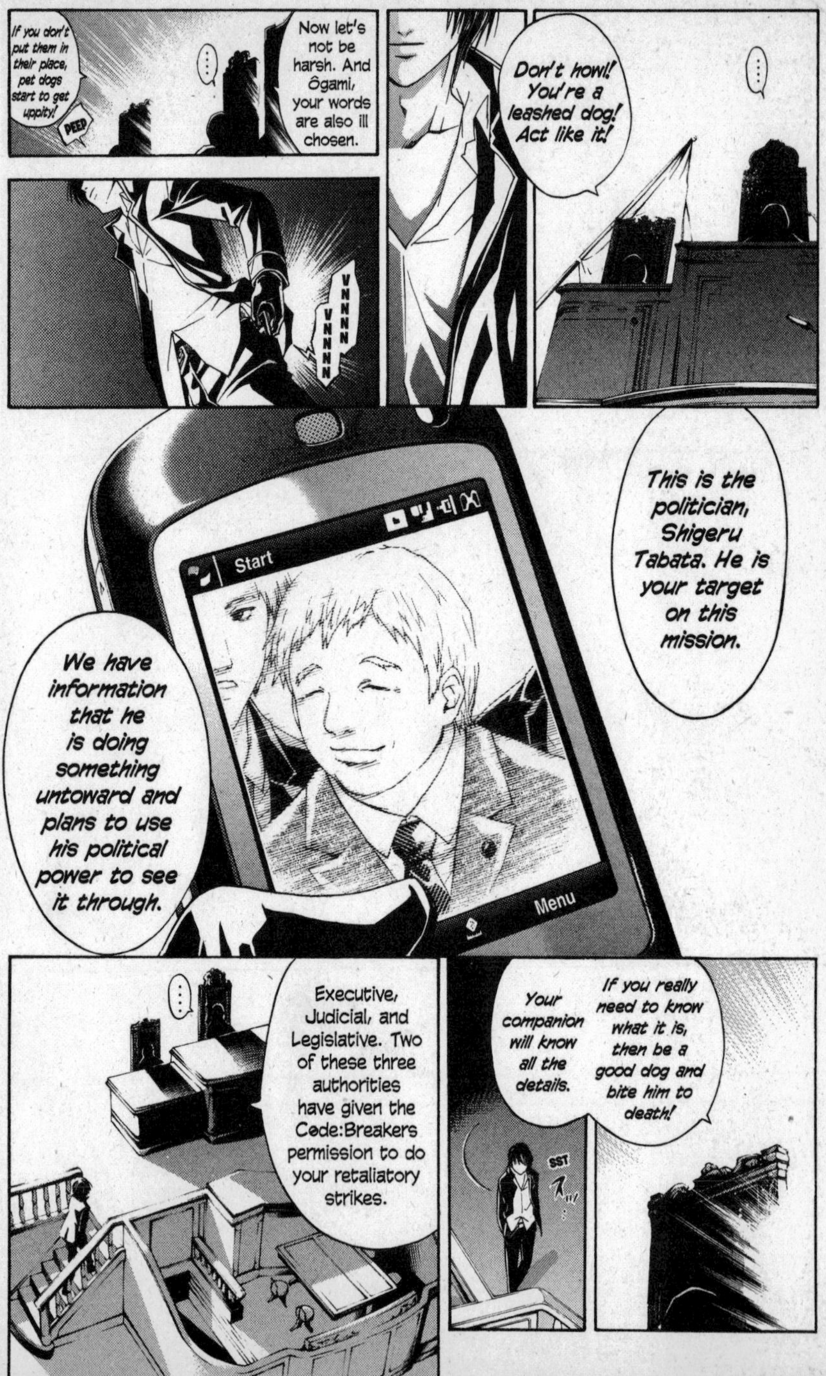
. . .
Don't howl! You're a leashed dog! Act like it!
Now let's not be harsh. And Ôgami, your words are also ill chosen.
. . .
If you don't put them in their place, pet dogs start to get uppity!
PEEP
VNNNN VNNNN
This is the politician, Shigeru Tabata. He is your target on this mission.
Start
Menu
We have information that he is doing something untoward and plans to use his political power to see it through.
If you really need to know what it is, then be a good dog and bite him to death!
Your companion will know all the details.
SST
Executive, Judicial, and Legislative. Two of these three authorities have given the Code:Breakers permission to do your retaliatory strikes.
. . .

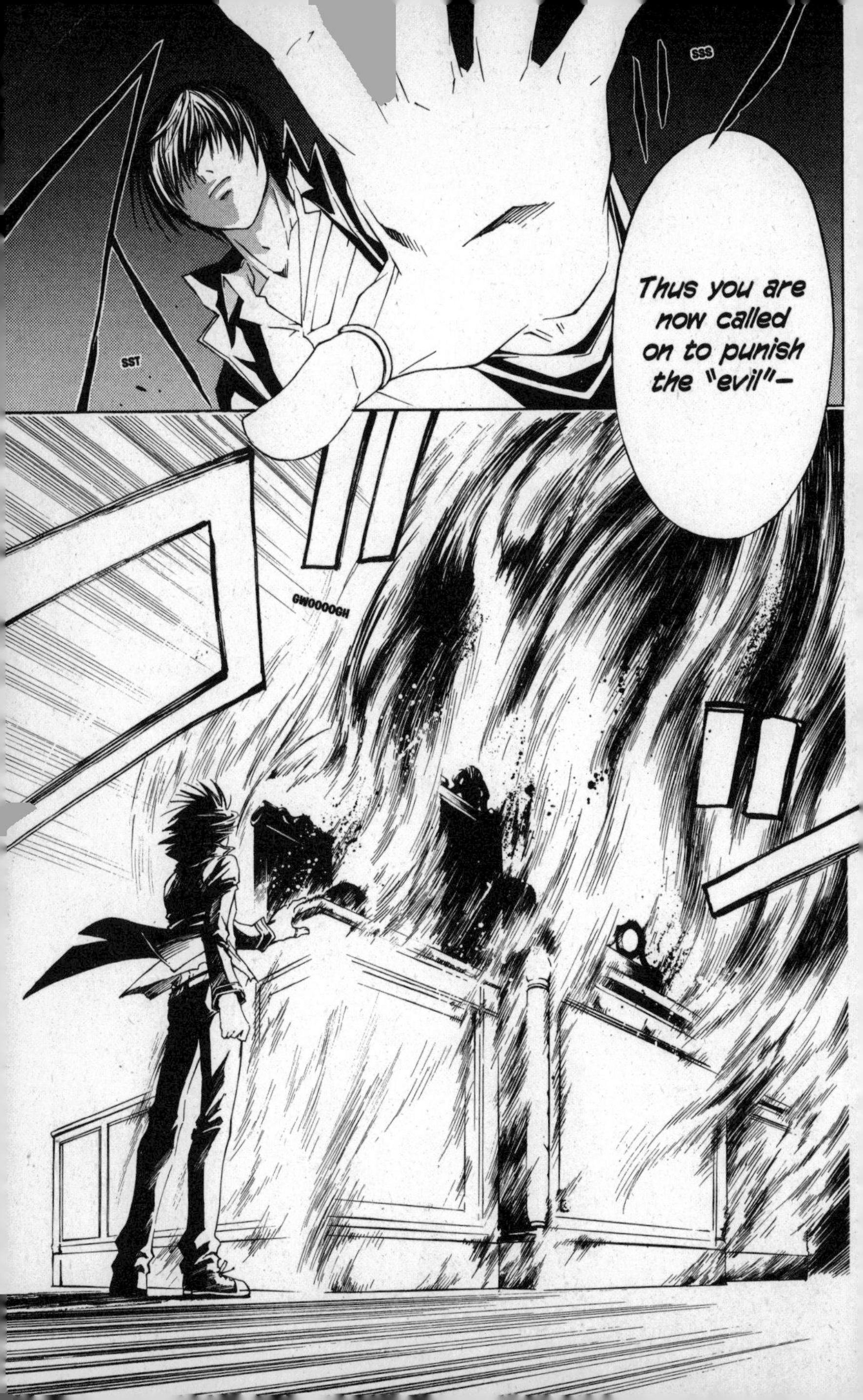
SSS
Thus you are now called on to punish the "evil"–
SST
GWOOOOGH

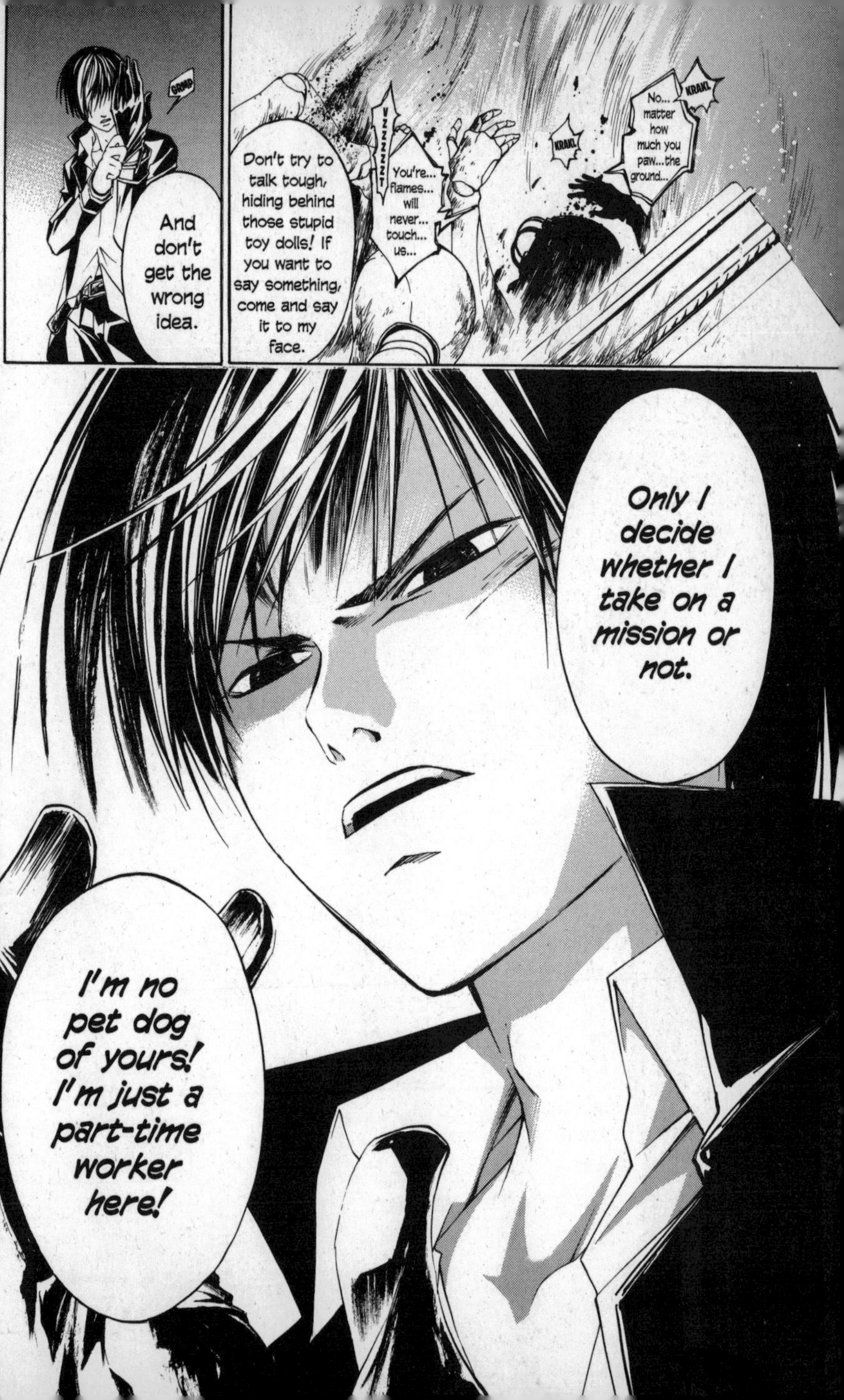
KRAK!
No... matter how much you paw...the ground...
KRAK!
VZZZZZZT
You're... flames... will never... touch... us...
Don't try to talk tough, hiding behind those stupid toy dolls! If you want to say something, come and say it to my face.
GRIND
And don't get the wrong idea.
Only I decide whether I take on a mission or not.
I'm no pet dog of yours! I'm just a part-time worker here!

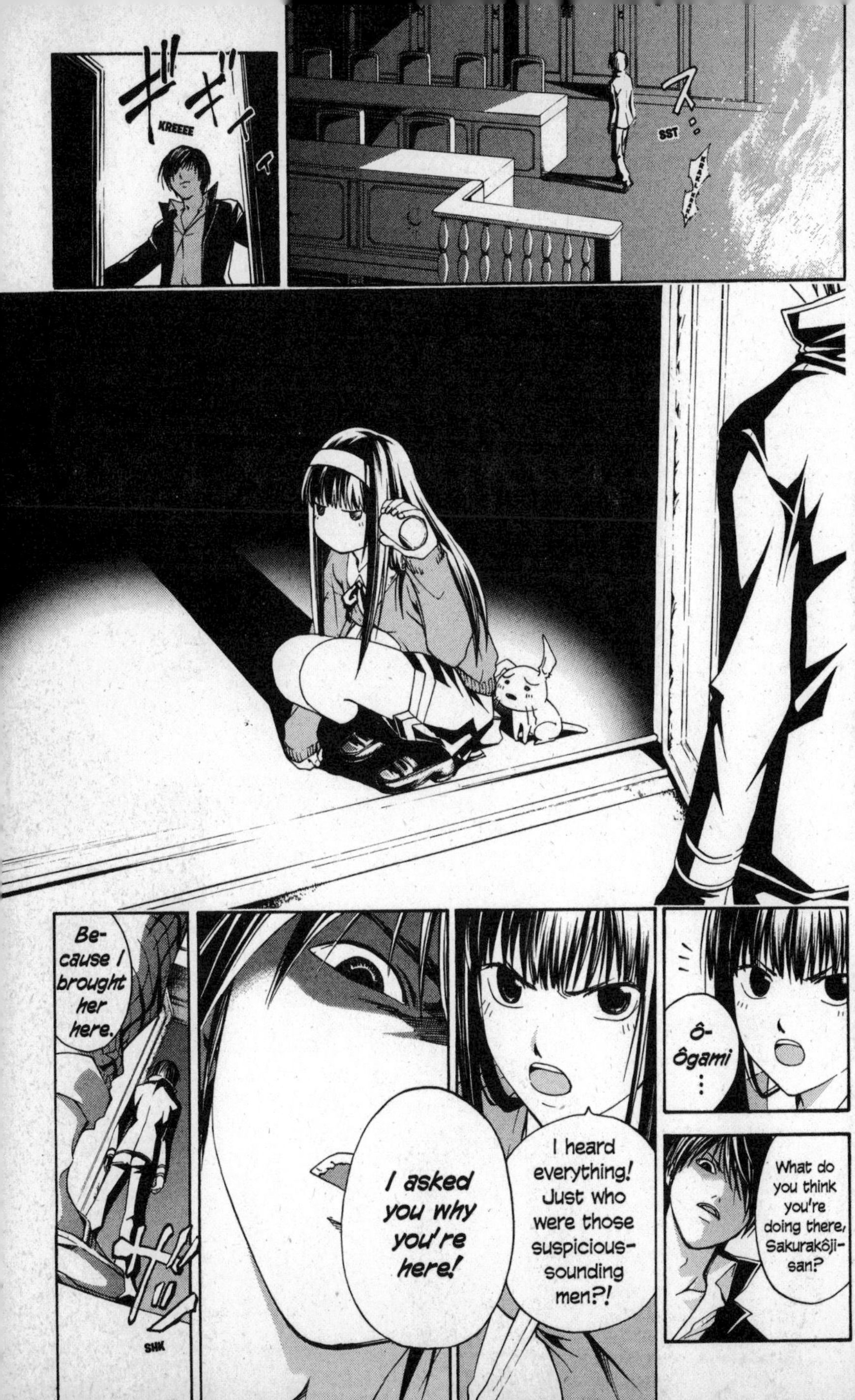
ス
SST
ギィィ
KREEEE
Ô-Ôgami...
What do you think you're doing there, Sakurakôji-san?
I heard everything! Just who were those suspicious-sounding men?!
I asked you why you're here!
Be-cause I brought her here.
SHK

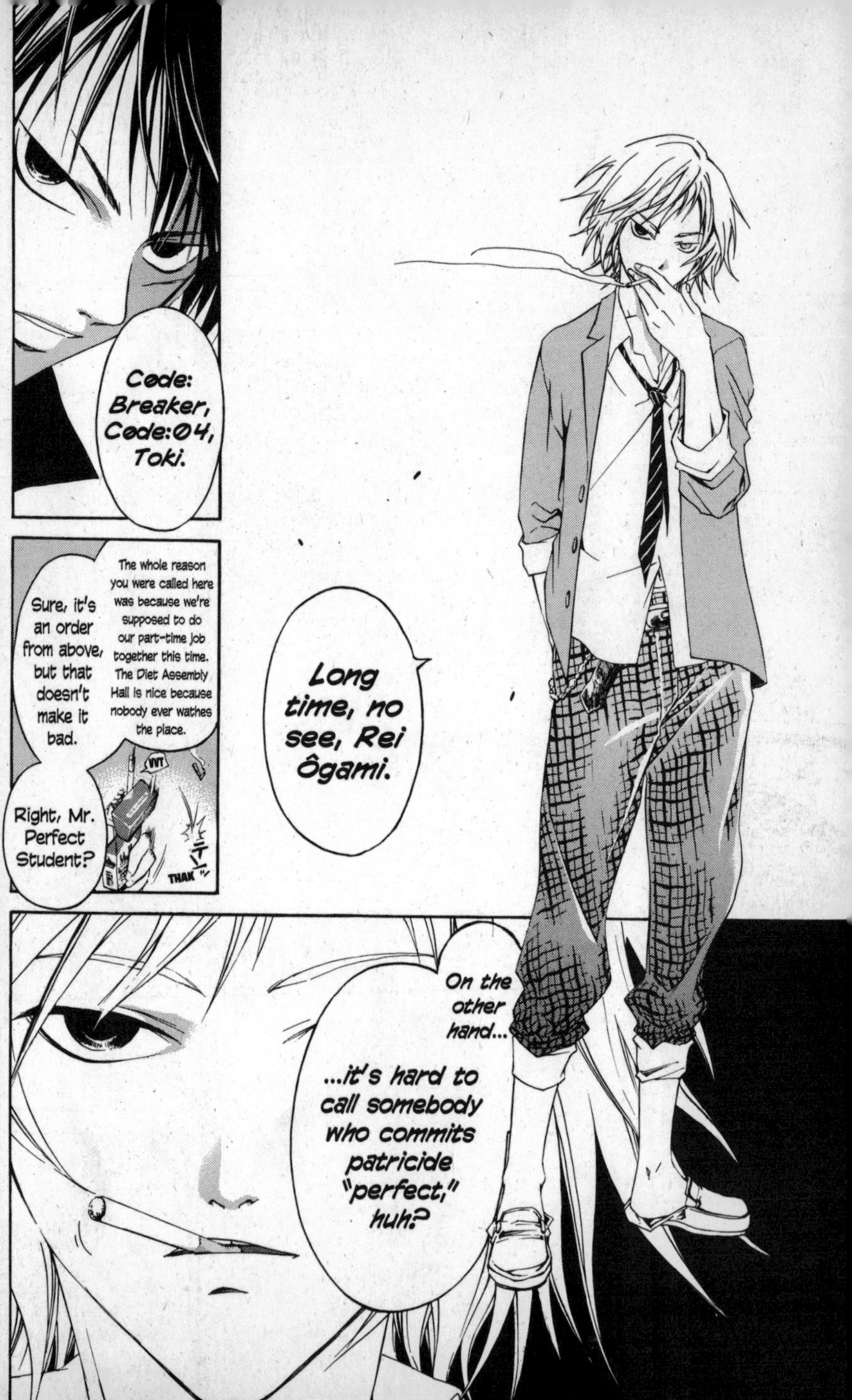
Long time, no see, Rei Ôgami.
Code: Breaker, Code:04, Toki.
The whole reason you were called here was because we're supposed to do our part-time job together this time. The Diet Assembly Hall is nice because nobody ever wathes the place.
Sure, it's an order from above, but that doesn't make it bad.
VVT
THAK
Right, Mr. Perfect Student?
On the other hand...
...it's hard to call somebody who commits patricide "perfect," huh?

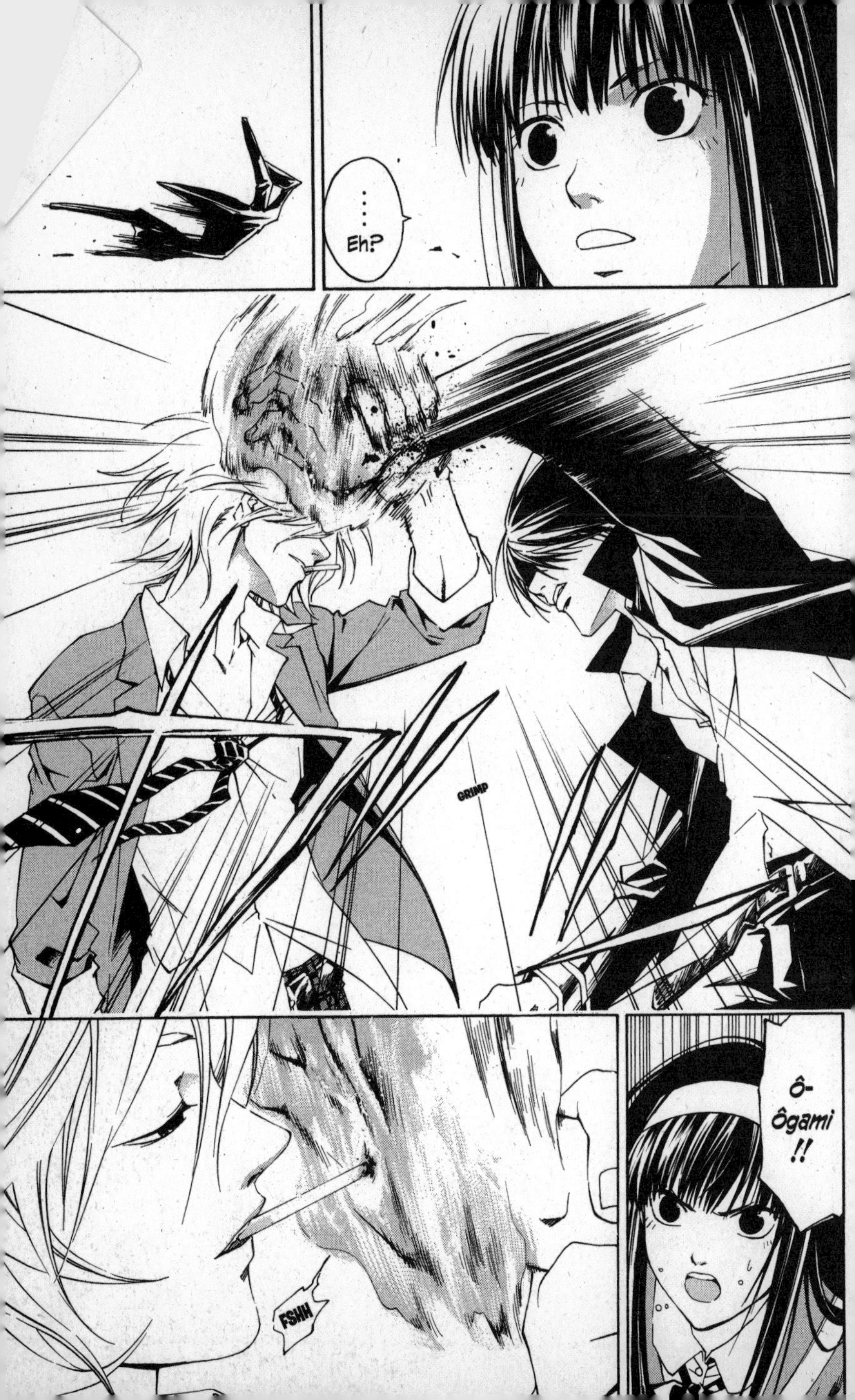

......Eh?
GRIMP
Ô-ôgami!!
FSHH

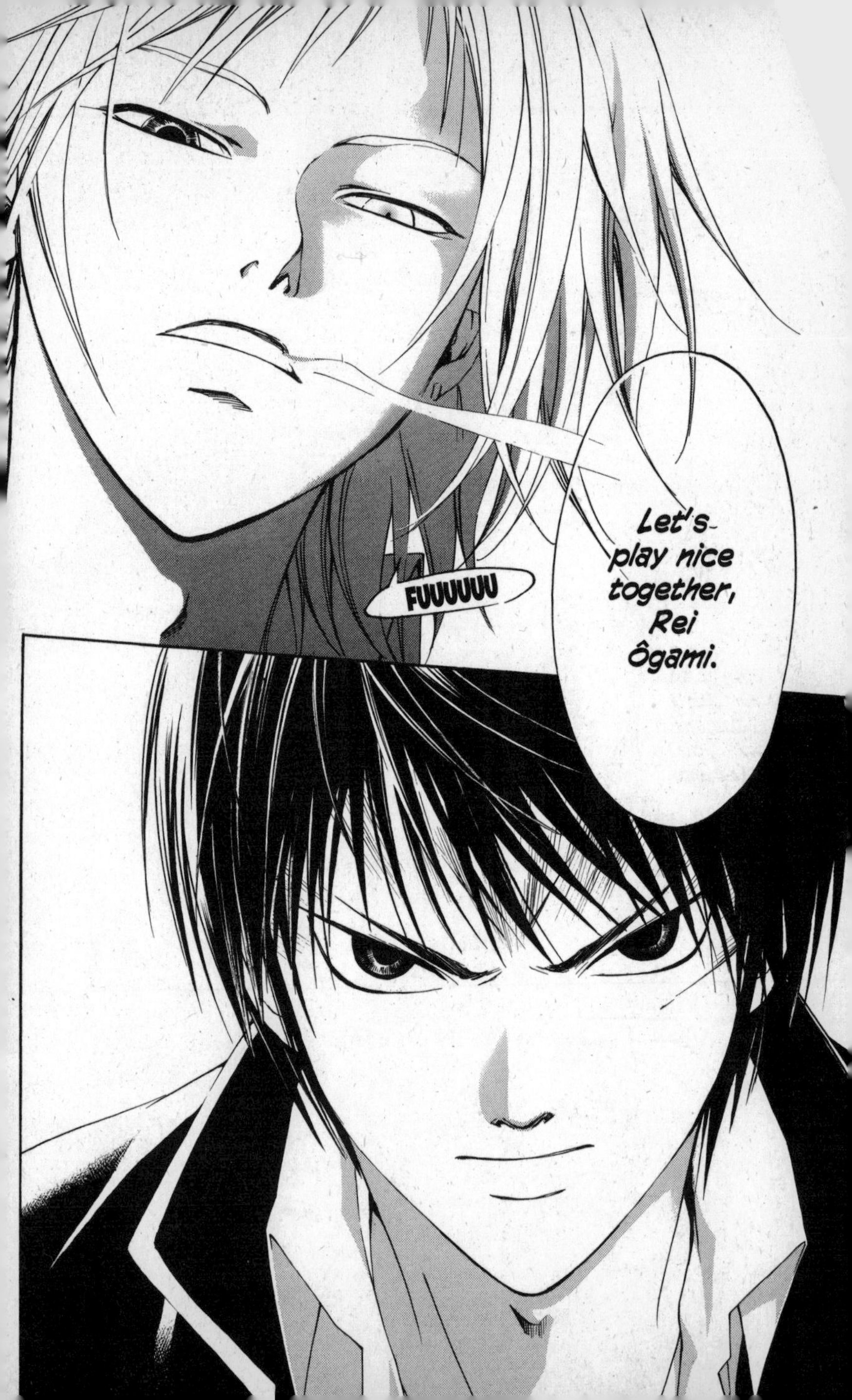
Let's-play nice together, Rei Ôgami.
FUUUUUU

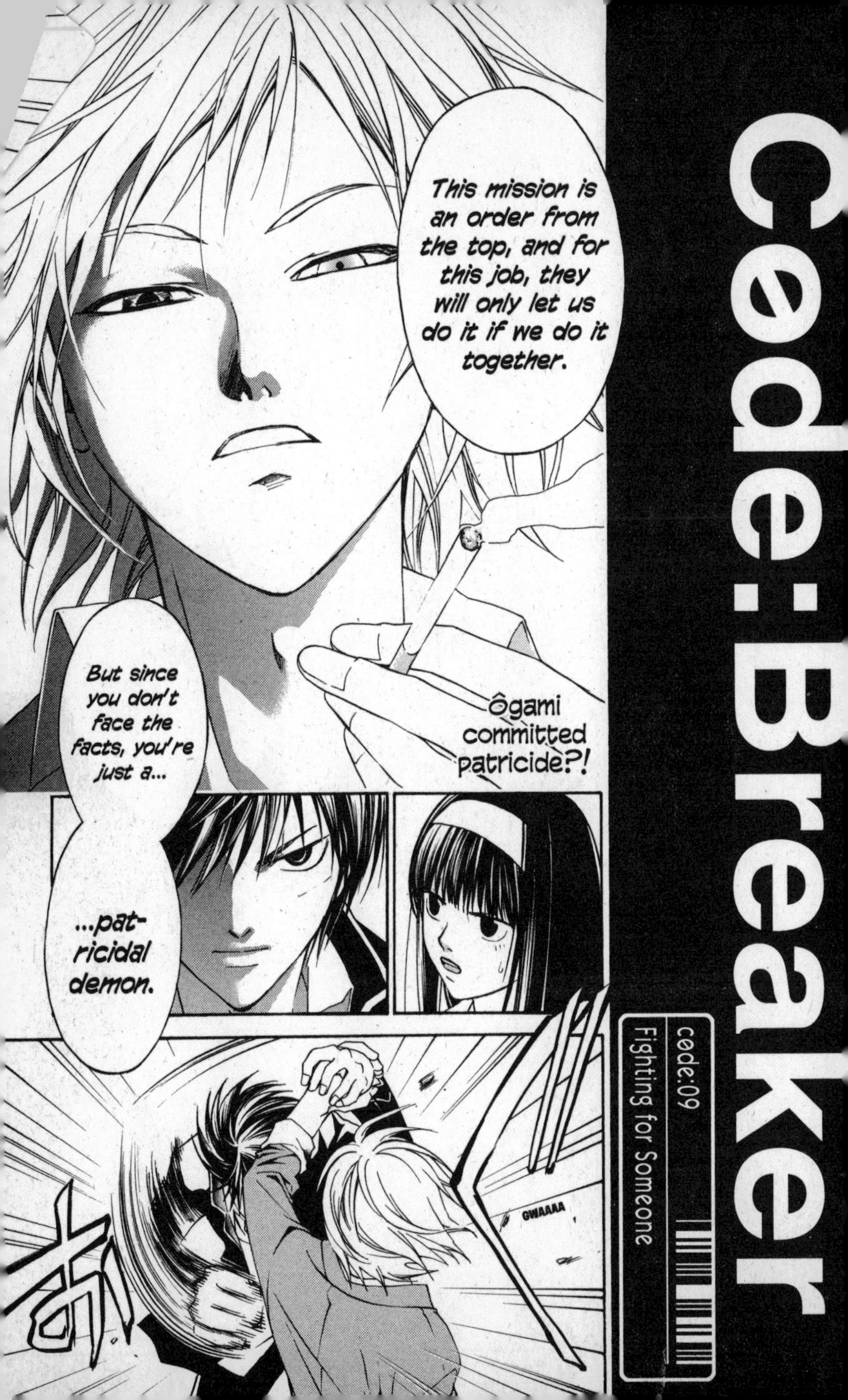

Cøde:Breaker
cøde:09
Fighting for Someone
This mission is an order from the top, and for this job, they will only let us do it if we do it together.
But since you don't face the facts, you're just a...
Ôgami committed patricide?!
...pat-ricidal demon.
GWAAAA

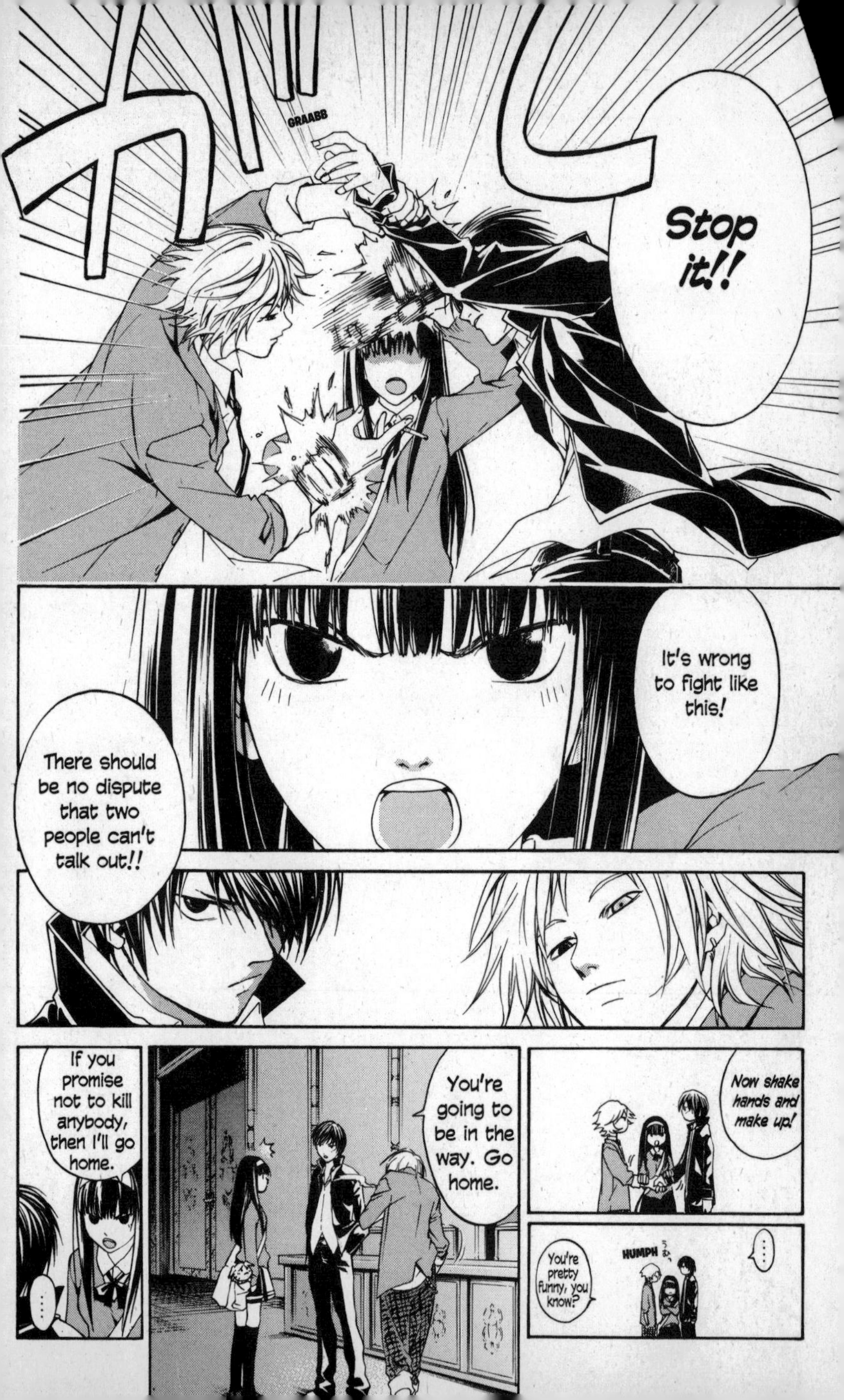

Stop it!!
GRAABB
It's wrong to fight like this!
There should be no dispute that two people can't talk out!!
Now shake hands and make up!
. . . .
HUMPH
You're pretty funny, you know?
You're going to be in the way. Go home.
If you promise not to kill anybody, then I'll go home.
. . . .

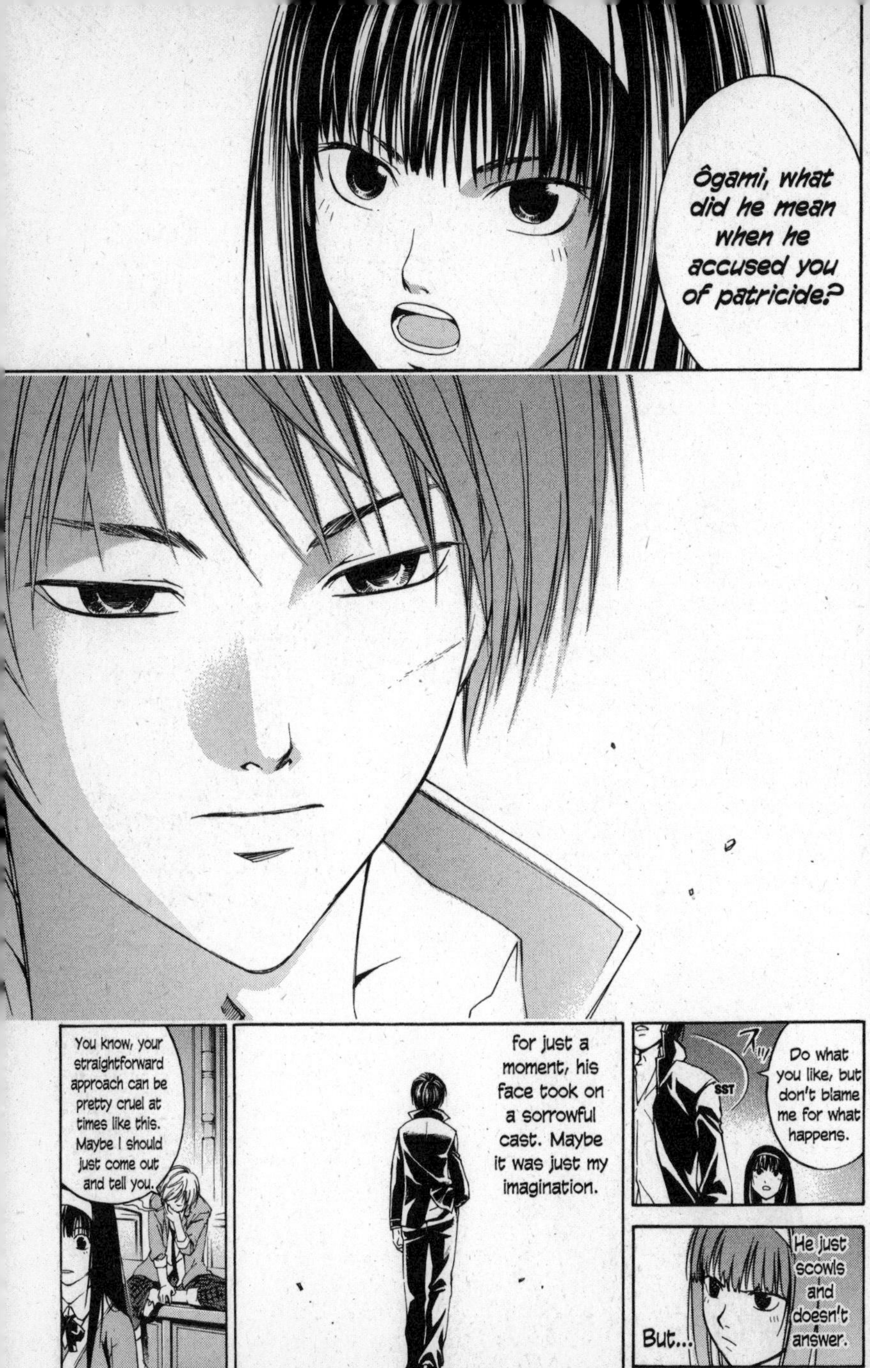
Ôgami, what did he mean when he accused you of patricide?
Do what you like, but don't blame me for what happens.
SST
He just scowls and doesn't answer.
But...
for just a moment, his face took on a sorrowful cast. Maybe it was just my imagination.
You know, your straightforward approach can be pretty cruel at times like this. Maybe I should just come out and tell you.

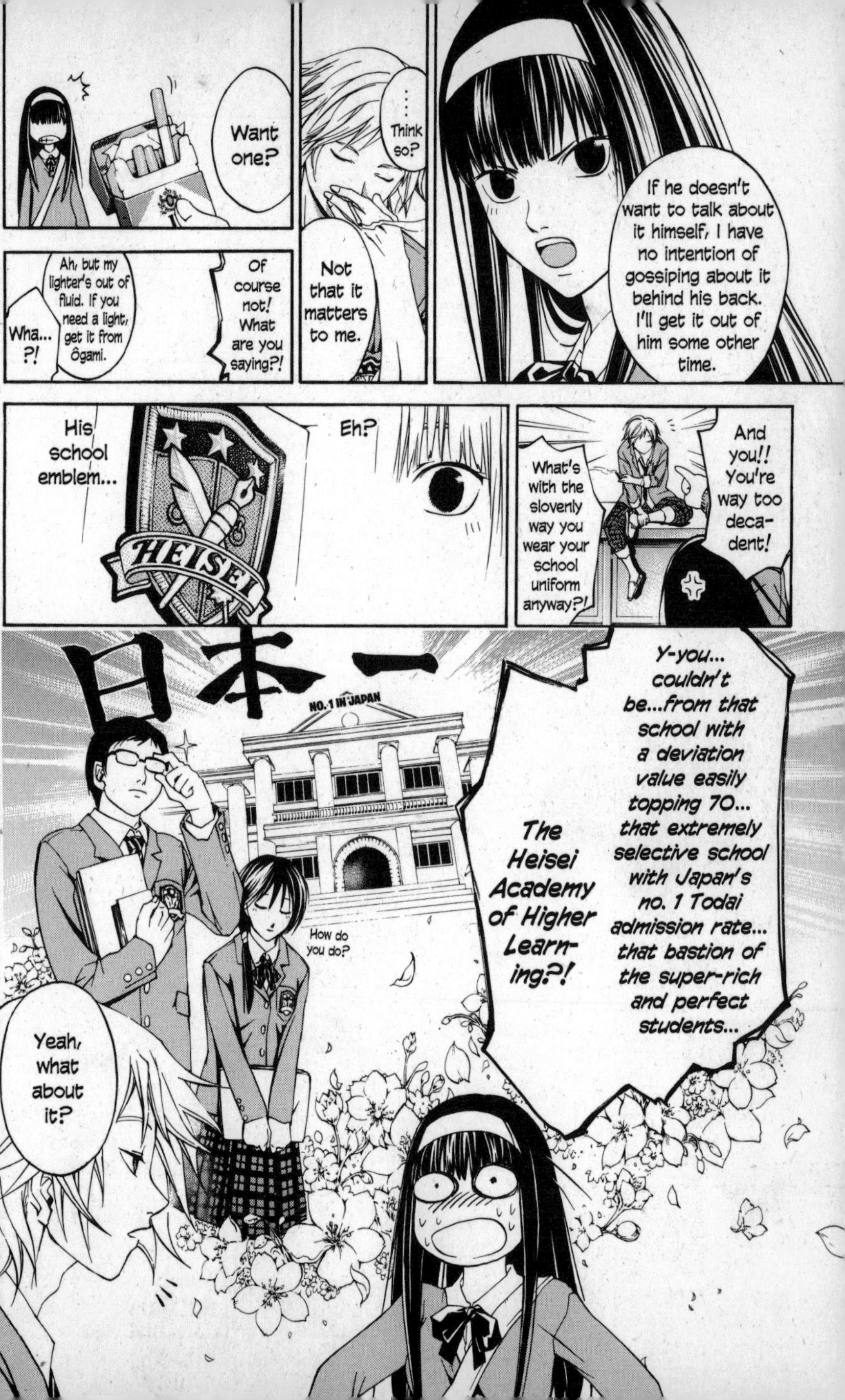

If he doesn't want to talk about it himself, I have no intention of gossiping about it behind his back. I'll get it out of him some other time.
....Think so?
Not that it matters to me.
Want one?
Of course not! What are you saying?!
Ah, but my lighter's out of fluid. If you need a light, get it from Ôgami.
Wha...?!
And you!! You're way too decadent!
What's with the slovenly way you wear your school uniform anyway?!
Eh?
His school emblem...
HEISEI
Y-you... couldn't be...from that school with a deviation value easily topping 70... that extremely selective school with Japan's no. 1 Todai admission rate... that bastion of the super-rich and perfect students...
The Heisei Academy of Higher Learn-ing?!
日本一
NO. 1 IN JAPAN
How do you do?
Yeah, what about it?

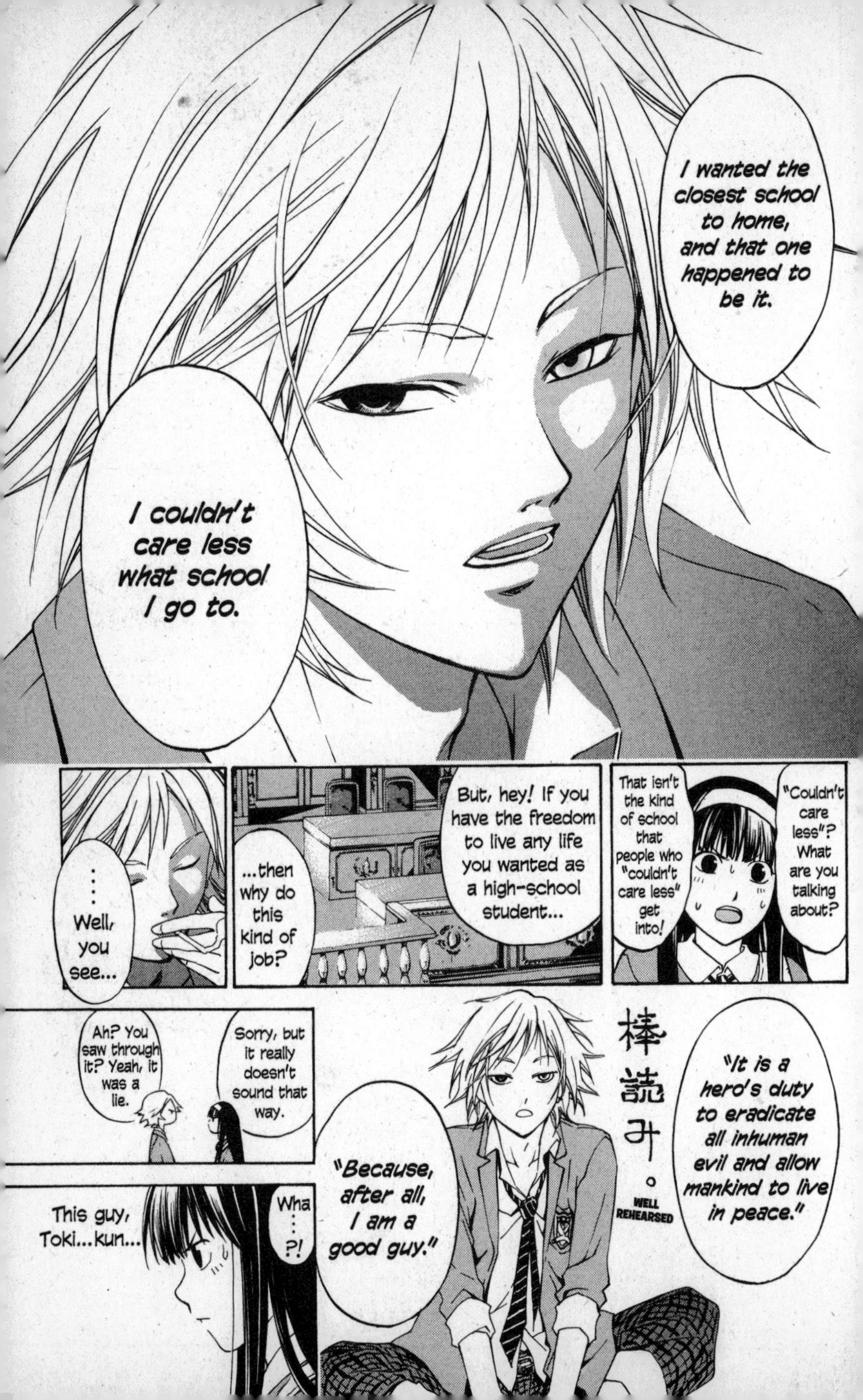
I wanted the closest school to home, and that one happened to be it.
I couldn't care less what school I go to.
"Couldn't care less"? What are you talking about?
That isn't the kind of school that people who "couldn't care less" get into!
But, hey! If you have the freedom to live any life you wanted as a high-school student...
...then why do this kind of job?
... Well, you see...
棒読み。
WELL REHEARSED
"It is a hero's duty to eradicate all inhuman evil and allow mankind to live in peace."
"Because, after all, I am a good guy."
Sorry, but it really doesn't sound that way.
Ah? You saw through it? Yeah, it was a lie.
Wha...?!
This guy, Toki...kun...

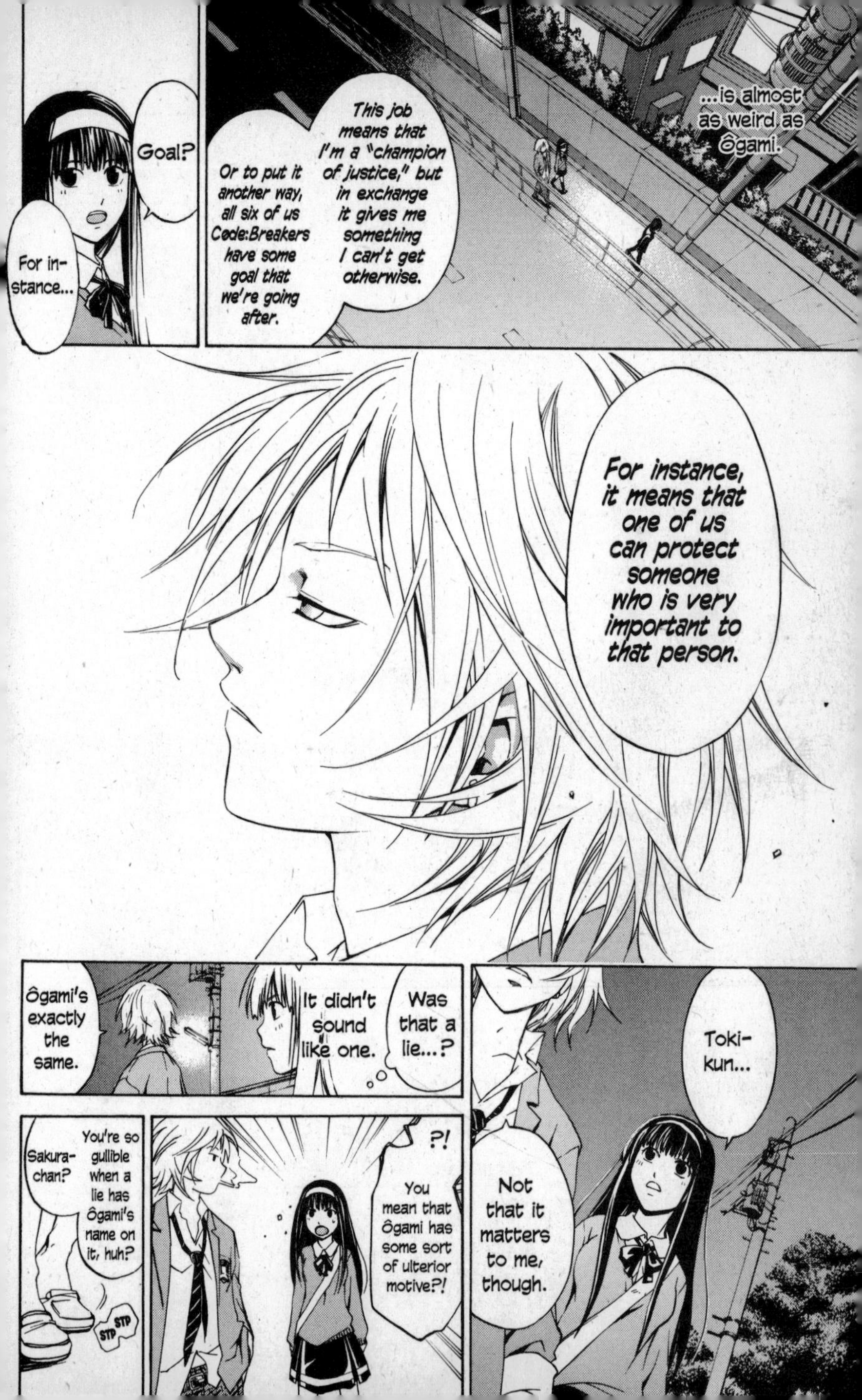
...is almost as weird as Ôgami.
This job means that I'm a "champion of justice," but in exchange it gives me something I can't get otherwise.
Or to put it another way, all six of us Code:Breakers have some goal that we're going after.
Goal?
For instance...
For instance, it means that one of us can protect someone who is very important to that person.
Toki-kun...
Not that it matters to me, though.
Was that a lie...?
It didn't sound like one.
Ôgami's exactly the same.
?!
You mean that Ôgami has some sort of ulterior motive?!
You're so gullible when a lie has Ôgami's name on it, huh?
Sakura-chan?
STP
STP

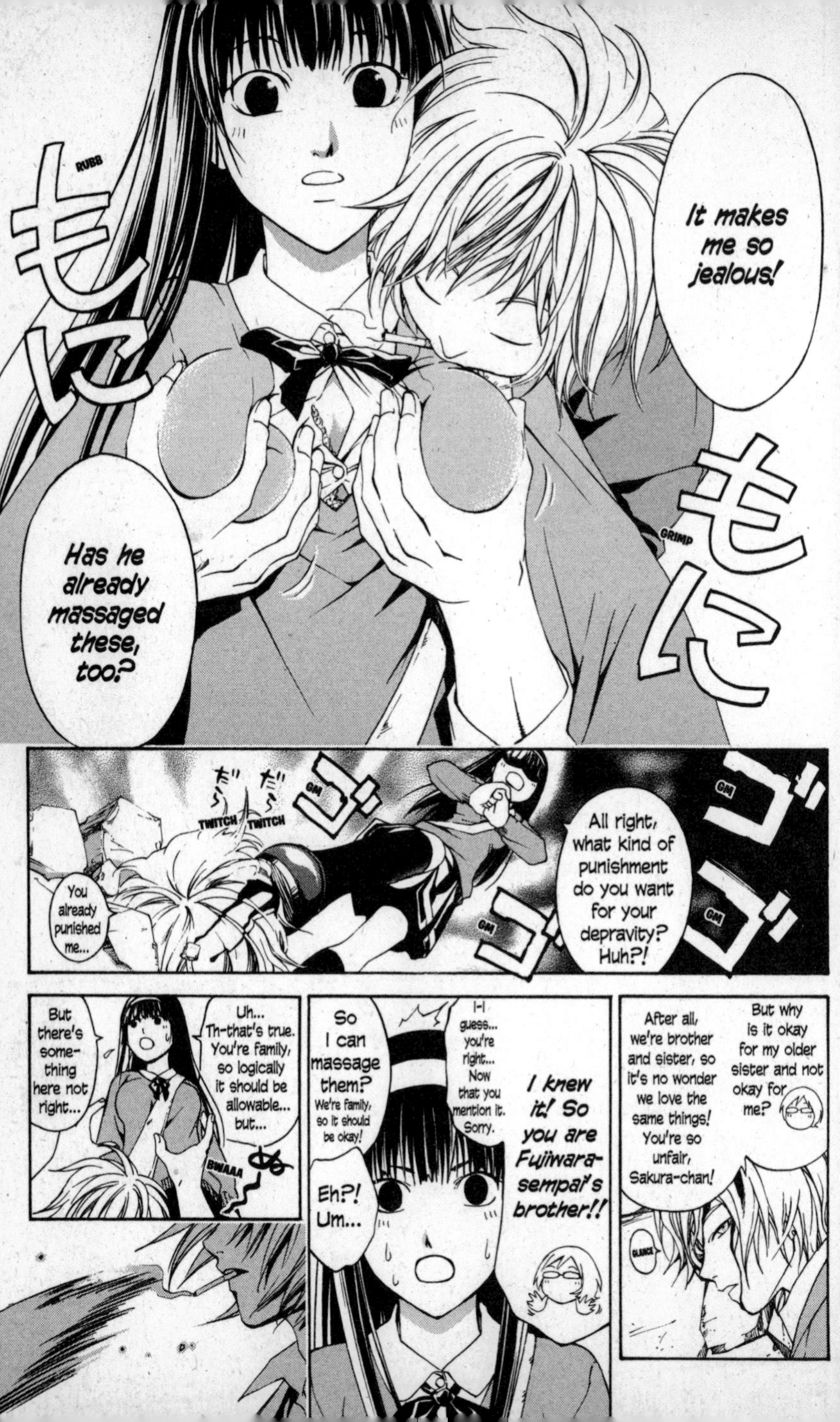

It makes me so jealous!
もに
GRIMP
RUBB
もに
Has he already massaged these, too?
ゴゴ
GM
GM
All right, what kind of punishment do you want for your depravity? Huh?!
ゴ
GM
GM
だら だら
TWITCH TWITCH
You already punished me...
But why is it okay for my older sister and not okay for me?
After all, we're brother and sister, so it's no wonder we love the same things! You're so unfair, Sakura-chan!
GLANCE
I-I guess... you're right... Now that you mention it. Sorry.
So I can massage them? We're family, so it should be okay!
I knew it! So you are Fujiwara-sempai's brother!!
Eh?! Um...
Uh... Th-that's true. You're family, so logically it should be allowable... but...
But there's something here not right...
BWAAA

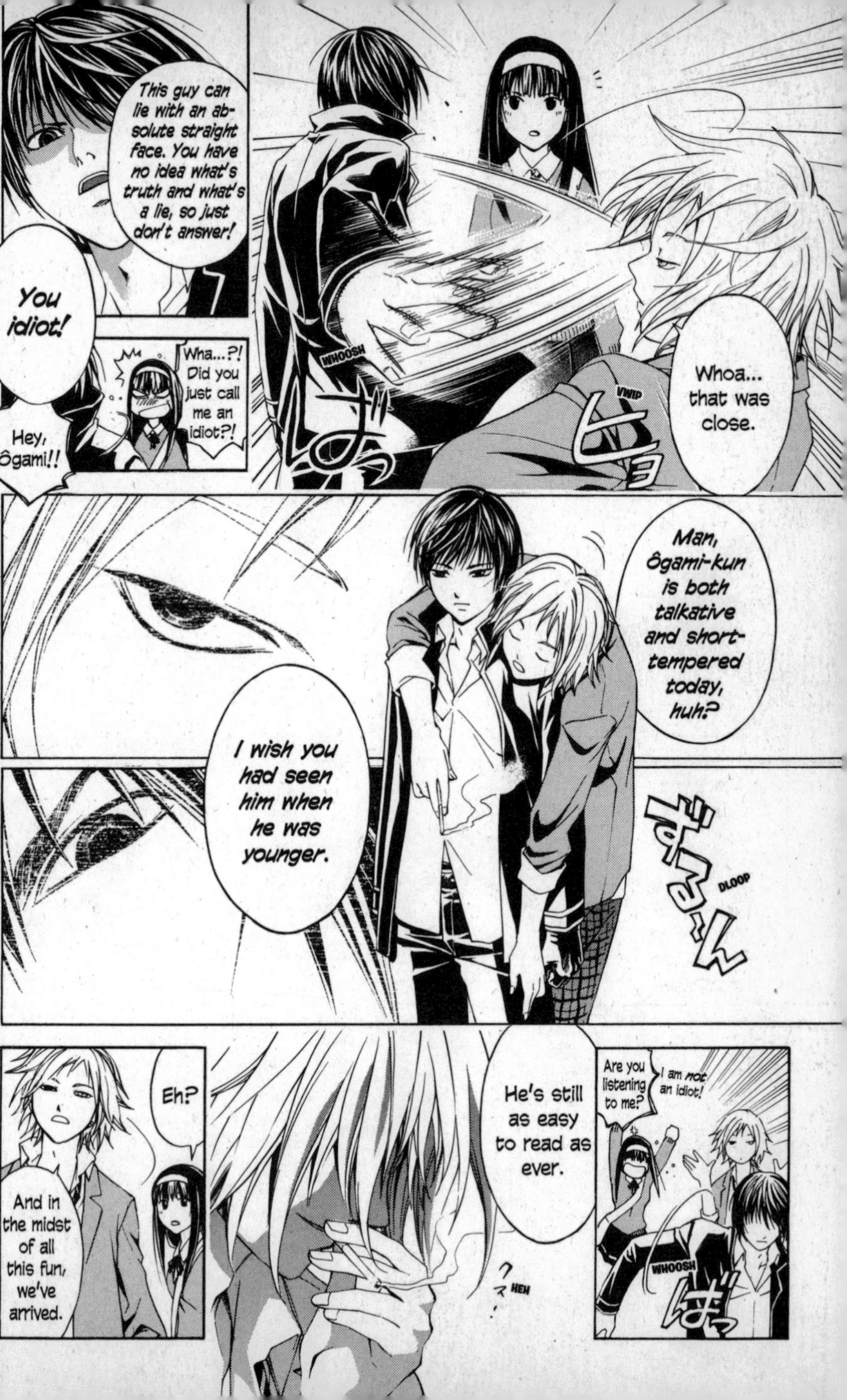
Whoa... that was close.
VWIP
WHOOSH
This guy can lie with an absolute straight face. You have no idea what's truth and what's a lie, so just don't answer!
You idiot!
Wha...?! Did you just call me an idiot?!
Hey, Ôgami!!
Man, Ôgami-kun is both talkative and short-tempered today, huh?
I wish you had seen him when he was younger.
DLOOP
I am *not* an idiot!
Are you listening to me?
WHOOSH
He's still as easy to read as ever.
HEH
Eh?
And in the midst of all this fun, we've arrived.

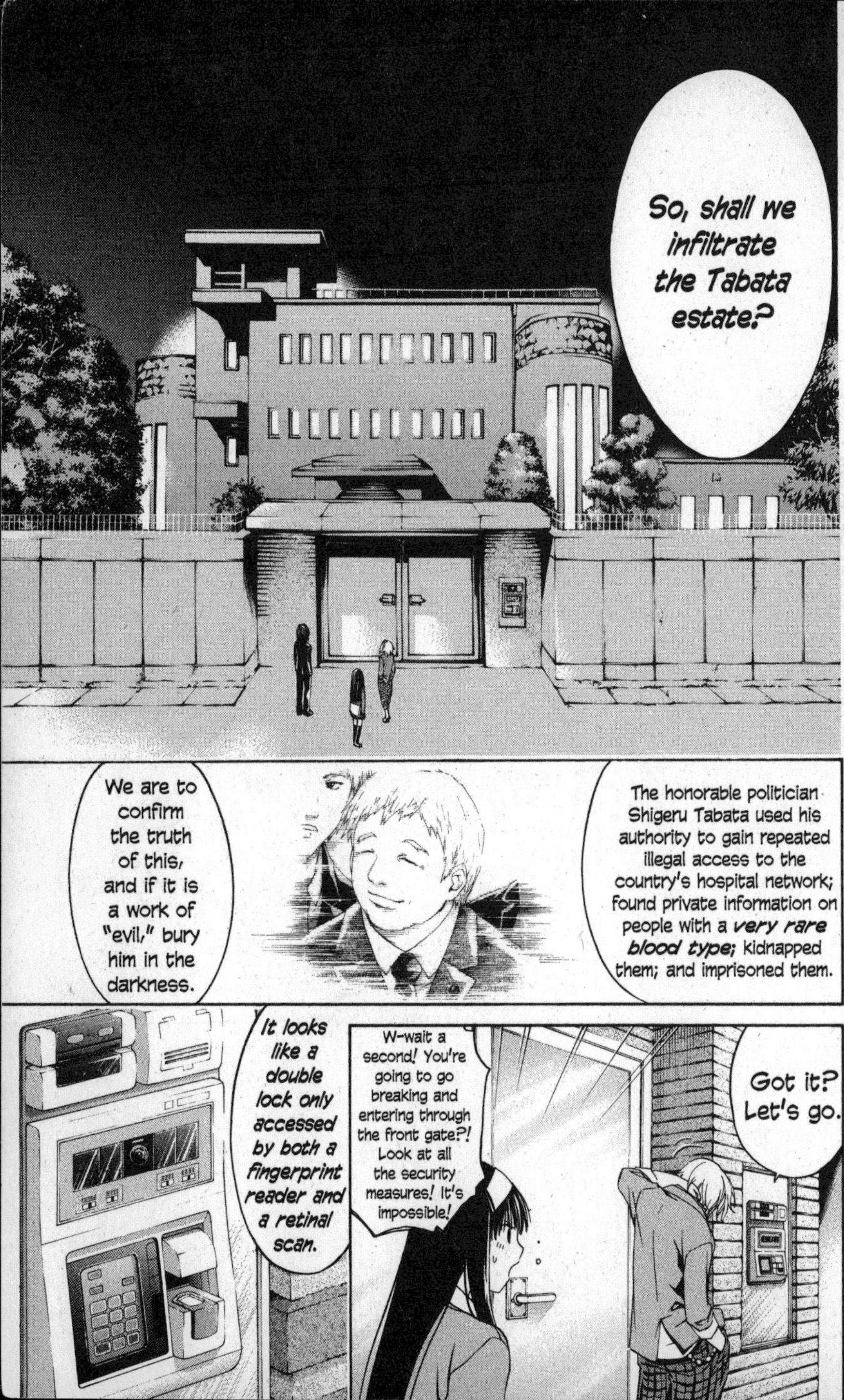
So, shall we infiltrate the Tabata estate?
The honorable politician Shigeru Tabata used his authority to gain repeated illegal access to the country's hospital network; found private information on people with a *very rare blood type;* kidnapped them; and imprisoned them.
We are to confirm the truth of this, and if it is a work of "evil," bury him in the darkness.
Got it? Let's go.
W-wait a second! You're going to go breaking and entering through the front gate?! Look at all the security measures! It's impossible!
It looks like a double lock only accessed by both a fingerprint reader and a retinal scan.

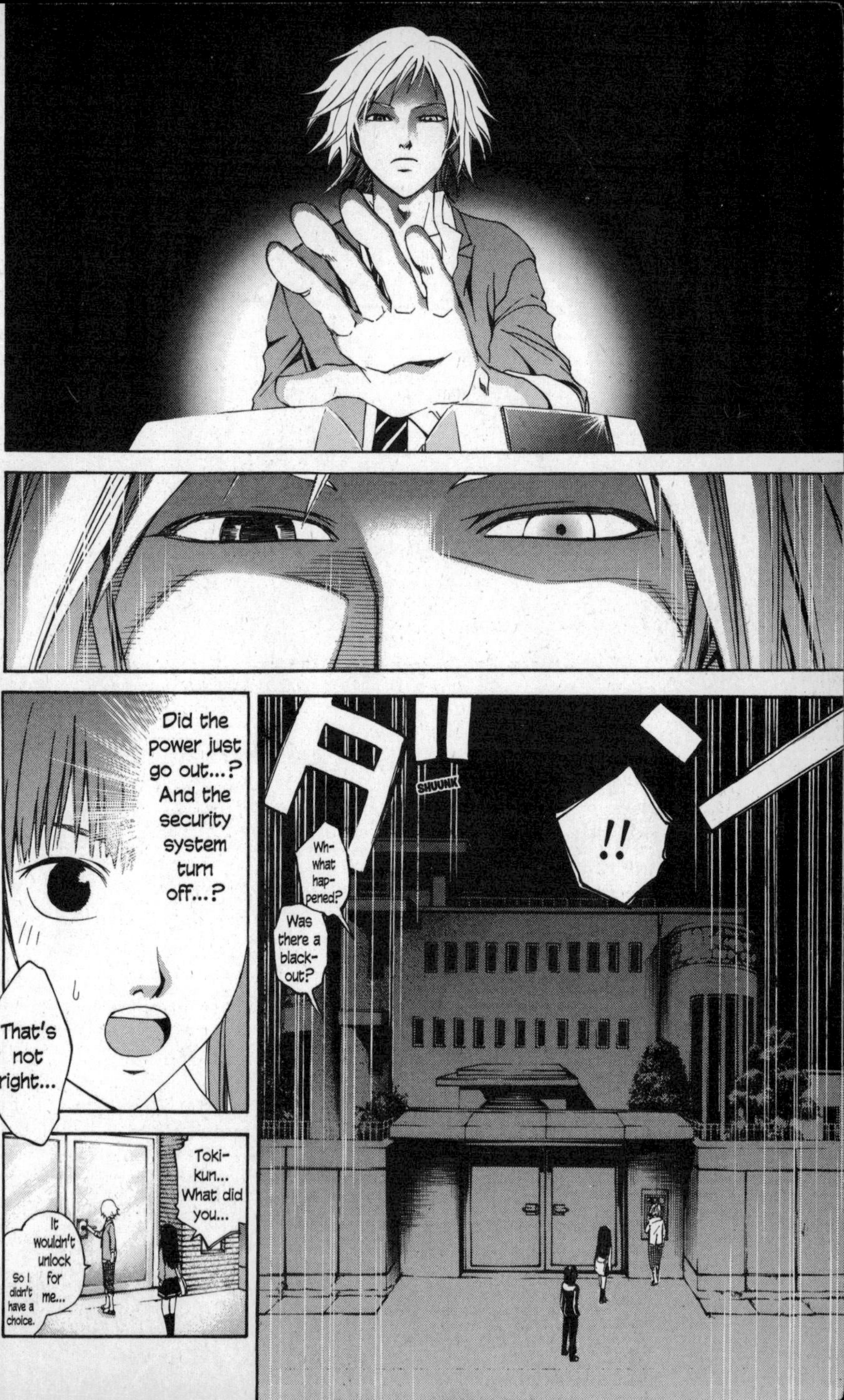
SHUUNK
Wh-what hap-pened?
Was there a black-out?
!!
Did the power just go out...? And the security system turn off...?
That's not right...
Toki-kun... What did you...
It wouldn't unlock for me...
So I didn't have a choice.

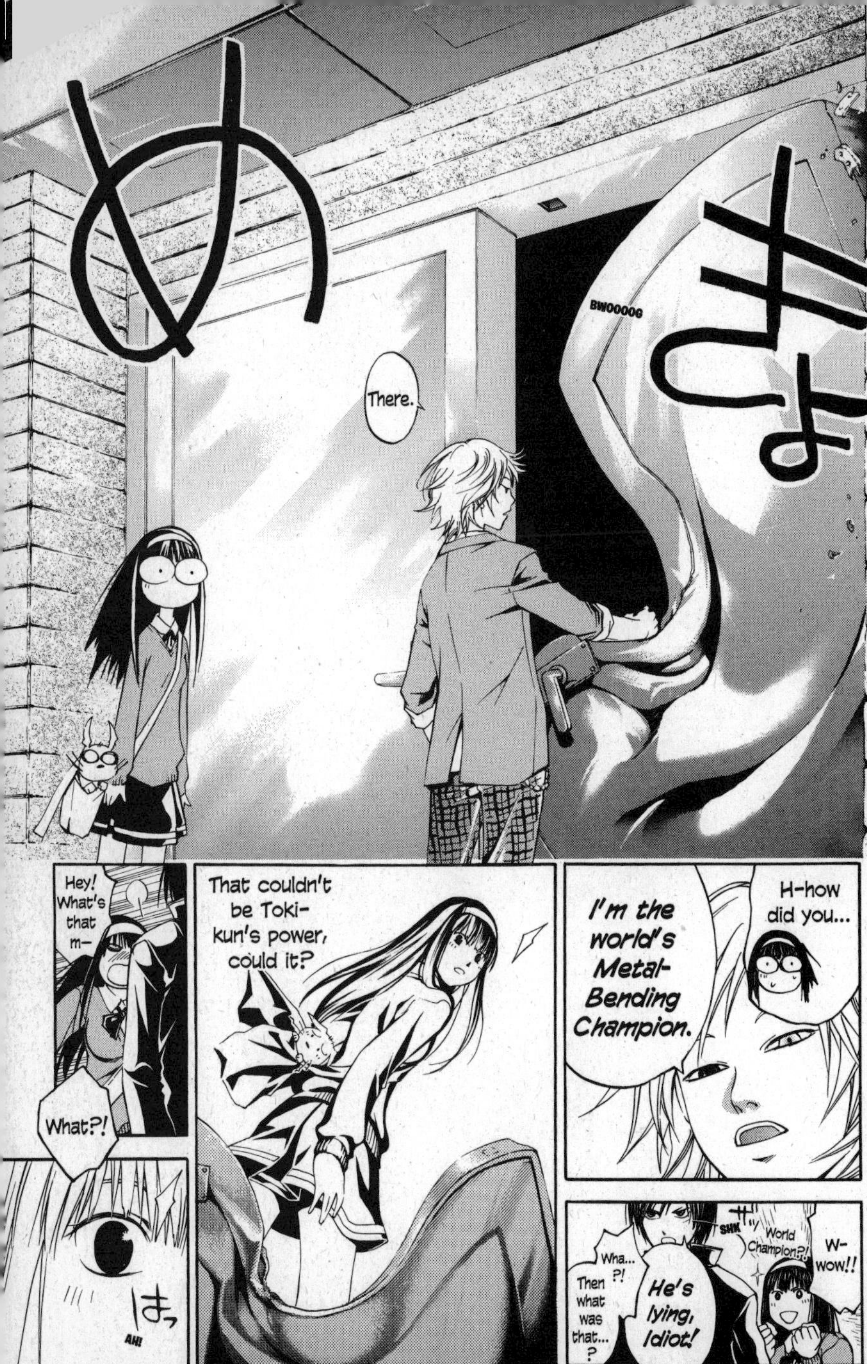
めぎょ
BWOOOOG
There.
H-how did you...
I'm the world's Metal-Bending Champion.
That couldn't be Toki-kun's power, could it?
Hey! What's that m—
What?!
W-wow!!
SHK
World Champion?!
He's lying, idiot!
Wha...?!
Then what was that...?
はっ
AH!

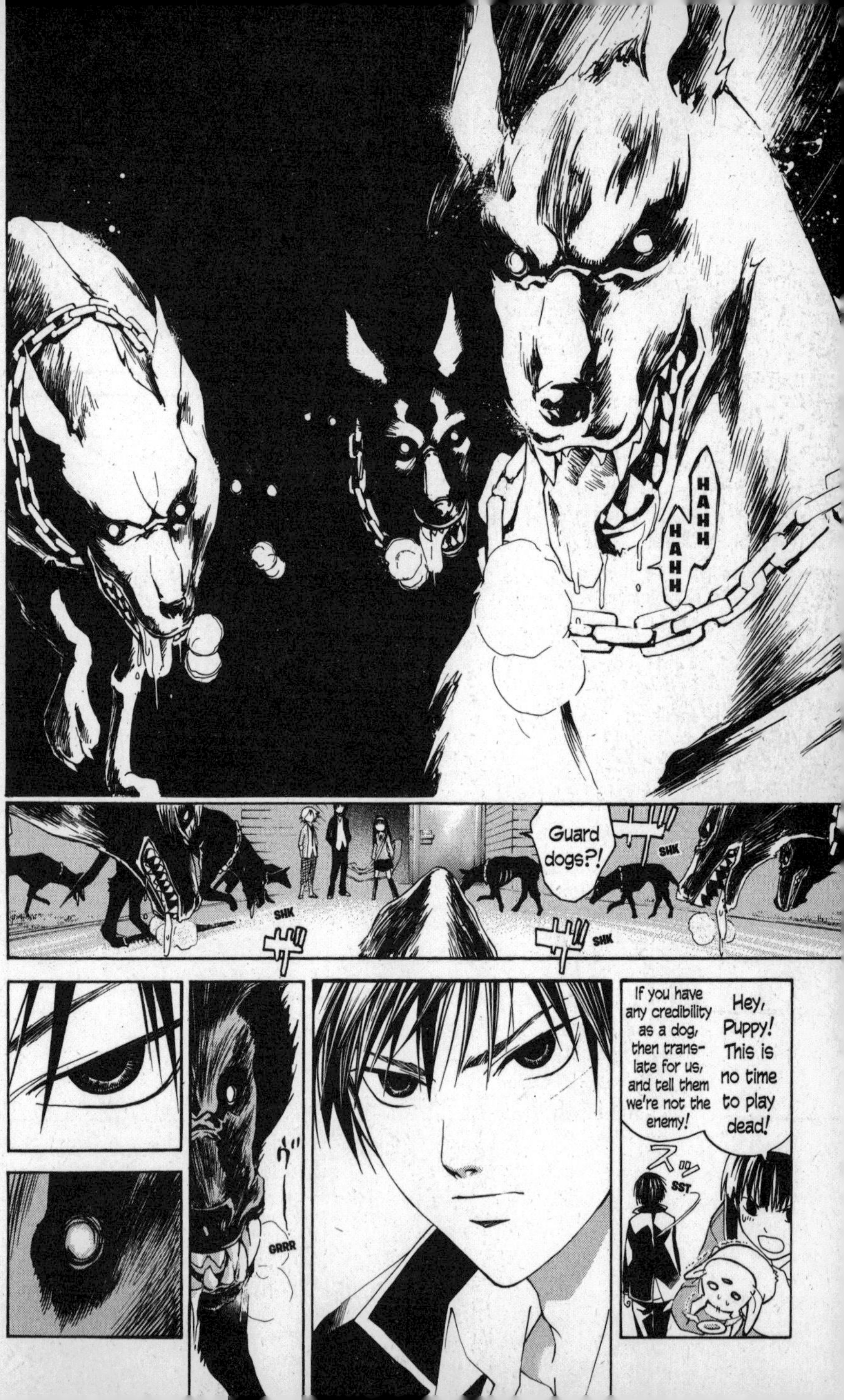
HAHH
HAHH
SHK
Guard dogs?!
SHK
SHK
Hey, Puppy! This is no time to play dead!
If you have any credibility as a dog, then trans-late for us, and tell them we're not the enemy!
SST
GRRR

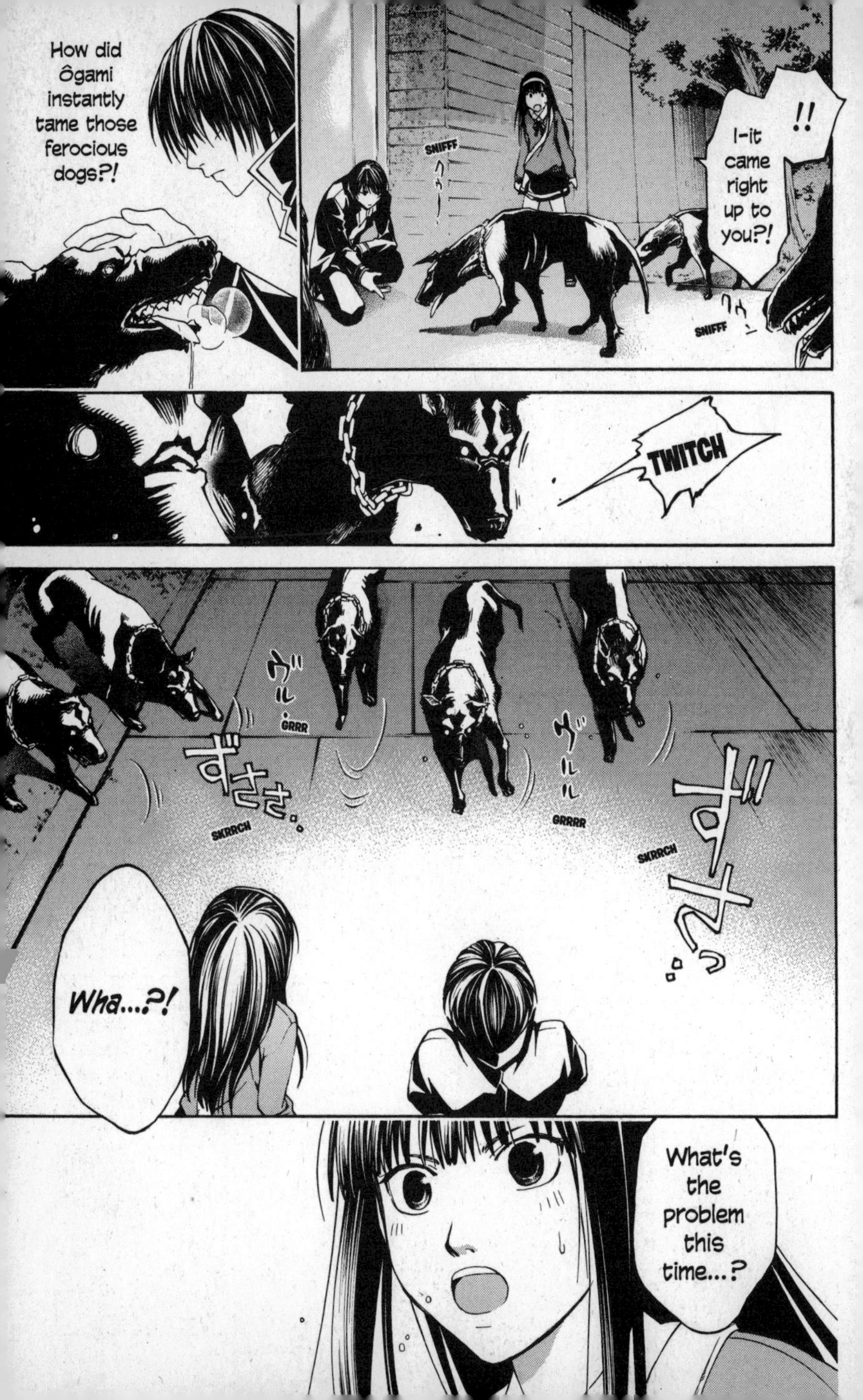
!!
I-it came right up to you?!
SNIFFF
SNIFFF
How did Ôgami instantly tame those ferocious dogs?!
TWITCH
ずさっ
SKRRCH
ヴルル
GRRRR
ヴル
GRRR
ずささ
SKRRCH
Wha...?!
What's the problem this time...?

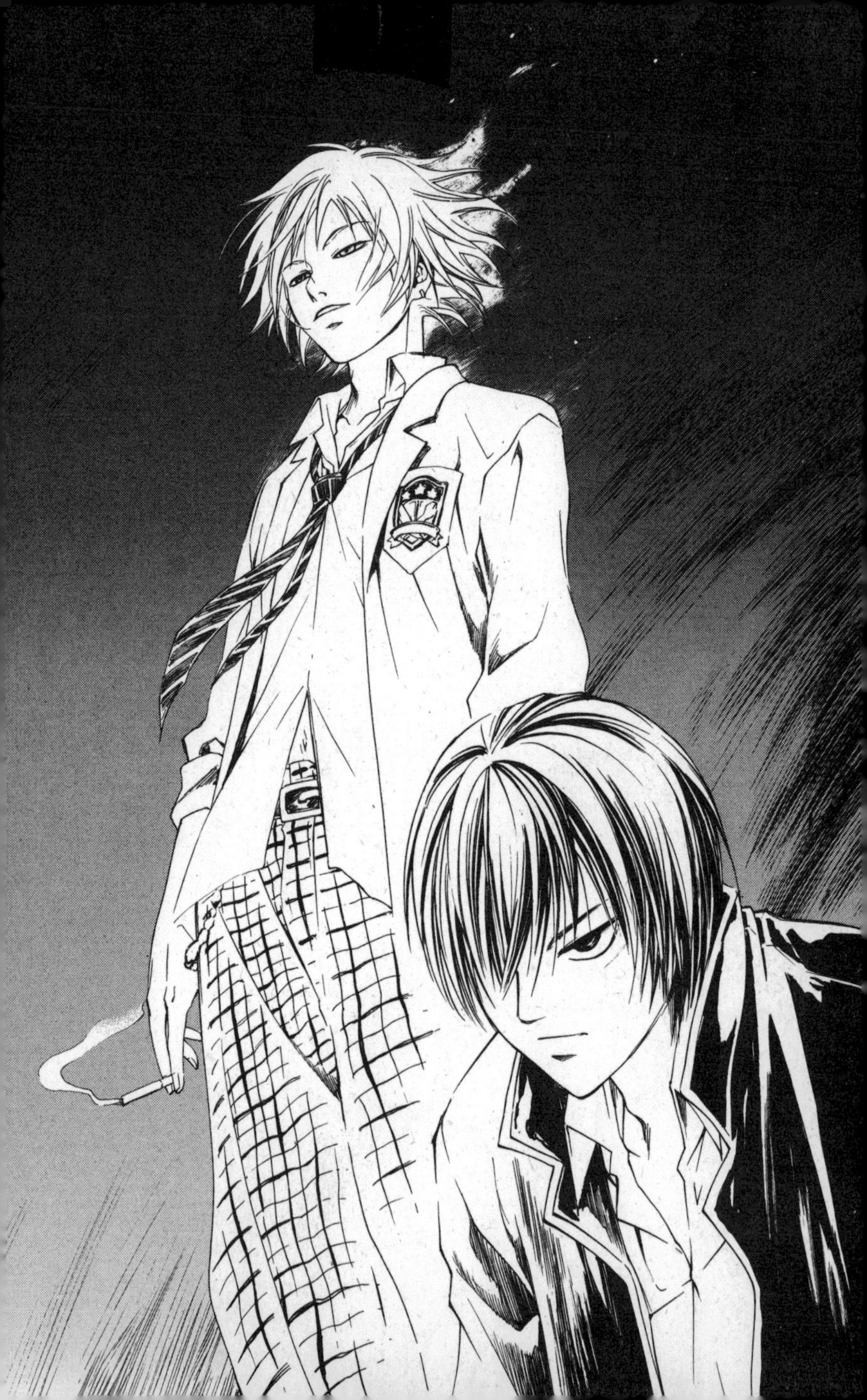

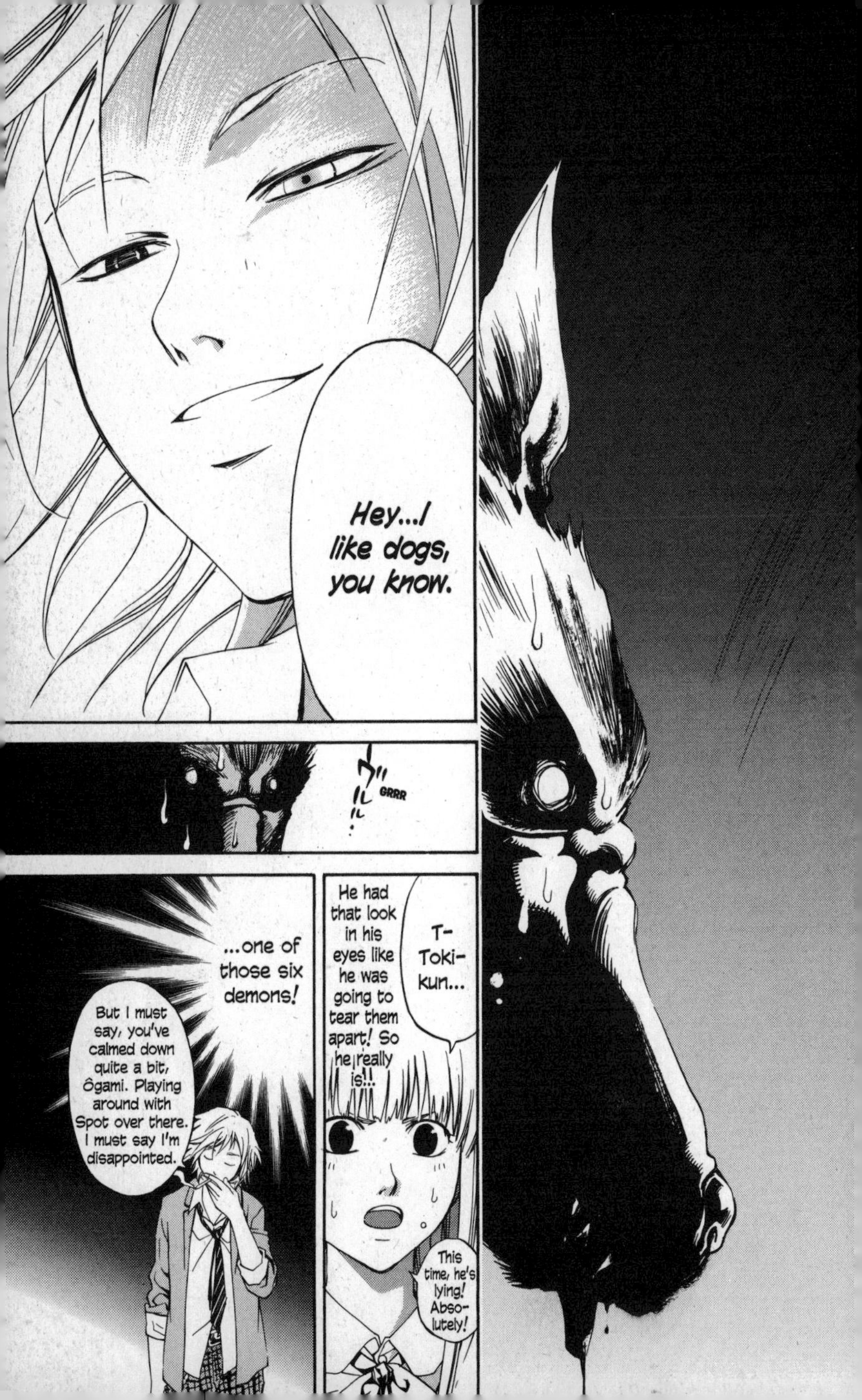

Hey...I like dogs, you know.
GRRR
T-Toki-kun...
He had that look in his eyes like he was going to tear them apart! So he really is...
This time, he's lying! Absolutely!
...one of those six demons!
But I must say, you've calmed down quite a bit, Ôgami. Playing around with Spot over there. I must say I'm disappointed.

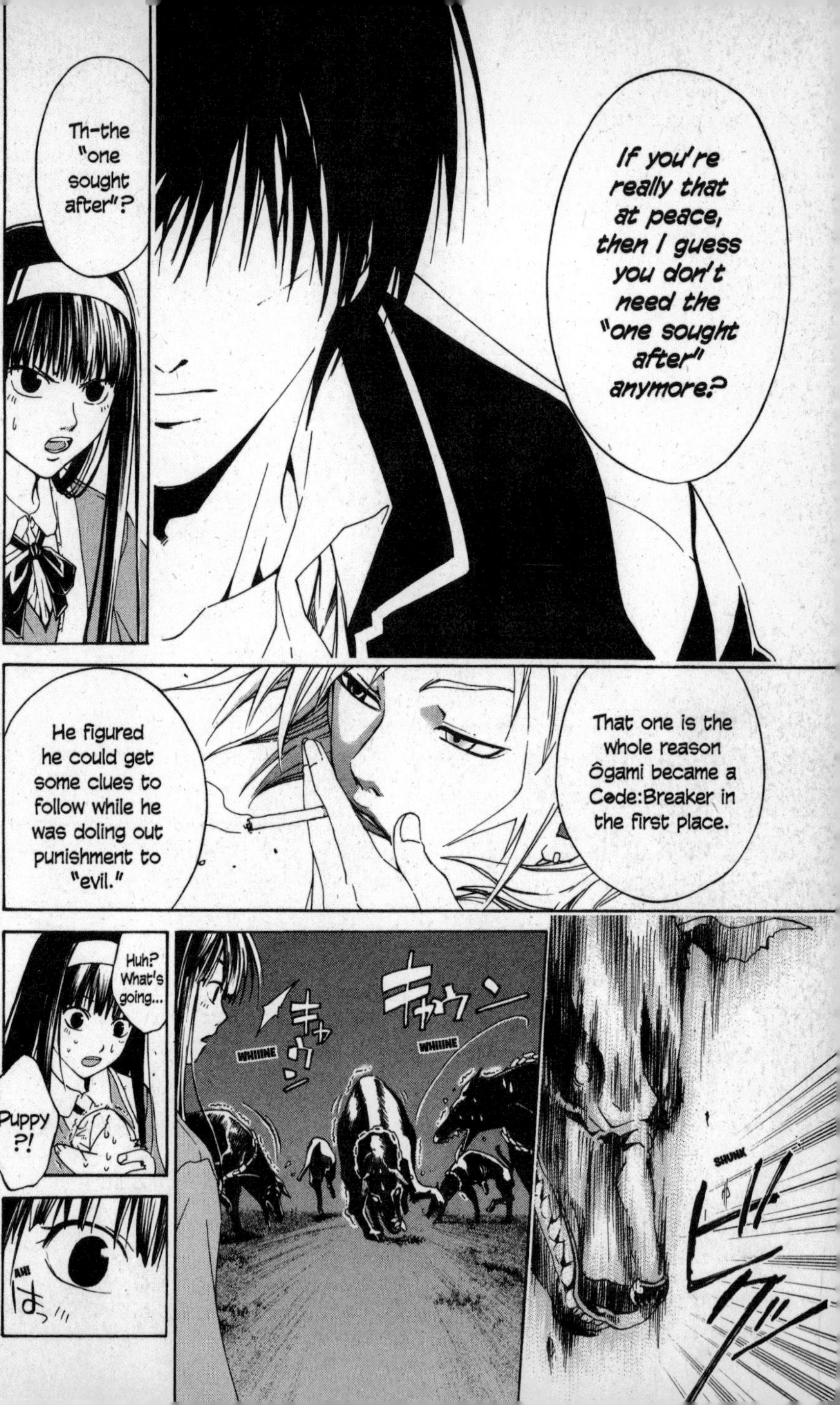

If you're really that at peace, then I guess you don't need the "one sought after" anymore?
Th-the "one sought after"?
That one is the whole reason Ôgami became a Code:Breaker in the first place.
He figured he could get some clues to follow while he was doling out punishment to "evil."
SHUNK
キャウン
WHIIINE
キャウン
WHIIINE
Huh? What's going...
Puppy?!
AH!
はっ

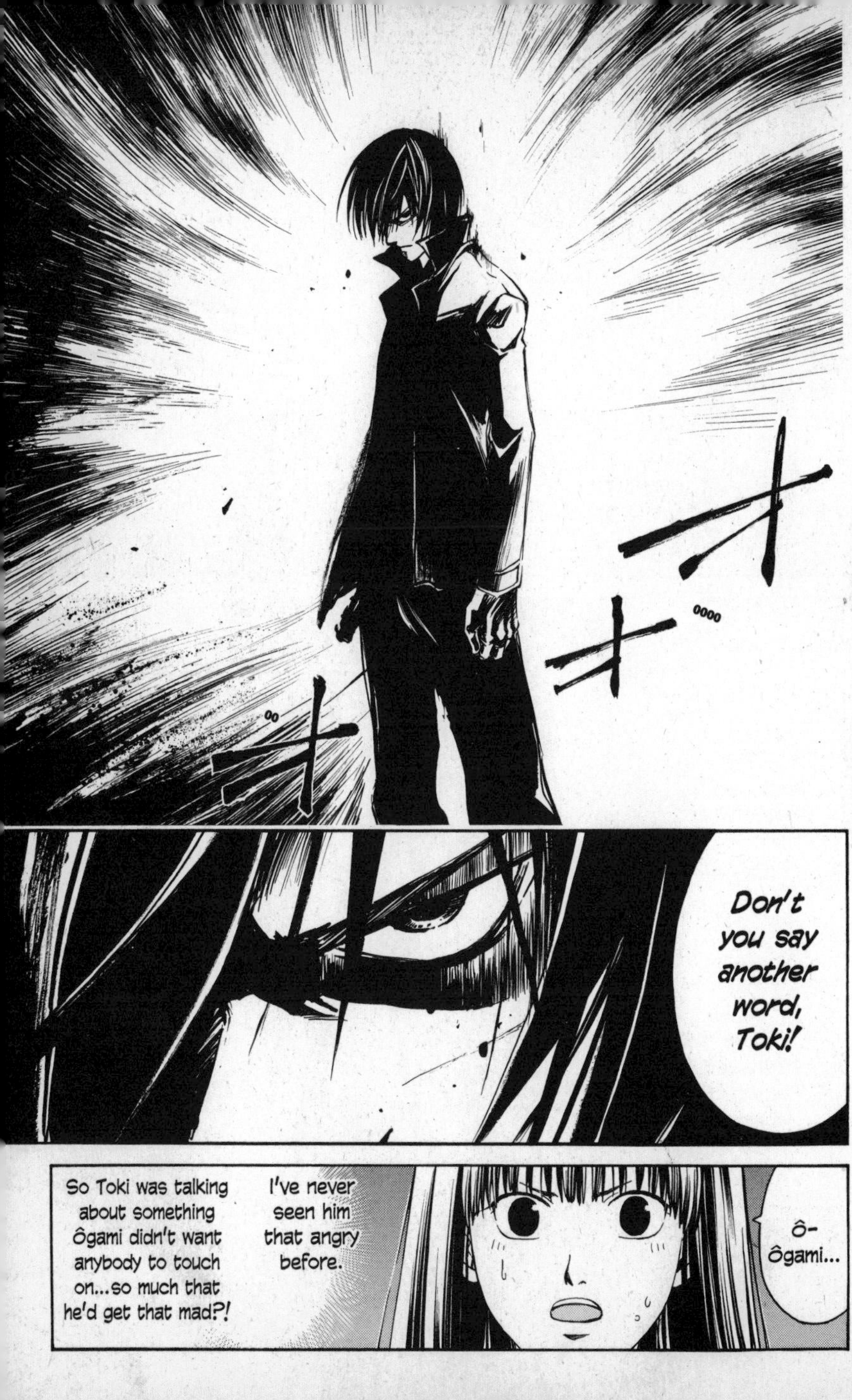
oooo
oo
Don't you say another word, Toki!
Ô- Ôgami...
I've never seen him that angry before.
So Toki was talking about something Ôgami didn't want anybody to touch on...so much that he'd get that mad?!

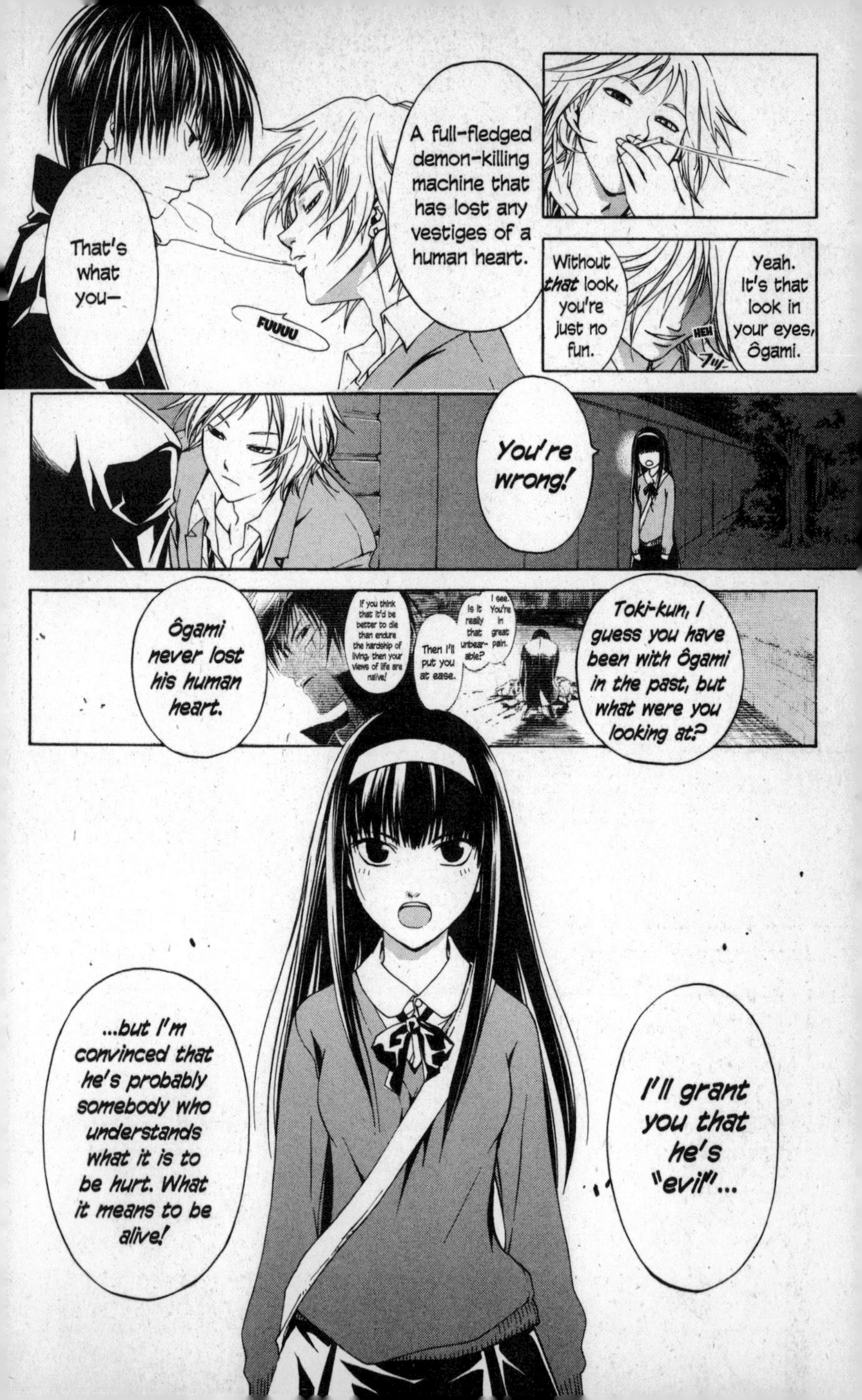
Yeah. It's that look in your eyes, Ôgami.
HEH
フッ
Without *that* look, you're just no fun.
A full-fledged demon-killing machine that has lost any vestiges of a human heart.
FUUUU
That's what you—
You're wrong!
Toki-kun, I guess you have been with Ôgami in the past, but what were you looking at?
I see. You're in great pain.
Is it really that unbearable?
Then I'll put you at ease.
If you think that it'd be better to die than endure the hardship of living, then your views of life are naive!
Ôgami never lost his human heart.
I'll grant you that he's "evil"...
...but I'm convinced that he's probably somebody who understands what it is to be hurt. What it means to be alive!

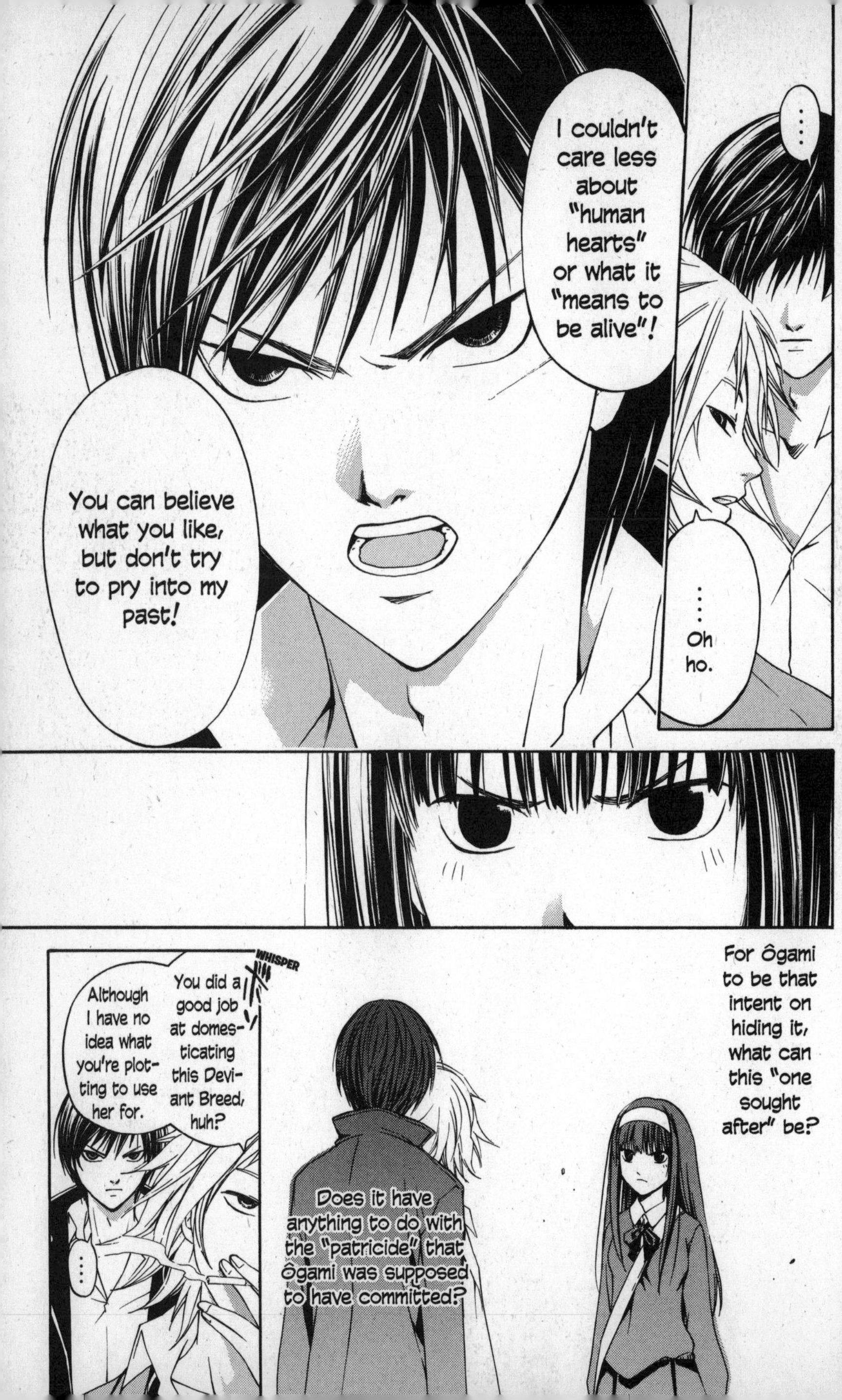
....
....Oh ho.
I couldn't care less about "human hearts" or what it "means to be alive"!
You can believe what you like, but don't try to pry into my past!
For Ôgami to be that intent on hiding it, what can this "one sought after" be?
Does it have anything to do with the "patricide" that Ôgami was supposed to have committed?
WHISPER
You did a good job at domesticating this Deviant Breed, huh?
Although I have no idea what you're plotting to use her for.
....

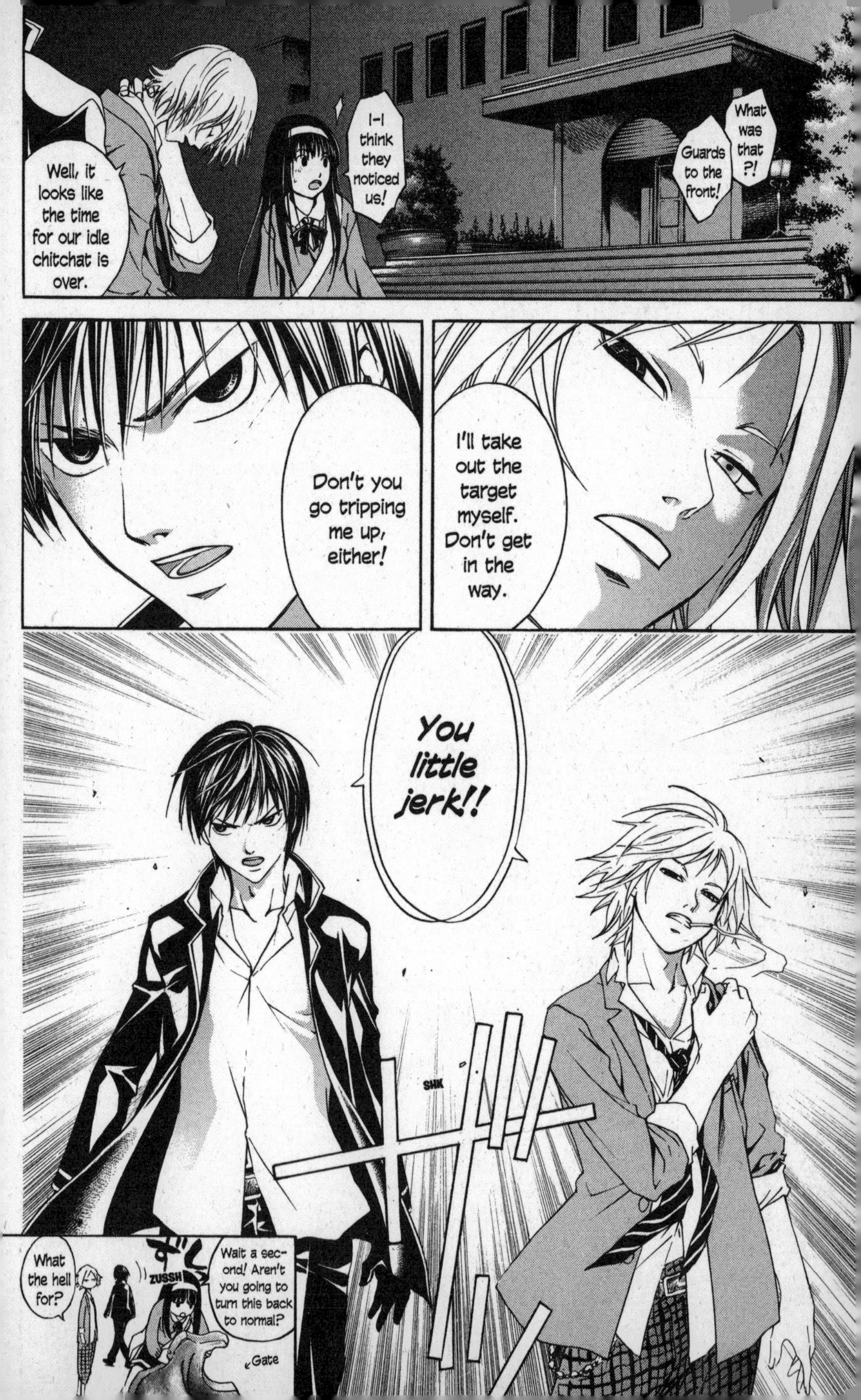
What was that?!
Guards to the front!
I-I think they noticed us!
Well, it looks like the time for our idle chitchat is over.
I'll take out the target myself. Don't get in the way.
Don't you go tripping me up, either!
You little jerk!!
SHK
Wait a second! Aren't you going to turn this back to normal?
ZUSSH
What the hell for?
Gate

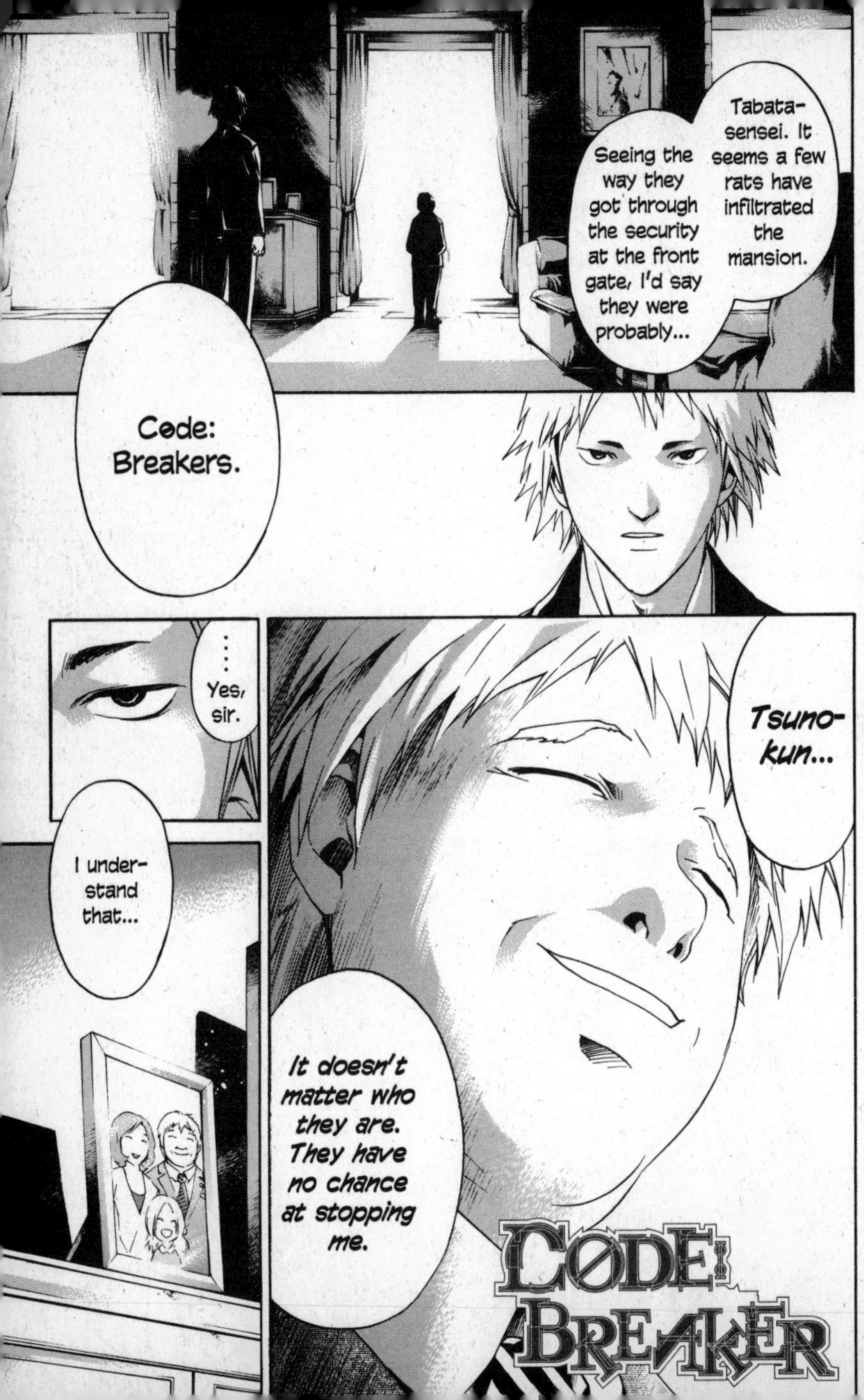
Tabata-sensei. It seems a few rats have infiltrated the mansion.
Seeing the way they got through the security at the front gate, I'd say they were probably...
Code: Breakers.
Tsuno-kun...
It doesn't matter who they are. They have no chance at stopping me.
... Yes, sir.
I understand that...
CODE:BREAKER

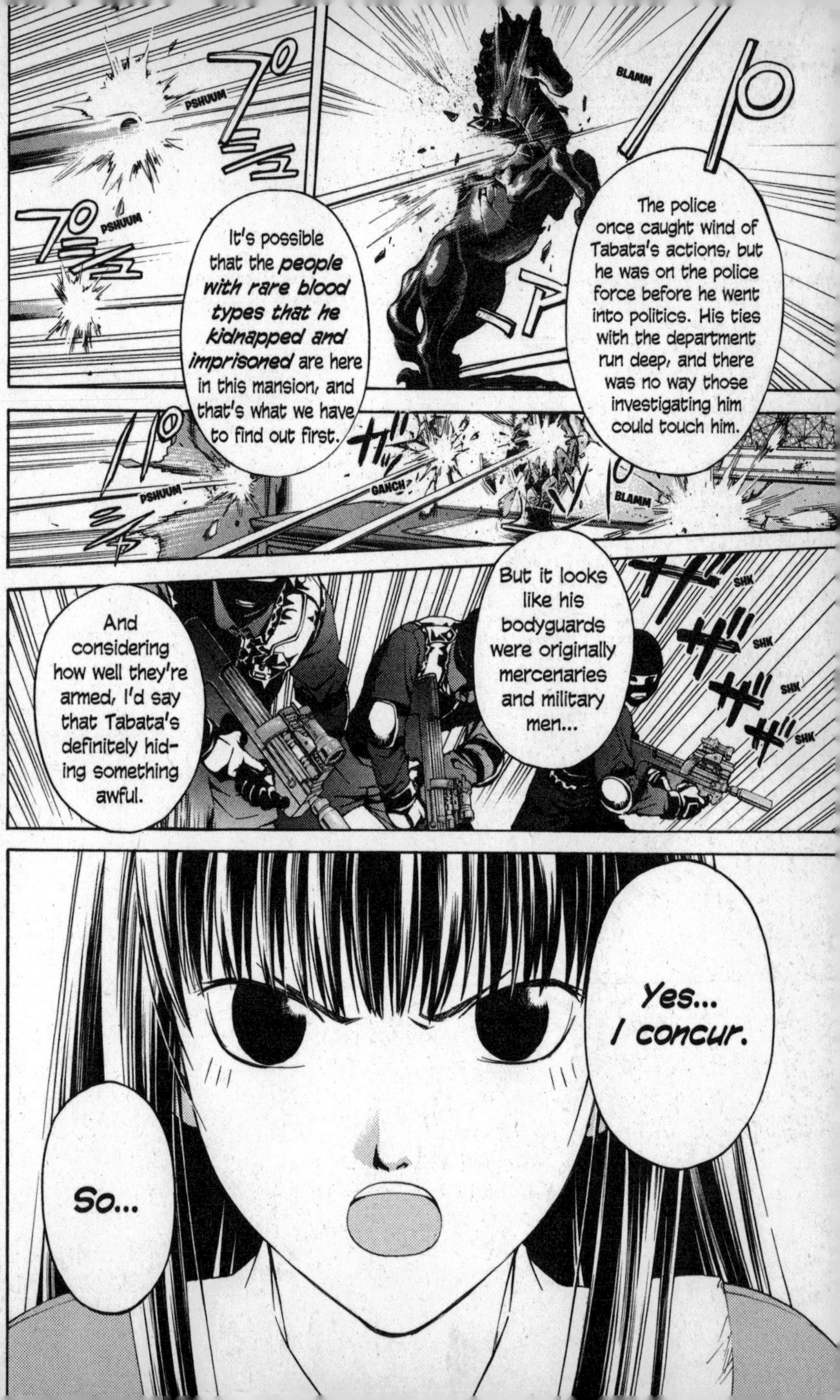
BLAMM
The police once caught wind of Tabata's actions, but he was on the police force before he went into politics. His ties with the department run deep, and there was no way those investigating him could touch him.
PSHUUM
It's possible that the *people with rare blood types that he kidnapped and imprisoned* are here in this mansion, and that's what we have to find out first.
PSHUUM
BLAMM
GANCH
PSHUUM
SHK
SHK
SHK
SHK
But it looks like his bodyguards were originally mercenaries and military men...
And considering how well they're armed, I'd say that Tabata's definitely hiding something awful.
Yes... I concur.
So...

code:10
Roaring on a Stormy Night

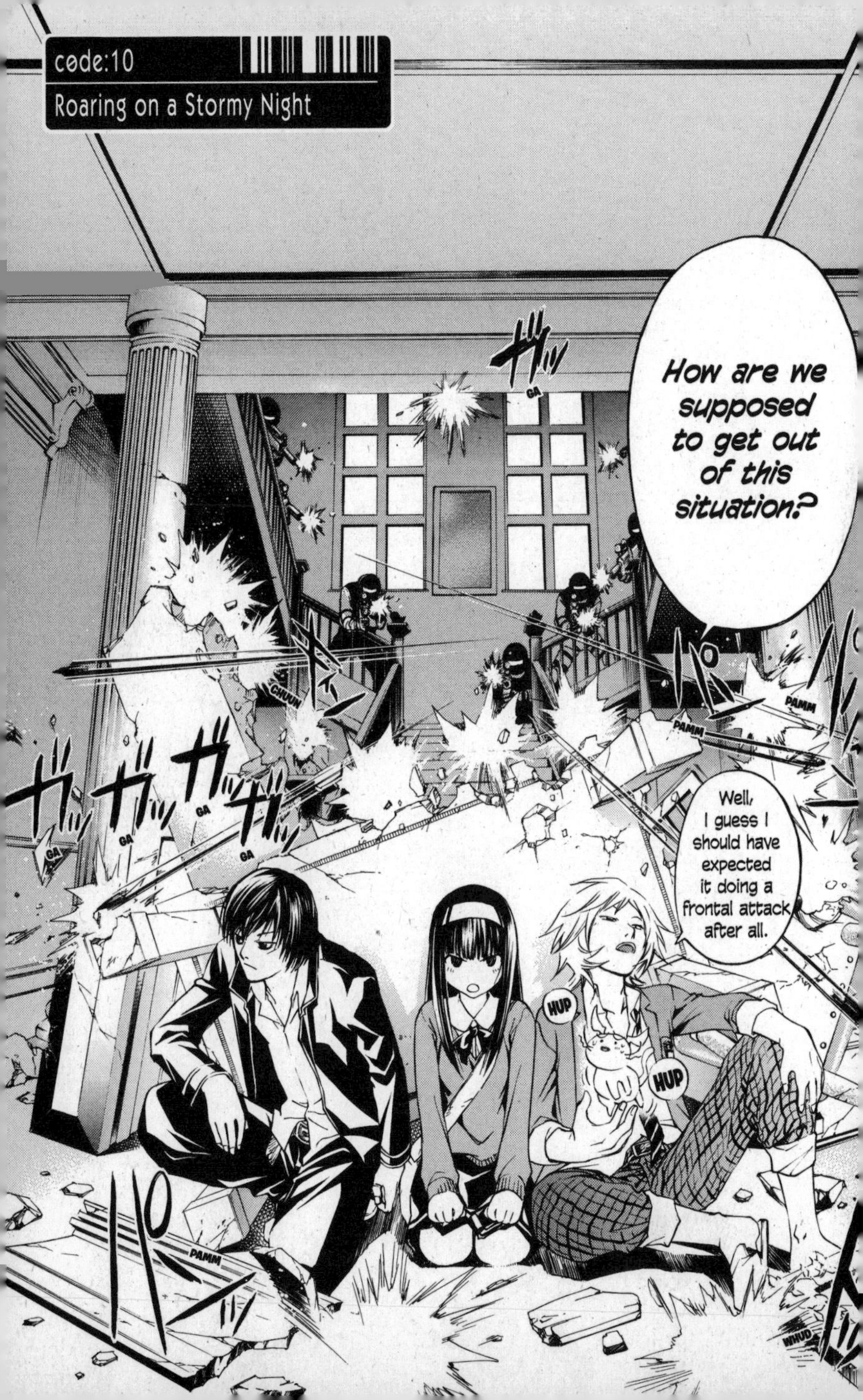
How are we supposed to get out of this situation?
GA
PAMM
PAMM
CHUUN
Well, I guess I should have expected it doing a frontal attack after all.
GA
GA
GA
GA
HUP
HUP
PAMM
WHUD

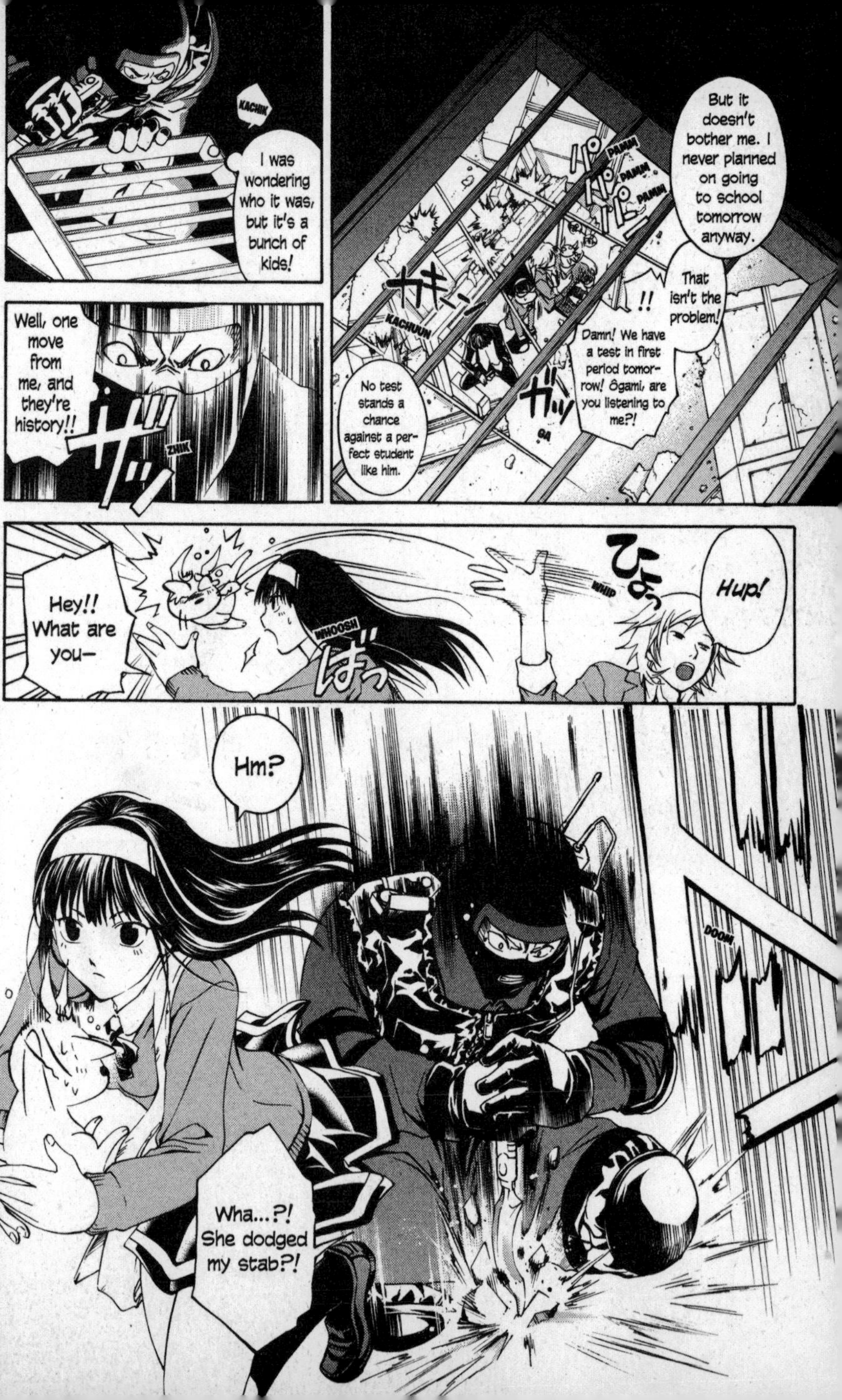

But it doesn't bother me. I never planned on going to school tomorrow anyway.
PAMM
PAMM
PAMM
That isn't the problem!
!!
Damn! We have a test in first period tomorrow! Ôgami, are you listening to me?!
KACHUUN
No test stands a chance against a perfect student like him.
GA
KACHIK
I was wondering who it was, but it's a bunch of kids!
Well, one move from me, and they're history!!
ZHIK
Hup!
ひょっ
WHIP
WHOOSH
ばっ
Hey!! What are you—
Hm?
DOOM
Wha...?! She dodged my stab?!

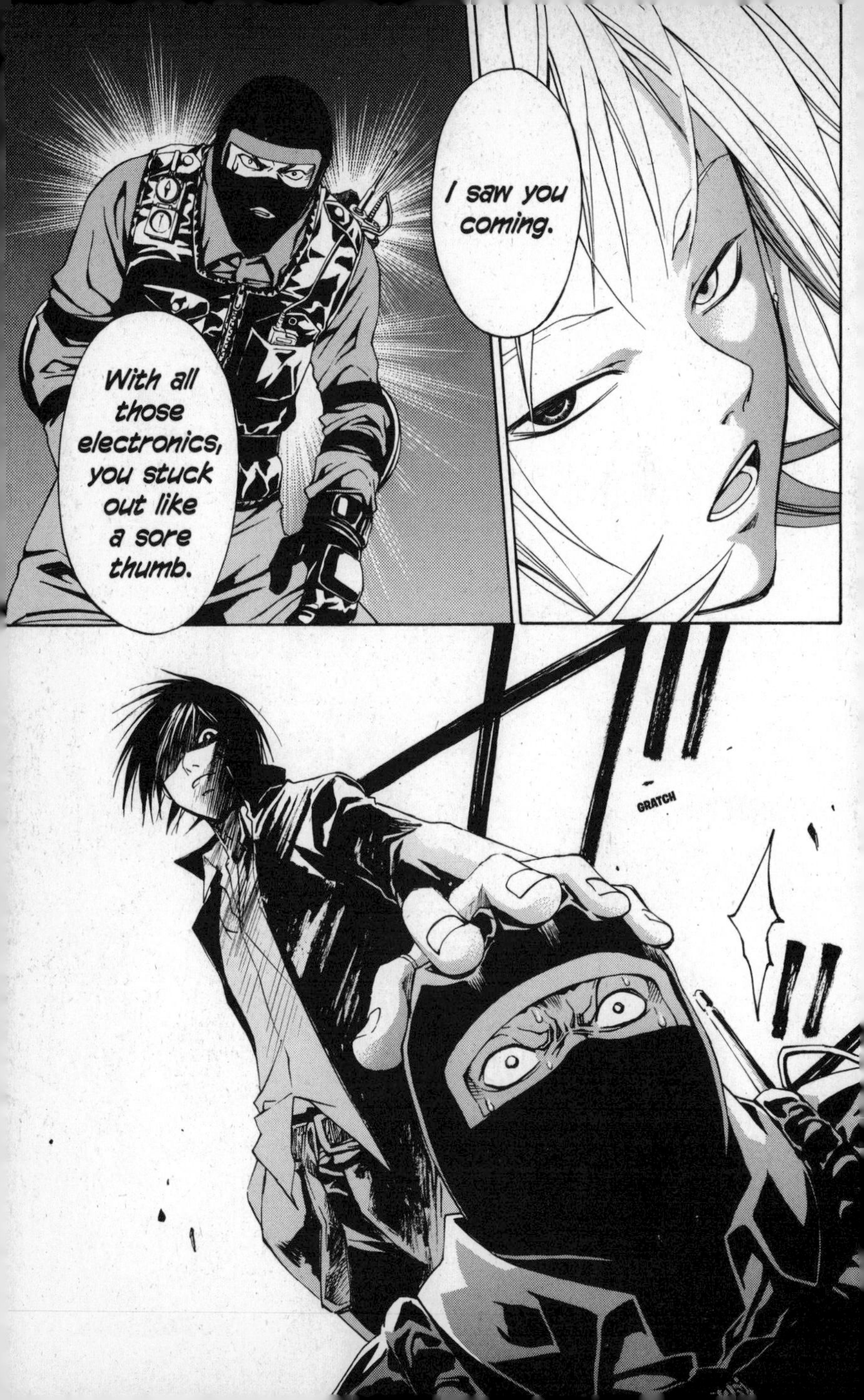
I saw you coming.
With all those electronics, you stuck out like a sore thumb.
GRATCH

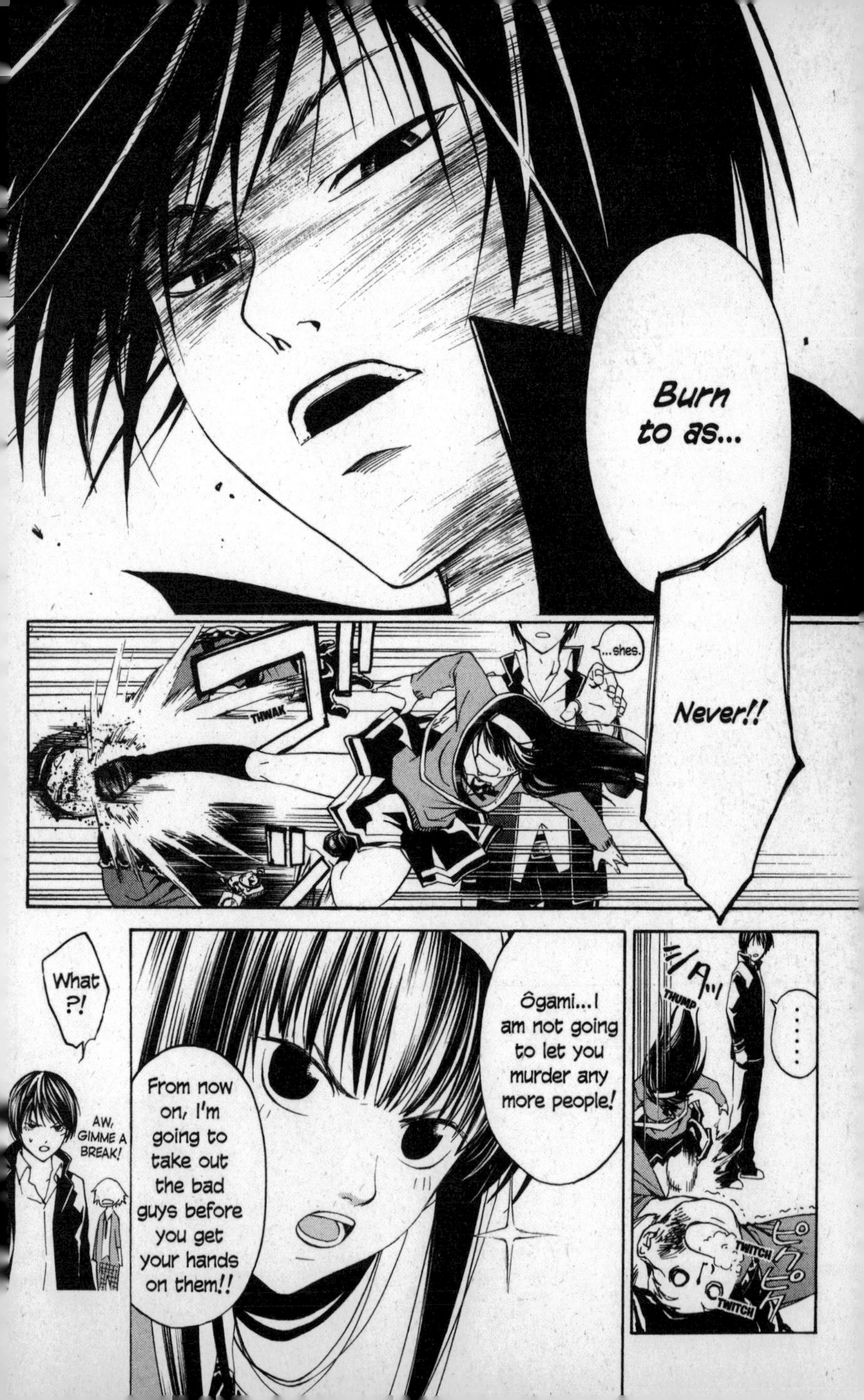

Burn to as...
Never!!
...shes.
THWAK
......
THUMP
TWITCH
TWITCH
Ôgami...I am not going to let you murder any more people!
From now on, I'm going to take out the bad guys before you get your hands on them!!
What ?!
AW, GIMME A BREAK!

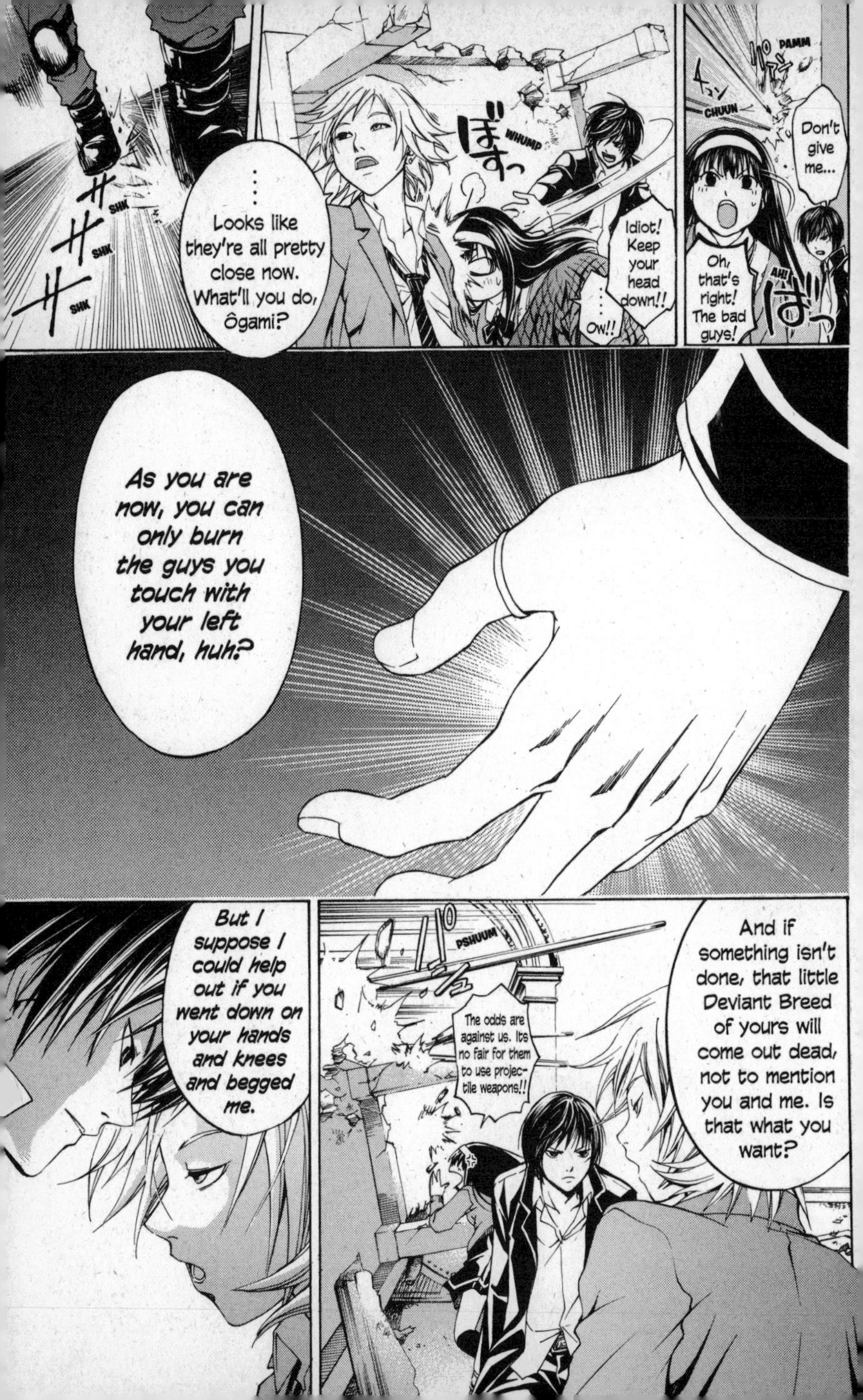
PAMM
CHUUN
Don't give me...
Oh, that's right! The bad guys!
AH!
WHUMP
Idiot! Keep your head down!!
... Ow!!
... Looks like they're all pretty close now. What'll you do, Ôgami?
SHK
SHK
SHK
As you are now, you can only burn the guys you touch with your left hand, huh?
And if something isn't done, that little Deviant Breed of yours will come out dead, not to mention you and me. Is that what you want?
PSHUUM
The odds are against us. Its no fair for them to use projectile weapons!!
But I suppose I could help out if you went down on your hands and knees and begged me.

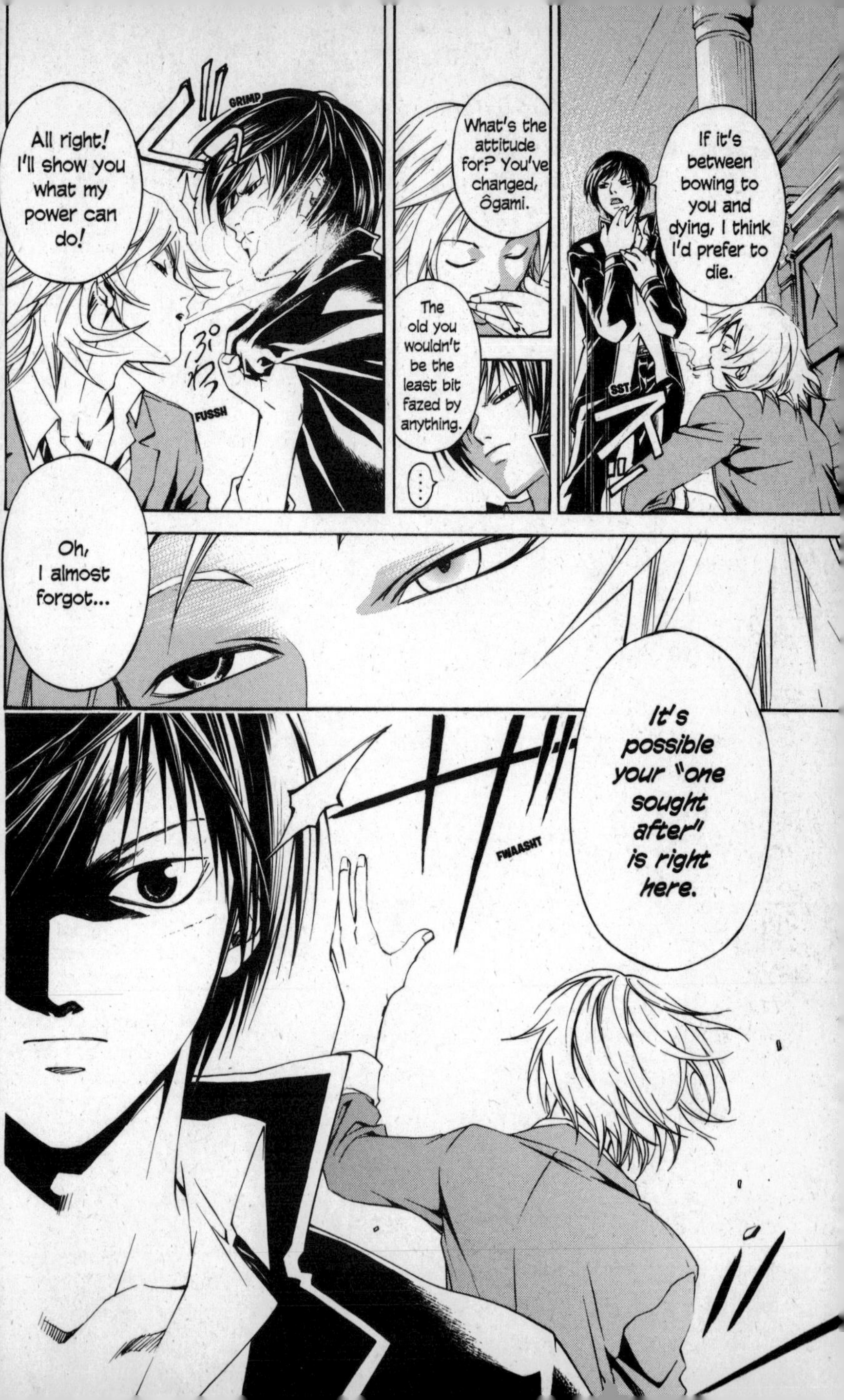
If it's between bowing to you and dying, I think I'd prefer to die.
SST
What's the attitude for? You've changed, Ôgami.
The old you wouldn't be the least bit fazed by anything.
...
GRIMP
All right! I'll show you what my power can do!
FUSSH
Oh, I almost forgot...
It's possible your "one sought after" is right here.
FWAASHT

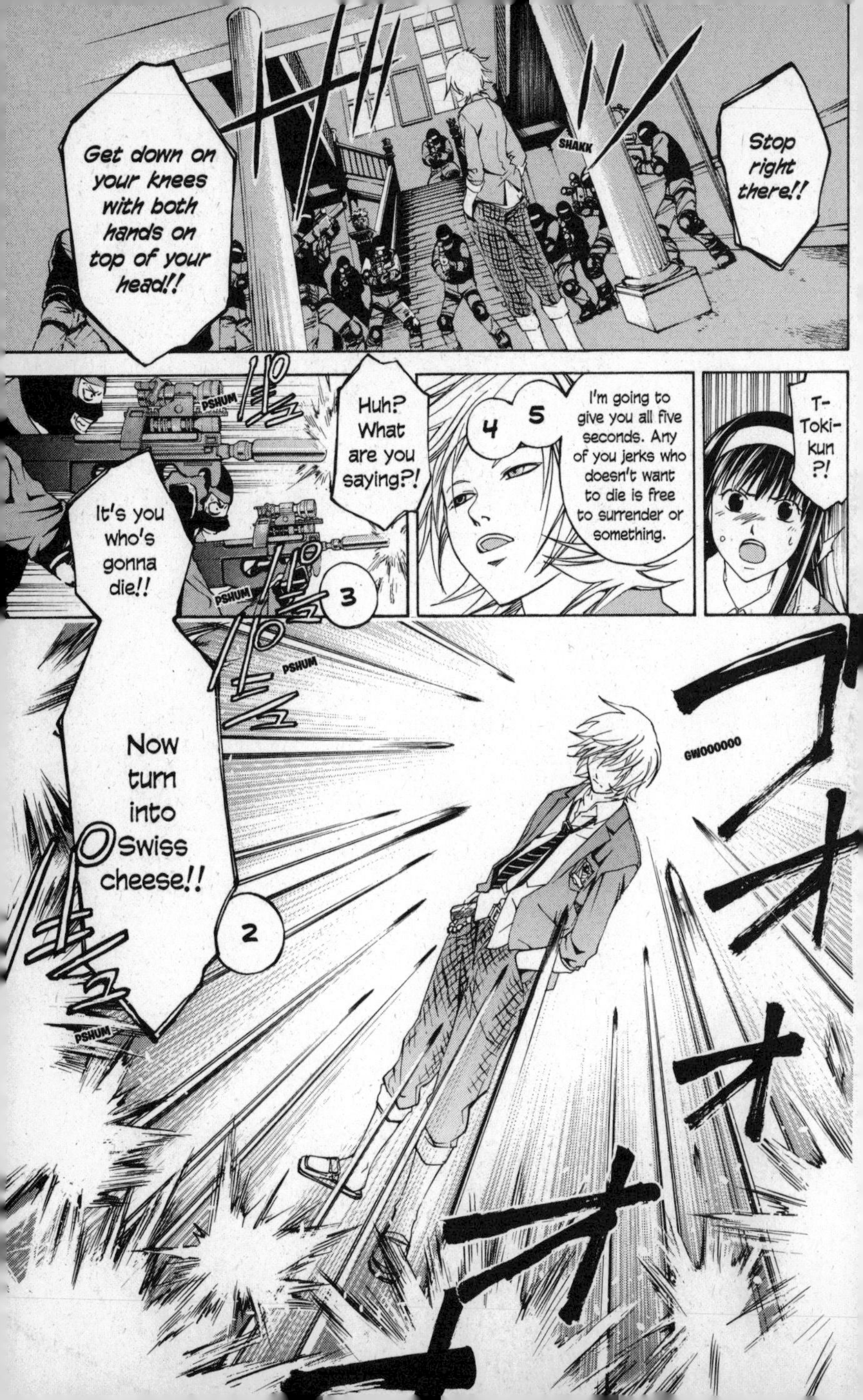
Stop right there!!
SHAKK
Get down on your knees with both hands on top of your head!!
T-Toki-kun?!
I'm going to give you all five seconds. Any of you jerks who doesn't want to die is free to surrender or something.
5
4
Huh? What are you saying?!
PSHUM
It's you who's gonna die!!
PSHUM
3
GWOOOOOO
PSHUM
Now turn into Swiss cheese!!
2
PSHUM

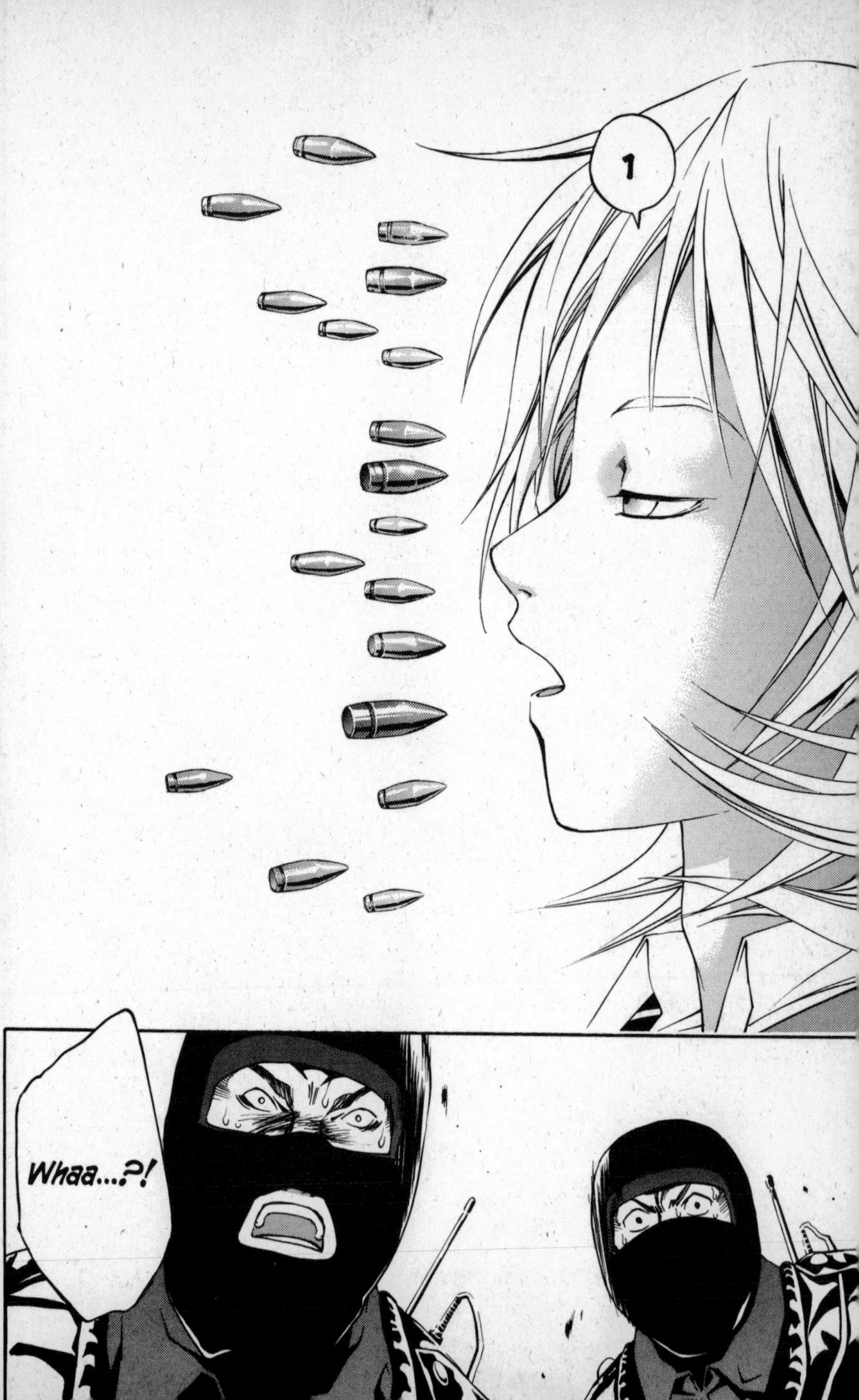
1
Whaa...?!

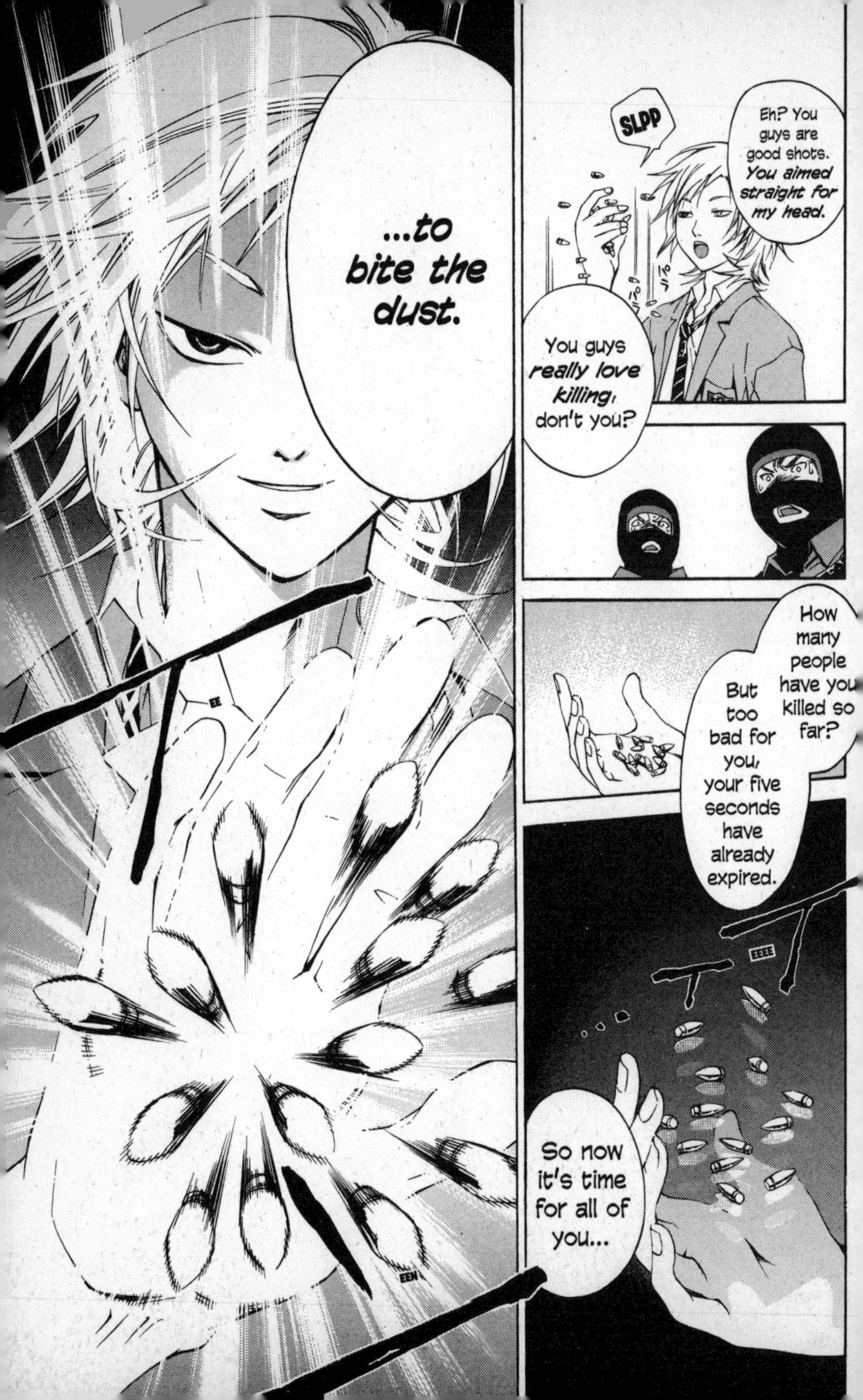
Eh? You guys are good shots. You aimed straight for my head.
SLPP
You guys really love killing, don't you?
How many people have you killed so far?
But too bad for you, your five seconds have already expired.
EEEE
So now it's time for all of you...
...to bite the dust.
EE
EEN

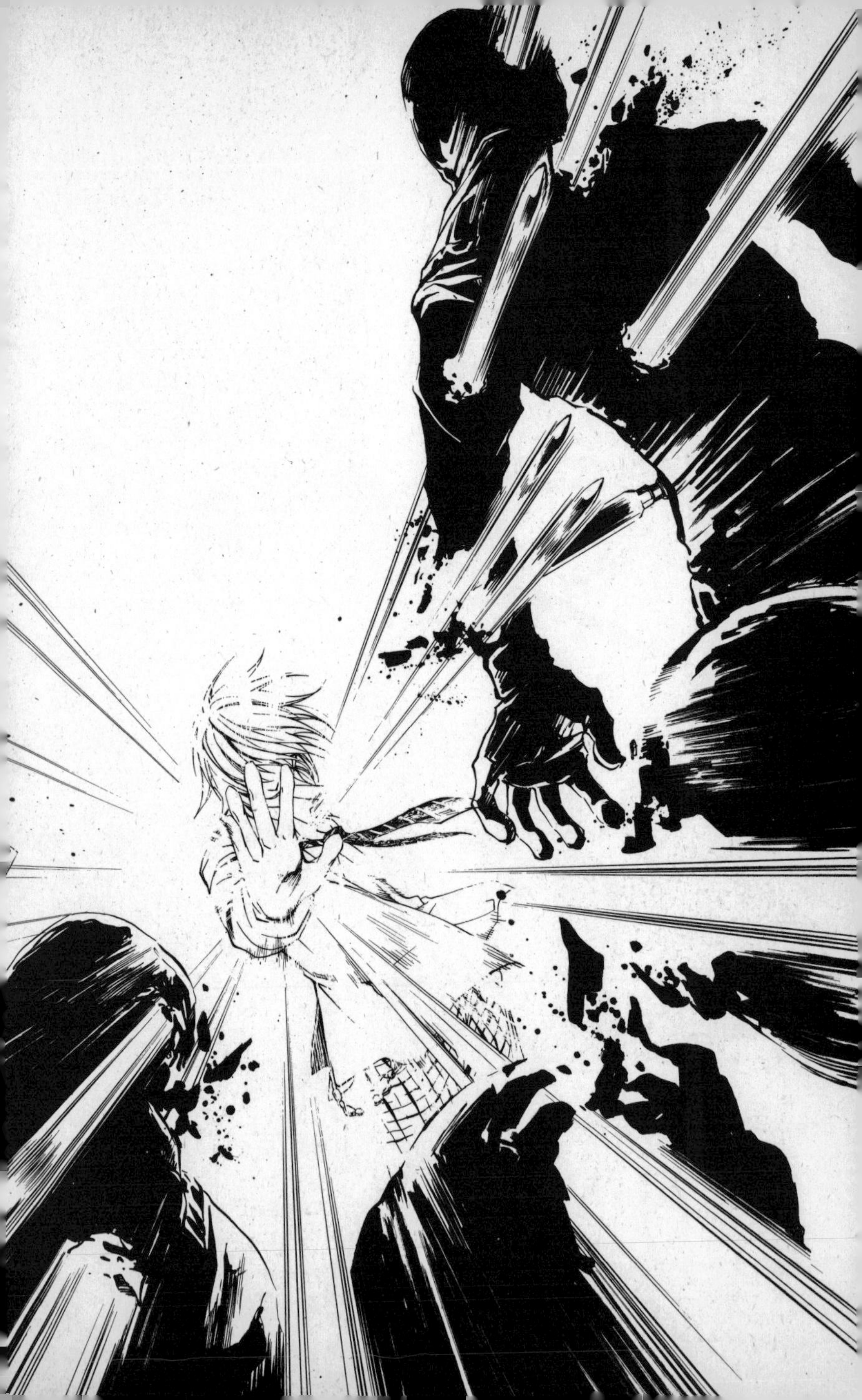

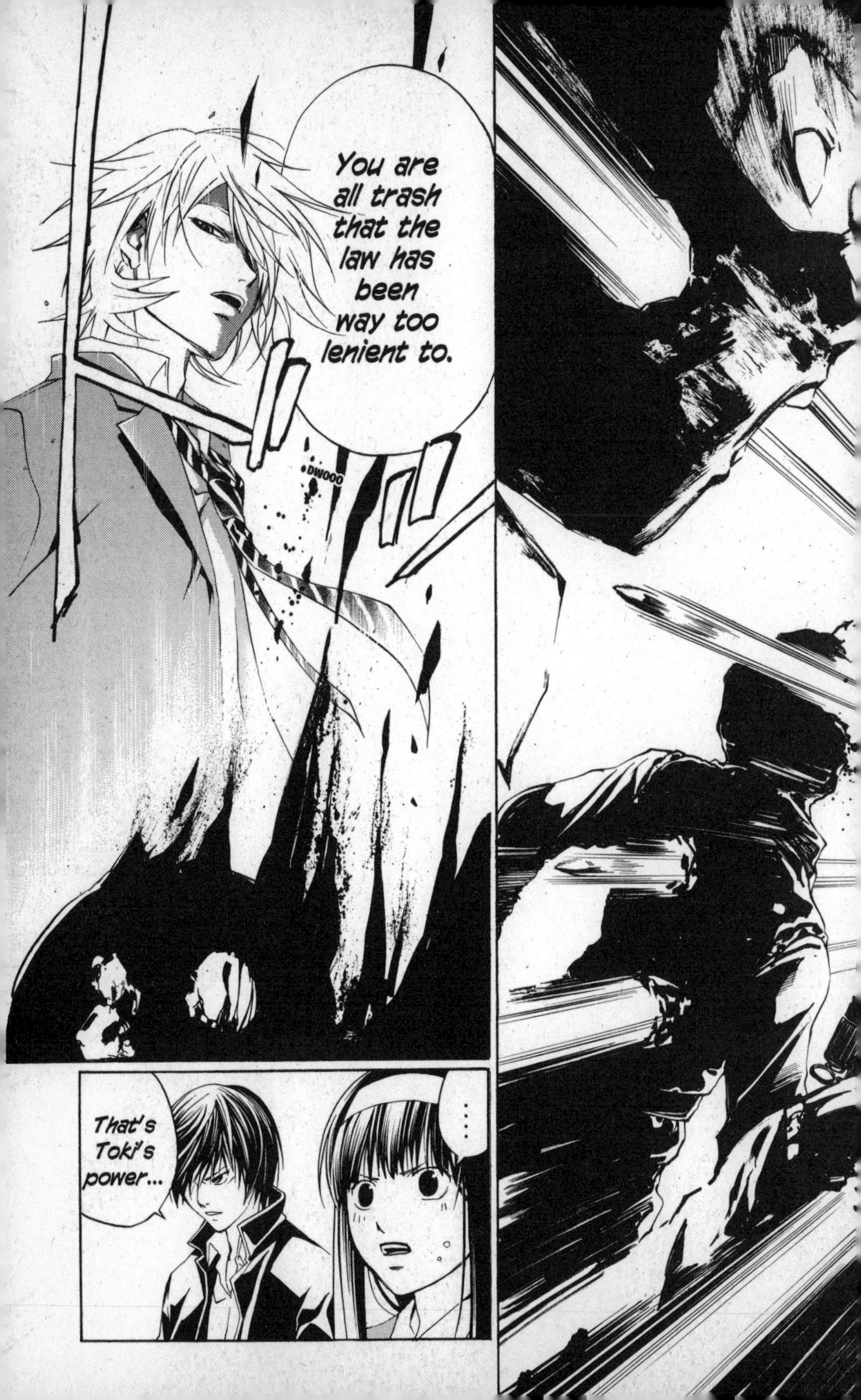
You are all trash that the law has been way too lenient to.
DWOOO
....
That's Toki's power...

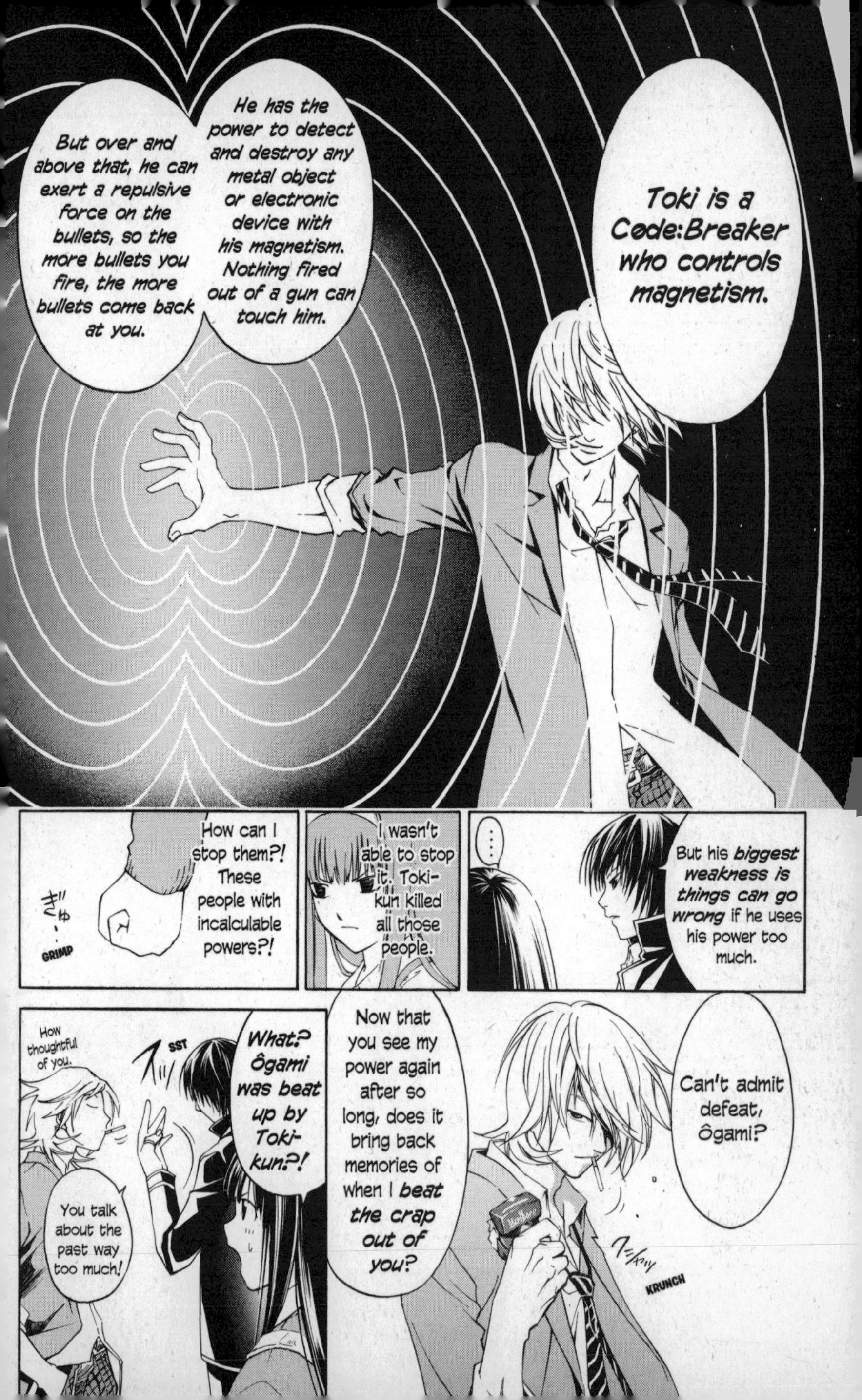

Toki is a Code:Breaker who controls magnetism.
He has the power to detect and destroy any metal object or electronic device with his magnetism. Nothing fired out of a gun can touch him.
But over and above that, he can exert a repulsive force on the bullets, so the more bullets you fire, the more bullets come back at you.
...
But his biggest weakness is things can go wrong if he uses his power too much.
I wasn't able to stop it. Toki-kun killed all those people.
How can I stop them?! These people with incalculable powers?!
GRIMP
Can't admit defeat, Ôgami?
KRUNCH
Now that you see my power again after so long, does it bring back memories of when I beat the crap out of you?
What? Ôgami was beat up by Toki-kun?!
SST
How thoughtful of you.
You talk about the past way too much!

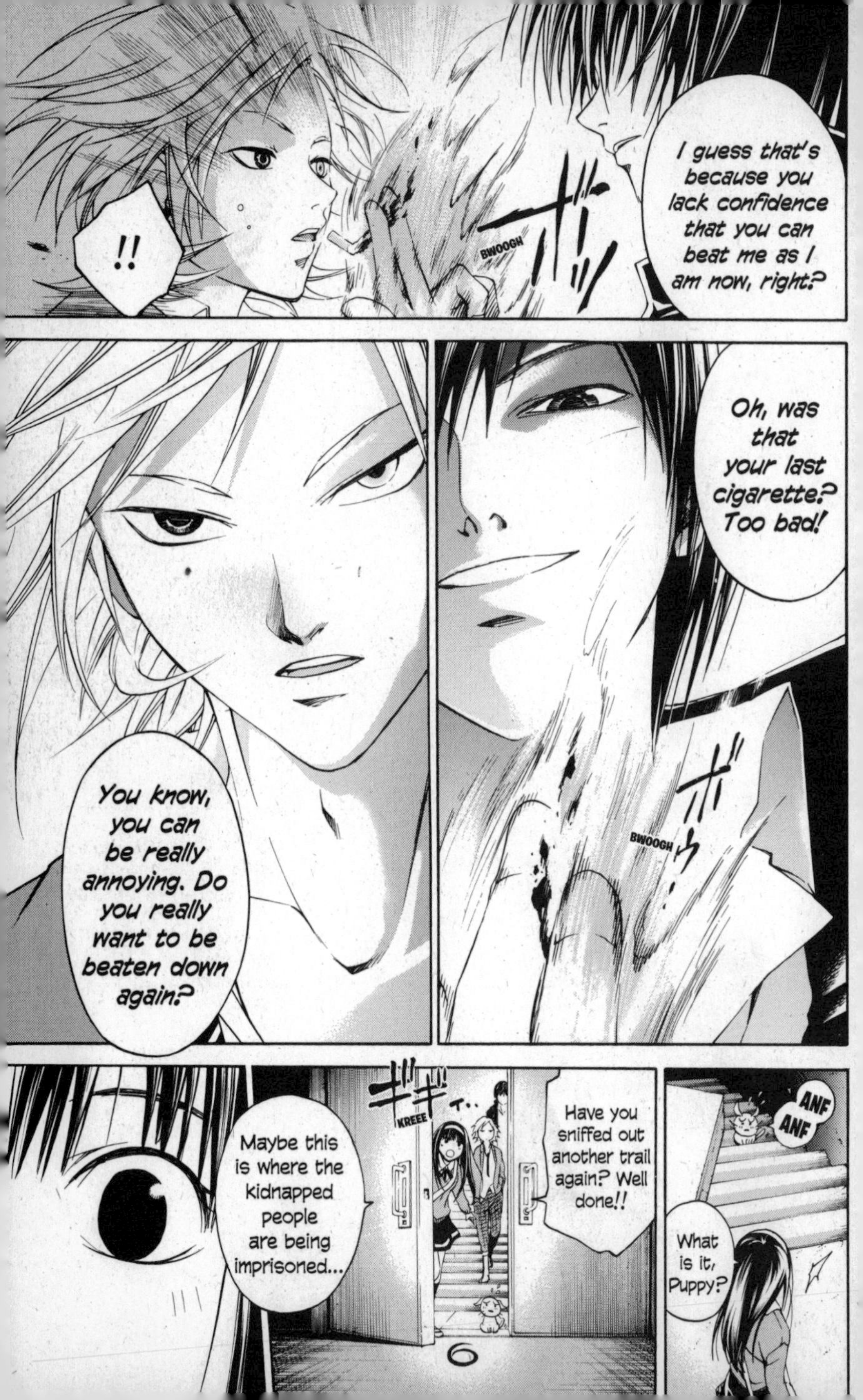
I guess that's because you lack confidence that you can beat me as I am now, right?
BWOOGH
!!
Oh, was that your last cigarette? Too bad!
BWOOGH
You know, you can be really annoying. Do you really want to be beaten down again?
ANF ANF
What is it, Puppy?
KREEE
Have you sniffed out another trail again? Well done!!
Maybe this is where the kidnapped people are being imprisoned...

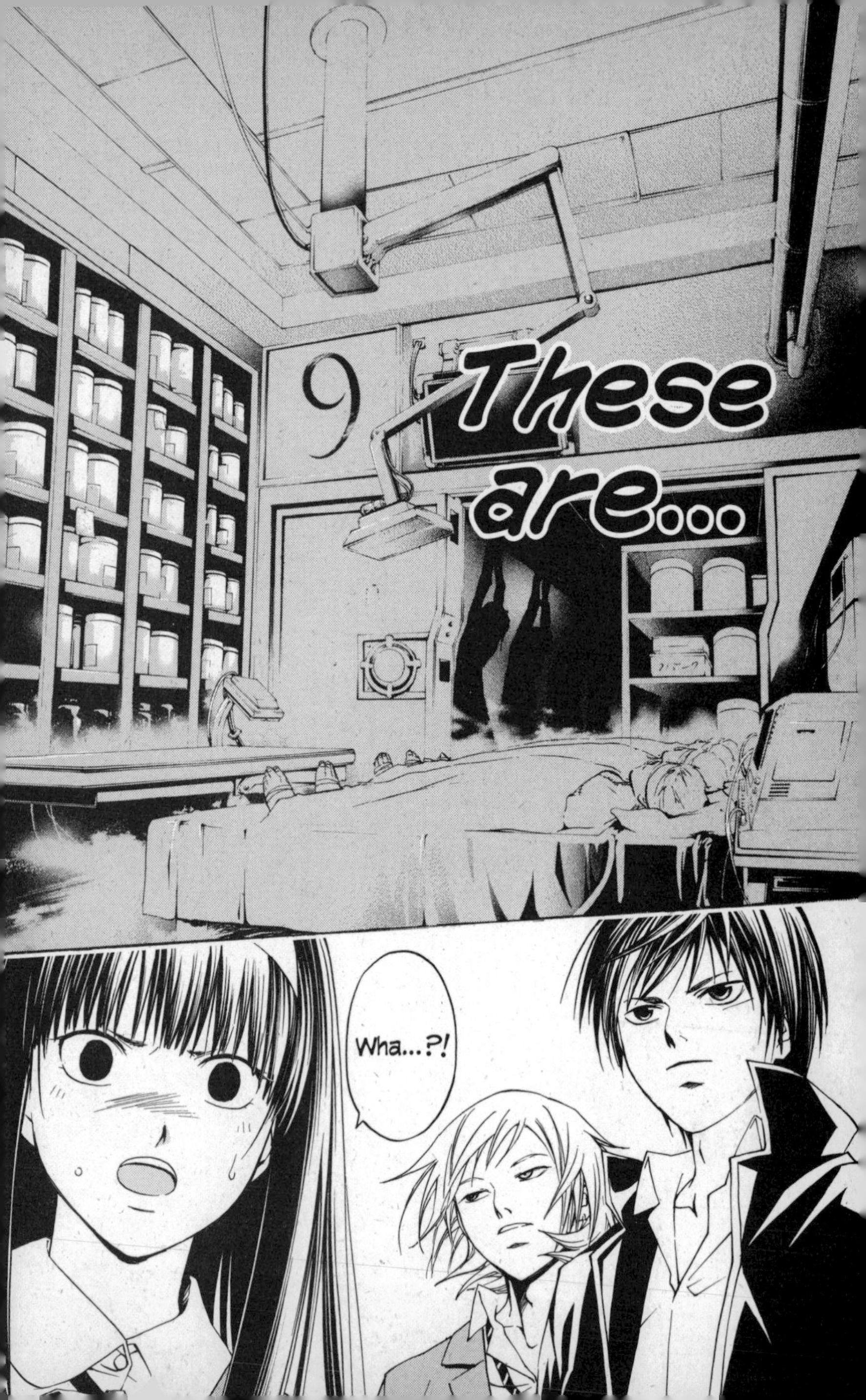
These are...
Wha...?!

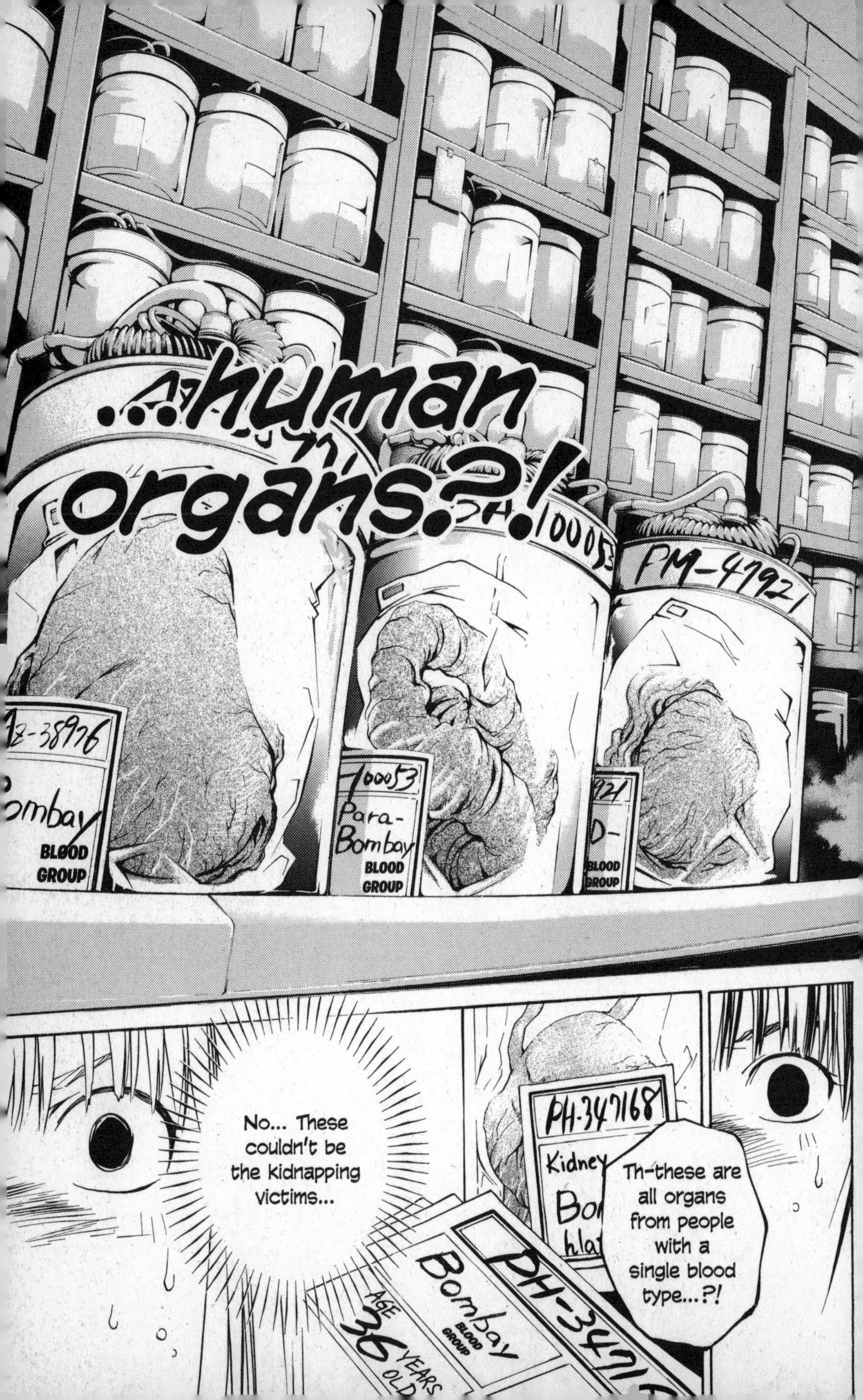
...human organs?!
PM-47921
100053
Para-Bombay
BLOOD GROUP
Bombay
BLOOD GROUP
Th-these are all organs from people with a single blood type...?!
PH-347168
Kidney
Bombay
BLOOD GROUP
AGE
36
YEARS OLD
No... These couldn't be the kidnapping victims...

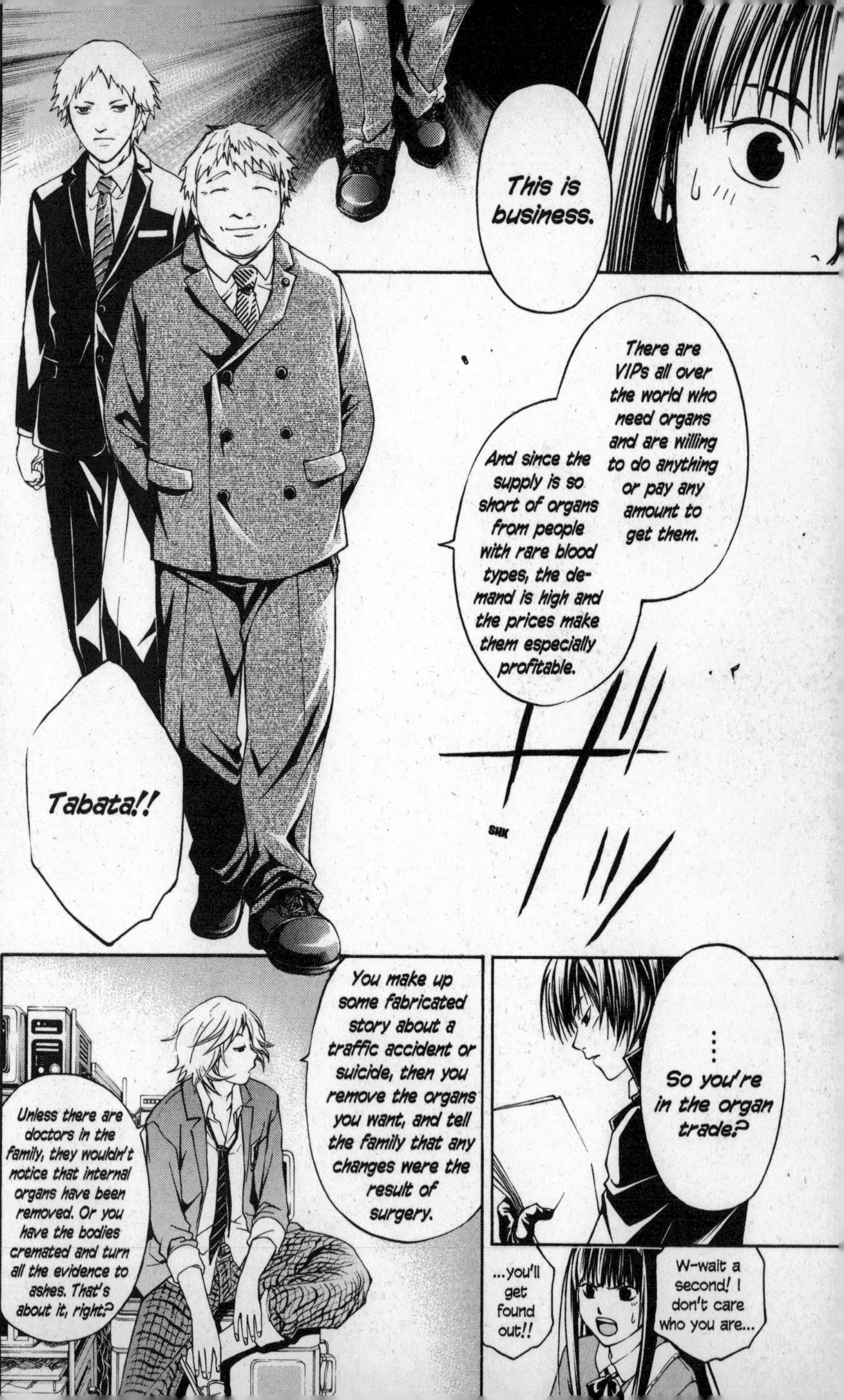
This is business.
There are VIPs all over the world who need organs and are willing to do anything or pay any amount to get them.
And since the supply is so short of organs from people with rare blood types, the demand is high and the prices make them especially profitable.
SHK
Tabata!!
... So you're in the organ trade?
W-wait a second! I don't care who you are...
...you'll get found out!!
You make up some fabricated story about a traffic accident or suicide, then you remove the organs you want, and tell the family that any changes were the result of surgery.
Unless there are doctors in the family, they wouldn't notice that internal organs have been removed. Or you have the bodies cremated and turn all the evidence to ashes. That's about it, right?

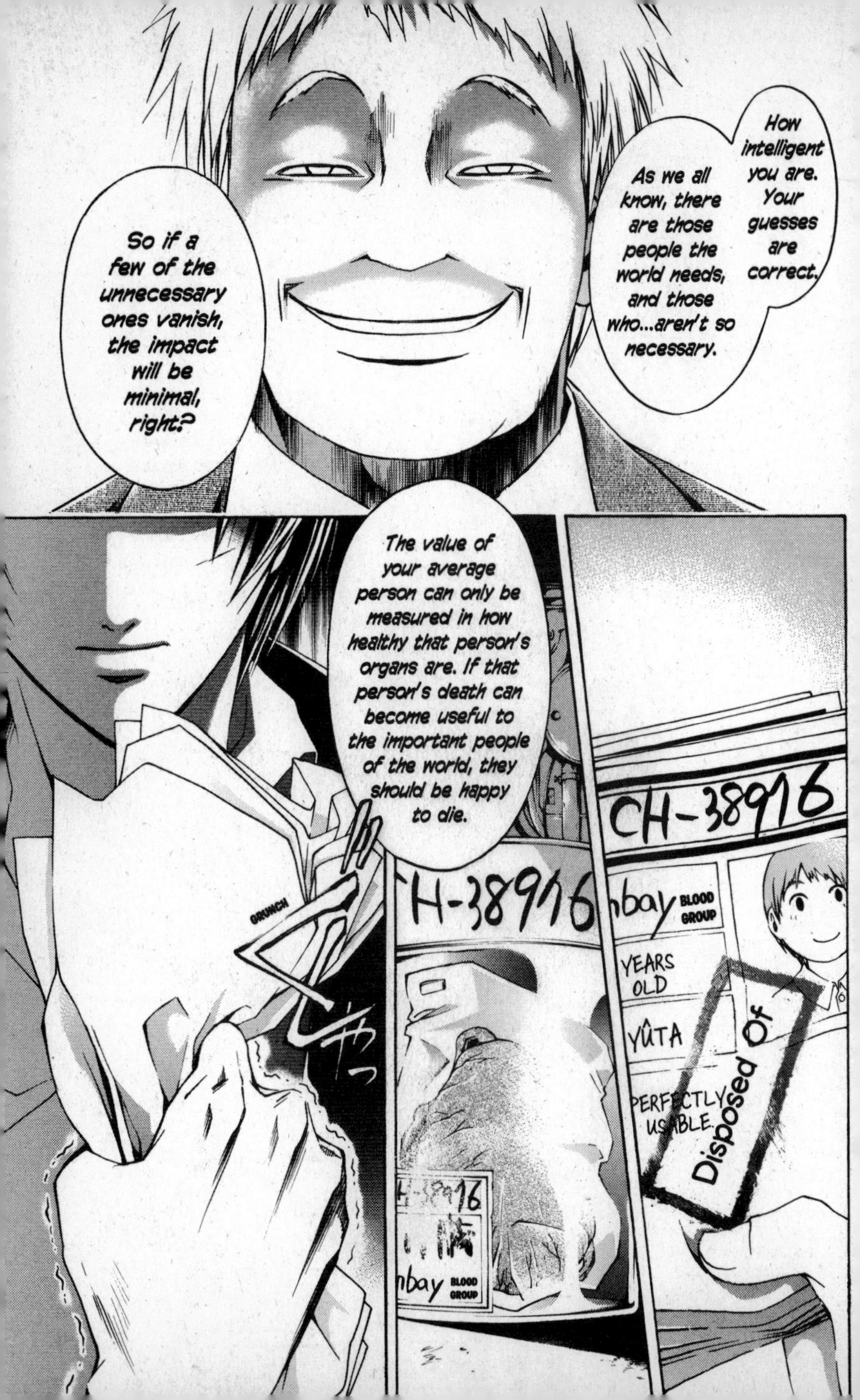
How intelligent you are. Your guesses are correct.
As we all know, there are those people the world needs, and those who...aren't so necessary.
So if a few of the unnecessary ones vanish, the impact will be minimal, right?
CH-38916
nbay
BLOOD GROUP
YEARS OLD
YÛTA
PERFECTLY USABLE.
Disposed Of
H-38916
nbay
BLOOD GROUP
The value of your average person can only be measured in how healthy that person's organs are. If that person's death can become useful to the important people of the world, they should be happy to die.
GRUNCH

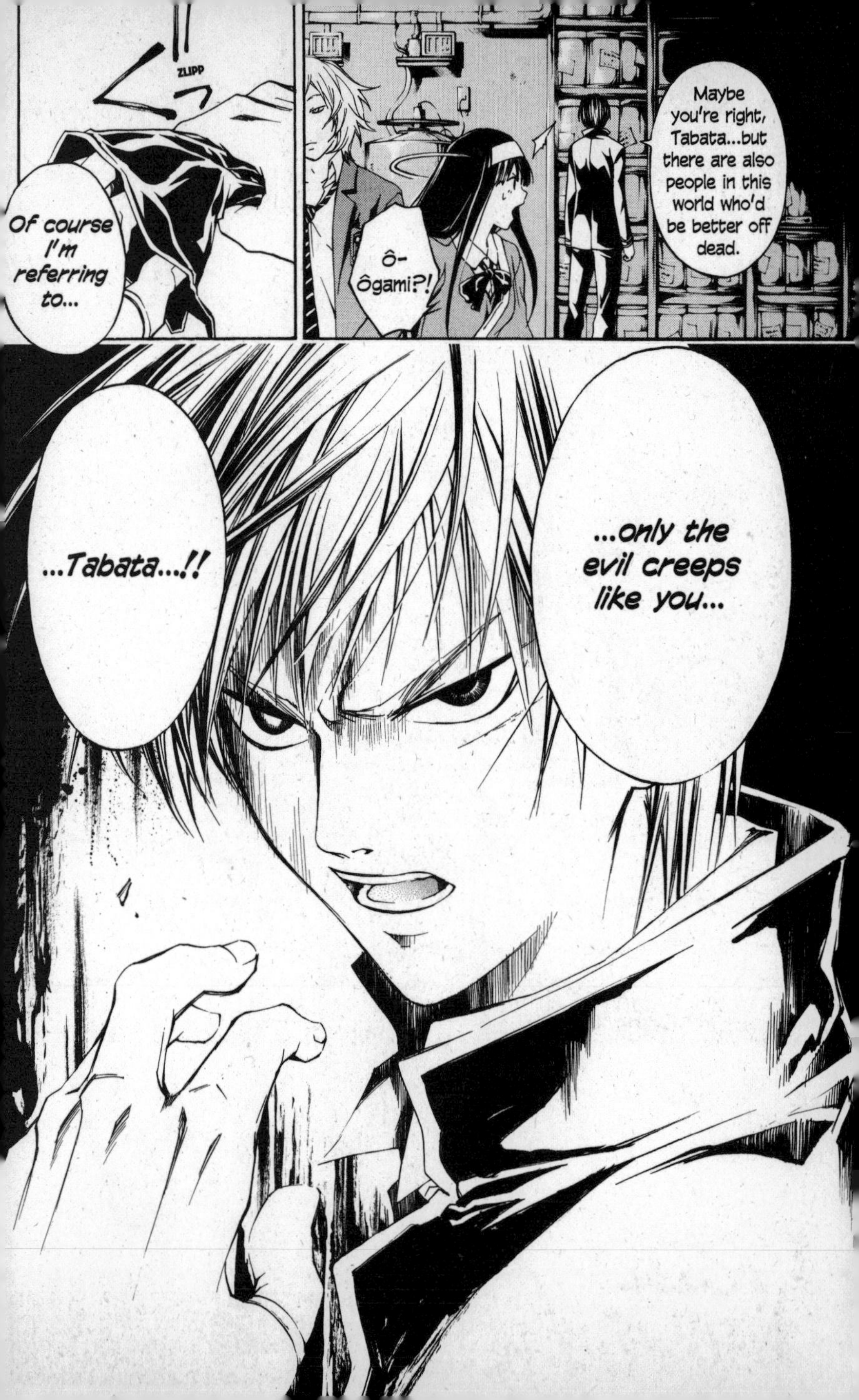
Maybe you're right, Tabata...but there are also people in this world who'd be better off dead.
Ô-Ôgami?!
ZLIPP
Of course I'm referring to...
...only the evil creeps like you...
...Tabata...!!

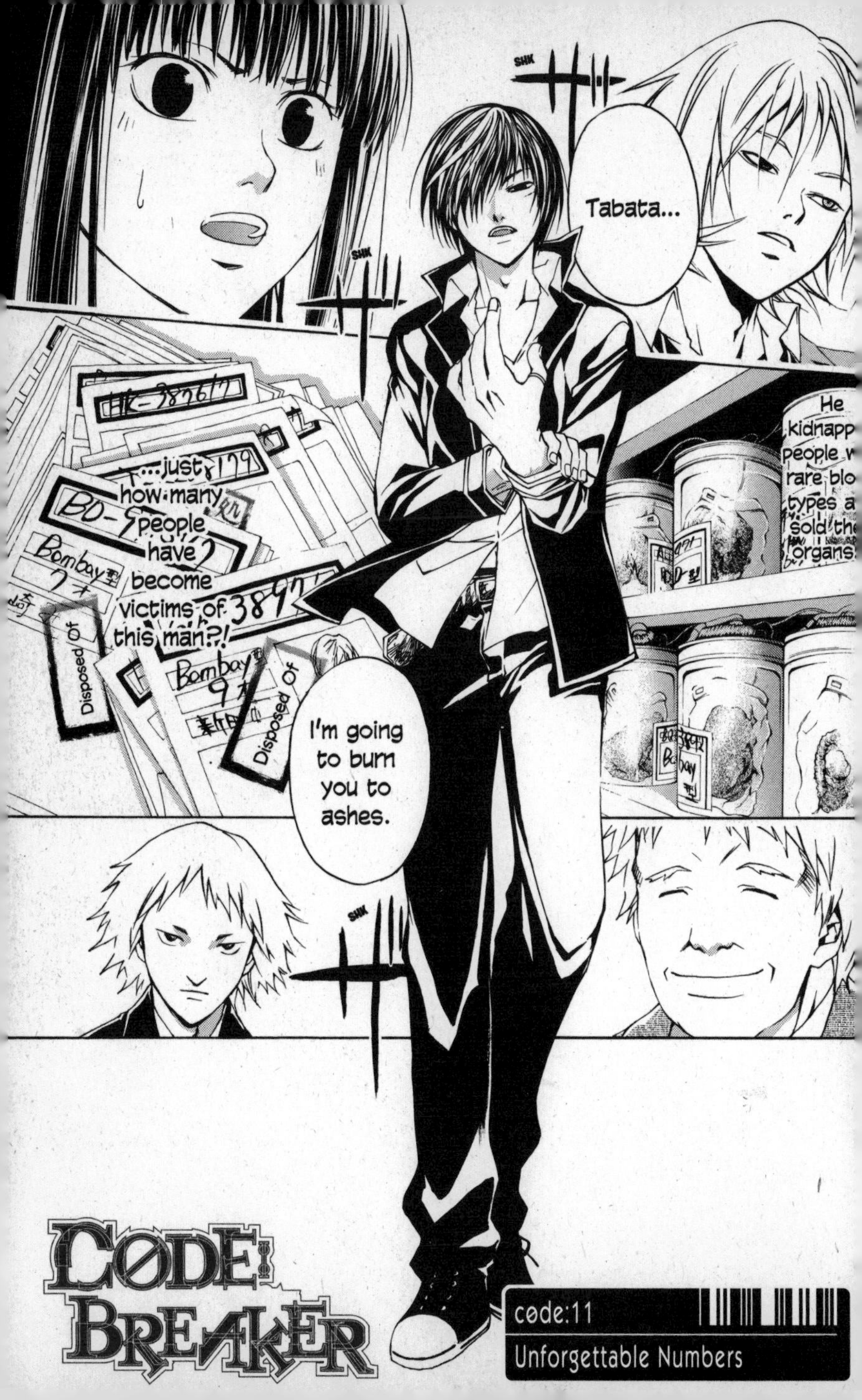
SHK
Tabata...
SHK
He kidnapp people w rare blo types a sold the organs.
...just how many people have become victims of this man?!
Disposed Of
Disposed Of
I'm going to burn you to ashes.
SHK
CODE:BREAKER
code:11
Unforgettable Numbers

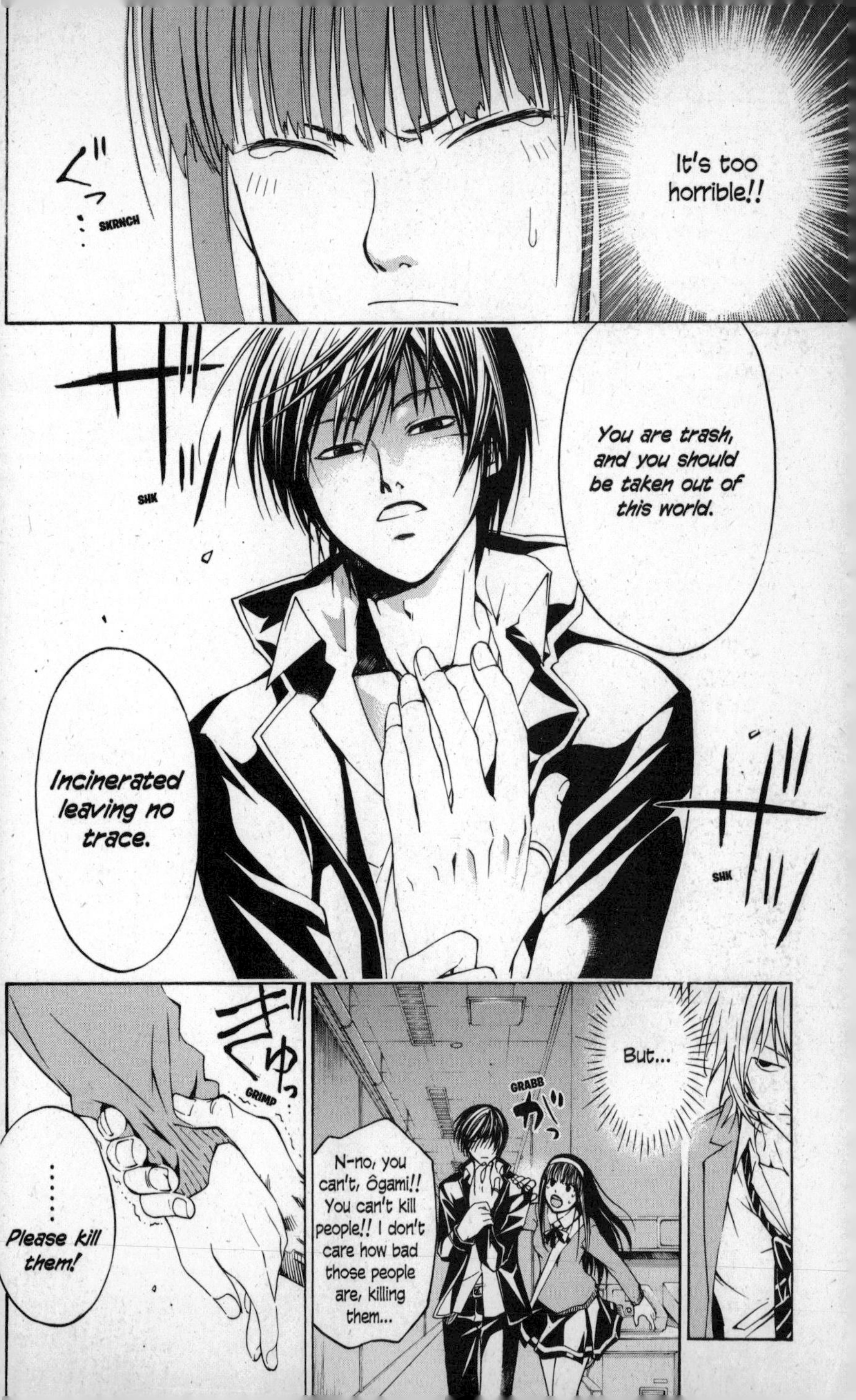
It's too horrible!!
ぐっ
SKRNCH
You are trash, and you should be taken out of this world.
SHK
Incinerated leaving no trace.
SHK
But...
GRABB
がっ
N-no, you can't, Ôgami!! You can't kill people!! I don't care how bad those people are, killing them...
ぎゅっ
GRIMP
......
Please kill them!

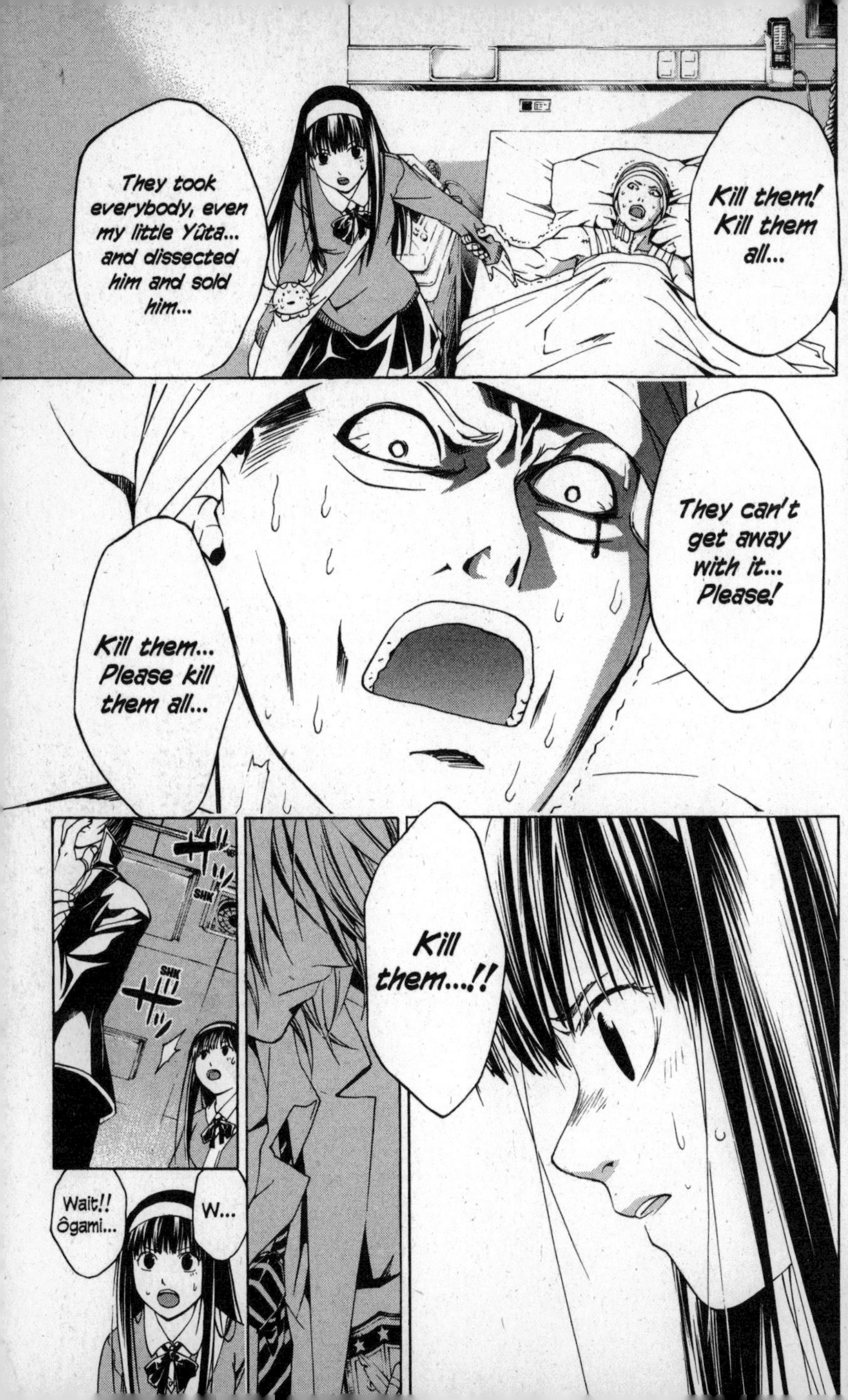
Kill them! Kill them all...
They took everybody, even my little Yûta... and dissected him and sold him...
They can't get away with it... Please!
Kill them... Please kill them all...
Kill them...!!
SHK
SHK
W...
Wait!! Ôgami...

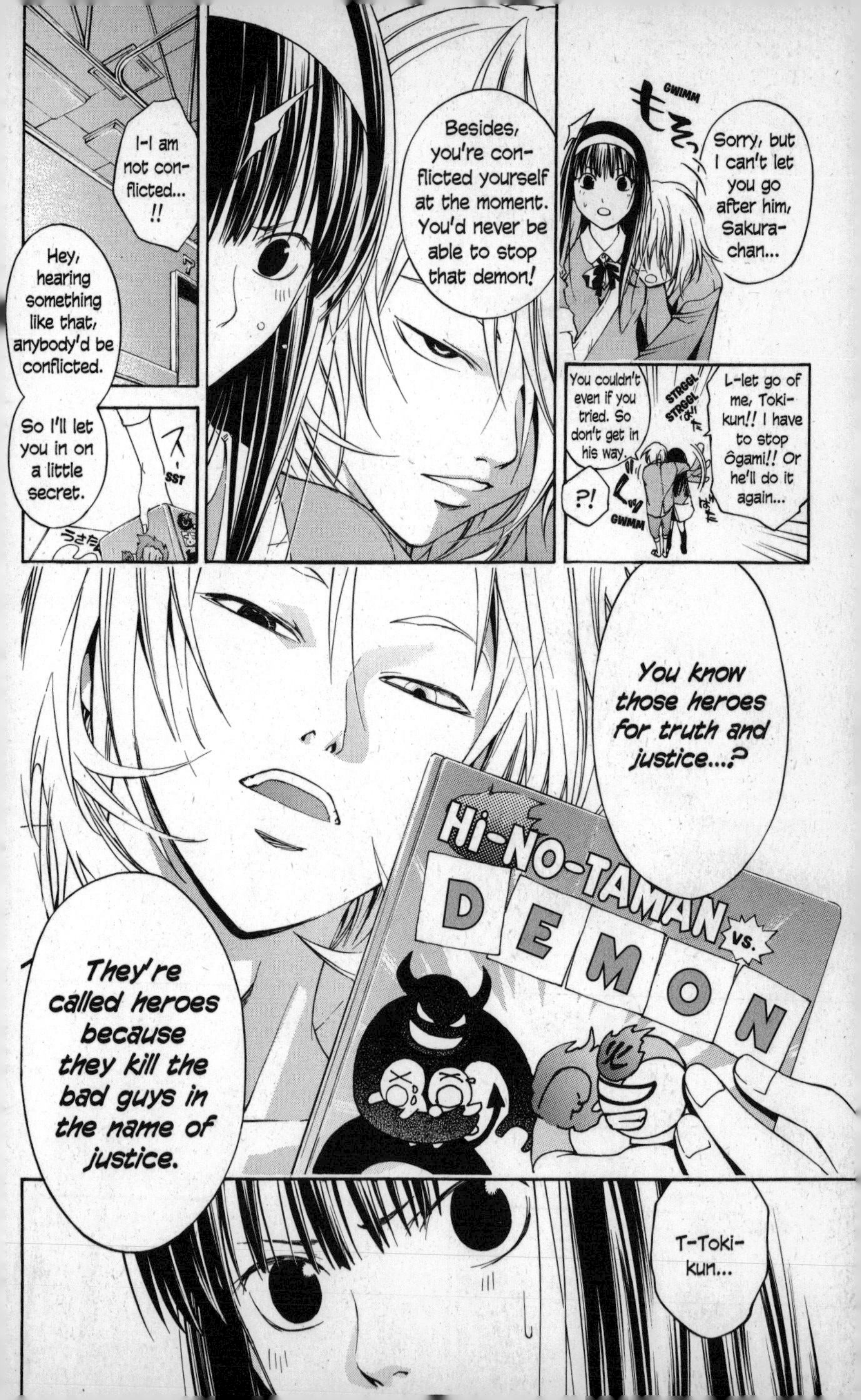
GWIMM
Sorry, but I can't let you go after him, Sakura-chan...
L-let go of me, Toki-kun!! I have to stop Ôgami!! Or he'll do it again...
STRGGL STRGGL
You couldn't even if you tried. So don't get in his way.
?!
GWMM
Besides, you're con-flicted yourself at the moment. You'd never be able to stop that demon!
I-I am not con-flicted...!!
Hey, hearing something like that, anybody'd be conflicted.
So I'll let you in on a little secret.
SST
You know those heroes for truth and justice...?
HI-NO-TAMAN VS. DEMON
They're called heroes because they kill the bad guys in the name of justice.
T-Toki-kun...

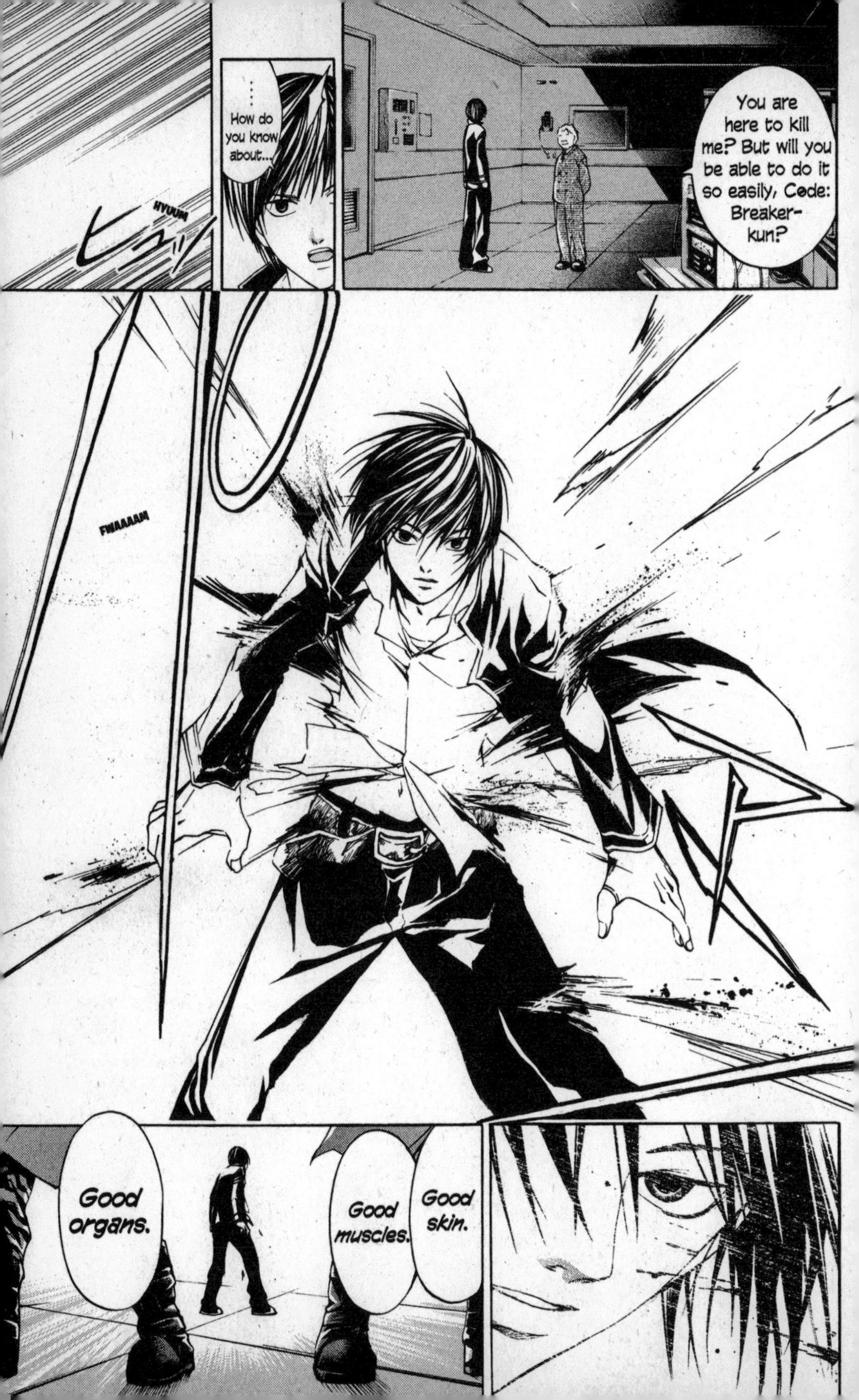
You are here to kill me? But will you be able to do it so easily, Code: Breaker-kun?
... How do you know about...
HYUUM
FWAAAAM
Good skin.
Good muscles.
Good organs.

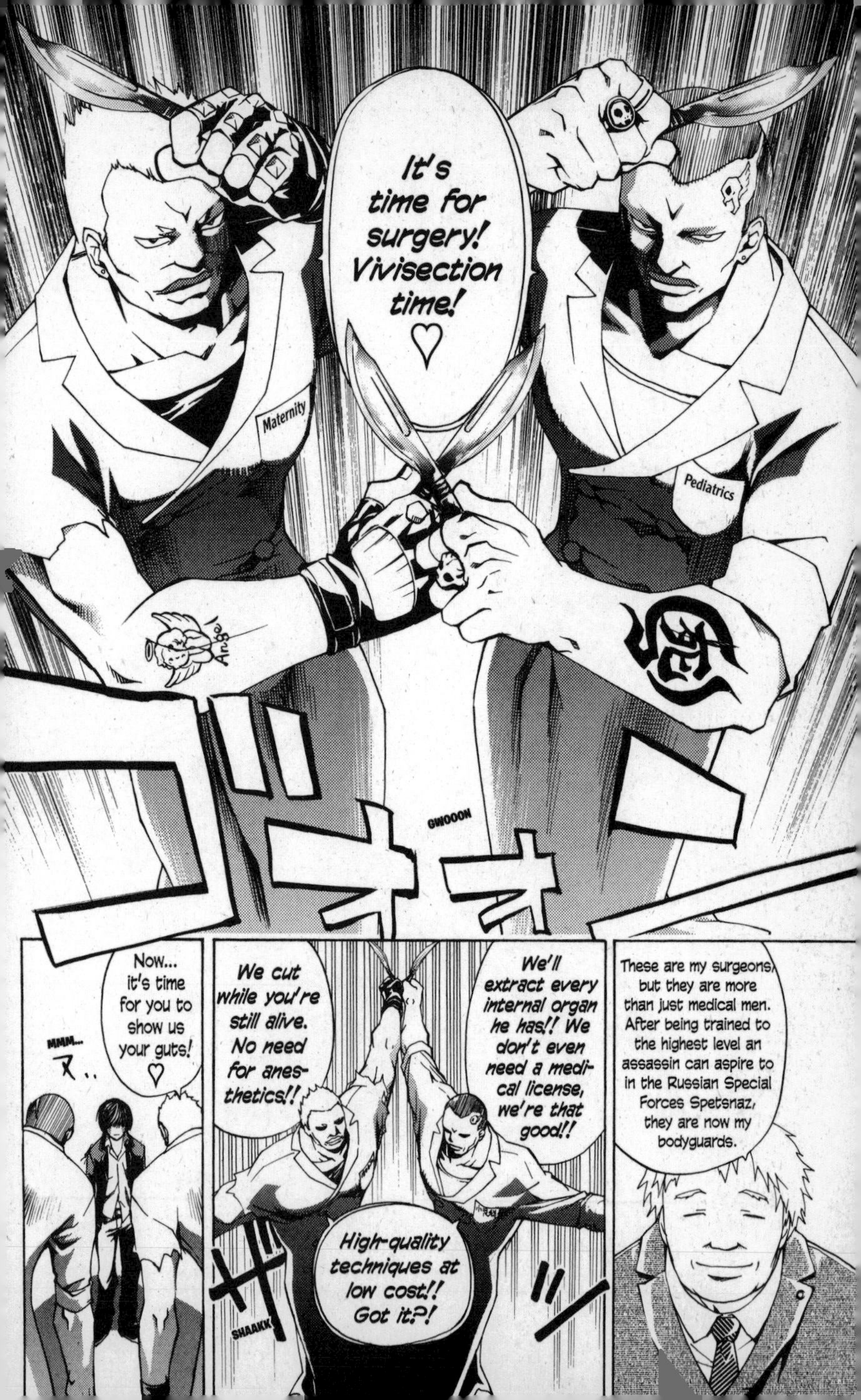
It's time for surgery! Vivisection time! ♡
Pediatrics
Maternity
Angel
GWOOON
These are my surgeons, but they are more than just medical men. After being trained to the highest level an assassin can aspire to in the Russian Special Forces Spetsnaz, they are now my bodyguards.
We'll extract every internal organ he has!! We don't even need a medical license, we're that good!!
We cut while you're still alive. No need for anesthetics!!
High-quality techniques at low cost!! Got it?!
SHAAKK
Now... it's time for you to show us your guts! ♡
MMM...

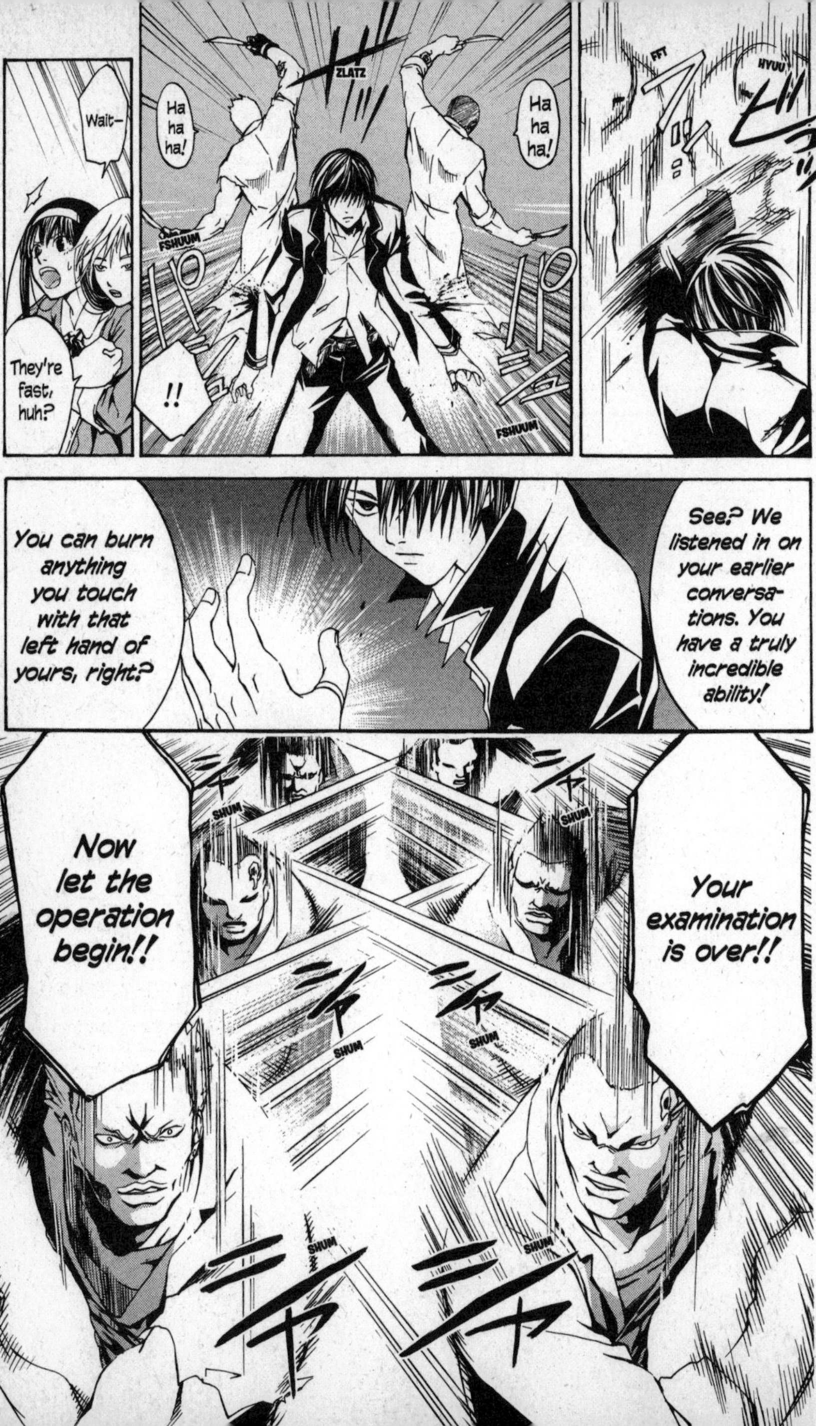
FFT
HYUU
ZLATZ
Ha ha ha!
Ha ha ha!
FSHUUM
!!
FSHUUM
Wait—
They're fast, huh?
See? We listened in on your earlier conversations. You have a truly incredible ability!
You can burn anything you touch with that left hand of yours, right?
SHUM
SHUM
Your examination is over!!
Now let the operation begin!!
SHUM
SHUM
SHUM
SHUM

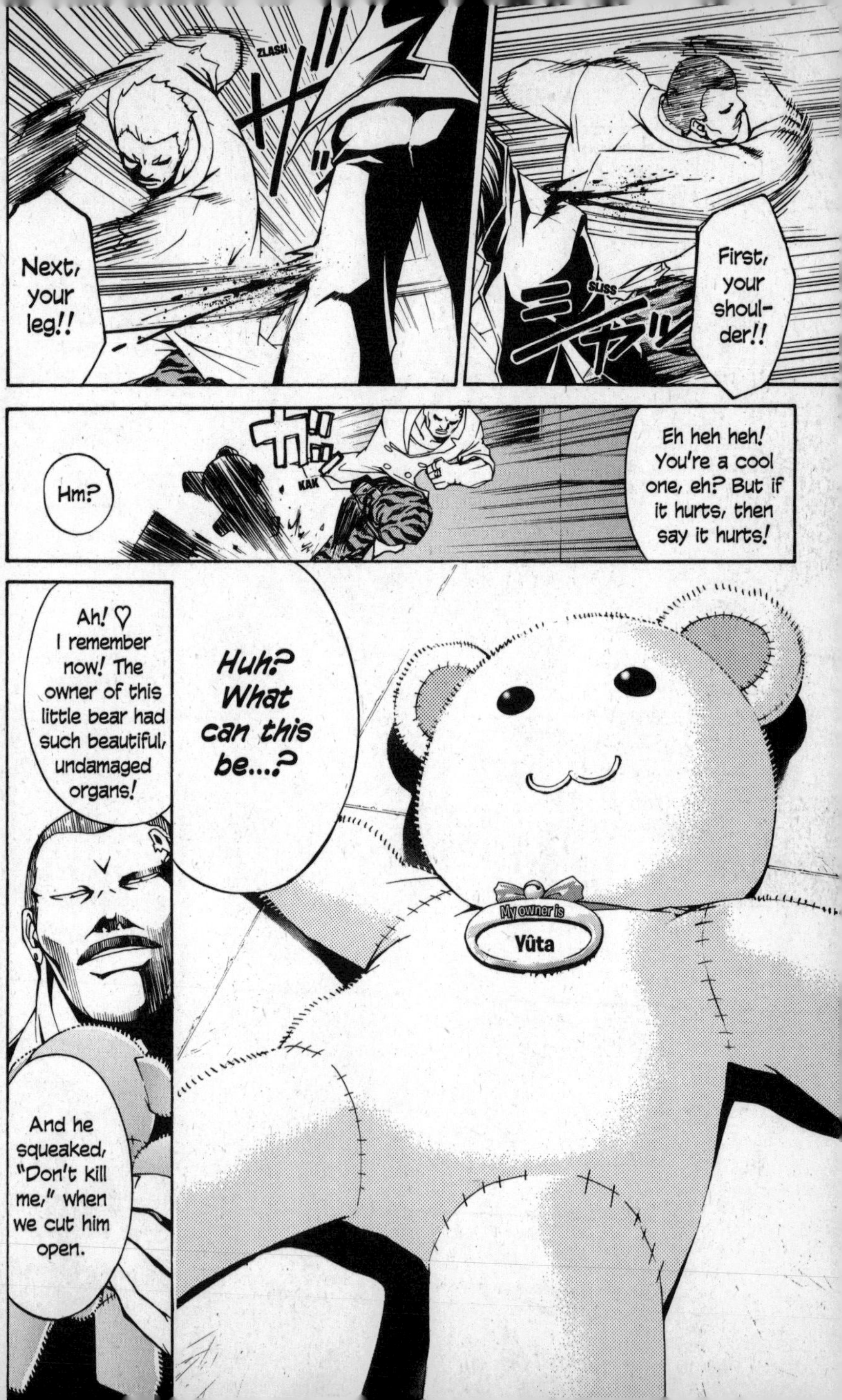
First, your shoul-der!!
SLISS
ZLASH
Next, your leg!!
Eh heh heh! You're a cool one, eh? But if it hurts, then say it hurts!
KAK
Hm?
Huh? What can this be...?
Ah! ♡ I remember now! The owner of this little bear had such beautiful, undamaged organs!
My owner is
Yûta
And he squeaked, "Don't kill me," when we cut him open.

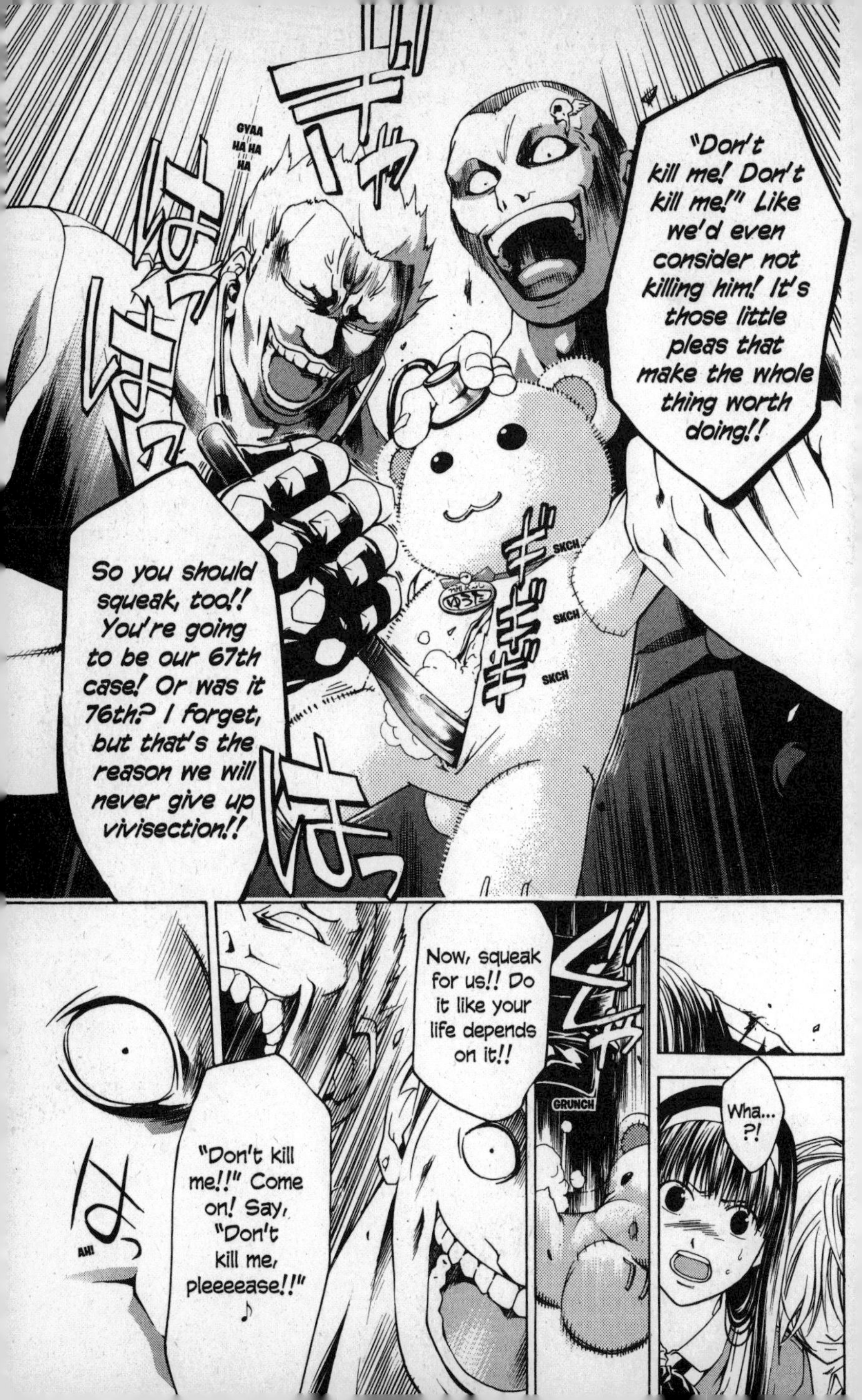

"Don't kill me! Don't kill me!" Like we'd even consider not killing him! It's those little pleas that make the whole thing worth doing!!
GYAA HA HA HA
SKCH
SKCH
SKCH
So you should squeak, too!! You're going to be our 67th case! Or was it 76th? I forget, but that's the reason we will never give up vivisection!!
Wha...?!
Now, squeak for us!! Do it like your life depends on it!!
GRUNCH
"Don't kill me!!" Come on! Say, "Don't kill me, pleeeease!!" ♪
AH!

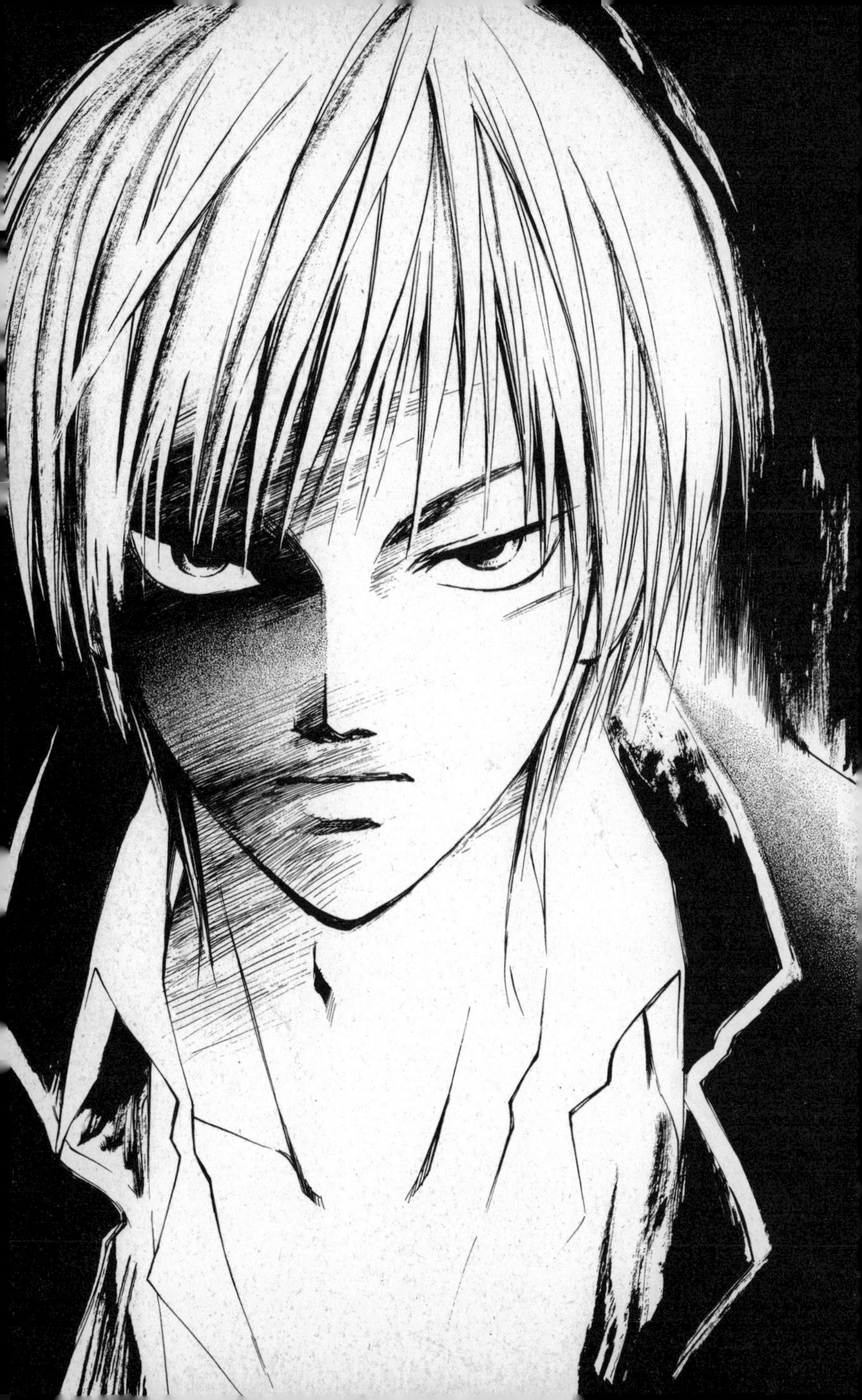

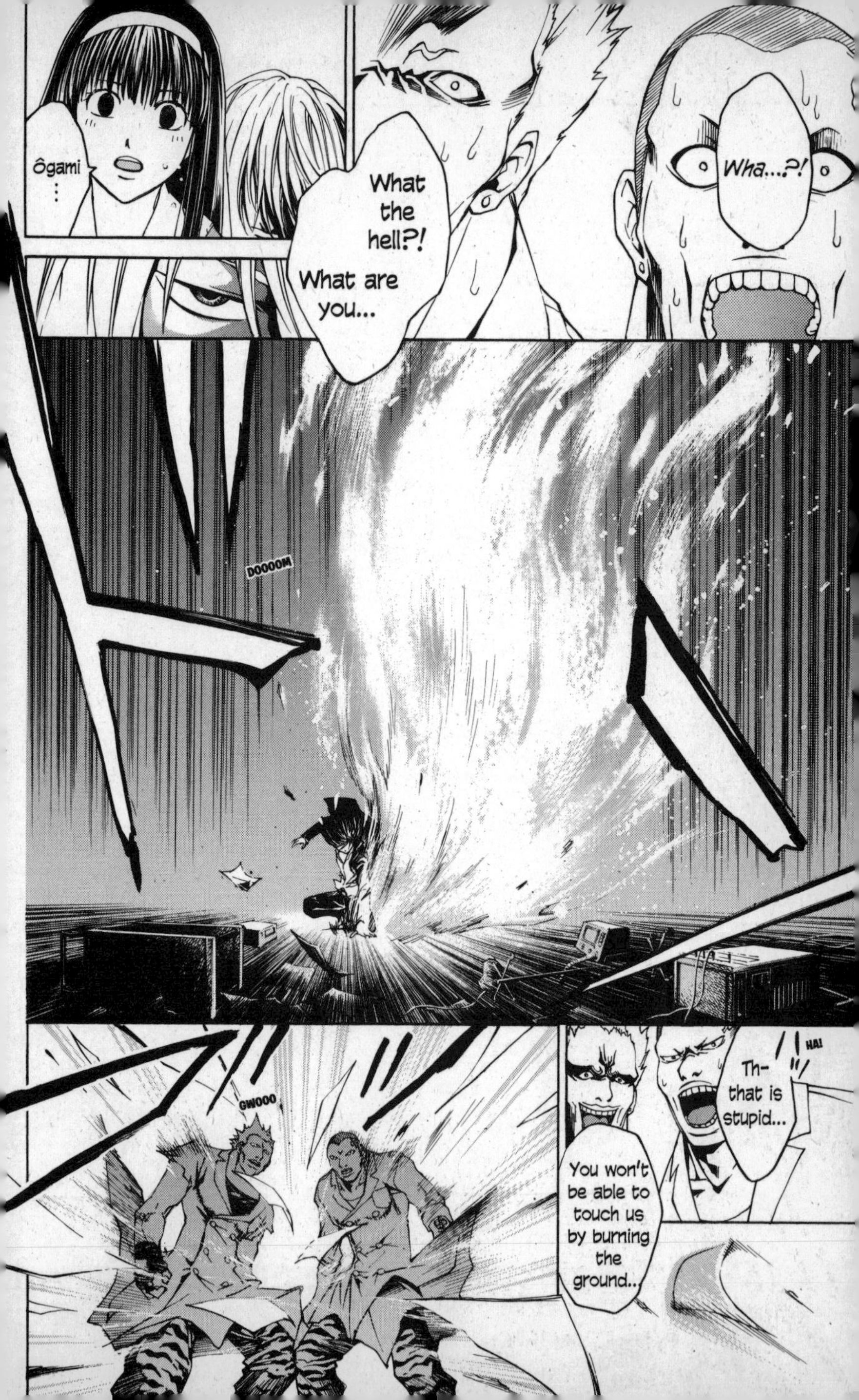
Wha...?!
What the hell?!
What are you...
Ôgami...
DOOOOM
HA!
Th-that is stupid...
You won't be able to touch us by burning the ground...
GWOOO

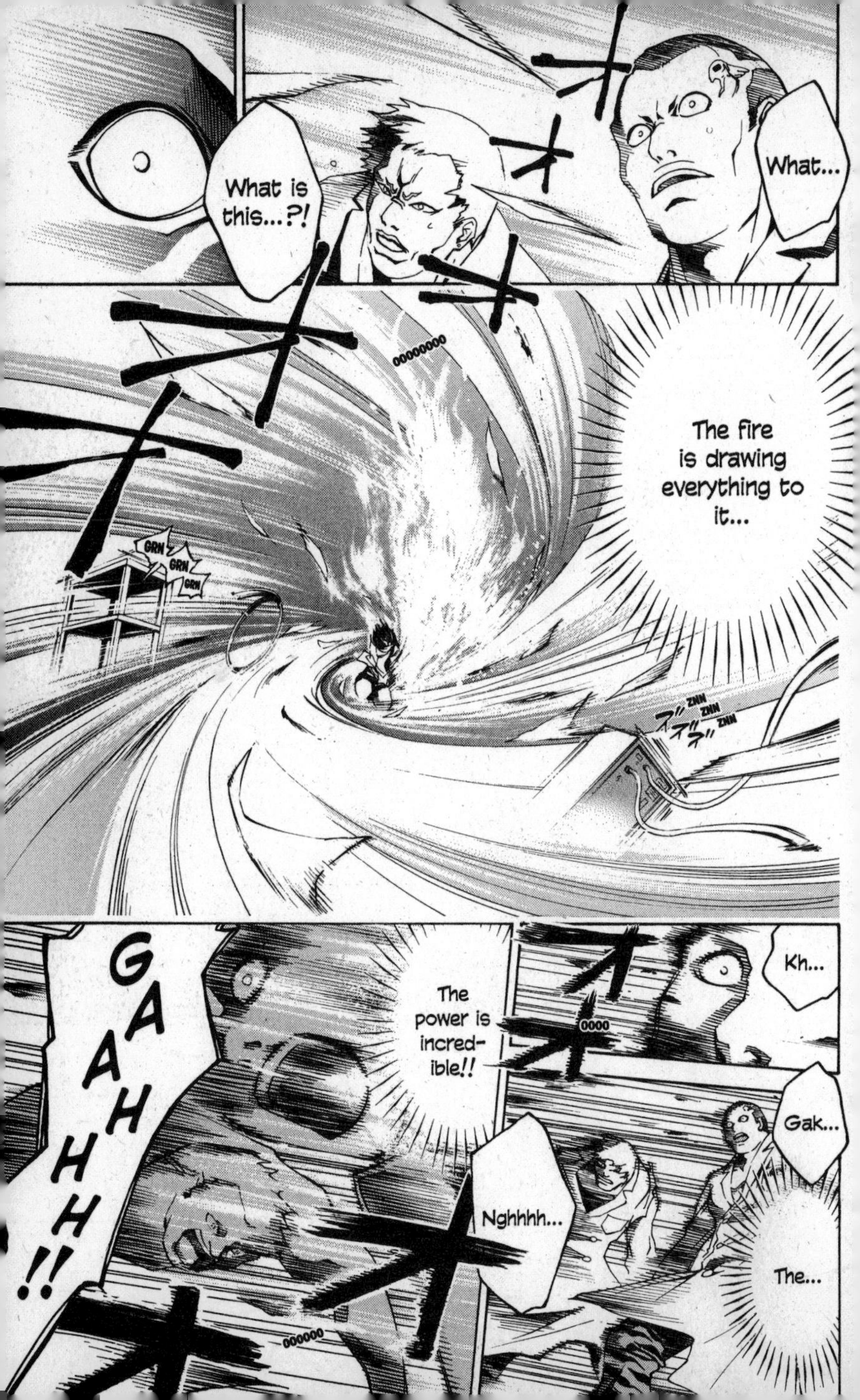
What...
What is this...?!
The fire is drawing everything to it...
oooooooo
ZNN
ZNN
ZNN
GRN
GRN
GRN
Kh...
oooo
Gak...
The...
The power is incredible!!
Nghhhh...
GAAHHHH!!
oooooo

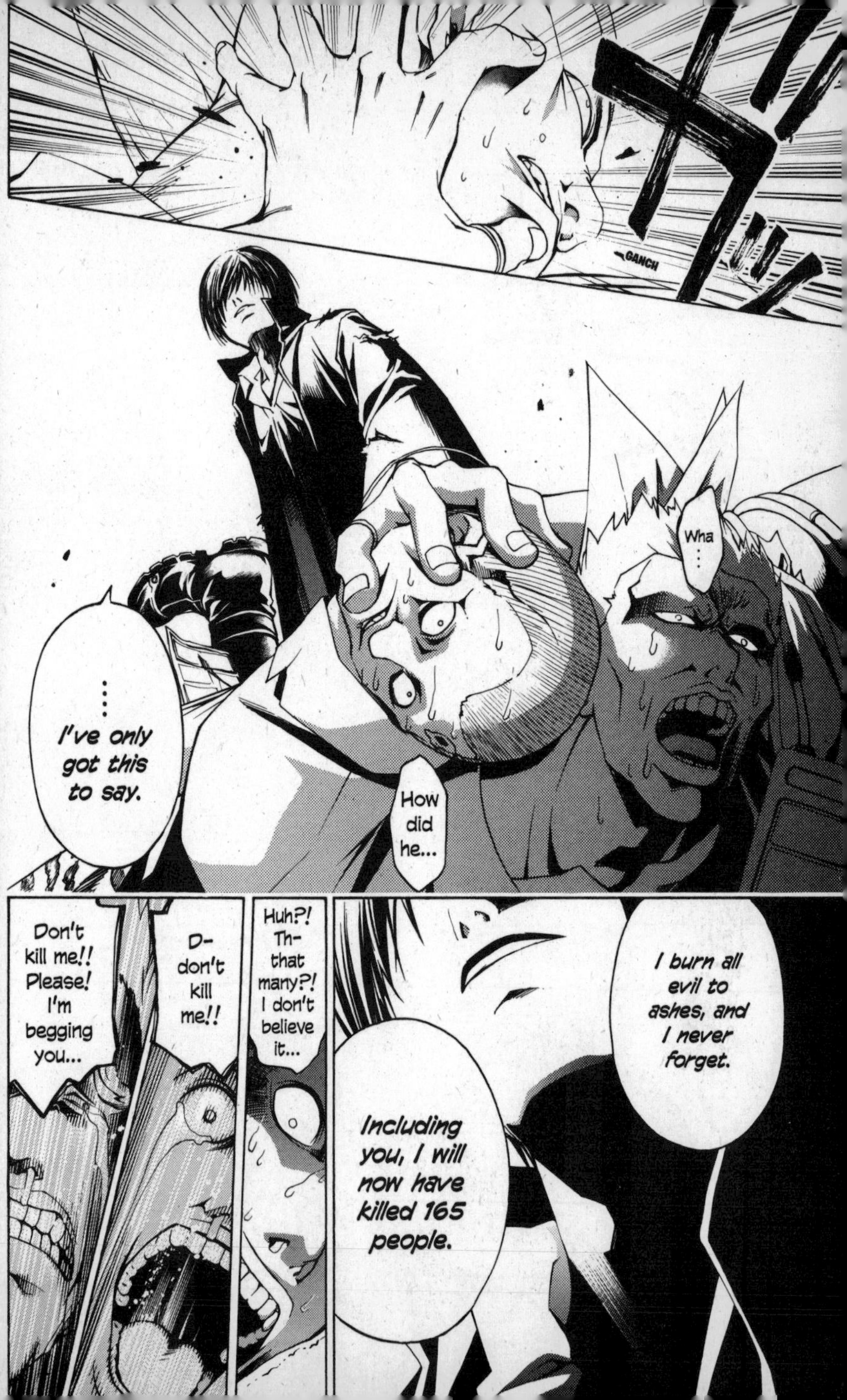
GANCH
Wha...
How did he...
... I've only got this to say.
I burn all evil to ashes, and I never forget.
Including you, I will now have killed 165 people.
Huh?! Th-that many?! I don't believe it...
D-don't kill me!!
Don't kill me!! Please! I'm begging you...

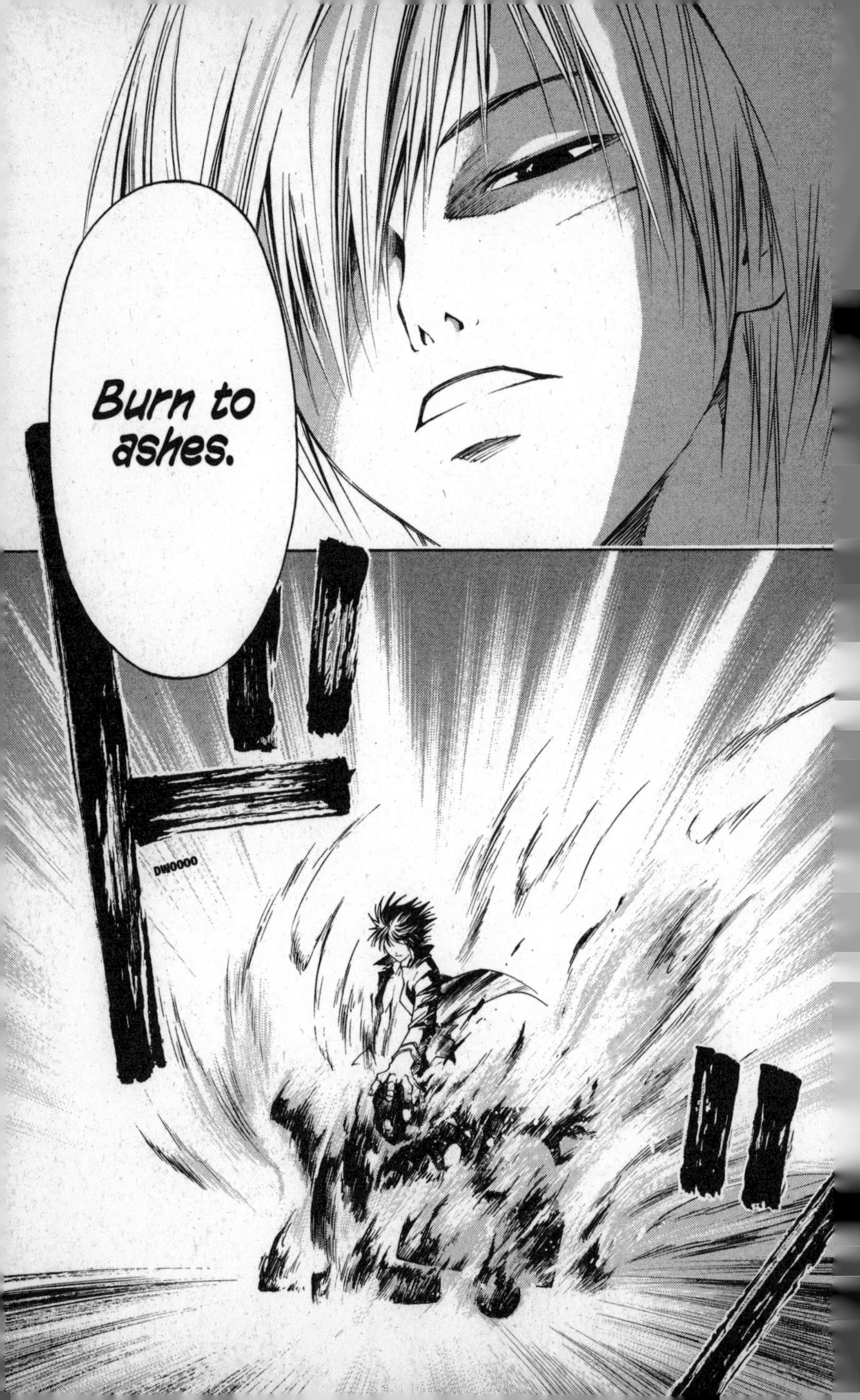
Burn to ashes.
DWOOOO

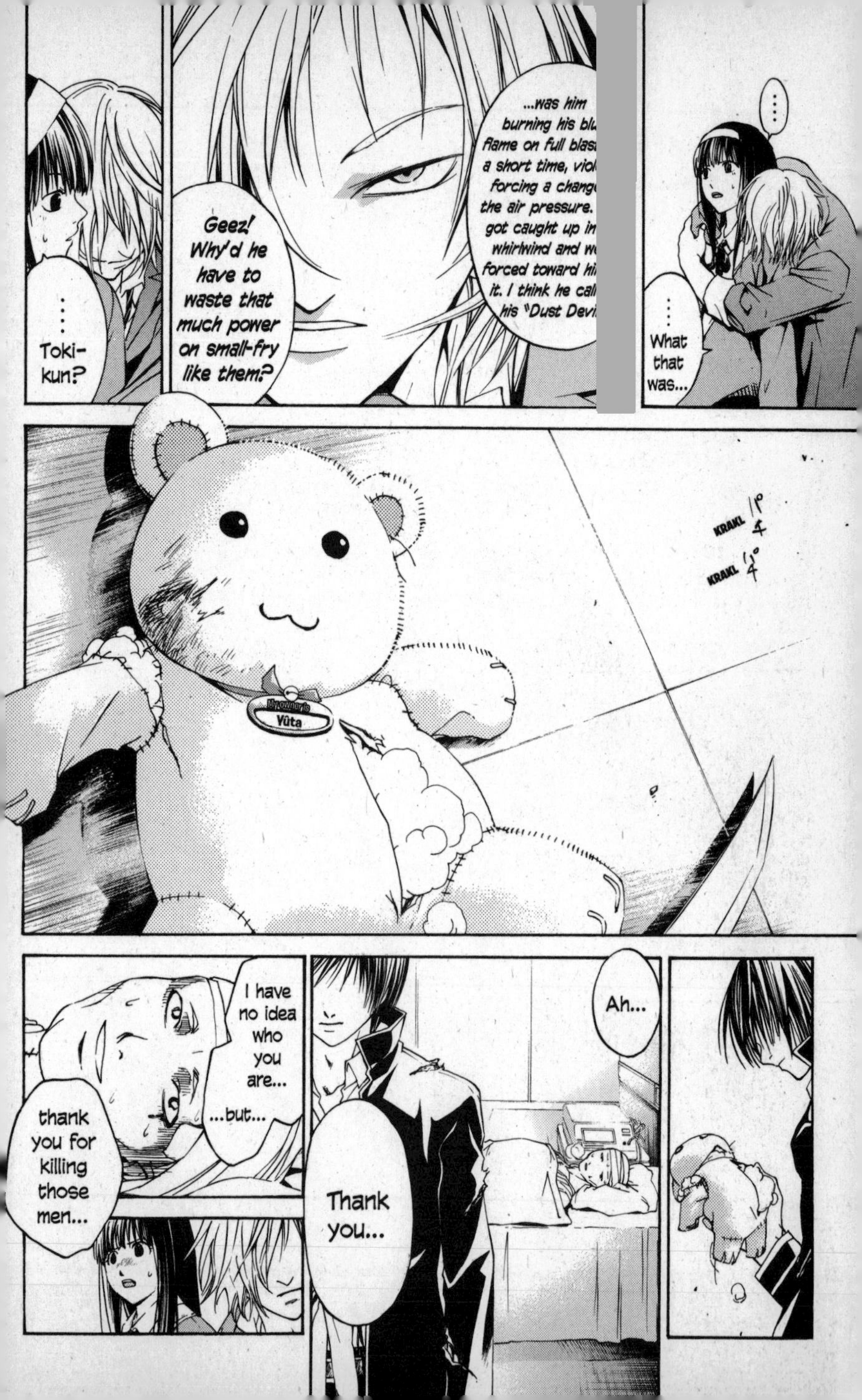
...
... What that was...
...was him burning his blu flame on full blas a short time, viol forcing a chang the air pressure. got caught up in whirlwind and we forced toward hi it. I think he cal his "Dust Devi
Geez! Why'd he have to waste that much power on small-fry like them?
... Toki-kun?
KRAKL
KRAKL
My owner is Yūta
Ah...
Thank you...
I have no idea who you are...
...but...
thank you for killing those men...

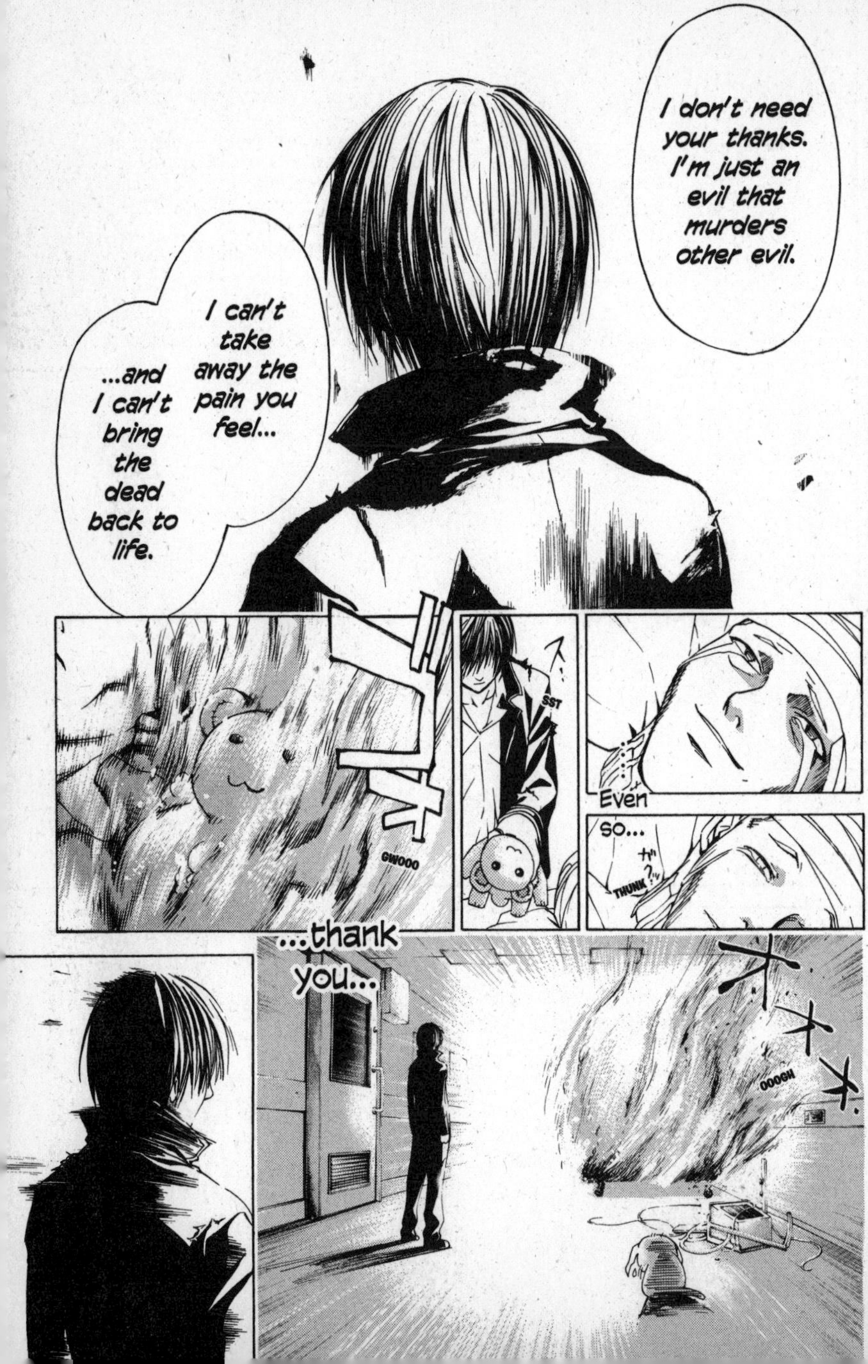
I don't need your thanks. I'm just an evil that murders other evil.
I can't take away the pain you feel...
...and I can't bring the dead back to life.
Even so...
THUNK
SST
GWOOO
...thank you...
OOOGH

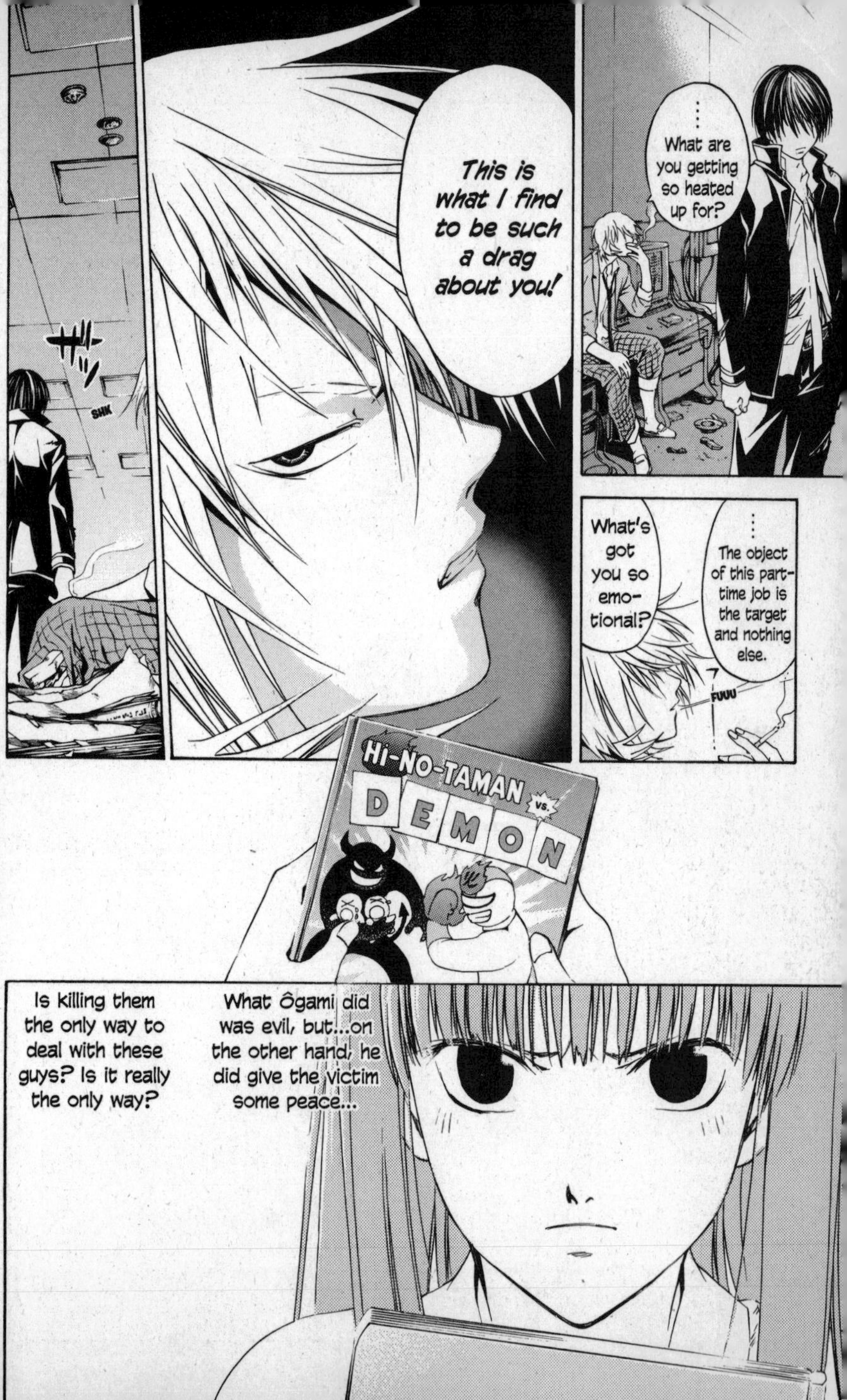

...
What are you getting so heated up for?
...
The object of this part-time job is the target and nothing else.
FUUU
What's got you so emotional?
This is what I find to be such a drag about you!
ザッ
SHK
HI-NO-TAMAN VS. DEMON
What Ôgami did was evil, but...on the other hand, he did give the victim some peace...
Is killing them the only way to deal with these guys? Is it really the only way?

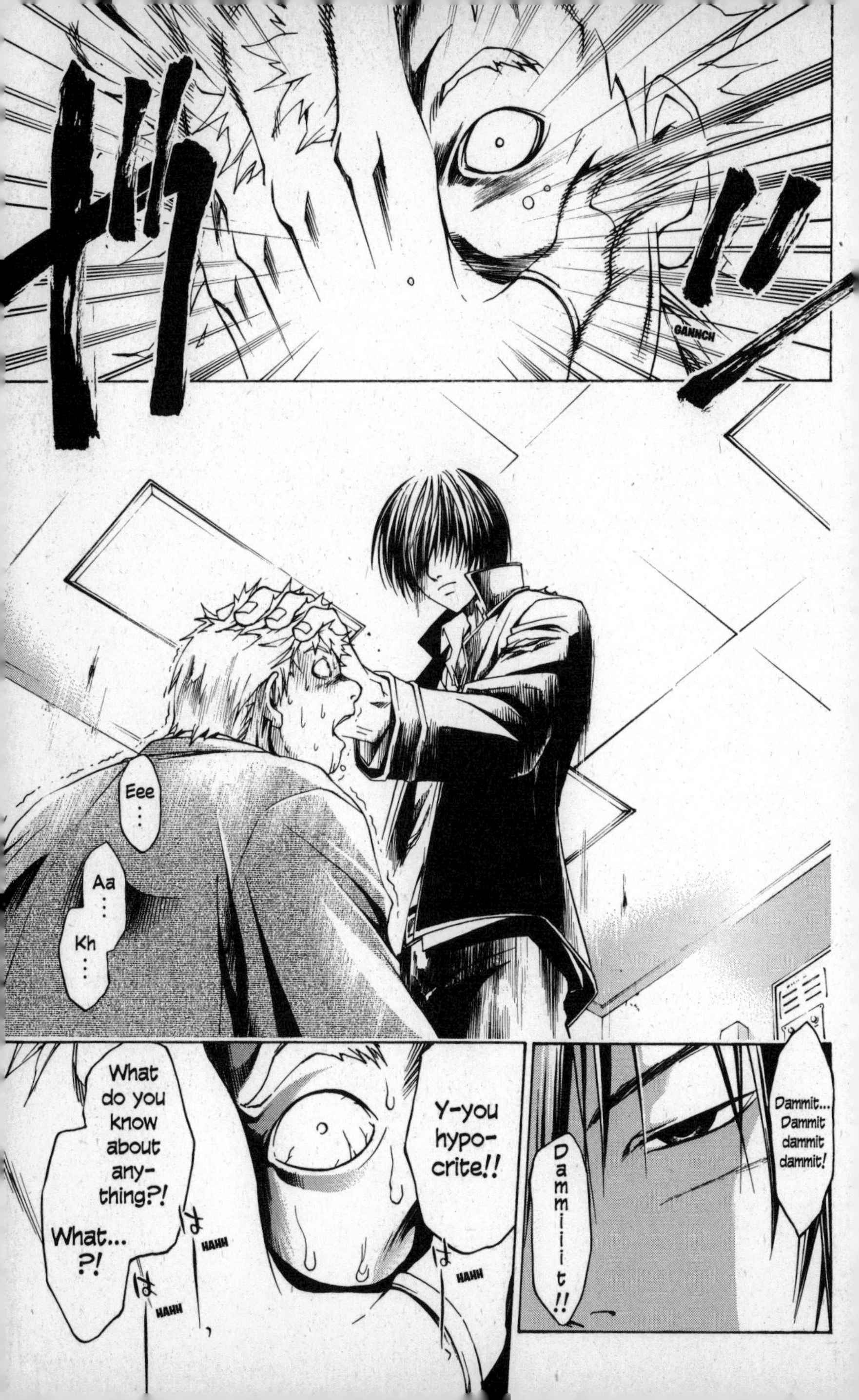
GANNCH
Eee...
Aa... Kh...
Dammit... Dammit dammit dammit!
Dammiiit!!
Y-you hypocrite!!
は HAHH
What do you know about anything?!
What...?!
は HAHH
は HAHH

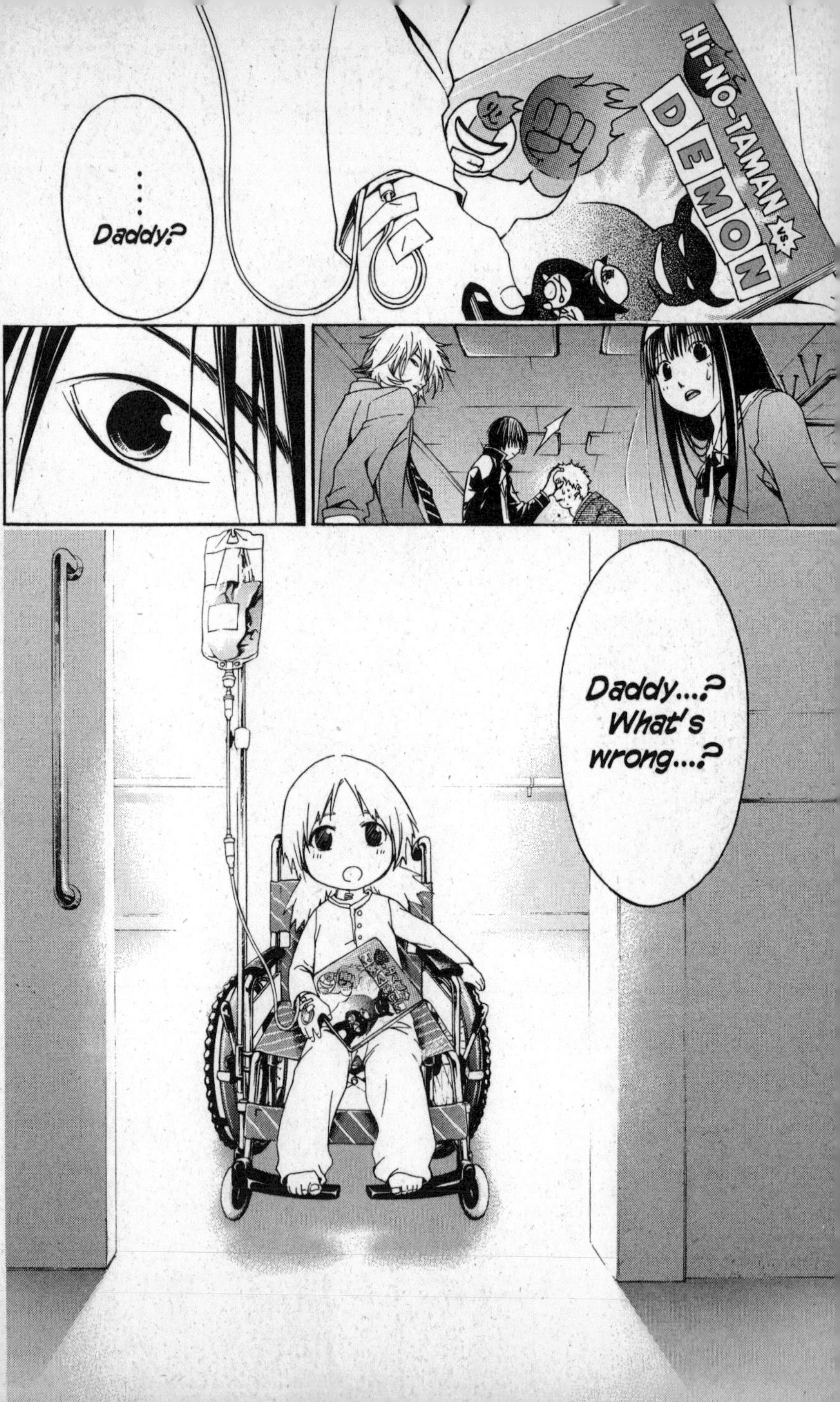
HI-NO-TAMAN vs. DEMON
......
Daddy?
Daddy...? What's wrong...?

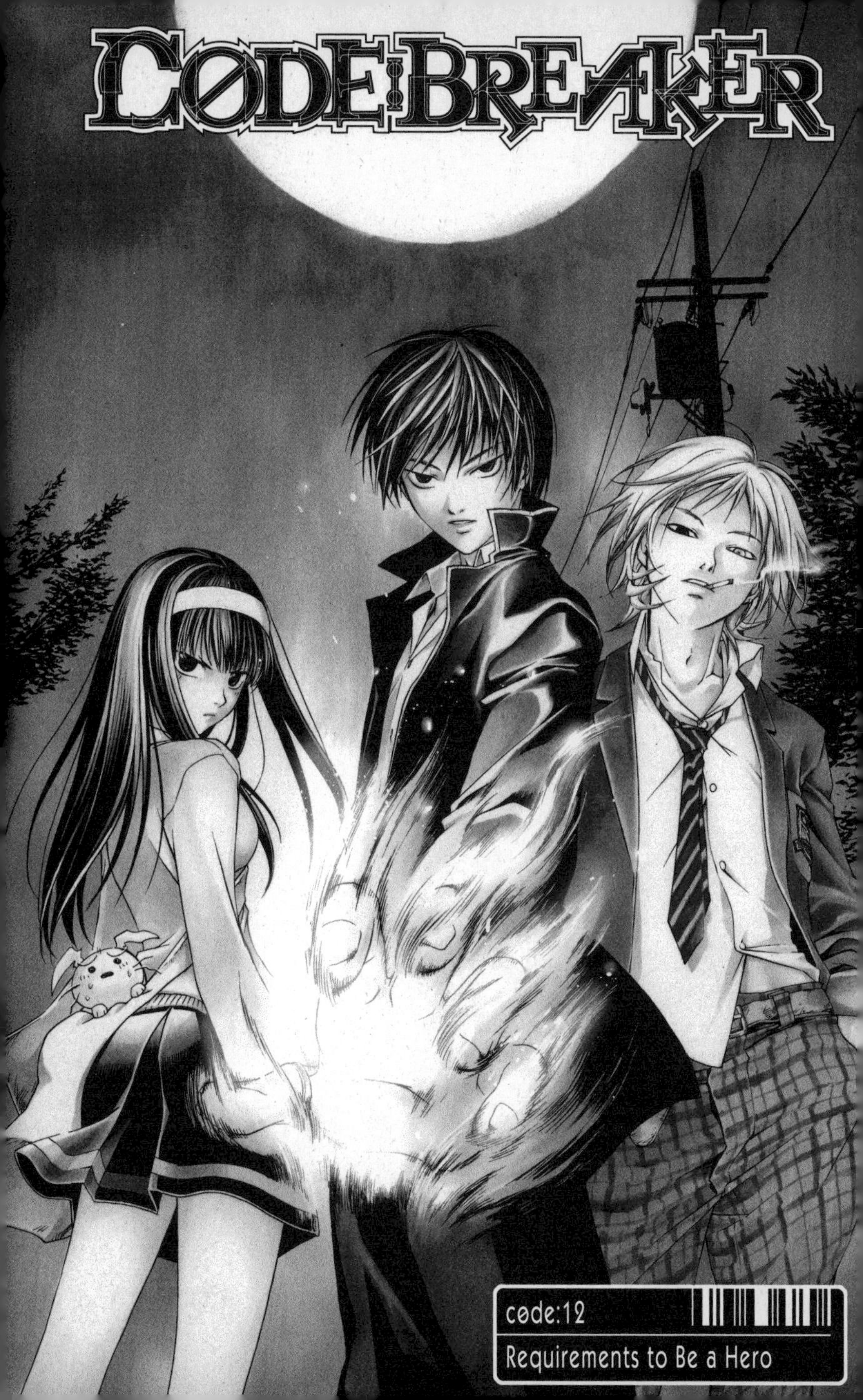
CODE:BREAKER
code:12
Requirements to Be a Hero

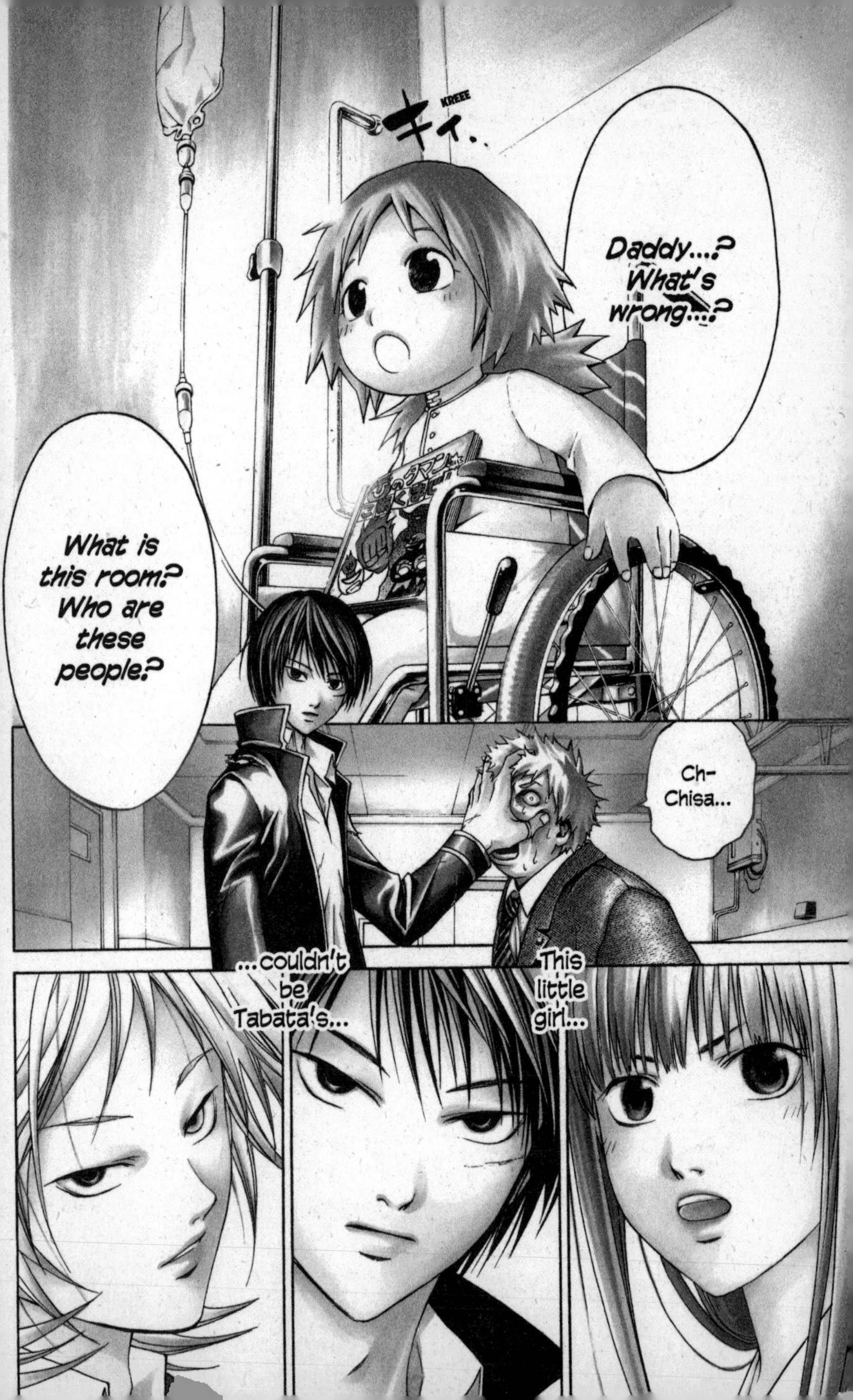
キィ..
KREEE
Daddy...? What's wrong...?
What is this room? Who are these people?
Ch- Chisa...
This little girl...
...couldn't be Tabata's...

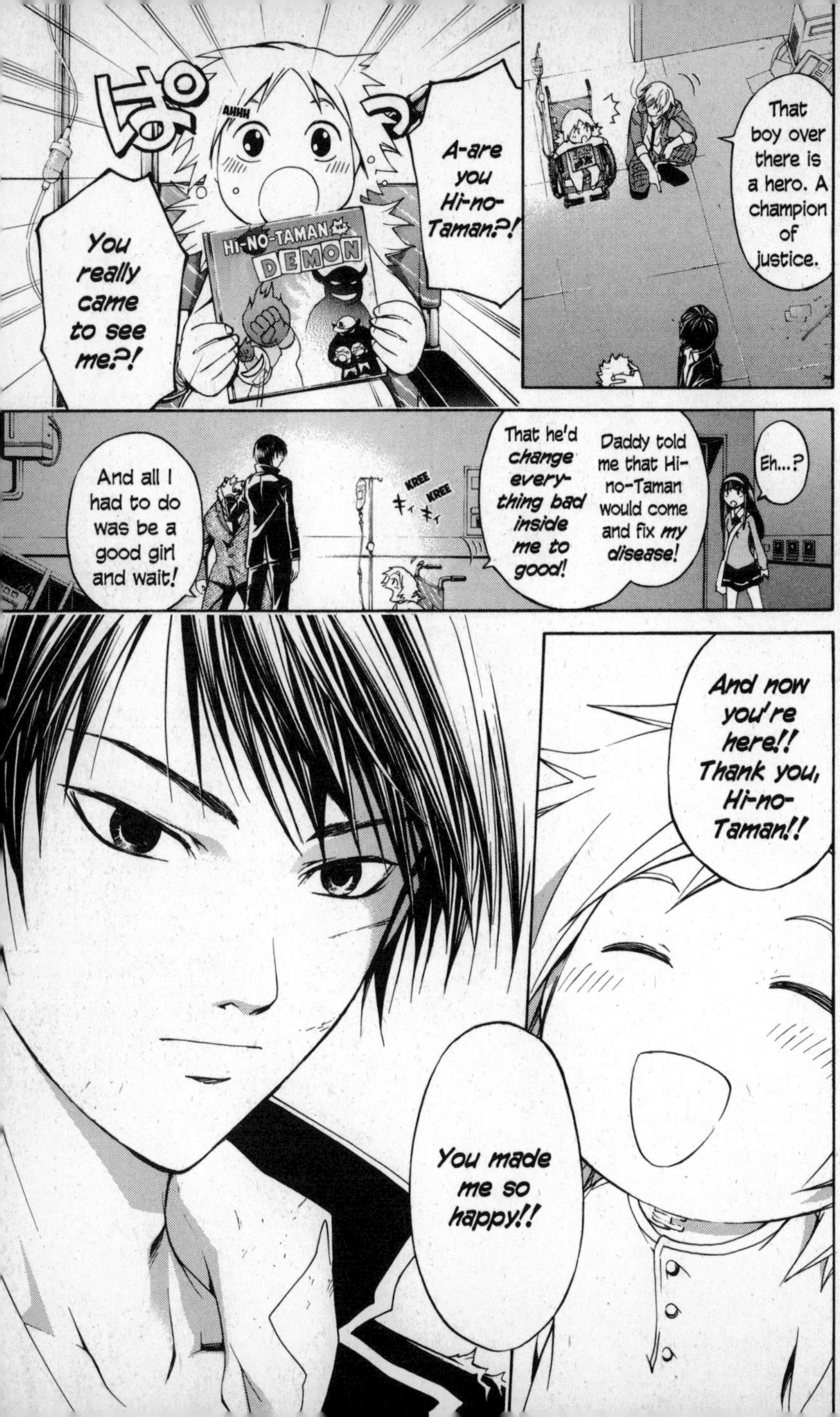
That boy over there is a hero. A champion of justice.
ぱっ
AHHH
A-are you Hi-no-Taman?!
HI-NO-TAMAN VS DEMON
You really came to see me?!
Eh...?
Daddy told me that Hi-no-Taman would come and fix my disease!
That he'd change every-thing bad inside me to good!
KREE KREE
キィ キィ
And all I had to do was be a good girl and wait!
And now you're here!! Thank you, Hi-no-Taman!!
You made me so happy!!

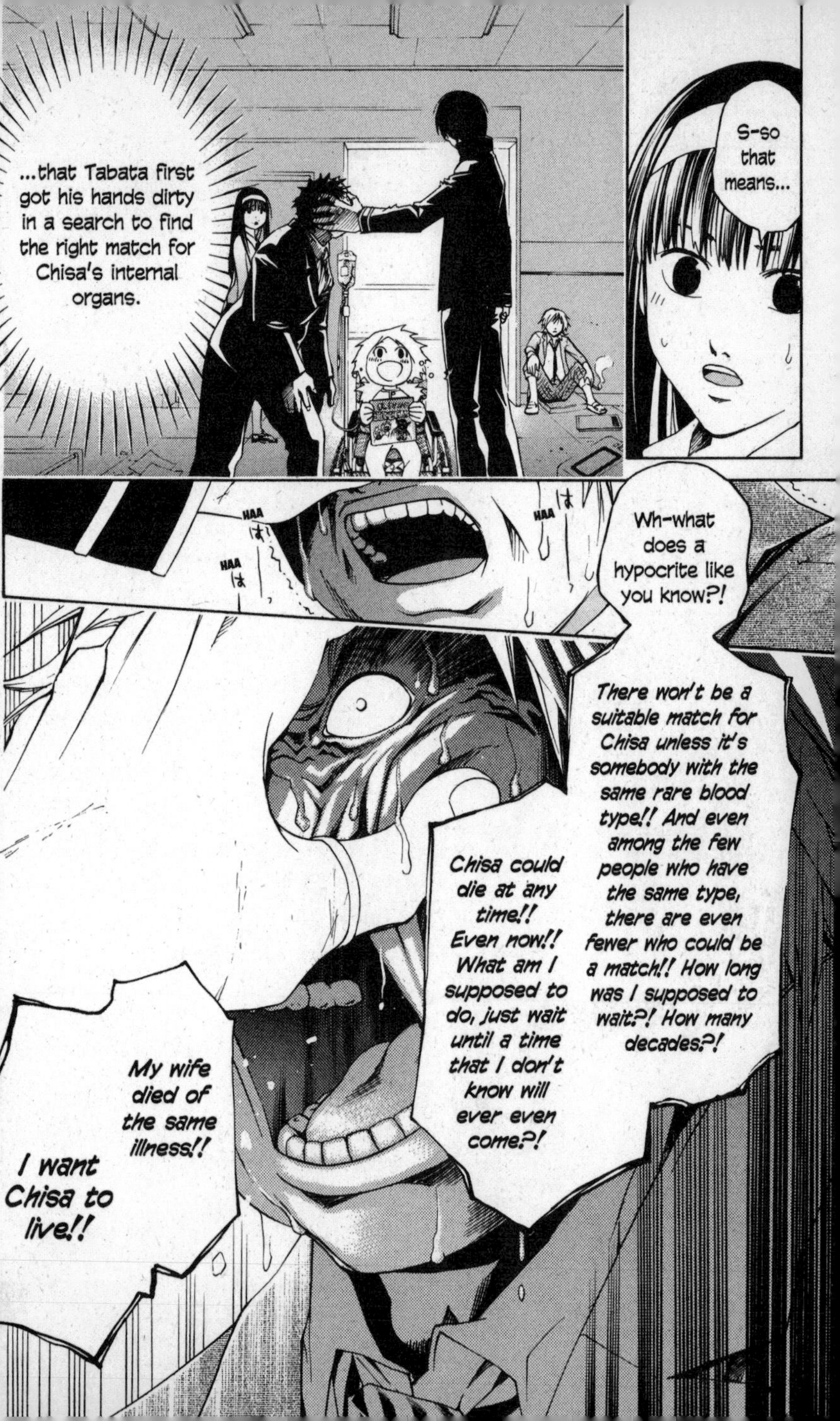
S-so that means...
...that Tabata first got his hands dirty in a search to find the right match for Chisa's internal organs.
Wh-what does a hypocrite like you know?!
HAA は
HAA は
HAA は
There won't be a suitable match for Chisa unless it's somebody with the same rare blood type!! And even among the few people who have the same type, there are even fewer who could be a match!! How long was I supposed to wait?! How many decades?!
Chisa could die at any time!! Even now!! What am I supposed to do, just wait until a time that I don't know will ever even come?!
My wife died of the same illness!!
I want Chisa to live!!

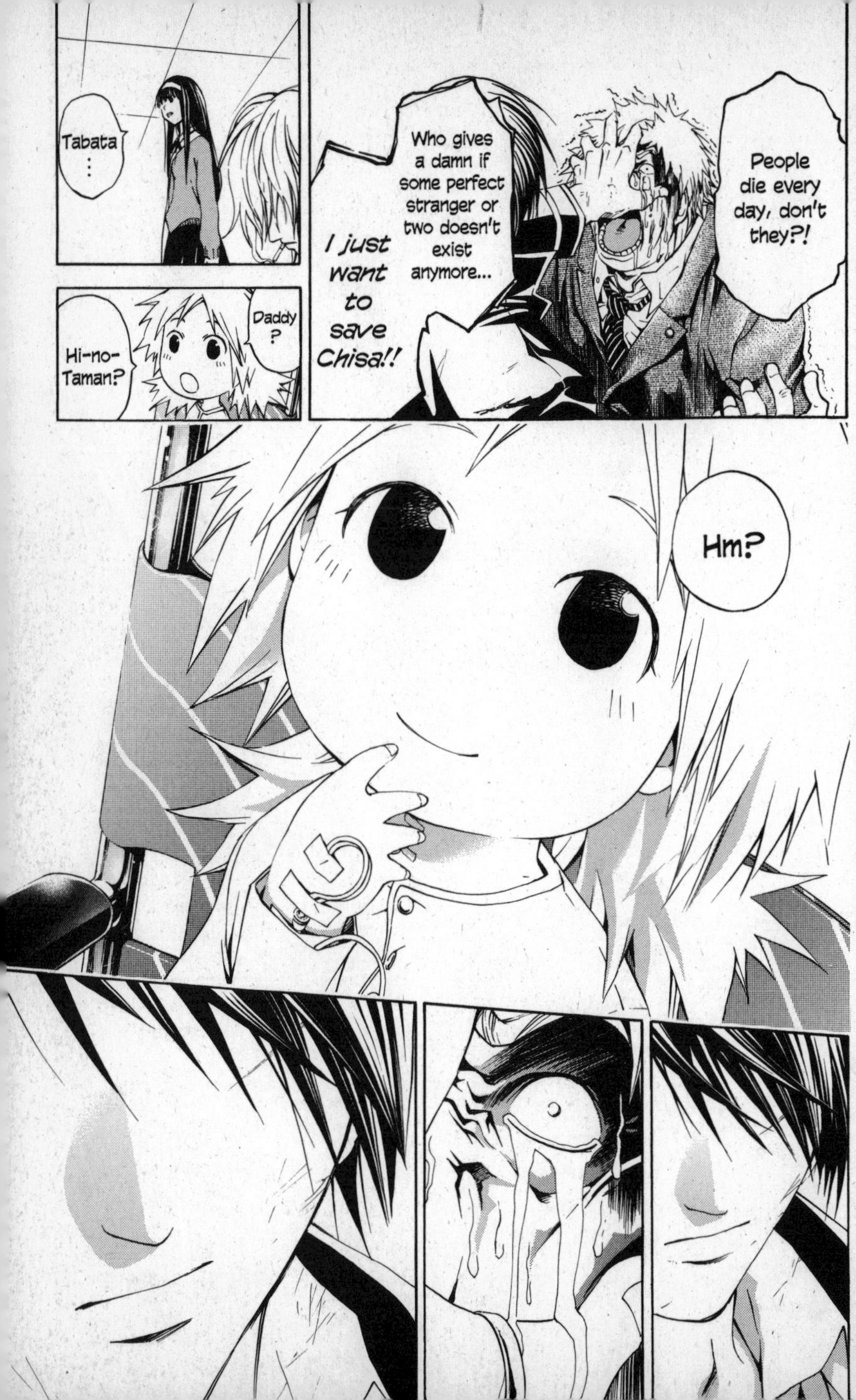
People die every day, don't they?!
Who gives a damn if some perfect stranger or two doesn't exist anymore...
I just want to save Chisa!!
Tabata . . .
Daddy?
Hi-no-Taman?
Hm?

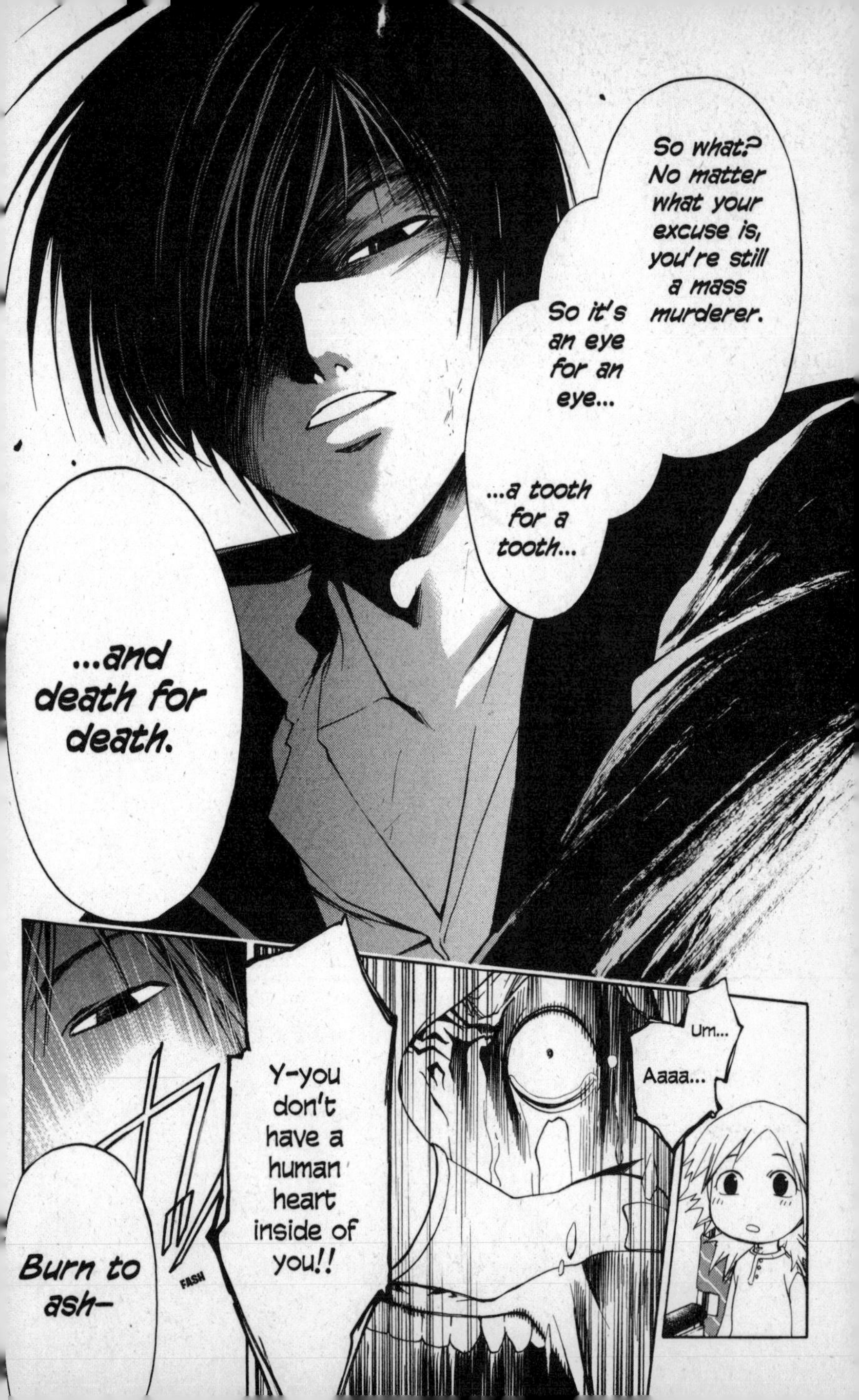
So what? No matter what your excuse is, you're still a mass murderer.
So it's an eye for an eye...
...a tooth for a tooth...
...and death for death.
Um...
Aaaa...
Y-you don't have a human heart inside of you!!
Burn to ash–
FASH

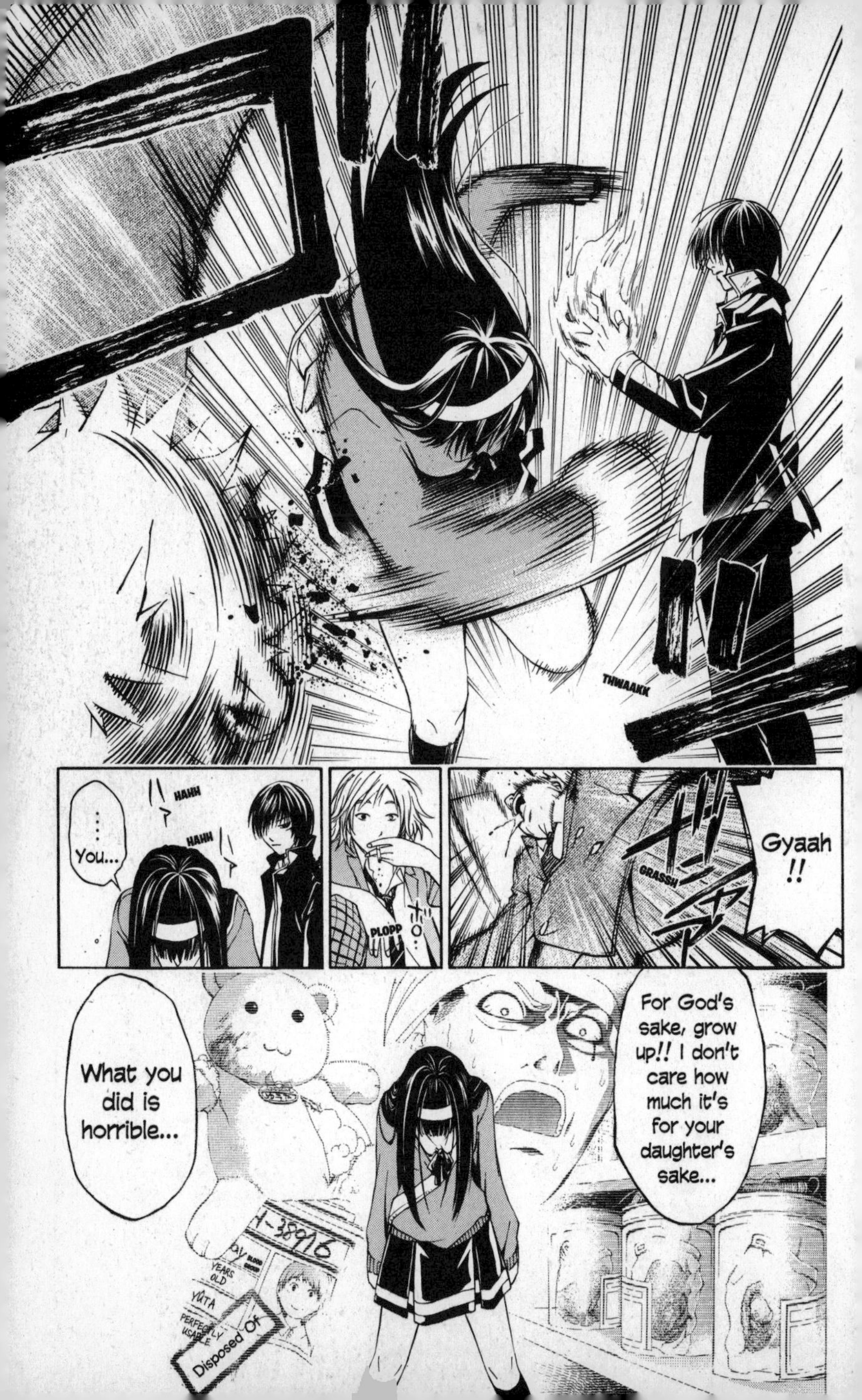
THWAAKK
Gyaah!!
GRASSH
PLOPP
HAHH
HAHH
...You...
For God's sake, grow up!! I don't care how much it's for your daughter's sake...
What you did is horrible...
1-38916
BLOOD GROUP
YEARS OLD
YŪTA
PERFECTLY USABLE
Disposed Of

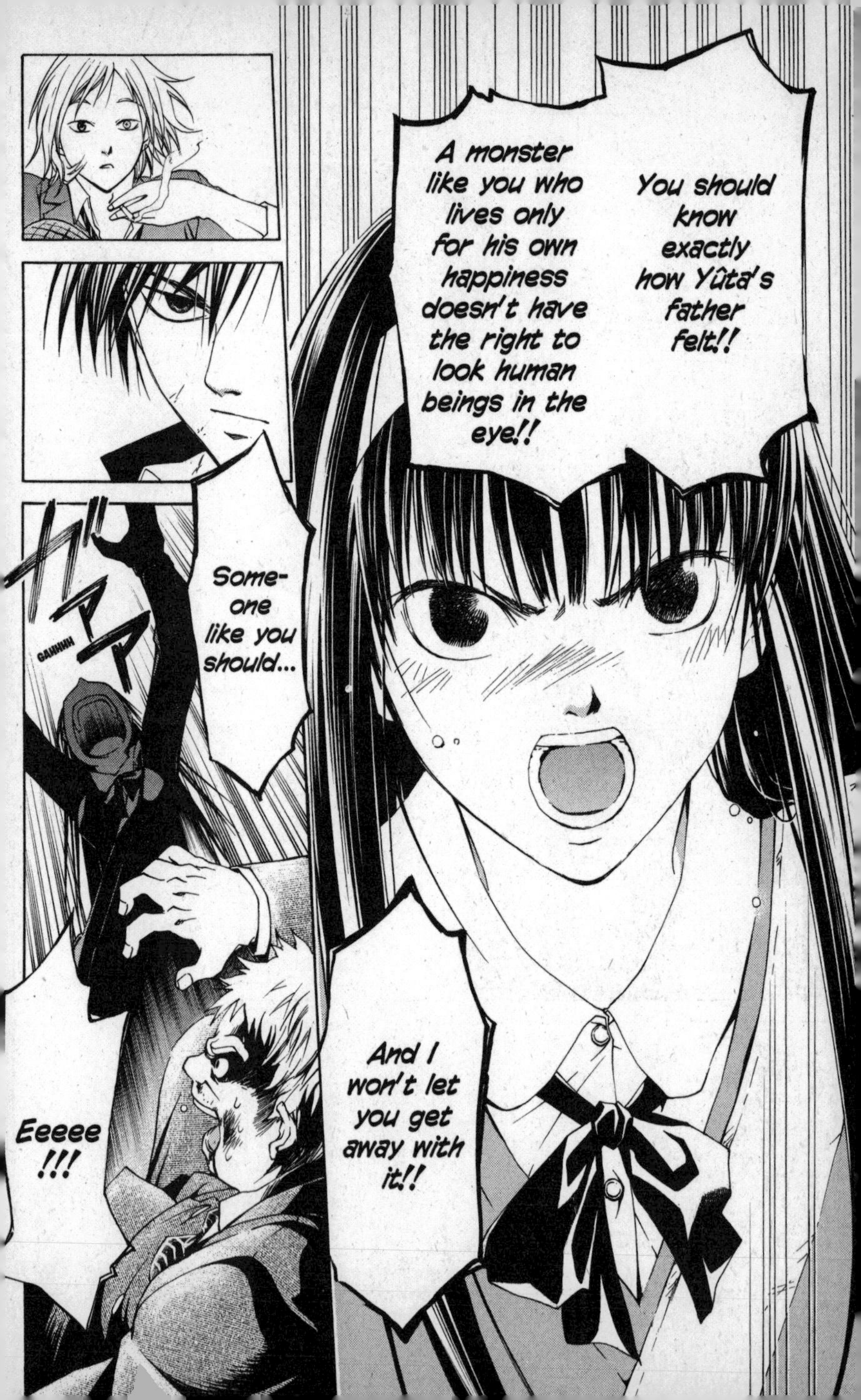

You should know exactly how Yûta's father felt!!
A monster like you who lives only for his own happiness doesn't have the right to look human beings in the eye!!
And I won't let you get away with it!!
Some-one like you should...
GAHHHH
Eeeee !!!

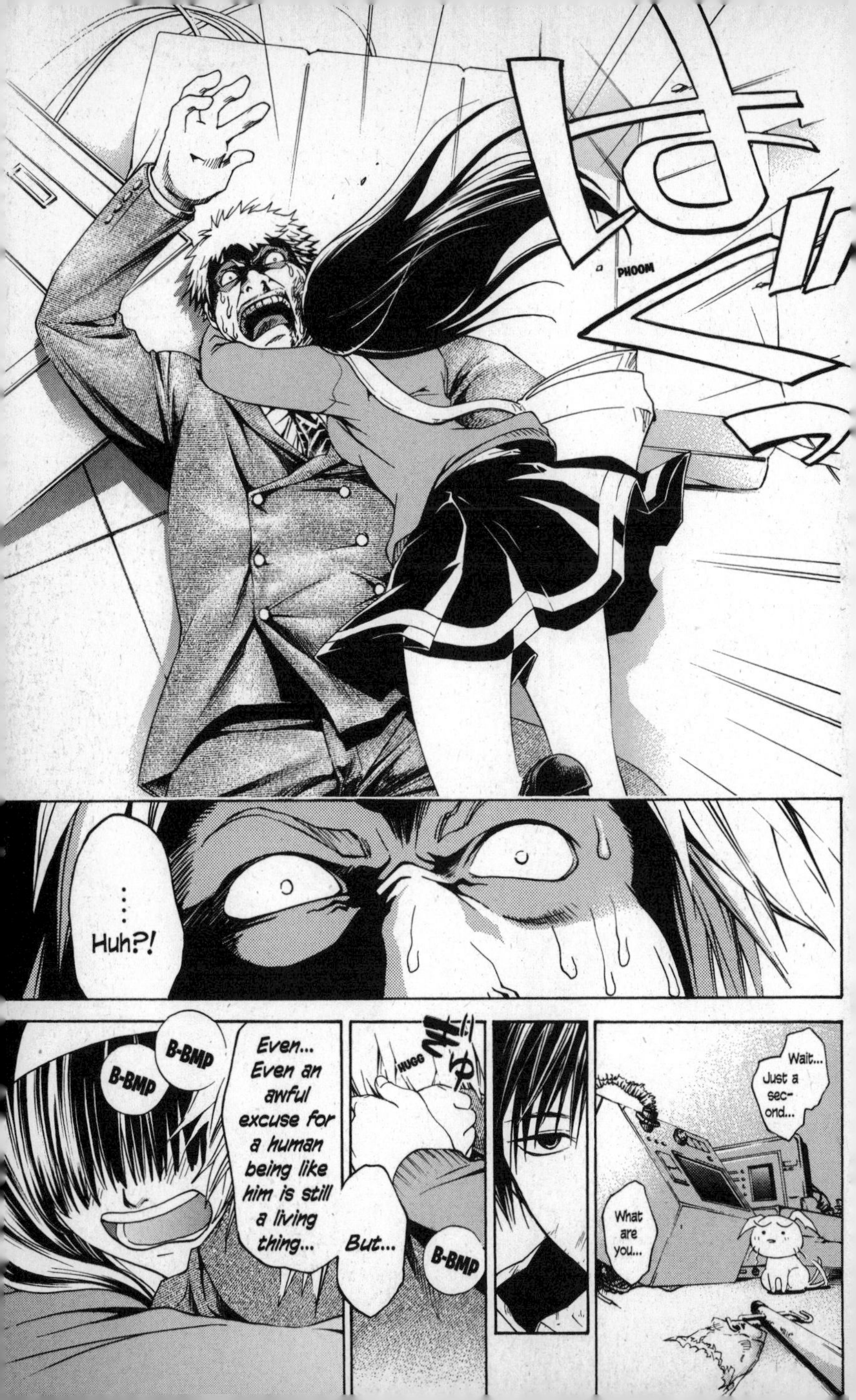
PHOOM
.....
Huh?!
Wait... Just a second...
What are you...
HUGG
B-BMP
But...
Even... Even an awful excuse for a human being like him is still a living thing...
B-BMP
B-BMP

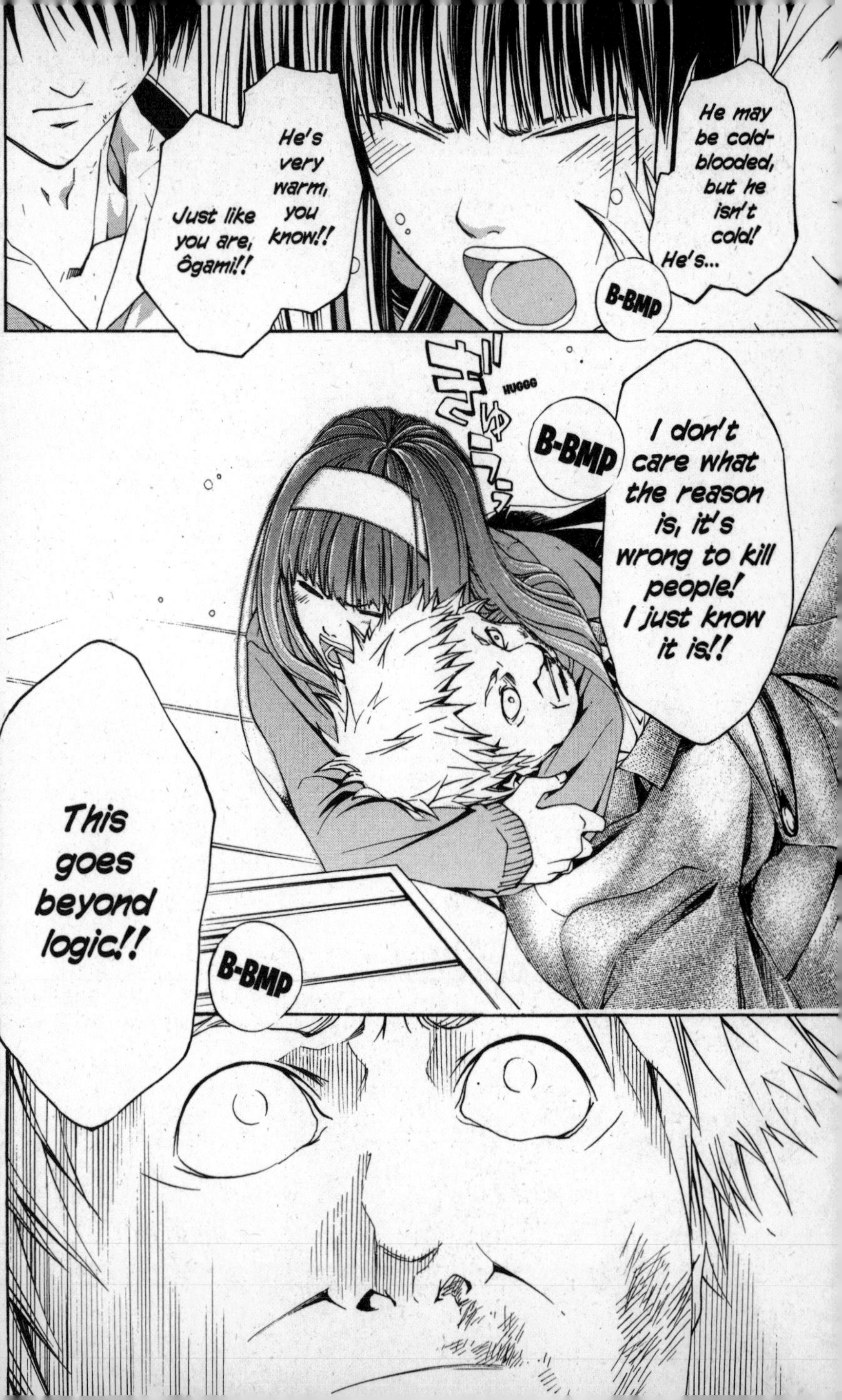
He may be cold-blooded, but he isn't cold! He's...
B-BMP
He's very warm, you know!!
Just like you are, ôgami!!
HUGGG
B-BMP
I don't care what the reason is, it's wrong to kill people! I just know it is!!
This goes beyond logic!!
B-BMP

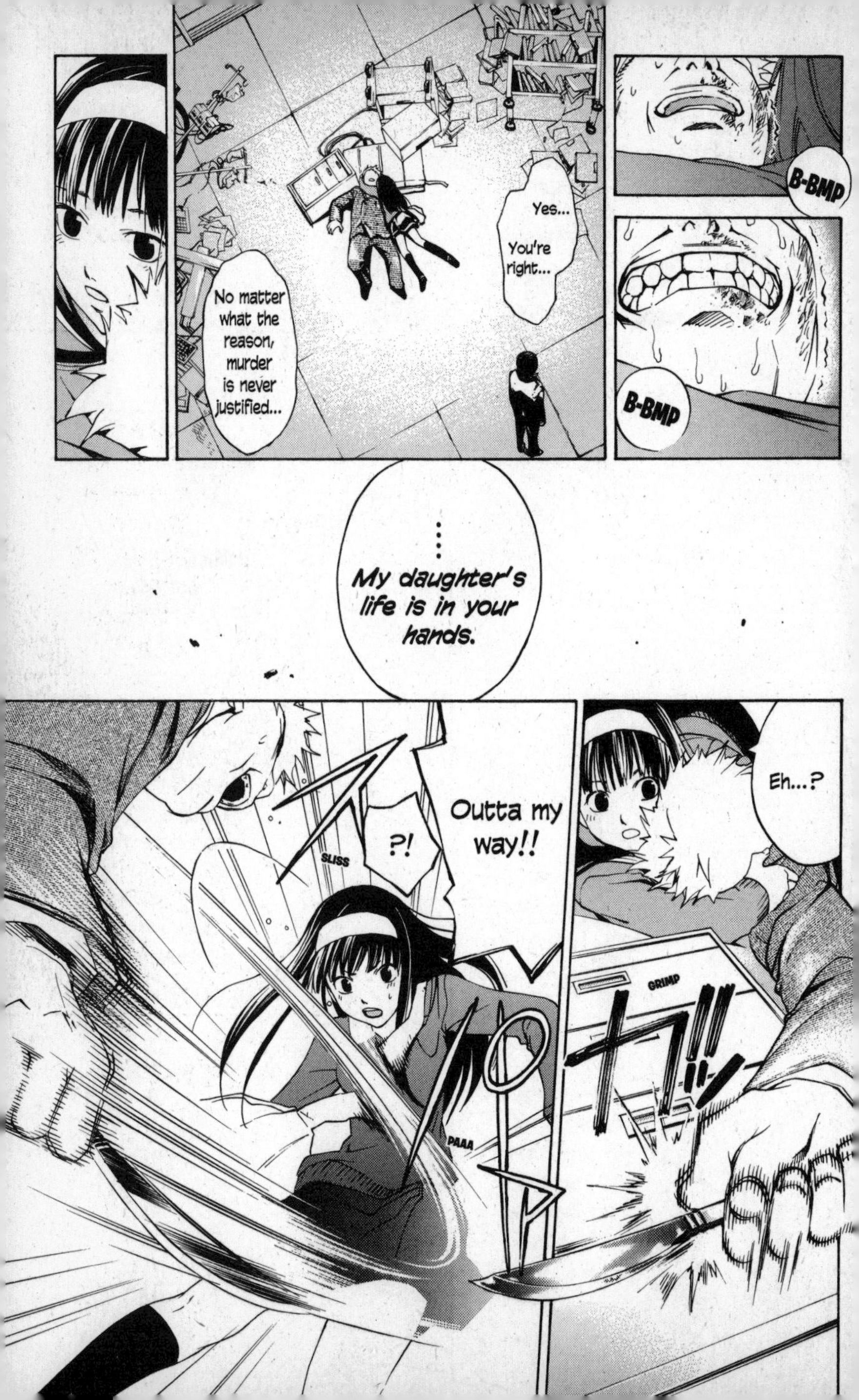
B-BMP
B-BMP
Yes...
You're right...
No matter what the reason, murder is never justified...
...
My daughter's life is in your hands.
Eh...?
Outta my way!!
?!
SLISS
GRIMP
PAAA

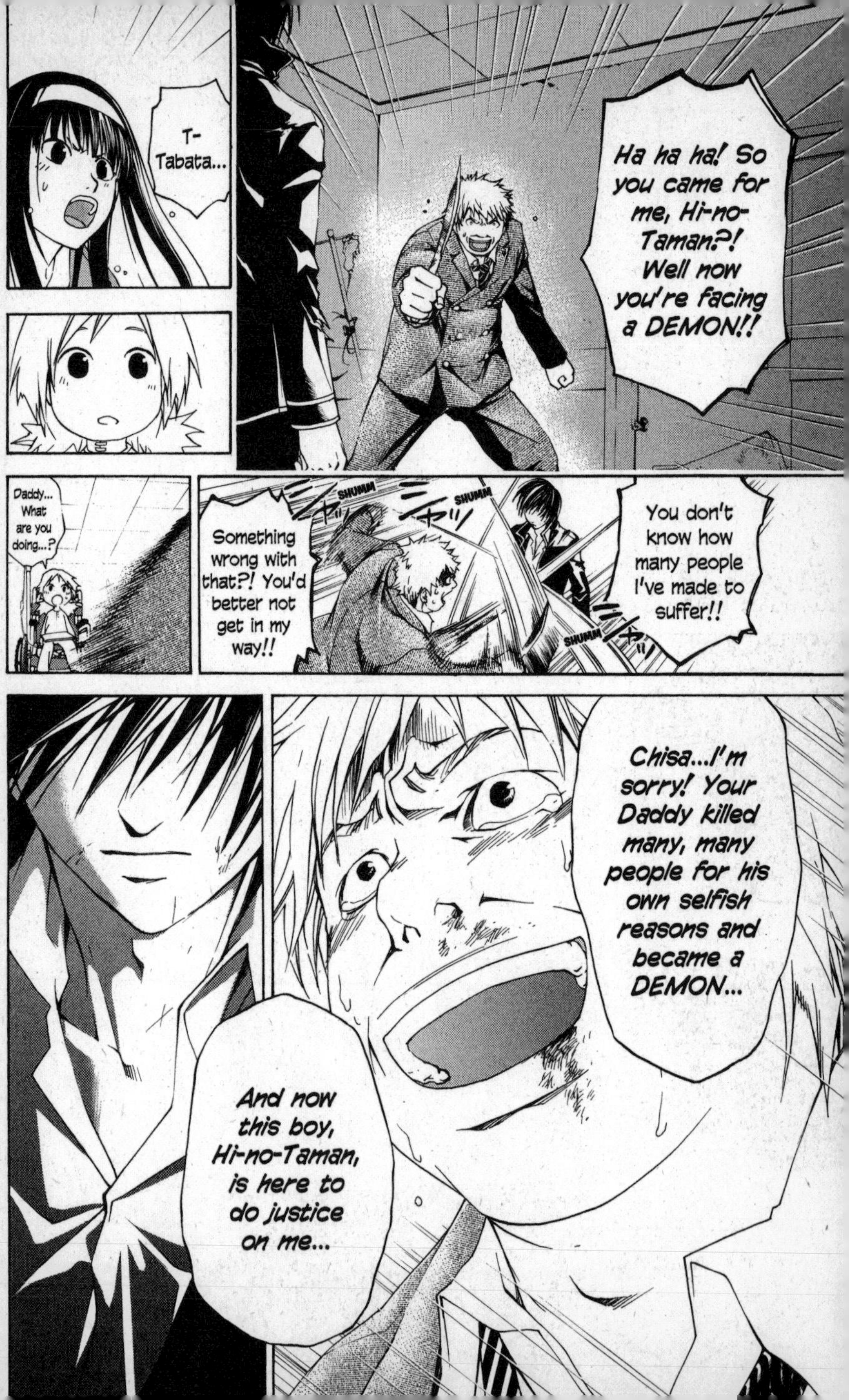
Ha ha ha! So you came for me, Hi-no-Taman?! Well now you're facing a DEMON!!
T-Tabata...
You don't know how many people I've made to suffer!!
SHUMM
SHUMM
SHUMM
Something wrong with that?! You'd better not get in my way!!
Daddy... What are you doing...?
Chisa...I'm sorry! Your Daddy killed many, many people for his own selfish reasons and became a DEMON...
And now this boy, Hi-no-Taman, is here to do justice on me...

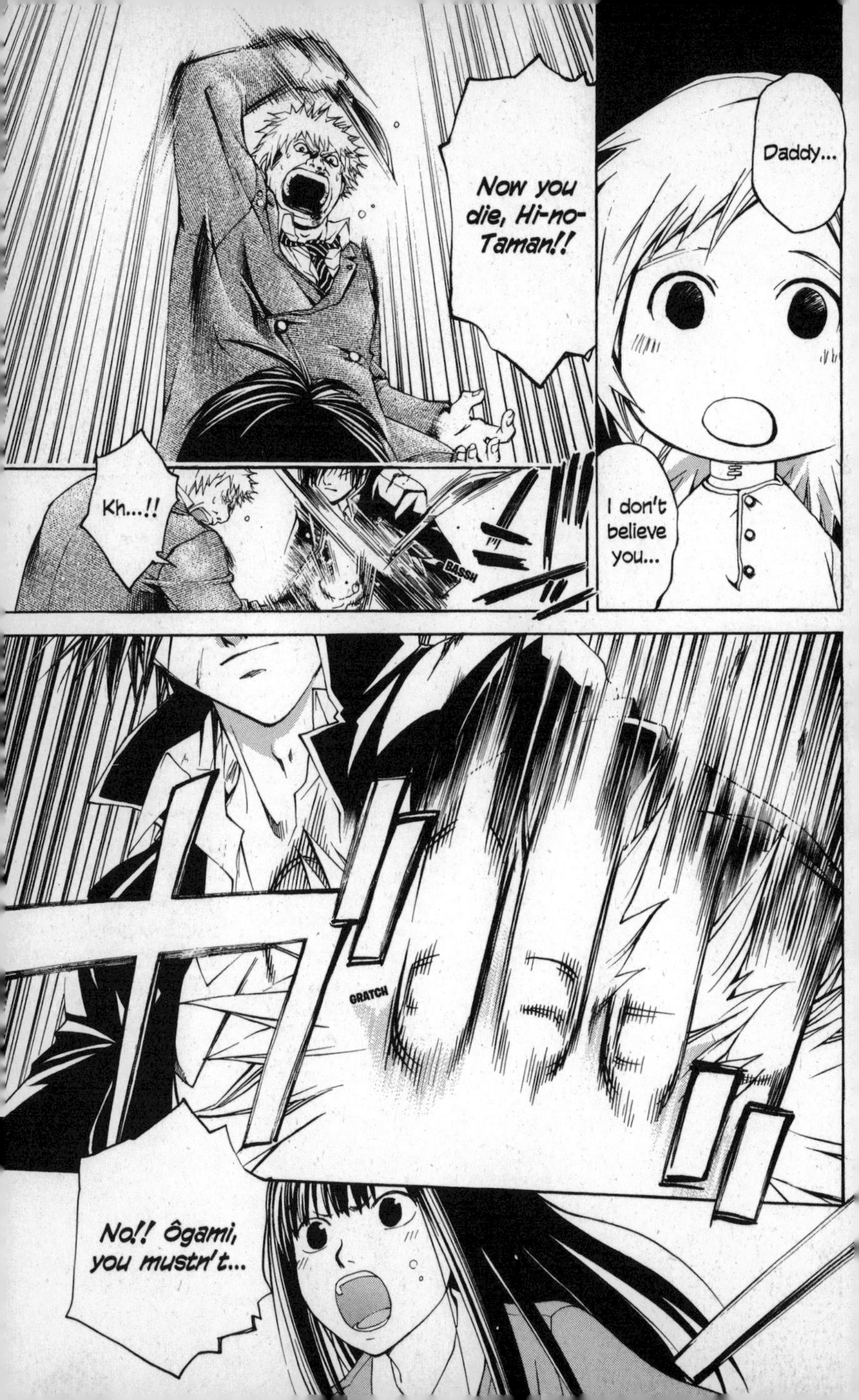
Daddy...
I don't believe you...
Now you die, Hi-no-Taman!!
Kh...!!
BASSH
GRATCH
No!! Ôgami, you mustn't...

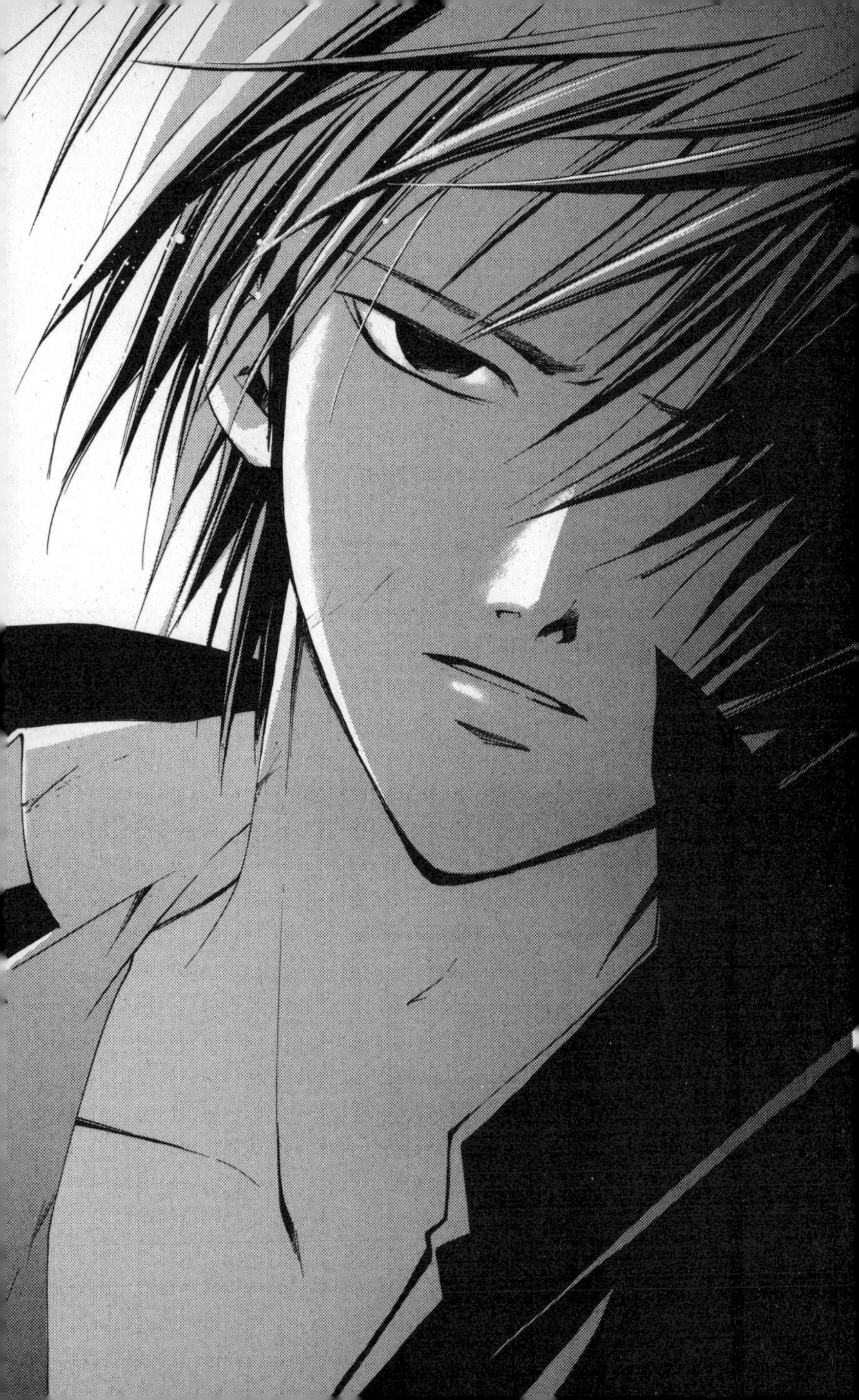

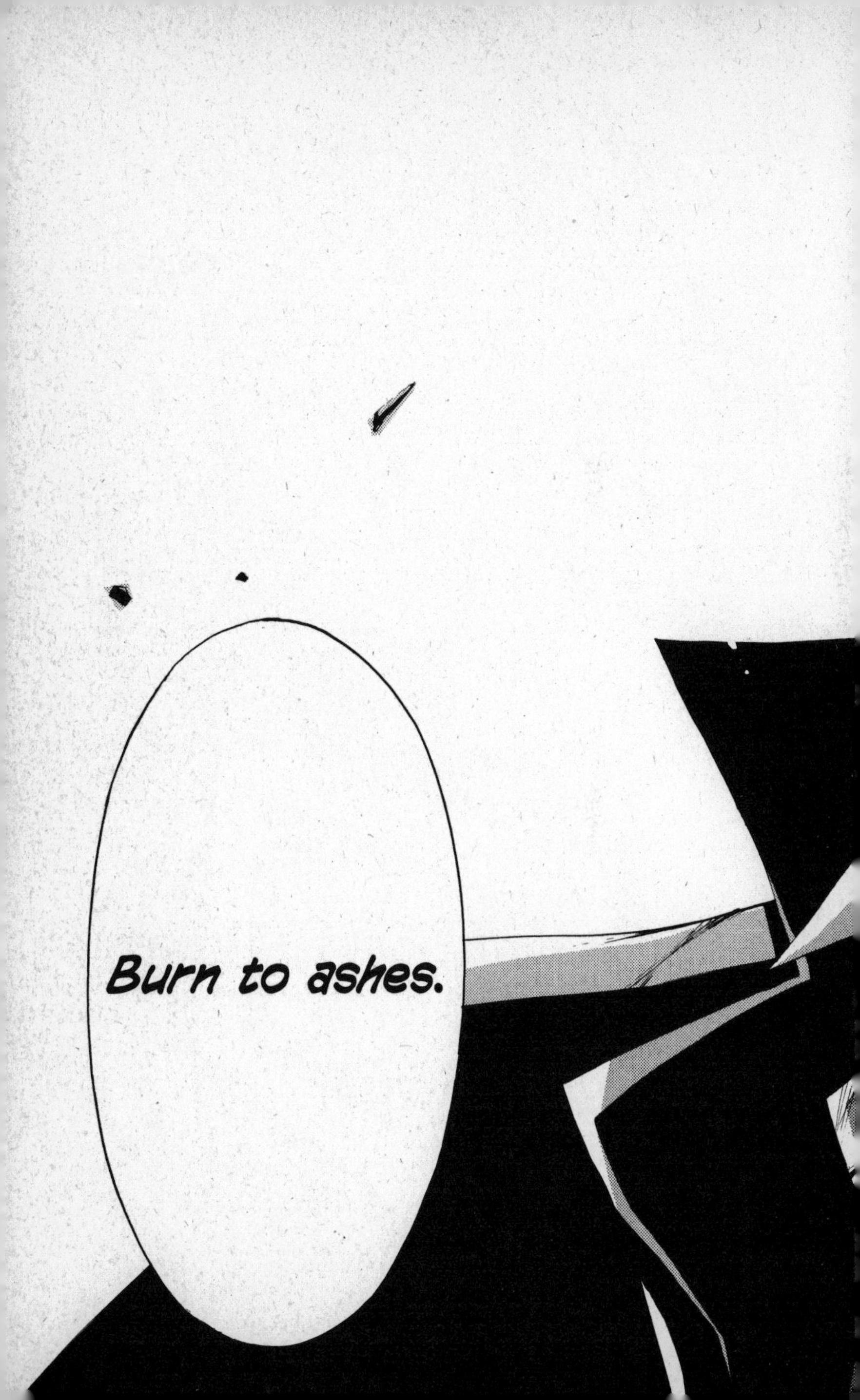
Burn to ashes.

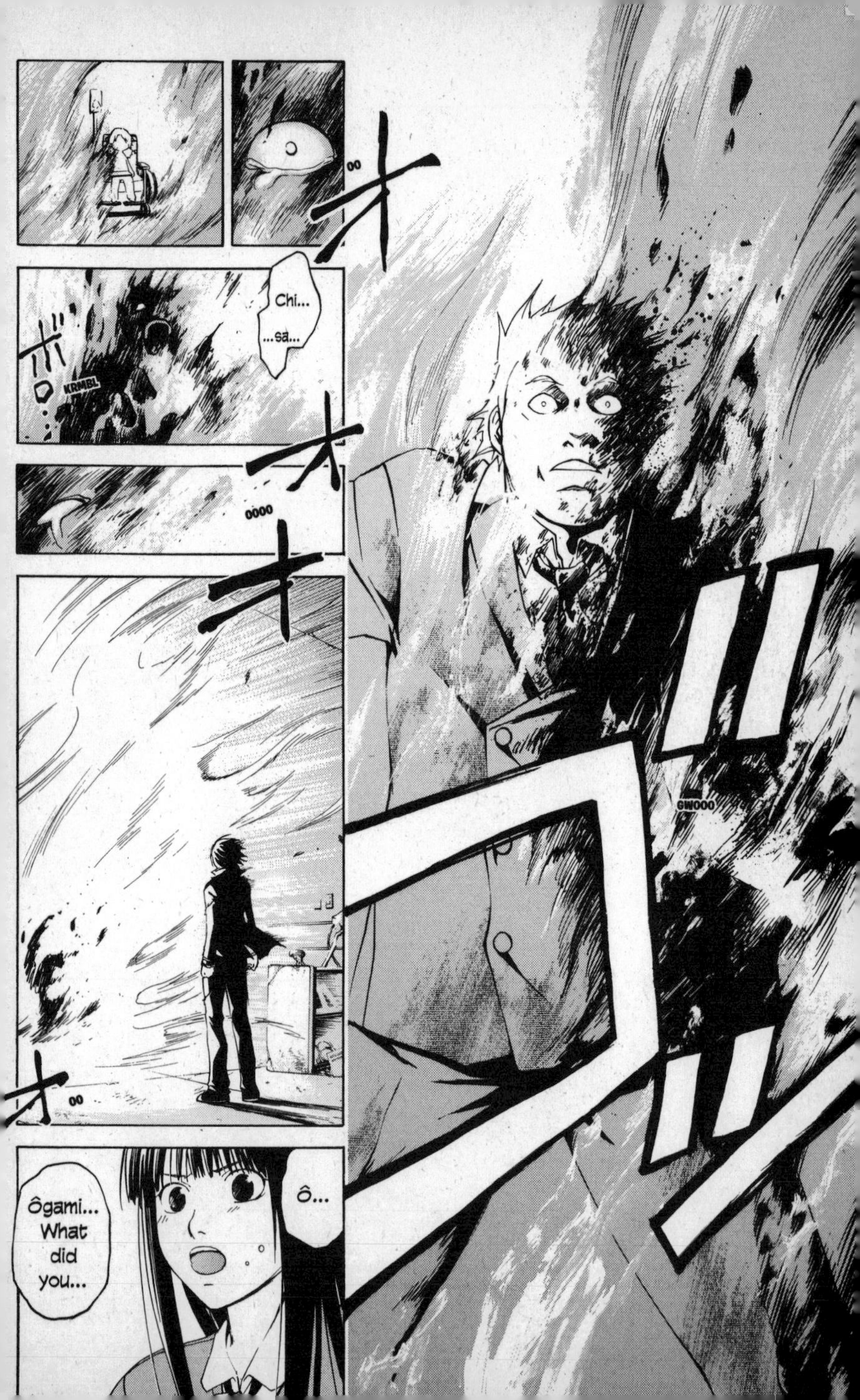
GWOOO
oo
Chi...
...sa...
KRMBL
oooo
oo
Ô...
Ôgami... What did you...

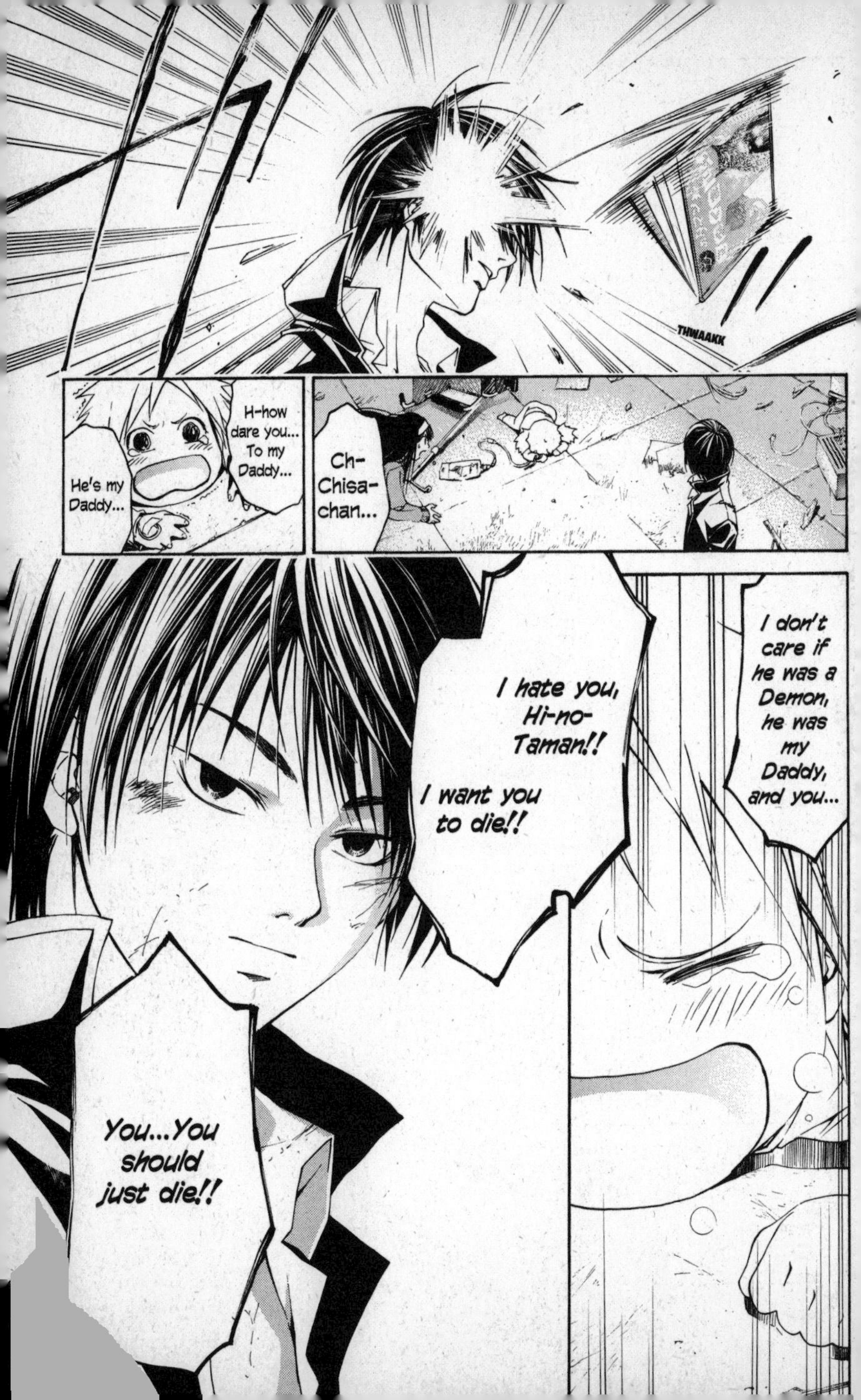
THWAAKK
Ch-Chisa-chan...
H-how dare you... To my Daddy...
He's my Daddy...
I don't care if he was a Demon, he was my Daddy, and you...
I hate you, Hi-no-Taman!!
I want you to die!!
You...You should just die!!

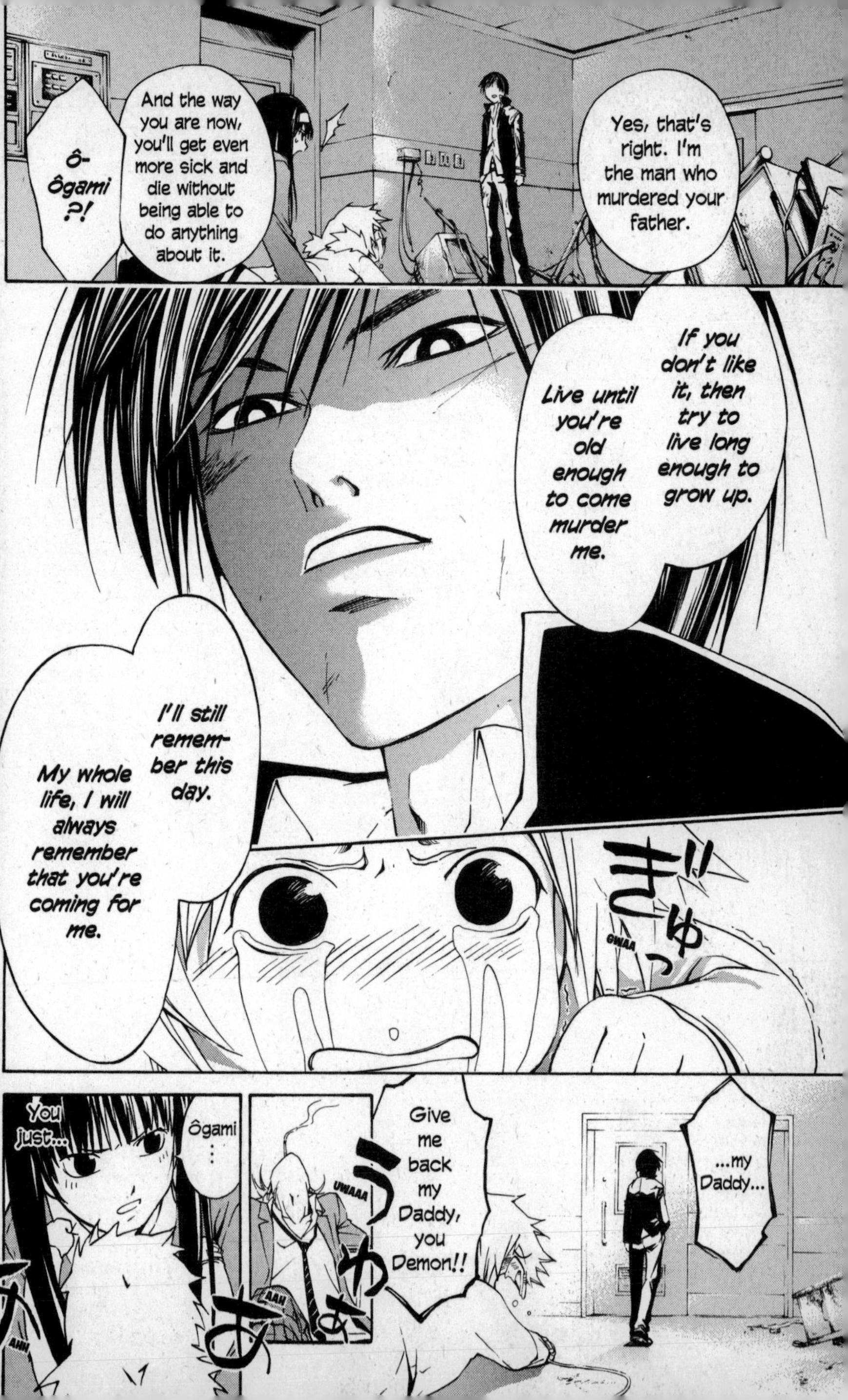
Yes, that's right. I'm the man who murdered your father.
And the way you are now, you'll get even more sick and die without being able to do anything about it.
Ô-Ôgami?!
If you don't like it, then try to live long enough to grow up.
Live until you're old enough to come murder me.
GWAA
I'll still remember this day.
My whole life, I will always remember that you're coming for me.
...my Daddy...
Give me back my Daddy, you Demon!!
UWAAA
AAH
Ôgami...
You just...
AHH

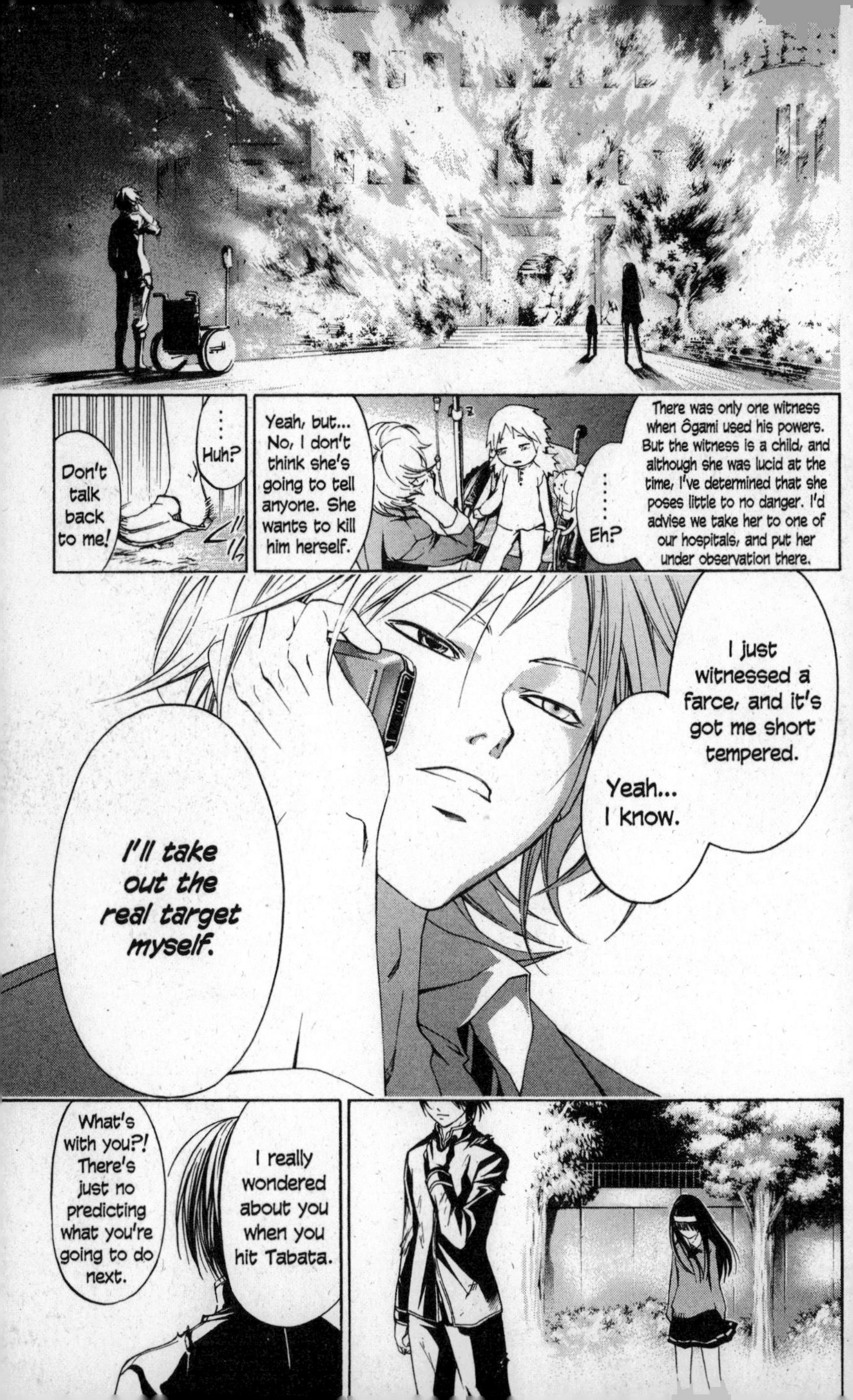
There was only one witness when Ôgami used his powers. But the witness is a child, and although she was lucid at the time, I've determined that she poses little to no danger. I'd advise we take her to one of our hospitals, and put her under observation there.
......Eh?
Yeah, but... No, I don't think she's going to tell anyone. She wants to kill him herself.
...Huh?
Don't talk back to me!
I just witnessed a farce, and it's got me short tempered.
Yeah... I know.
I'll take out the real target myself.
I really wondered about you when you hit Tabata.
What's with you?! There's just no predicting what you're going to do next.

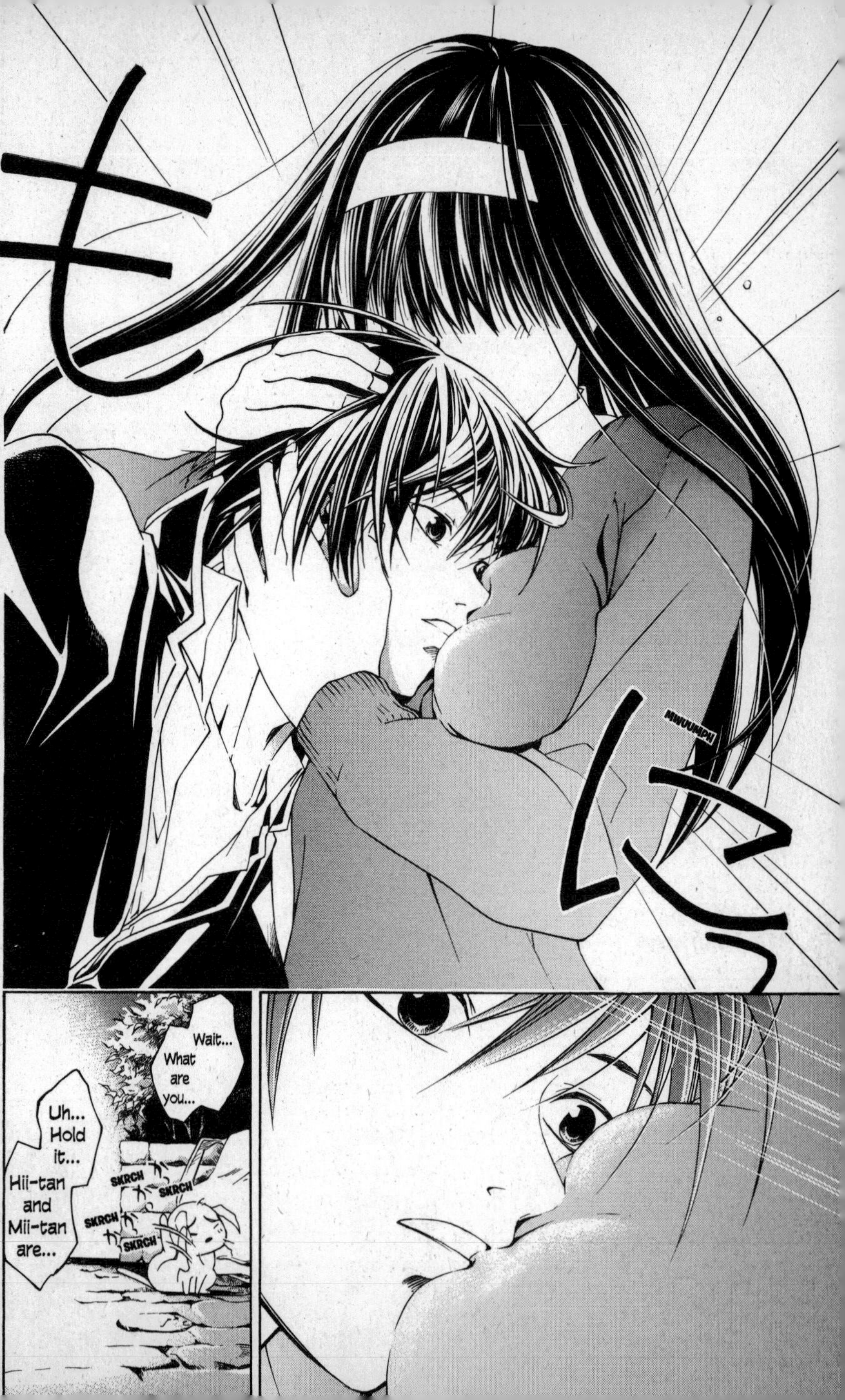
MNUUUMPH
Wait... What are you...
Uh... Hold it... Hii-tan and Mii-tan are...
SKRCH
SKRCH
SKRCH
SKRCH

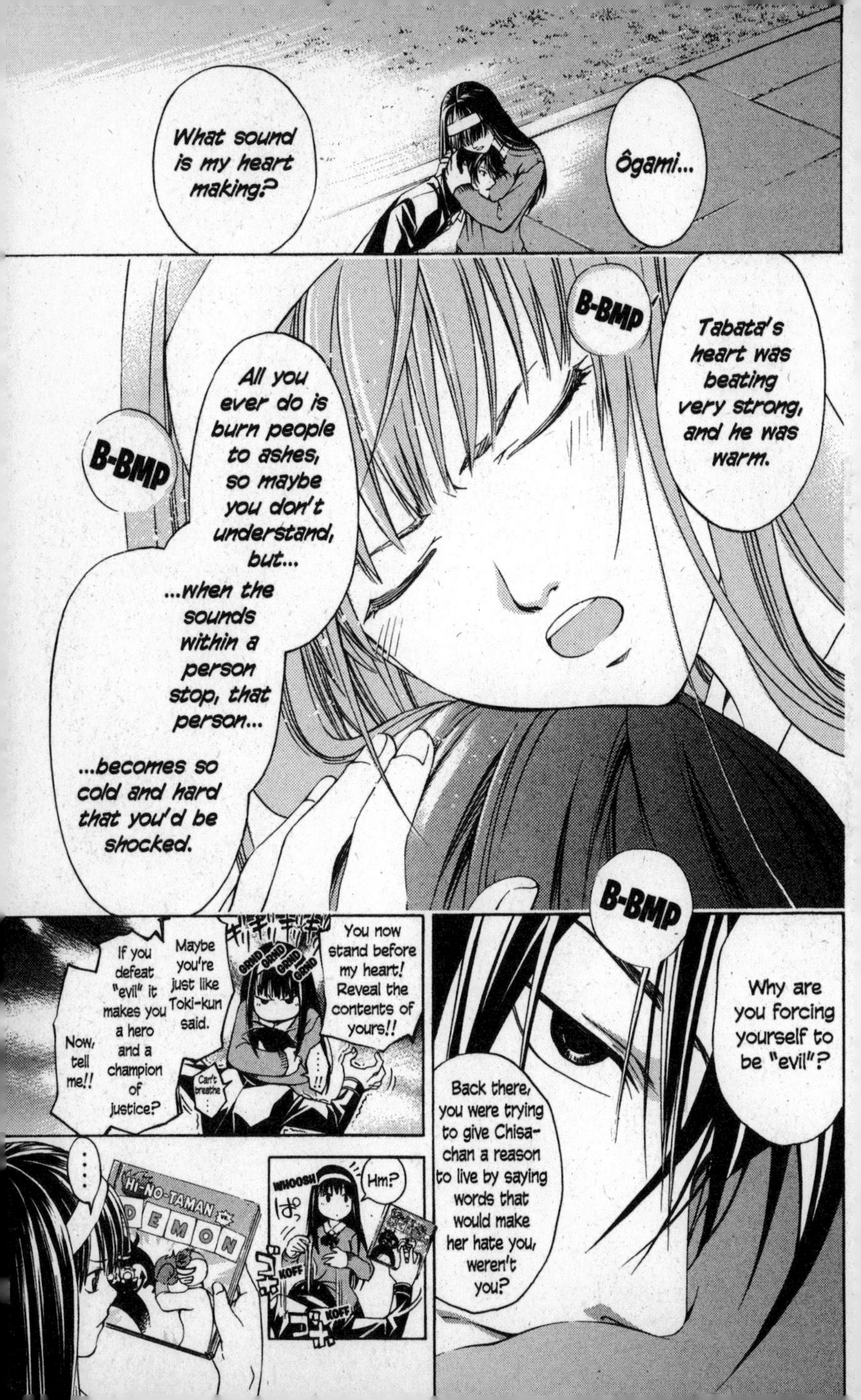
Ôgami...
What sound is my heart making?
B-BMP
Tabata's heart was beating very strong, and he was warm.
All you ever do is burn people to ashes, so maybe you don't understand, but...
B-BMP
...when the sounds within a person stop, that person...
...becomes so cold and hard that you'd be shocked.
B-BMP
Why are you forcing yourself to be "evil"?
Back there, you were trying to give Chisa-chan a reason to live by saying words that would make her hate you, weren't you?
You now stand before my heart! Reveal the contents of yours!!
GRND GRND GRND GRND
Maybe you're just like Toki-kun said.
If you defeat "evil" it makes you a hero and a champion of justice?
Now, tell me!!
Can't breathe...
!!
Hm?
WHOOSH
KOFF
KOFF
....
HI-NO-TAMAN
DEMON

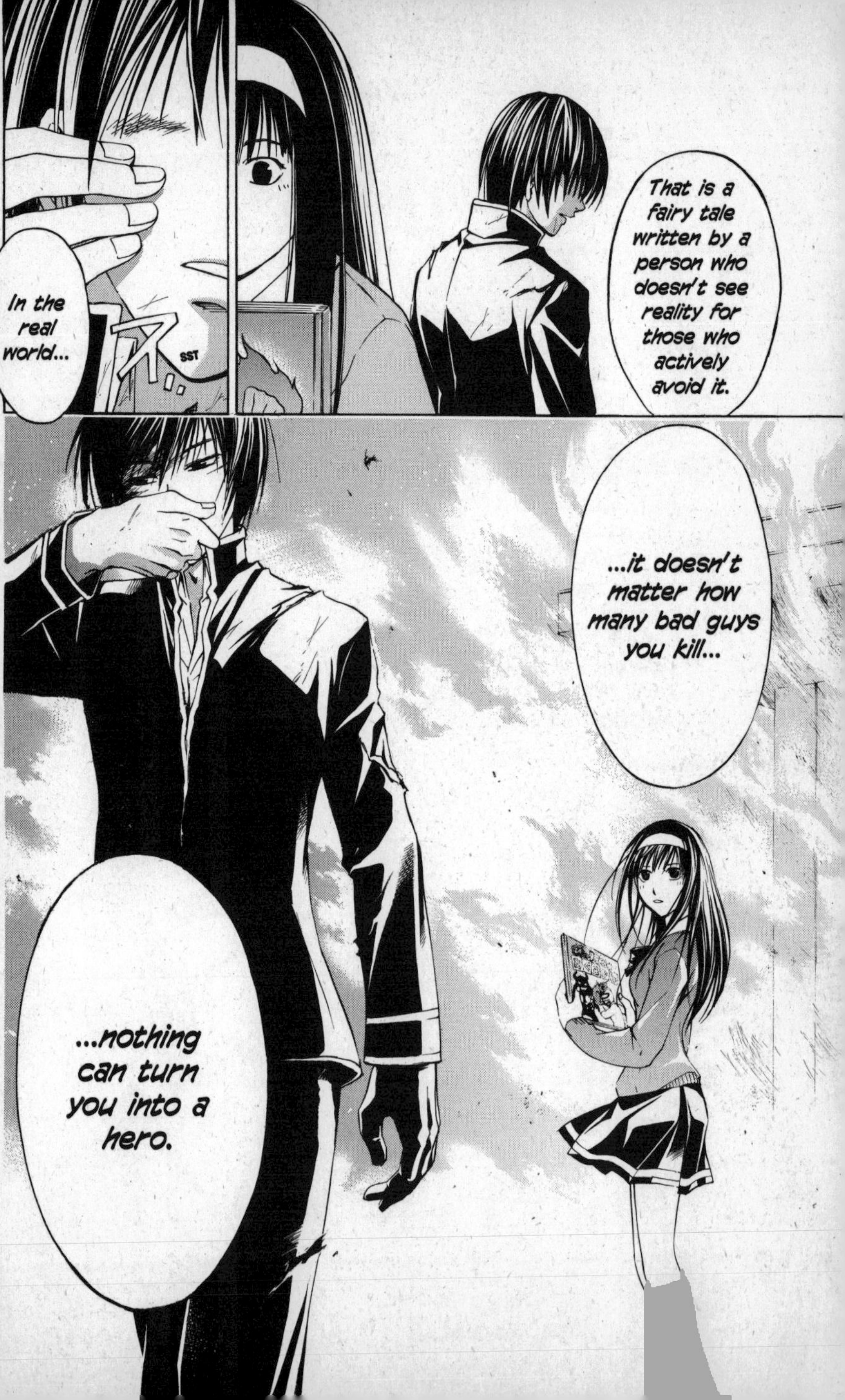
That is a fairy tale written by a person who doesn't see reality for those who actively avoid it.
In the real world...
SST
...it doesn't matter how many bad guys you kill...
...nothing can turn you into a hero.

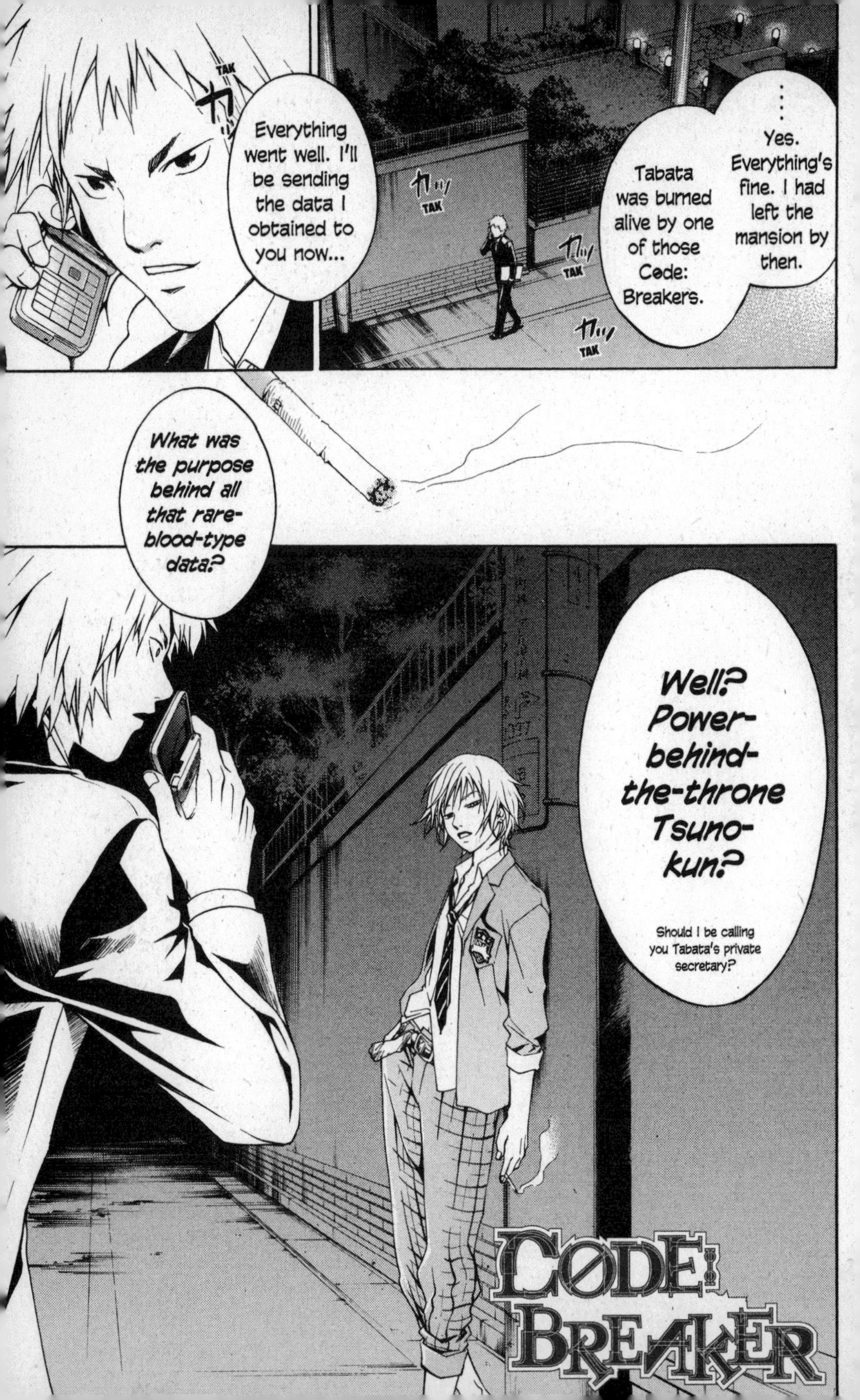
TAK
TAK
TAK
... Yes. Everything's fine. I had left the mansion by then.
Tabata was burned alive by one of those Code: Breakers.
TAK
Everything went well. I'll be sending the data I obtained to you now...
What was the purpose behind all that rare-blood-type data?
Well? Power-behind-the-throne Tsuno-kun?
Should I be calling you Tabata's private secretary?
CODE:BREAKER

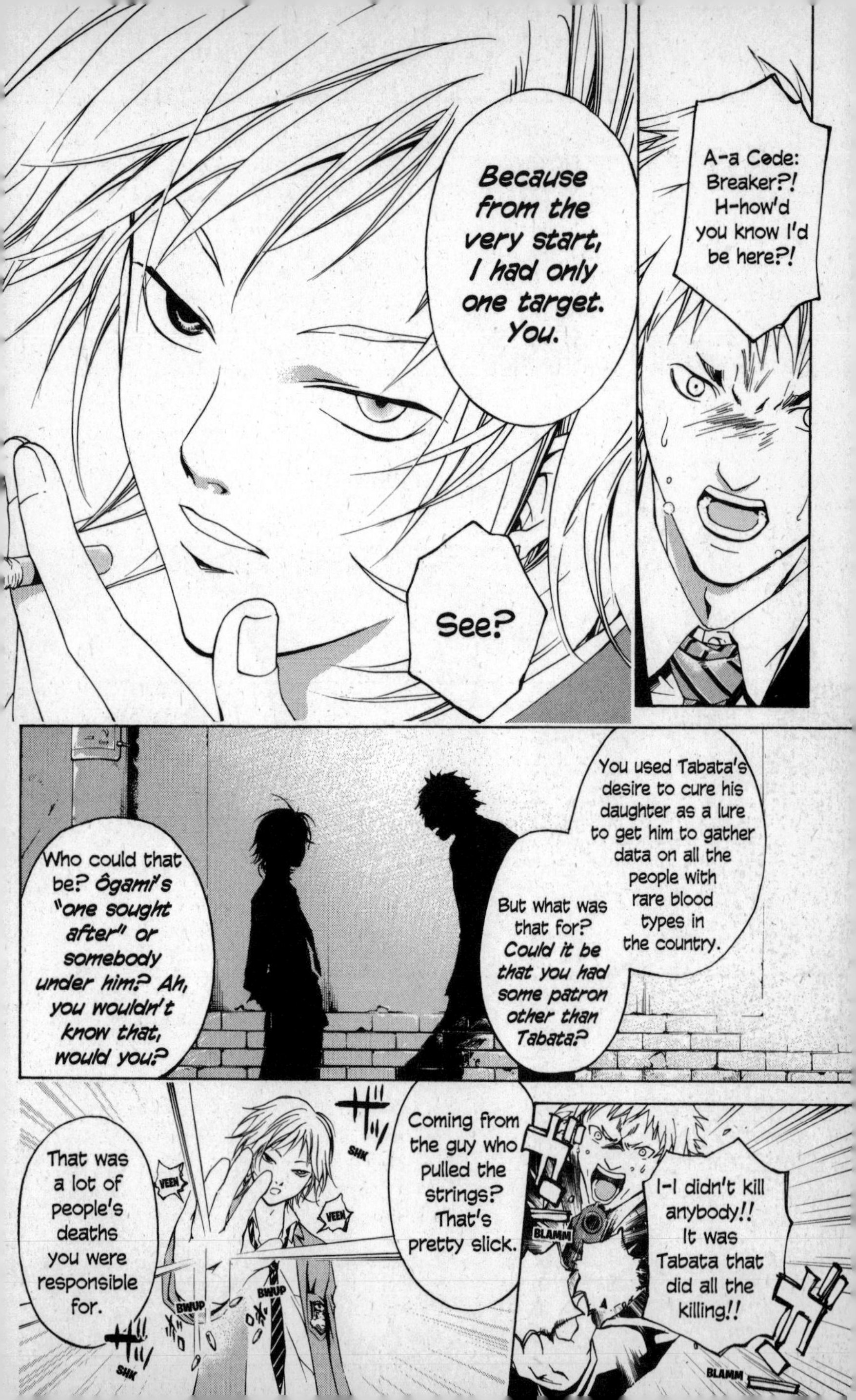
A-a Code: Breaker?! H-how'd you know I'd be here?!
Because from the very start, I had only one target. You.
See?
You used Tabata's desire to cure his daughter as a lure to get him to gather data on all the people with rare blood types in the country.
But what was that for? Could it be that you had some patron other than Tabata?
Who could that be? Ôgami's "one sought after" or somebody under him? Ah, you wouldn't know that, would you?
BLAMM
I-I didn't kill anybody!! It was Tabata that did all the killing!!
BLAMM
SHK
Coming from the guy who pulled the strings? That's pretty slick.
VEEN
VEEN
That was a lot of people's deaths you were responsible for.
BWUP
BWUP
SHK

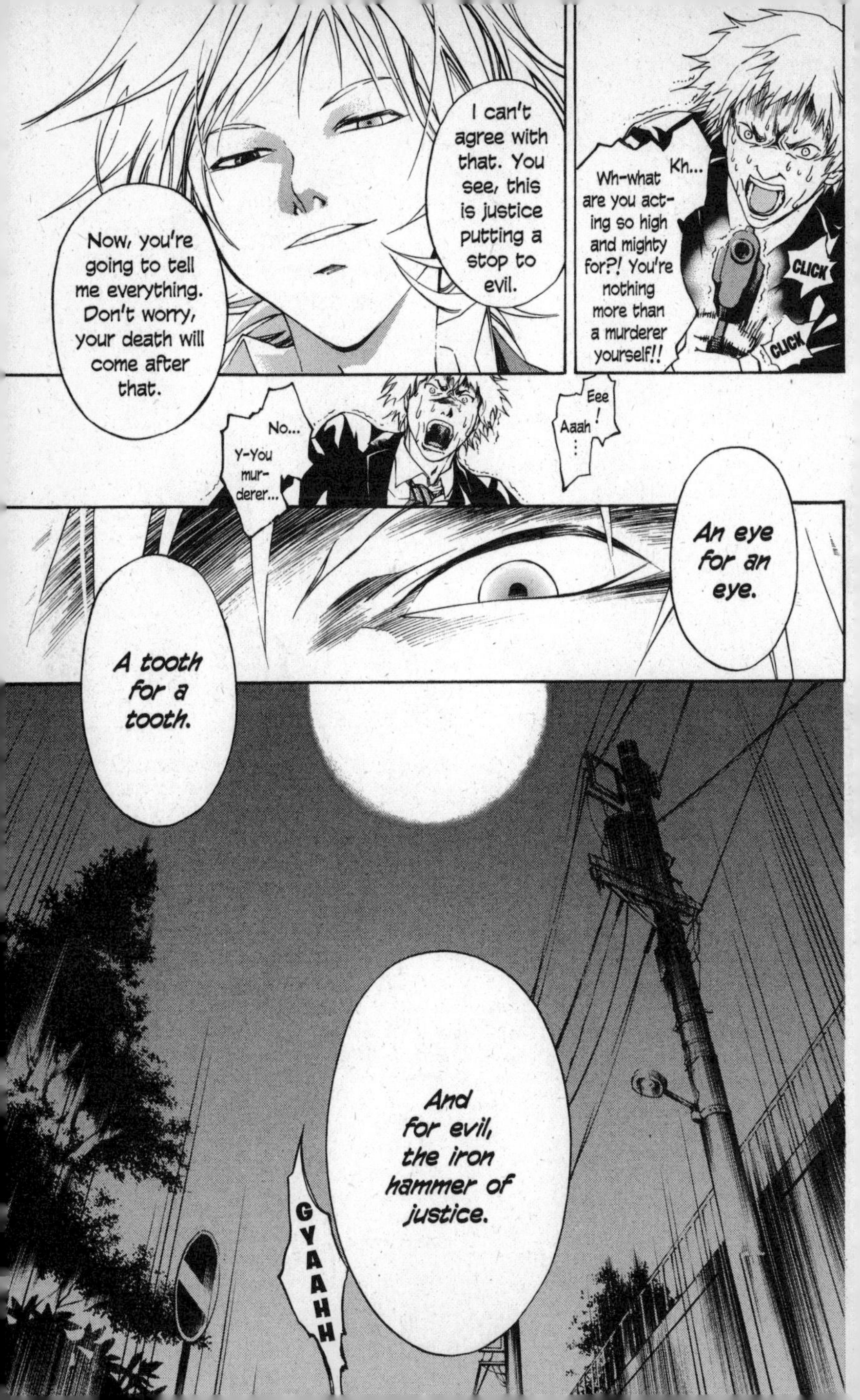
Kh...
Wh-what are you act-ing so high and mighty for?! You're nothing more than a murderer yourself!!
CLICK
CLICK
I can't agree with that. You see, this is justice putting a stop to evil.
Now, you're going to tell me everything. Don't worry, your death will come after that.
Eee! Aaah...
No...
Y-You mur-derer...
An eye for an eye.
A tooth for a tooth.
And for evil, the iron hammer of justice.
GYAAHH

code:13
Ôgami's Secret

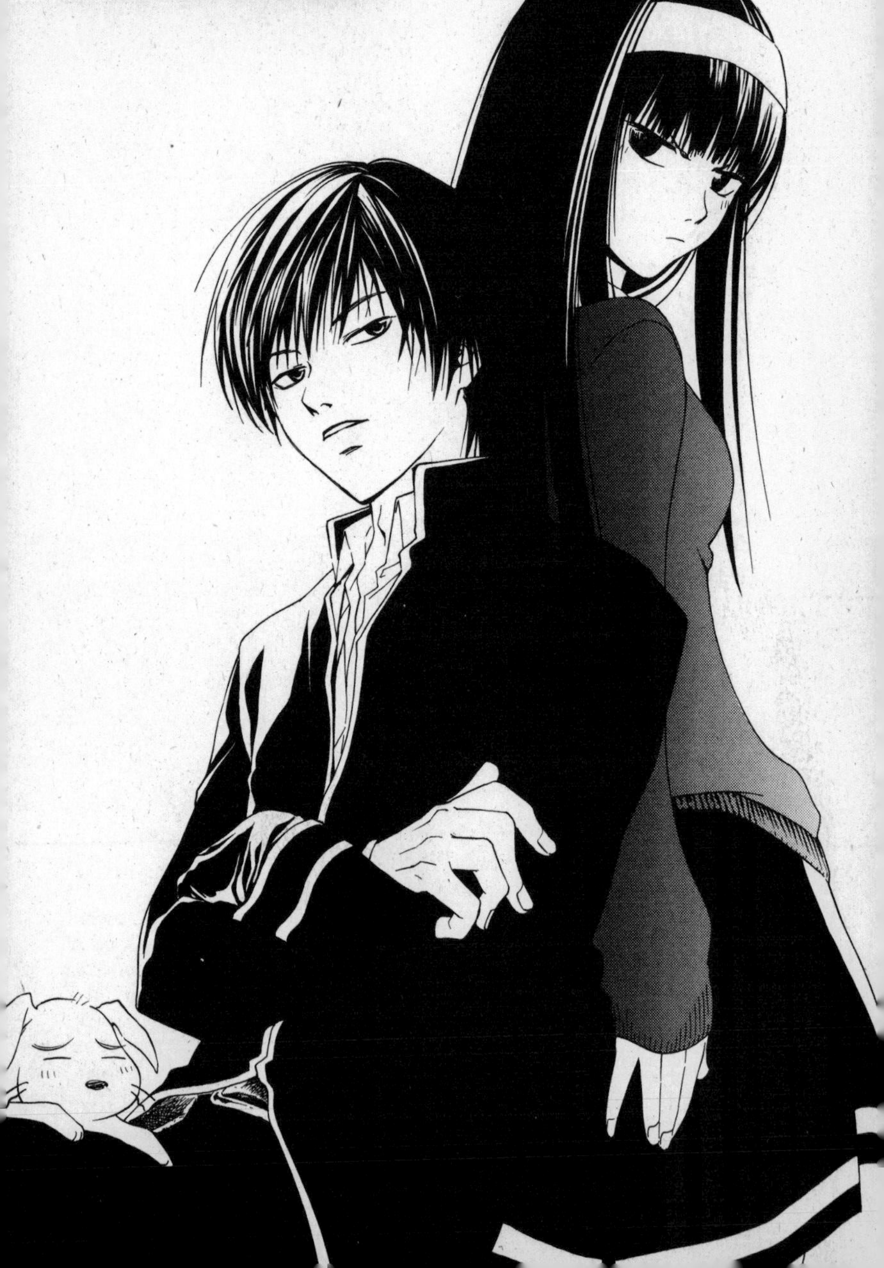

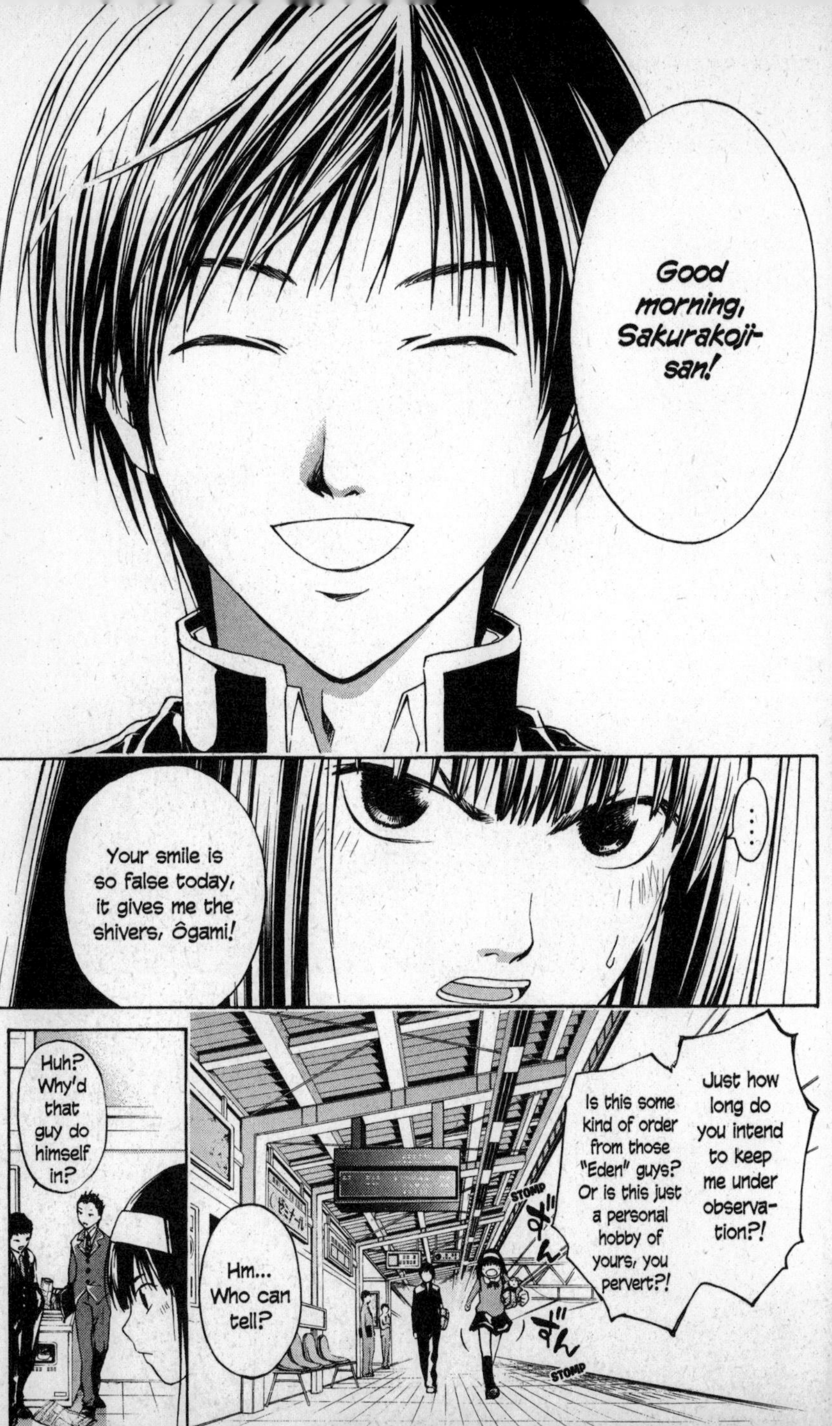
Good morning, Sakurakoji-san!
....
Your smile is so false today, it gives me the shivers, Ôgami!
Just how long do you intend to keep me under observation?!
Is this some kind of order from those "Eden" guys? Or is this just a personal hobby of yours, you pervert?!
STOMP
STOMP
Hm... Who can tell?
Huh? Why'd that guy do himself in?

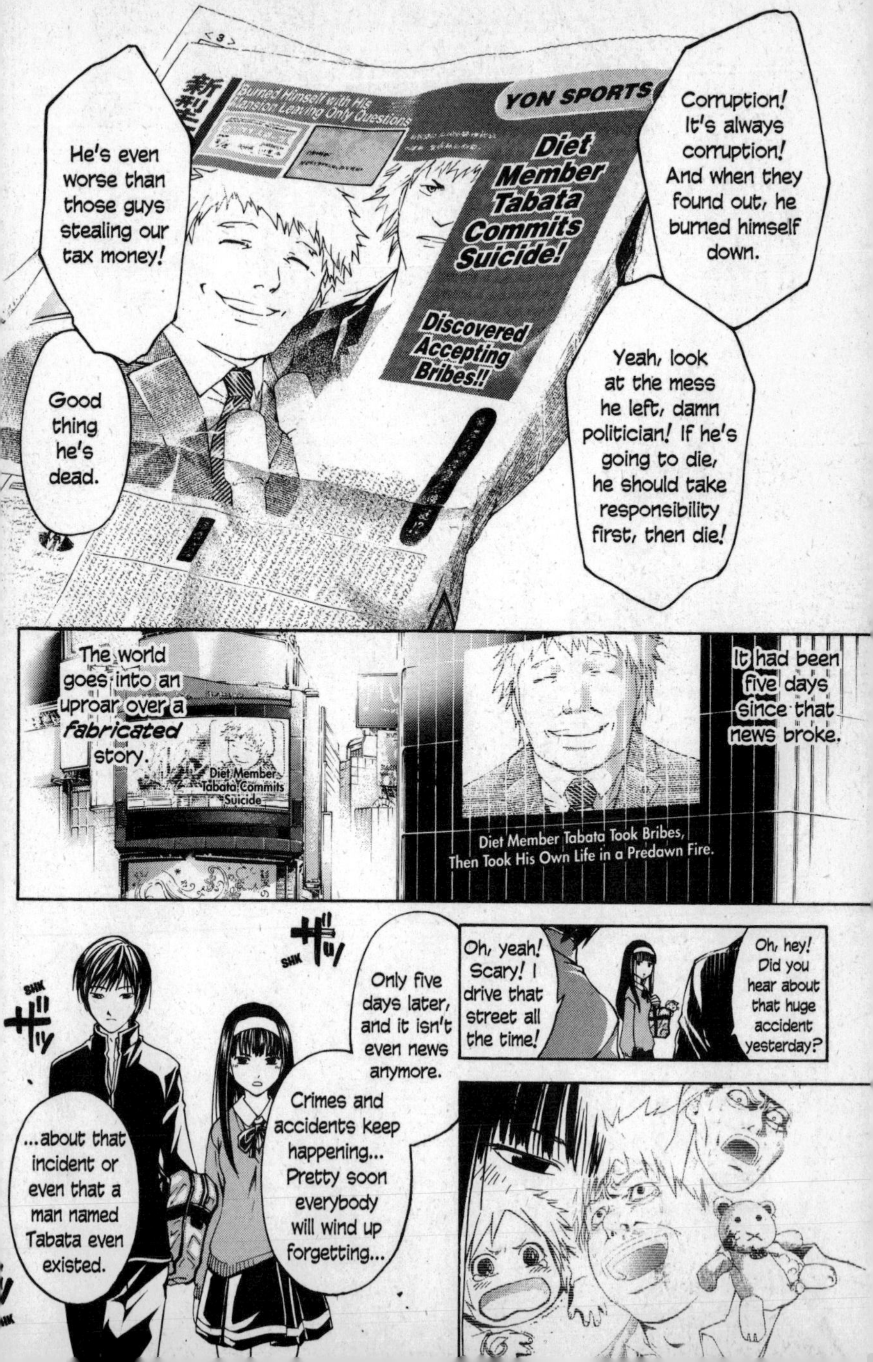

YON SPORTS
Diet Member Tabata Commits Suicide!
Discovered Accepting Bribes!!
Burned Himself with His Mansion Leaving Only Questions
Corruption! It's always corruption! And when they found out, he burned himself down.
Yeah, look at the mess he left, damn politician! If he's going to die, he should take responsibility first, then die!
He's even worse than those guys stealing our tax money!
Good thing he's dead.
It had been five days since that news broke.
Diet Member Tabata Took Bribes, Then Took His Own Life in a Predawn Fire.
The world goes into an uproar over a *fabricated* story.
Diet Member Tabata Commits Suicide
Oh, hey! Did you hear about that huge accident yesterday?
Oh, yeah! Scary! I drive that street all the time!
SHK
Only five days later, and it isn't even news anymore.
Crimes and accidents keep happening... Pretty soon everybody will wind up forgetting...
SHK
...about that incident or even that a man named Tabata even existed.

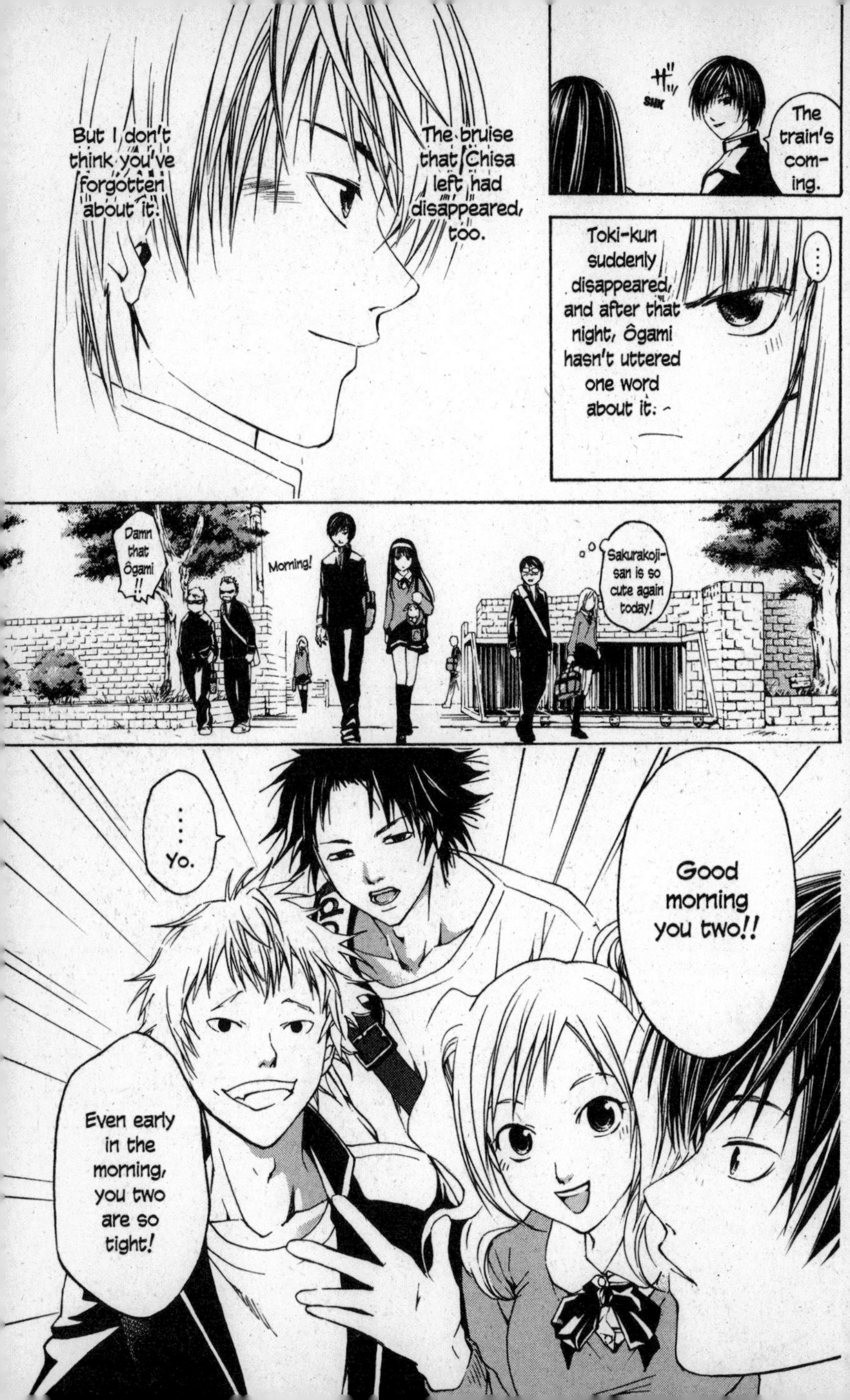
SHK
The train's coming.
Toki-kun suddenly disappeared, and after that night, Ôgami hasn't uttered one word about it.
......
The bruise that Chisa left had disappeared, too.
But I don't think you've forgotten about it.
Sakurakoji-san is so cute again today!
Morning!
Damn that Ôgami!!
Good morning you two!!
.... Yo.
Even early in the morning, you two are so tight!

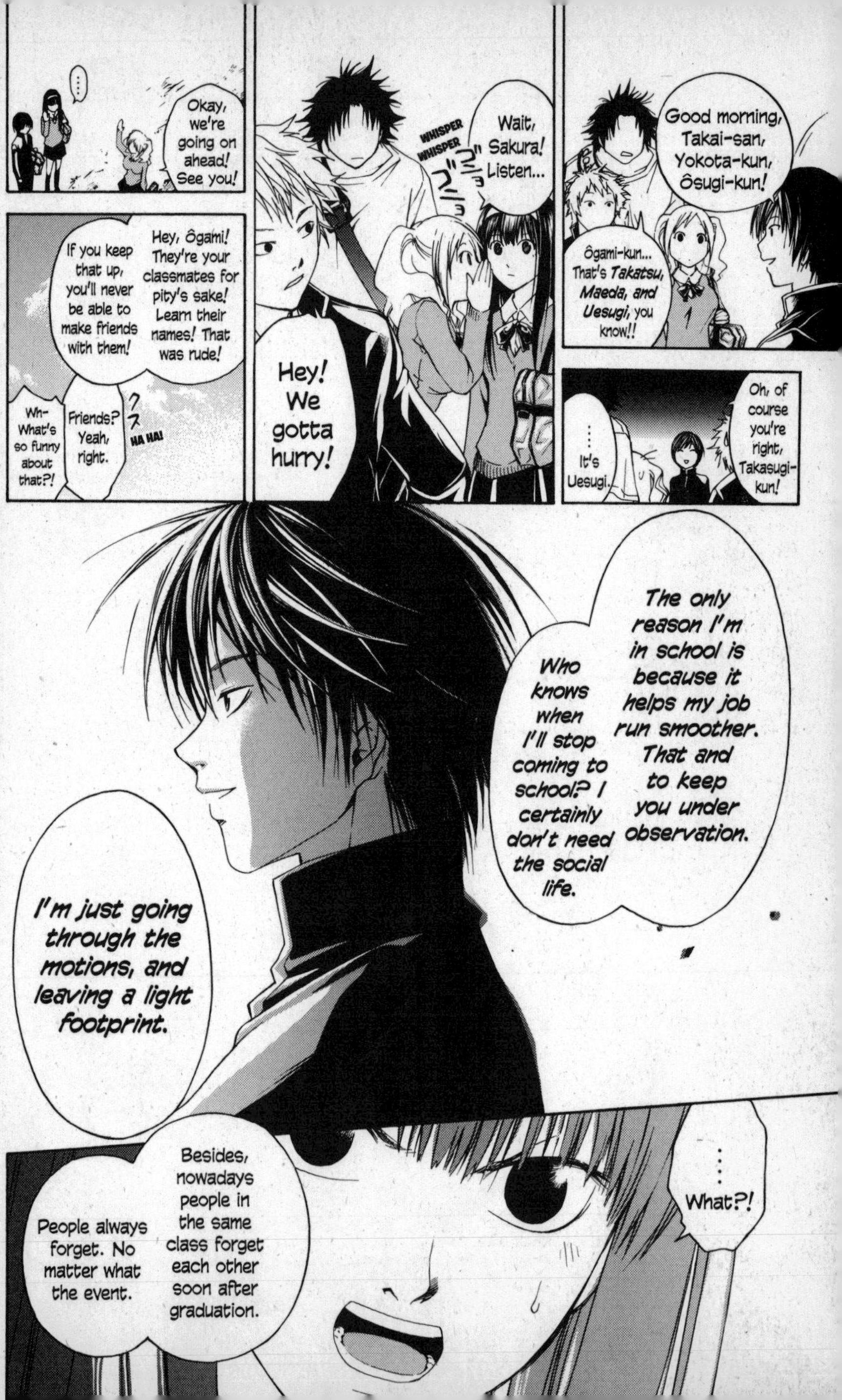
Good morning, Takai-san, Yokota-kun, Ôsugi-kun!
Ôgami-kun... That's Takatsu, Maeda, and Uesugi, you know!!
Oh, of course you're right, Takasugi-kun!
...It's Uesugi.
WHISPER WHISPER
ゴニョゴニョ
Wait, Sakura! Listen...
Hey! We gotta hurry!
Okay, we're going on ahead! See you!
...
Hey, Ôgami! They're your classmates for pity's sake! Learn their names! That was rude!
If you keep that up, you'll never be able to make friends with them!
クス
HA HA!
Friends? Yeah, right.
Wh- What's so funny about that?!
The only reason I'm in school is because it helps my job run smoother. That and to keep you under observation.
Who knows when I'll stop coming to school? I certainly don't need the social life.
I'm just going through the motions, and leaving a light footprint.
...What?!
Besides, nowadays people in the same class forget each other soon after graduation.
People always forget. No matter what the event.

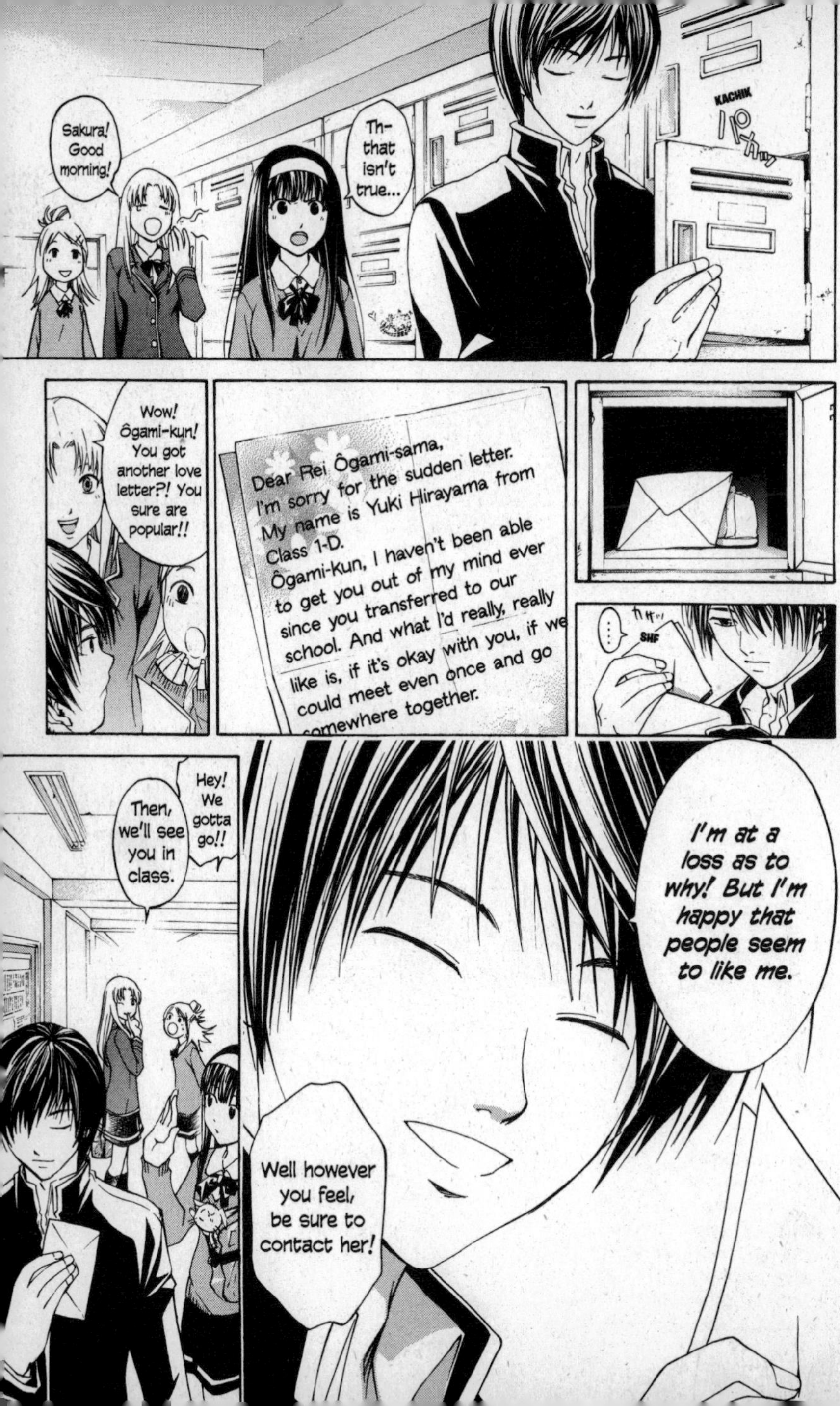
KACHIK
Th- that isn't true...
Sakura! Good morning!
...
SHF
Dear Rei Ôgami-sama,
I'm sorry for the sudden letter.
My name is Yuki Hirayama from Class 1-D.
Ôgami-Kun, I haven't been able to get you out of my mind ever since you transferred to our school. And what I'd really, really like is, if it's okay with you, if we could meet even once and go somewhere together.
Wow! Ôgami-kun! You got another love letter?! You sure are popular!!
I'm at a loss as to why! But I'm happy that people seem to like me.
Well however you feel, be sure to contact her!
Hey! We gotta go!!
Then, we'll see you in class.

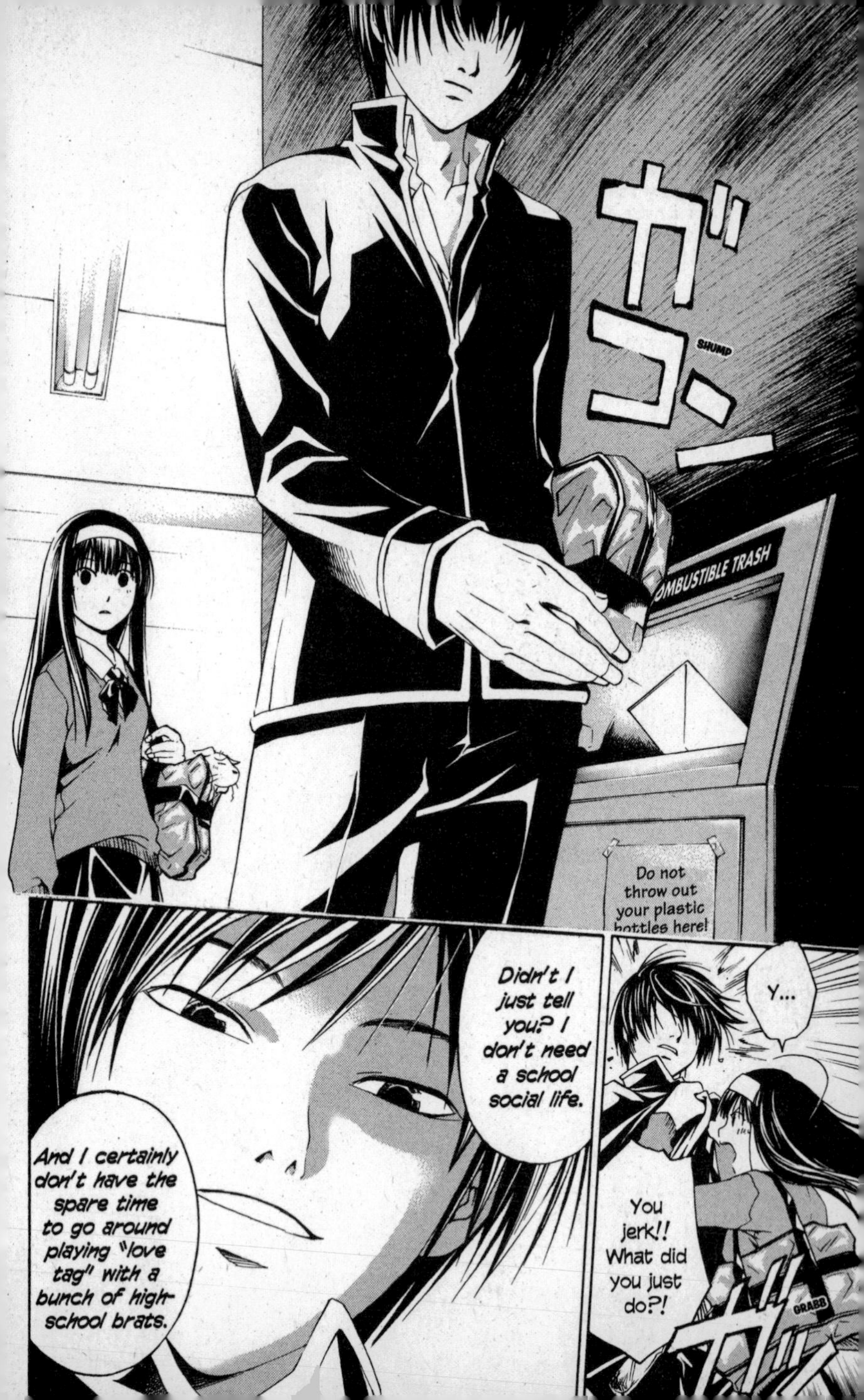
ガゴー
SHUMP
OMBUSTIBLE TRASH
Do not throw out your plastic bottles here!
Y...
You jerk!! What did you just do?!
GRABB
Didn't I just tell you? I don't need a school social life.
And I certainly don't have the spare time to go around playing "love tag" with a bunch of high-school brats.

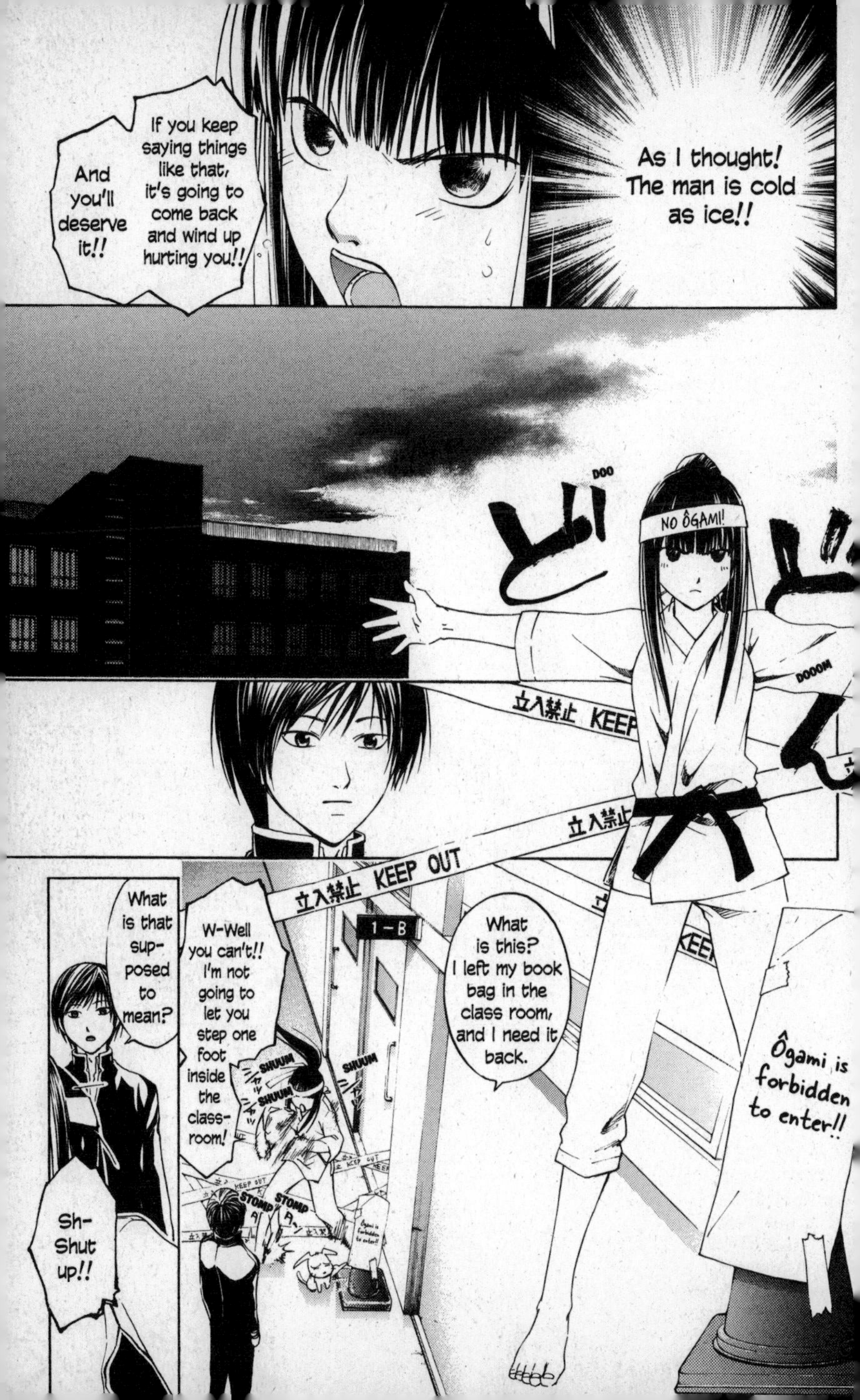
As I thought! The man is cold as ice!!
If you keep saying things like that, it's going to come back and wind up hurting you!!
And you'll deserve it!!
DOO
NO ÔGAMI!
DOOOM
立入禁止 KEEP
立入禁止
立入禁止 KEEP OUT
1-B
Ôgami is forbidden to enter!!
What is this? I left my book bag in the class room, and I need it back.
SHUUM
SHUUM
SHUUM
W-Well you can't!! I'm not going to let you step one foot inside the class-room!
STOMP
STOMP
What is that sup-posed to mean?
Sh-Shut up!!

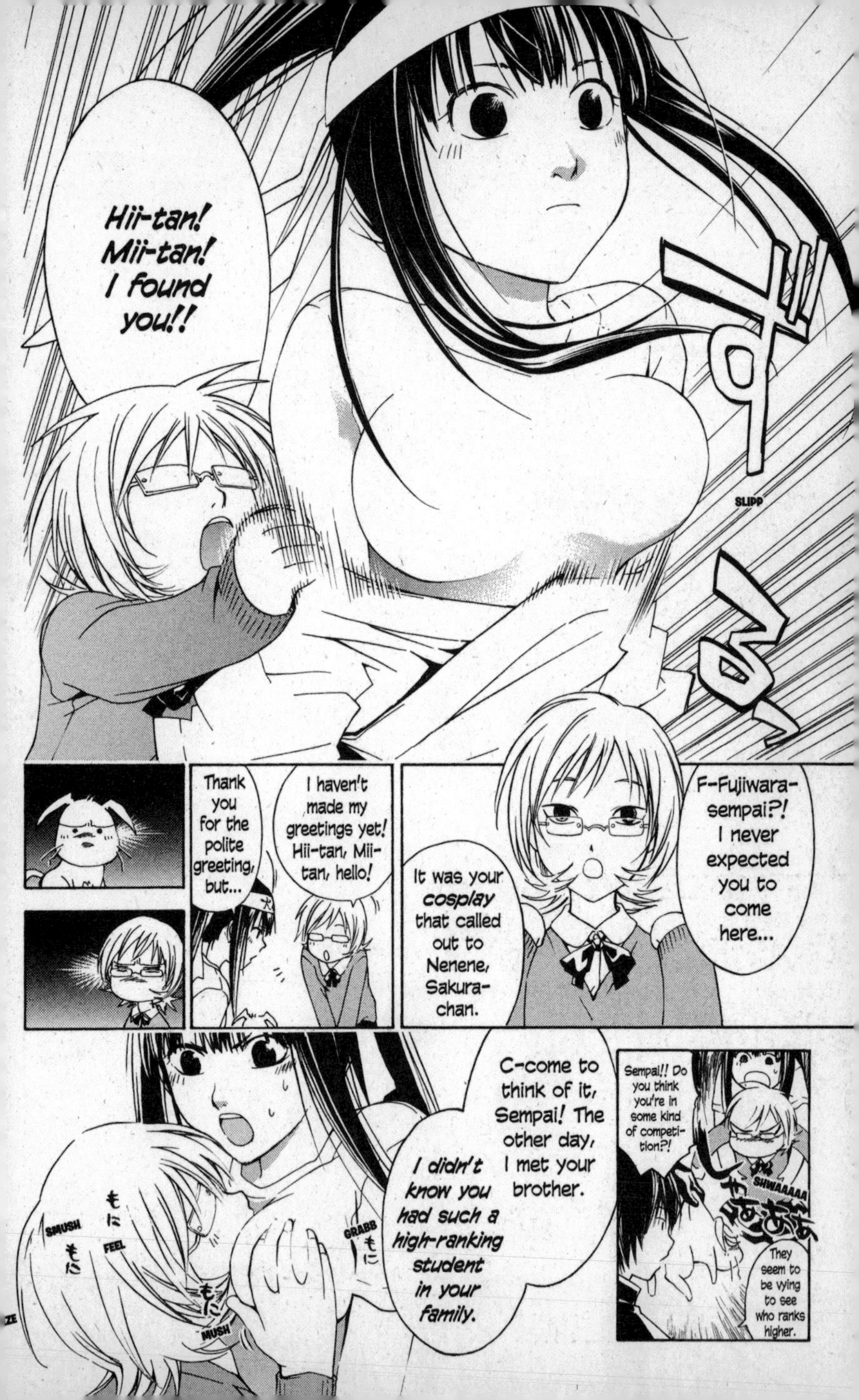
Hii-tan! Mii-tan! I found you!!
SLIPP
F-Fujiwara-sempai?! I never expected you to come here...
It was your cosplay that called out to Nenene, Sakura-chan.
I haven't made my greetings yet! Hii-tan, Mii-tan, hello!
Thank you for the polite greeting, but...
Sempai!! Do you think you're in some kind of competition?!
SHWAAAAA
They seem to be vying to see who ranks higher.
C-come to think of it, Sempai! The other day, I met your brother.
I didn't know you had such a high-ranking student in your family.
GRABB
もに
SMUSH
もに
FEEL
もに
MUSH
もに

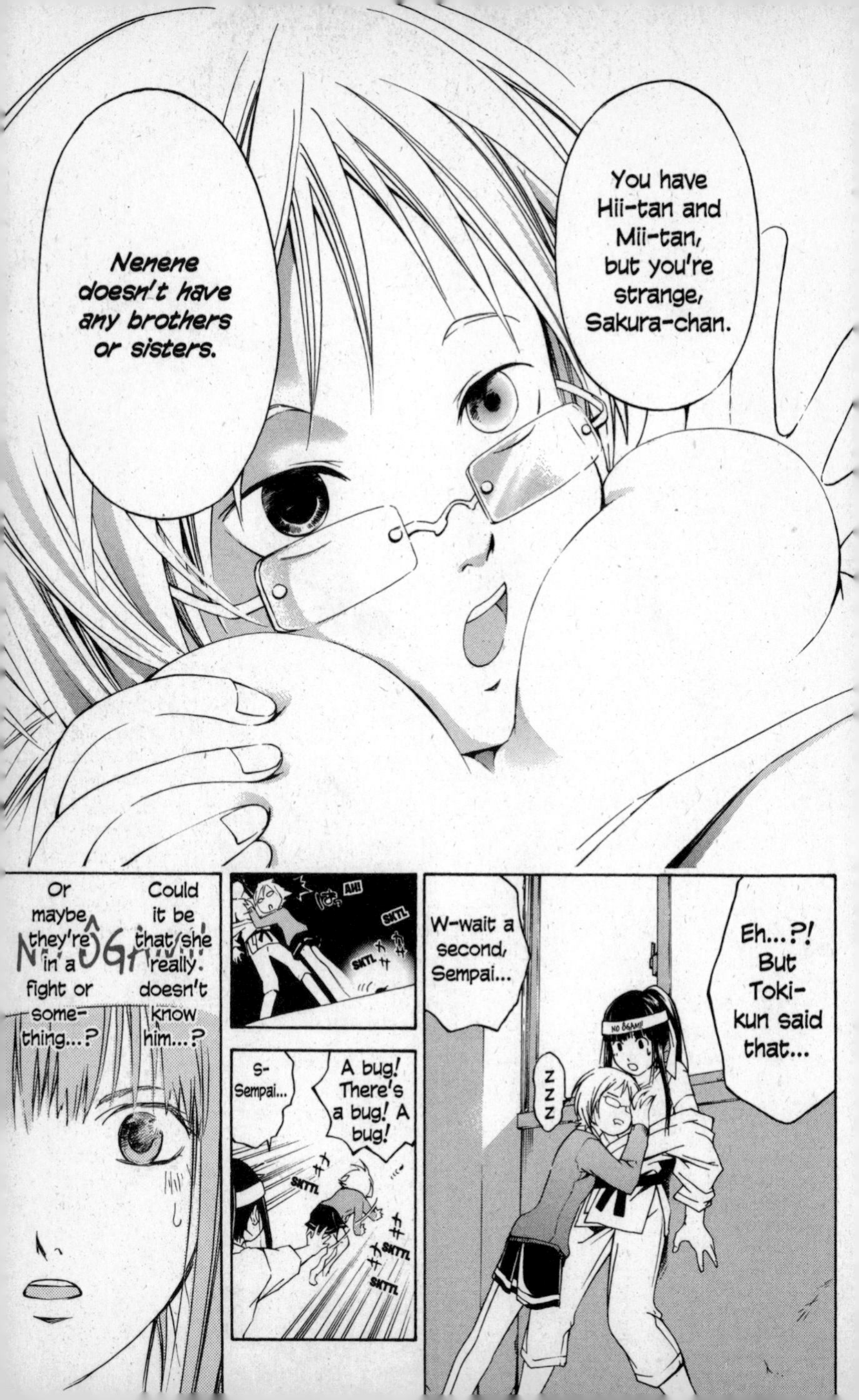
You have Hii-tan and Mii-tan, but you're strange, Sakura-chan.
Nenene doesn't have any brothers or sisters.
Eh...?! But Toki-kun said that...
W-wait a second, Sempai...
ZZZ
AH!
SKTL
SKTL
A bug! There's a bug! A bug!
S-Sempai...
SKTTL
SKTTL
SKTTL
Could it be that she really doesn't know him...?
Or maybe they're in a fight or some-thing...?

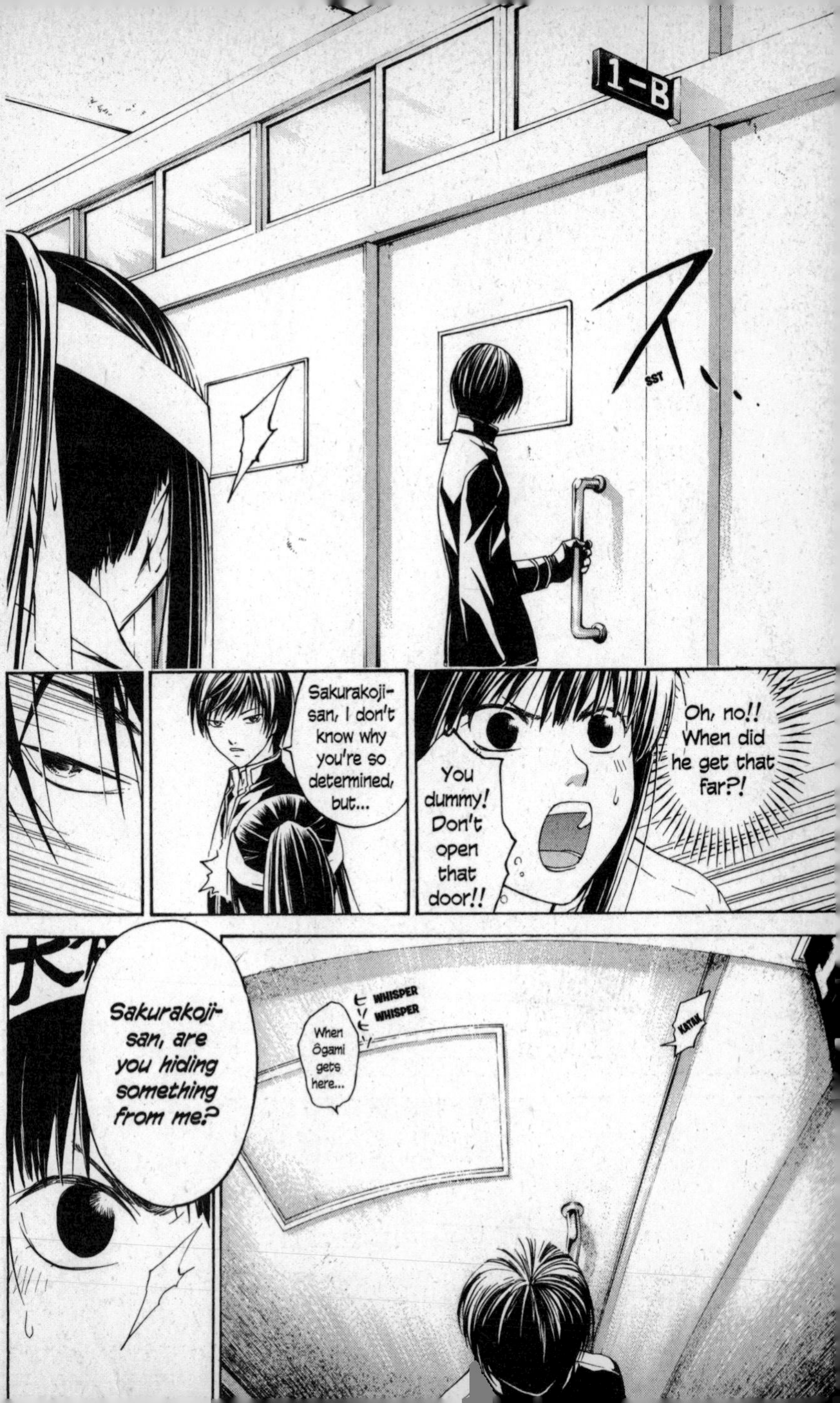
1-B
SST
Oh, no!! When did he get that far?!
You dummy! Don't open that door!!
Sakurakoji-san, I don't know why you're so determined, but...
KATAN
WHISPER WHISPER
When Ōgami gets here...
Sakurakoji-san, are you hiding something from me?

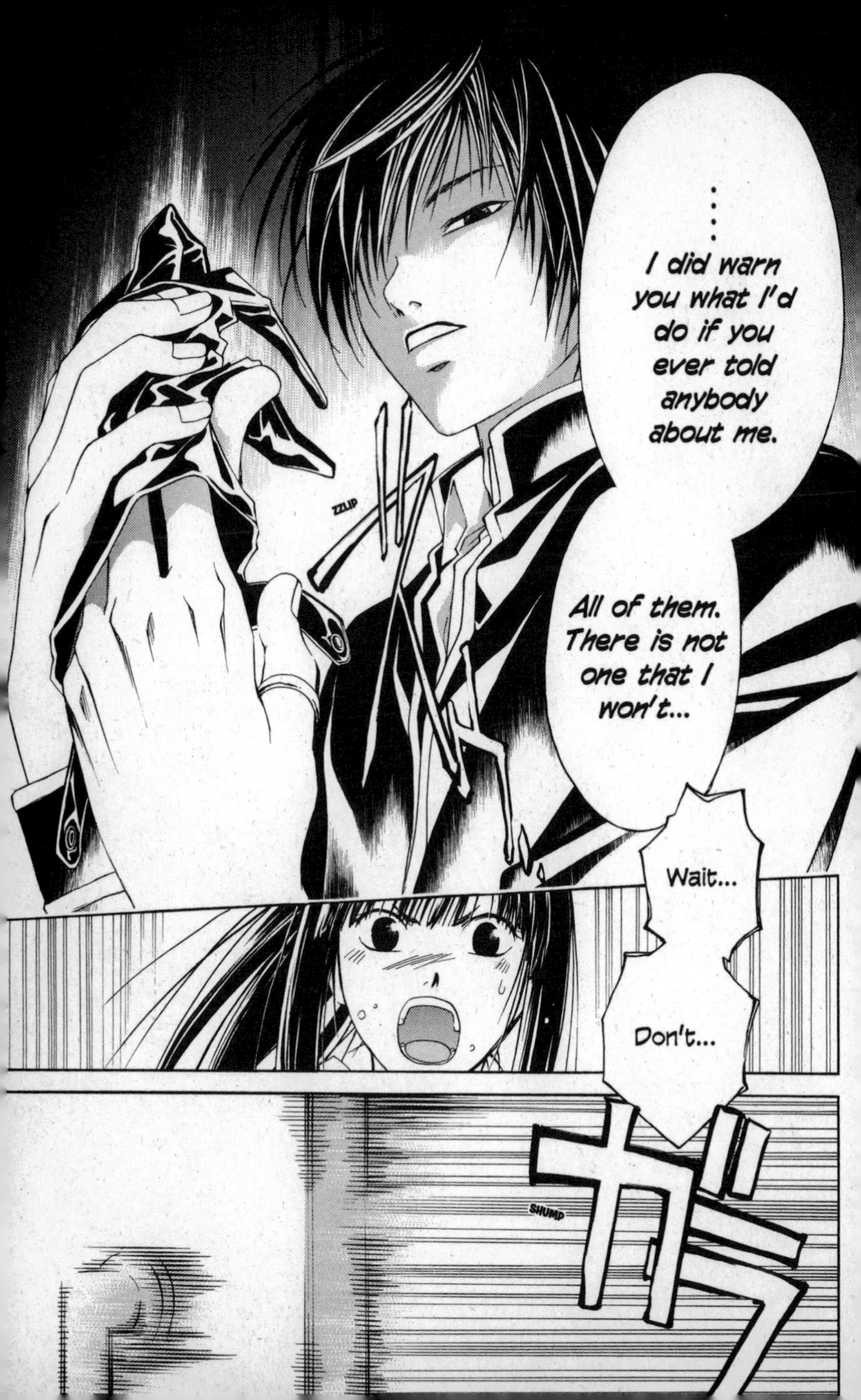
...
I did warn you what I'd do if you ever told anybody about me.
ZZLIP
All of them. There is not one that I won't...
Wait...
Don't...
SHUMP
ガラ

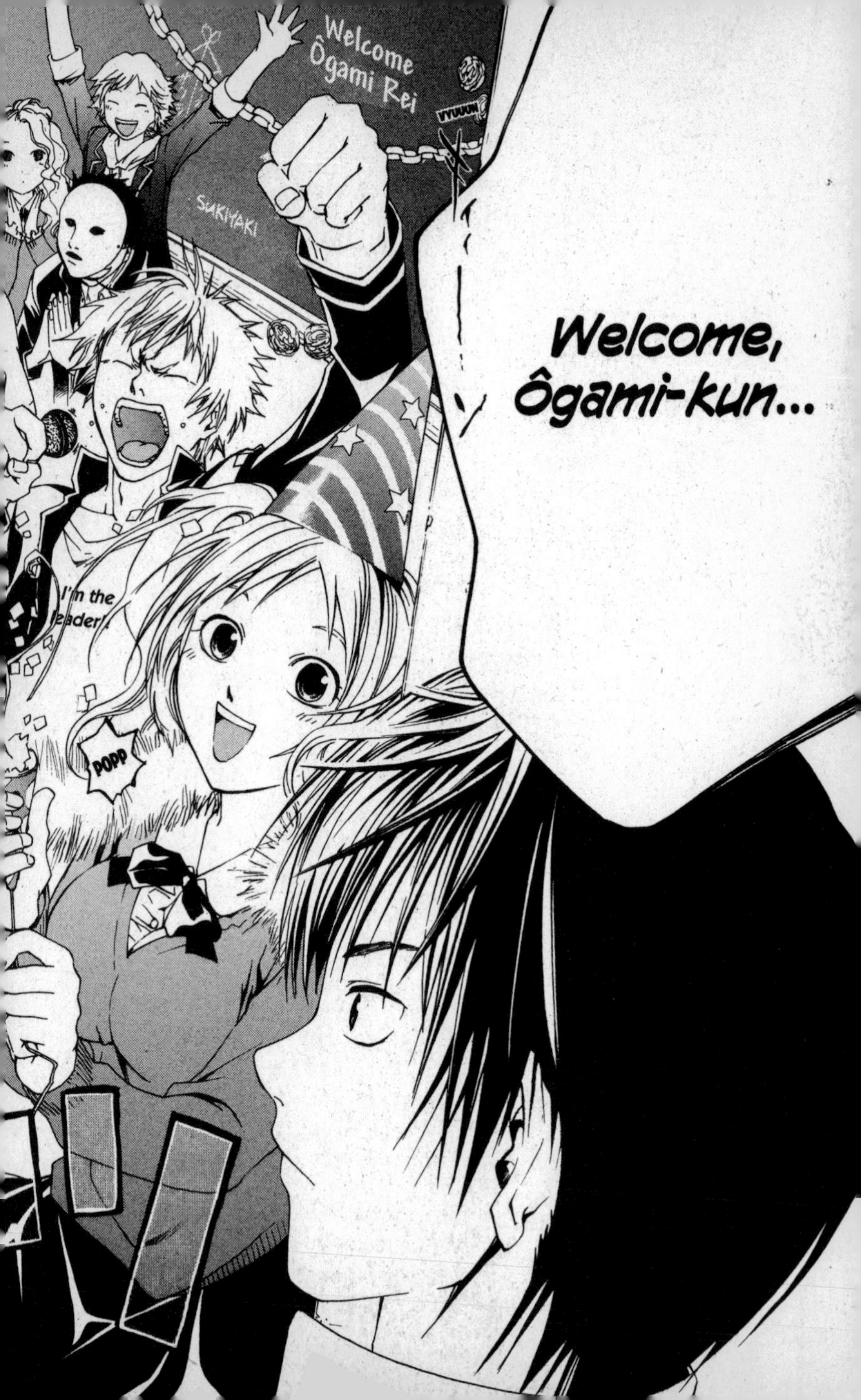
Welcome Ôgami Rei
VYUUUN
SUKIYAKI
Welcome, Ôgami-kun...
I'm the leader!
POPP

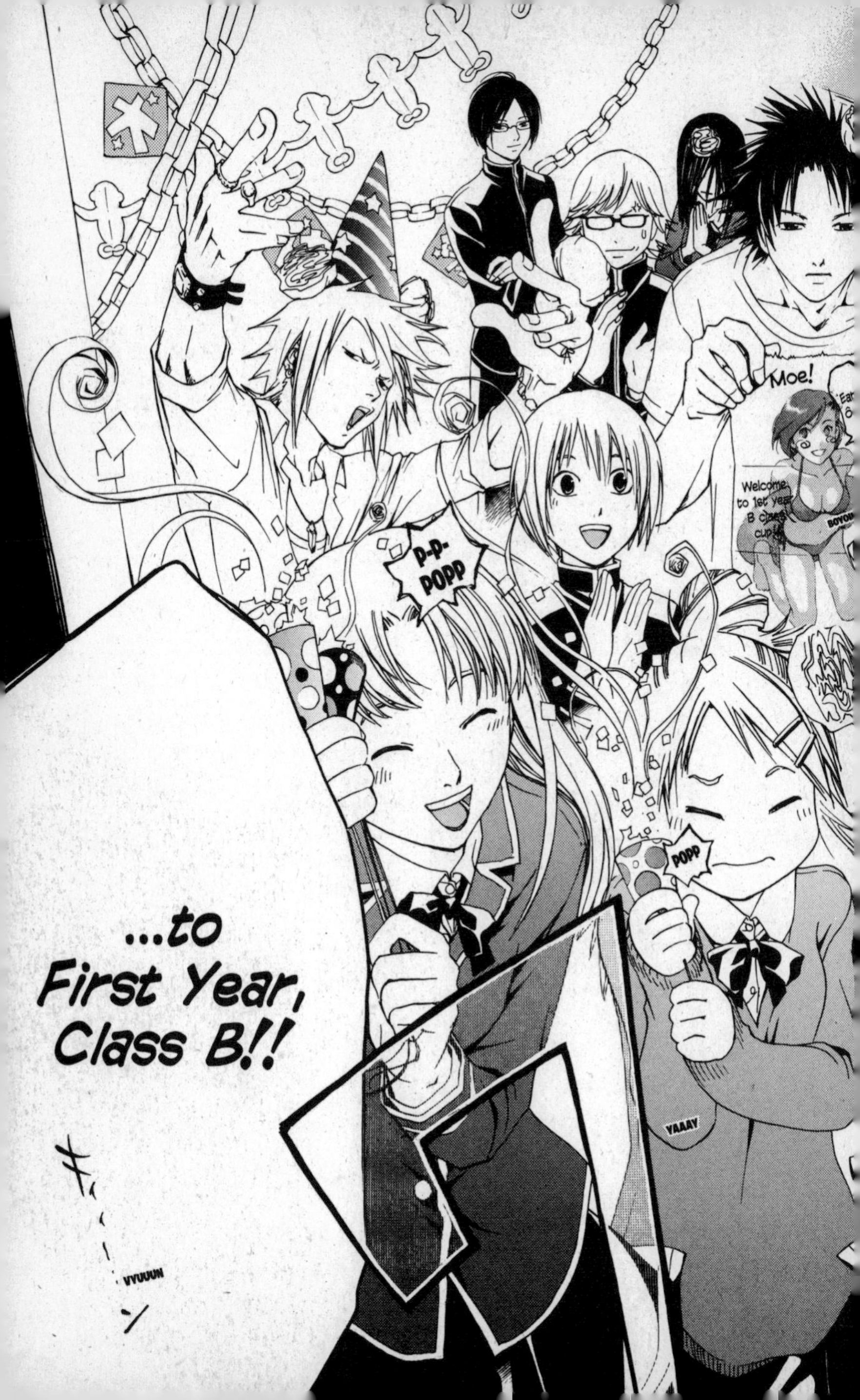
Moe!
Welcome to 1st year
P-P-POPP
POPP
YAAAY
...to First Year, Class B!!
VVUUUN

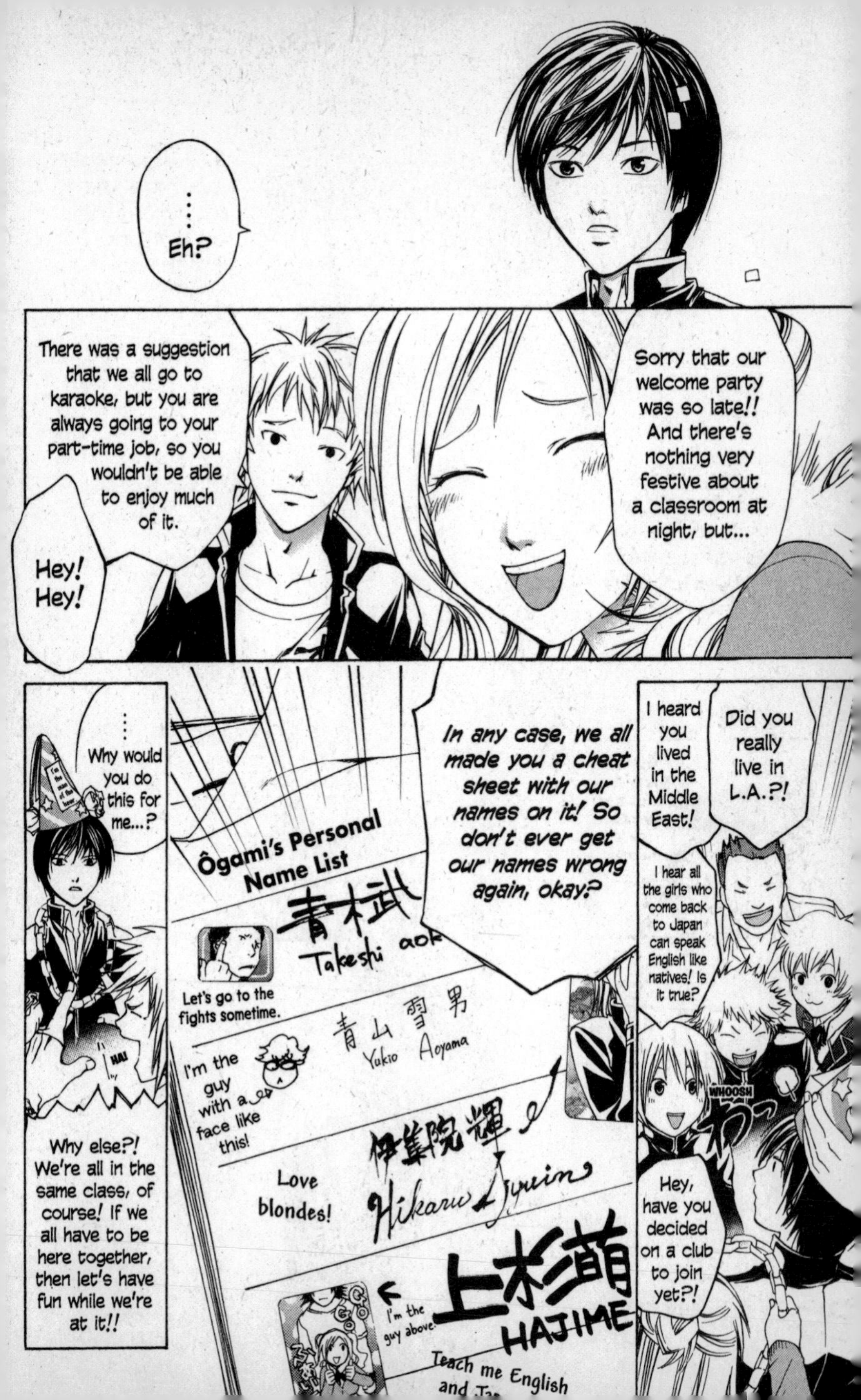
...
Eh?
Sorry that our welcome party was so late!! And there's nothing very festive about a classroom at night, but...
There was a suggestion that we all go to karaoke, but you are always going to your part-time job, so you wouldn't be able to enjoy much of it.
Hey! Hey!
Did you really live in L.A.?!
I heard you lived in the Middle East!
I hear all the girls who come back to Japan can speak English like natives! Is it true?
WHOOSH
Hey, have you decided on a club to join yet?!
In any case, we all made you a cheat sheet with our names on it! So don't ever get our names wrong again, okay?
Ôgami's Personal Name List
青木武
Takeshi aok
Let's go to the fights sometime.
青山雪男
Yukio Aoyama
I'm the guy with a face like this!
伊集院輝
Hikaru Ijyuin
Love blondes!
上杉萌
HAJIME
I'm the guy above.
Teach me English and Ja
...
Why would you do this for me...?
HAI
Why else?! We're all in the same class, of course! If we all have to be here together, then let's have fun while we're at it!!

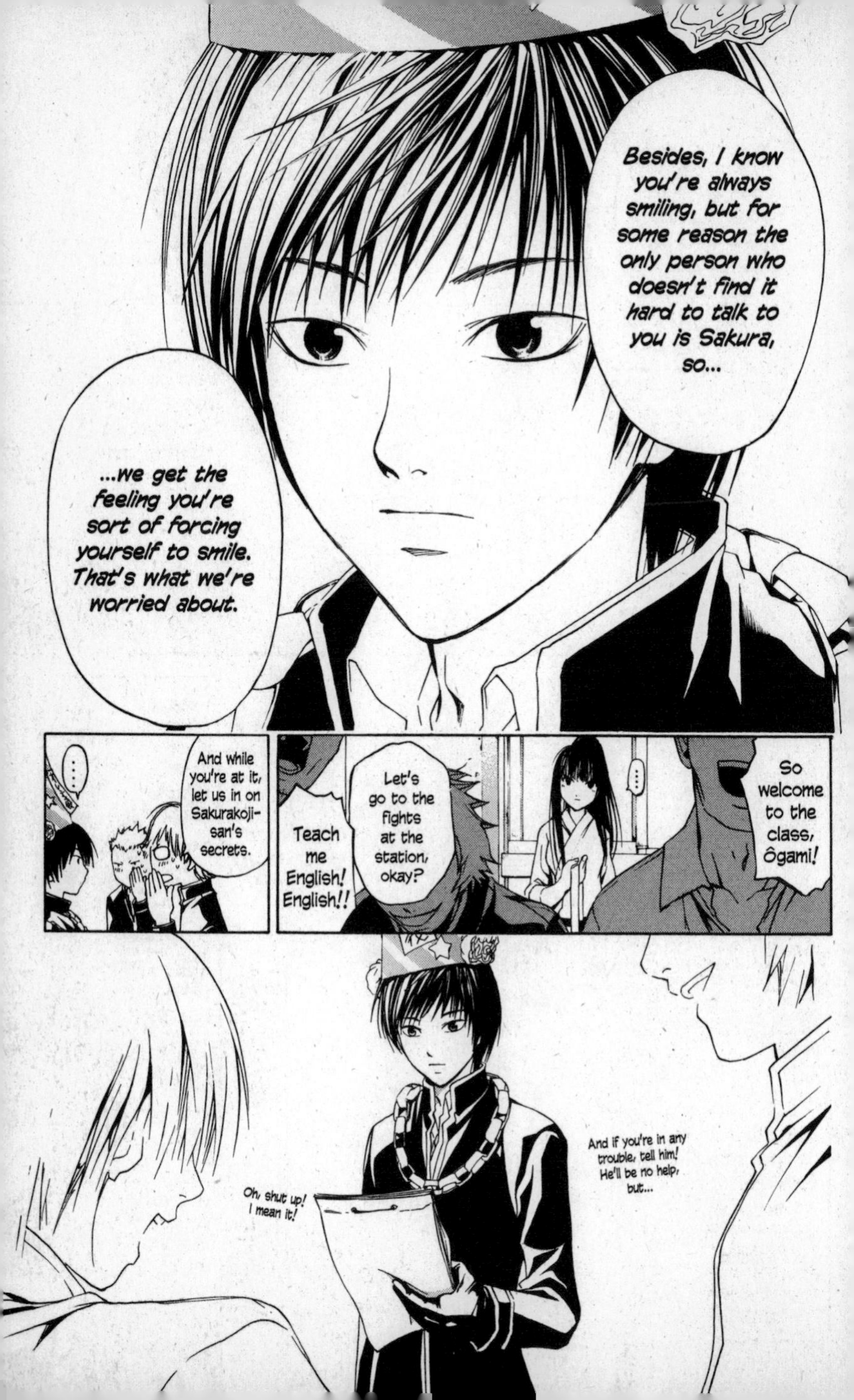
Besides, I know you're always smiling, but for some reason the only person who doesn't find it hard to talk to you is Sakura, so...
...we get the feeling you're sort of forcing yourself to smile. That's what we're worried about.
So welcome to the class, Ôgami!
...
Let's go to the fights at the station, okay?
Teach me English! English!!
And while you're at it, let us in on Sakurakoji-san's secrets.
...
And if you're in any trouble, tell him! He'll be no help, but...
Oh, shut up! I mean it!

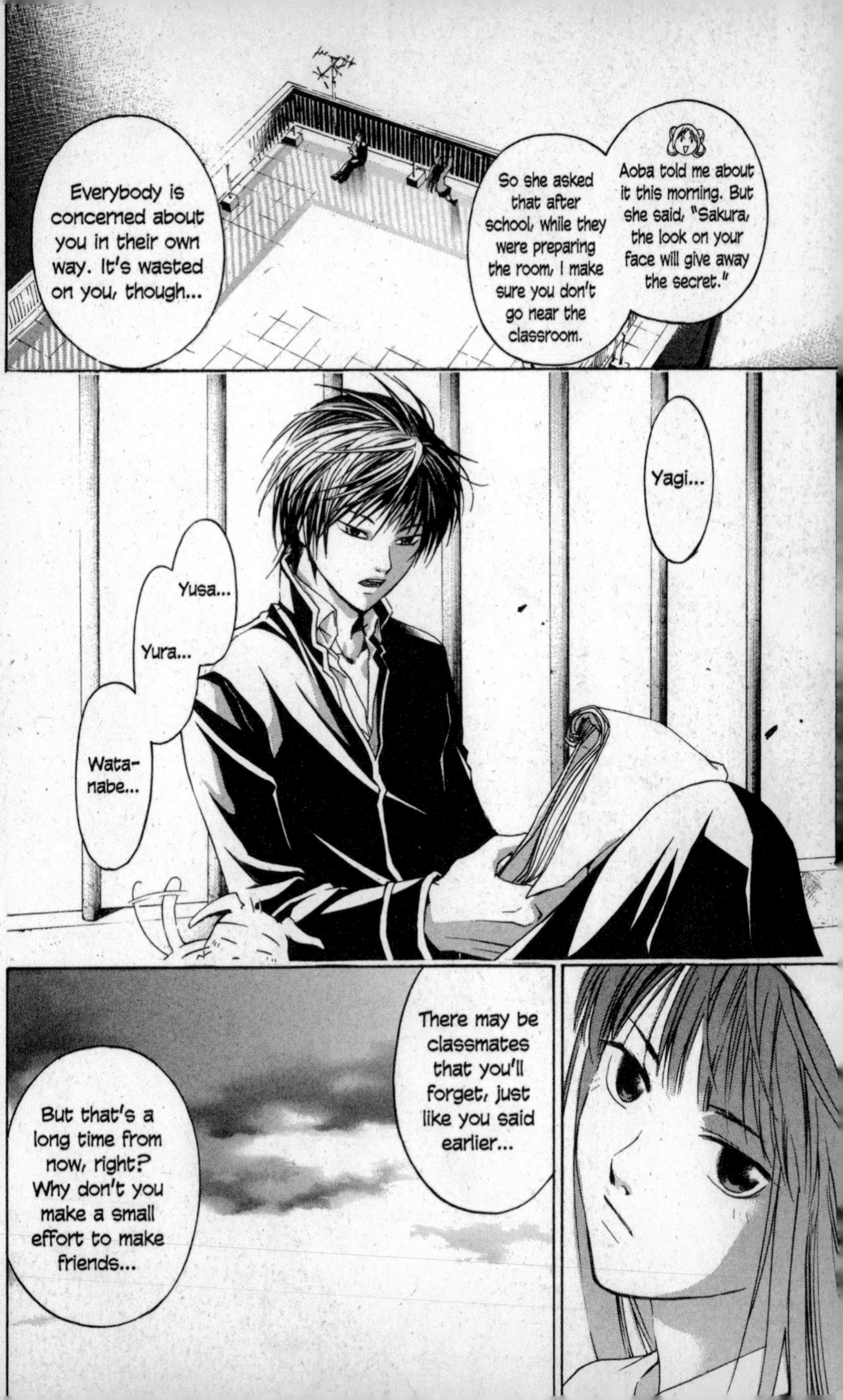
Aoba told me about it this morning. But she said, "Sakura, the look on your face will give away the secret."
So she asked that after school, while they were preparing the room, I make sure you don't go near the classroom.
Everybody is concerned about you in their own way. It's wasted on you, though...
Yagi...
Yusa...
Yura...
Wata-nabe...
There may be classmates that you'll forget, just like you said earlier...
But that's a long time from now, right? Why don't you make a small effort to make friends...

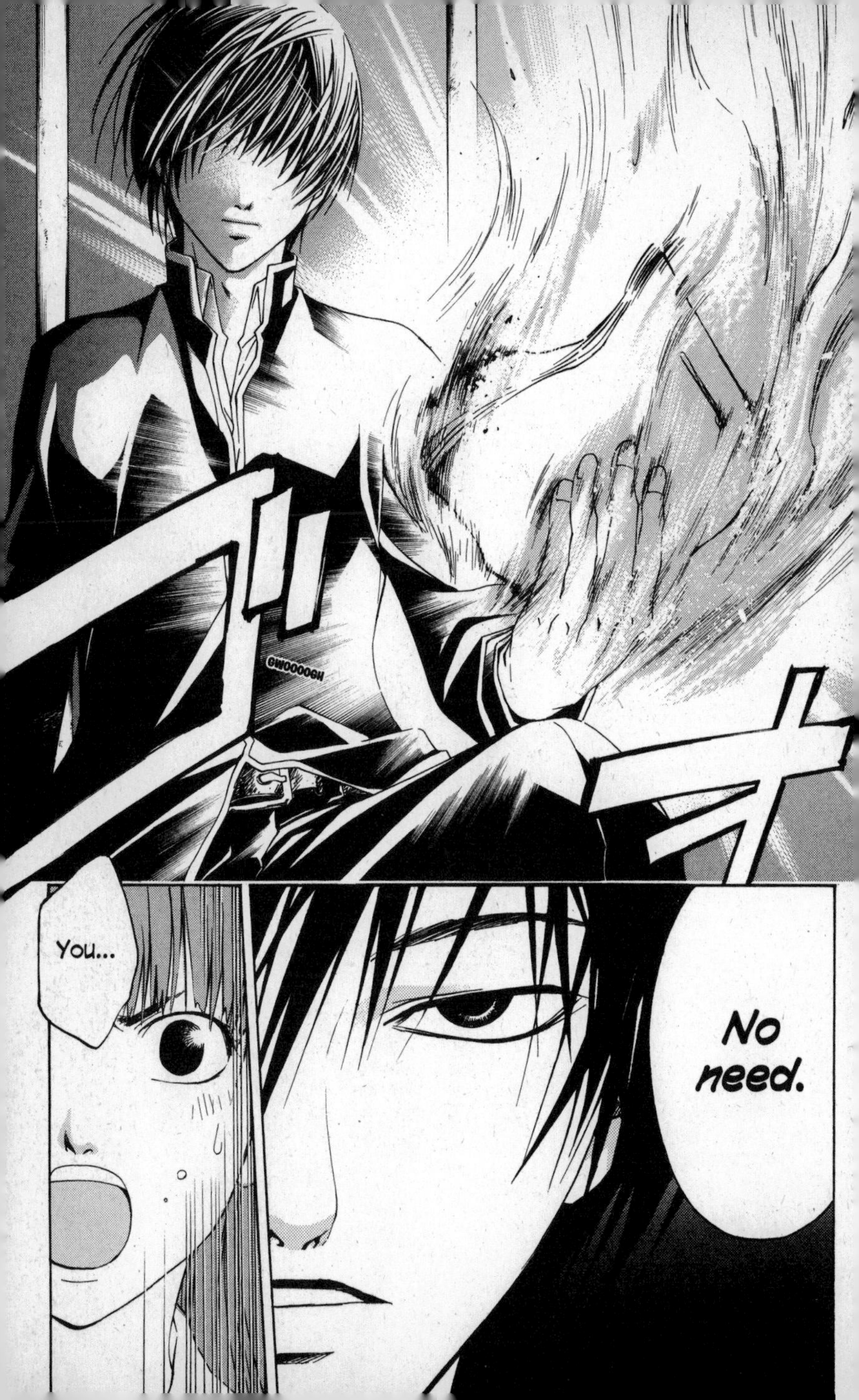
GWOOOOGH
No need.
You...

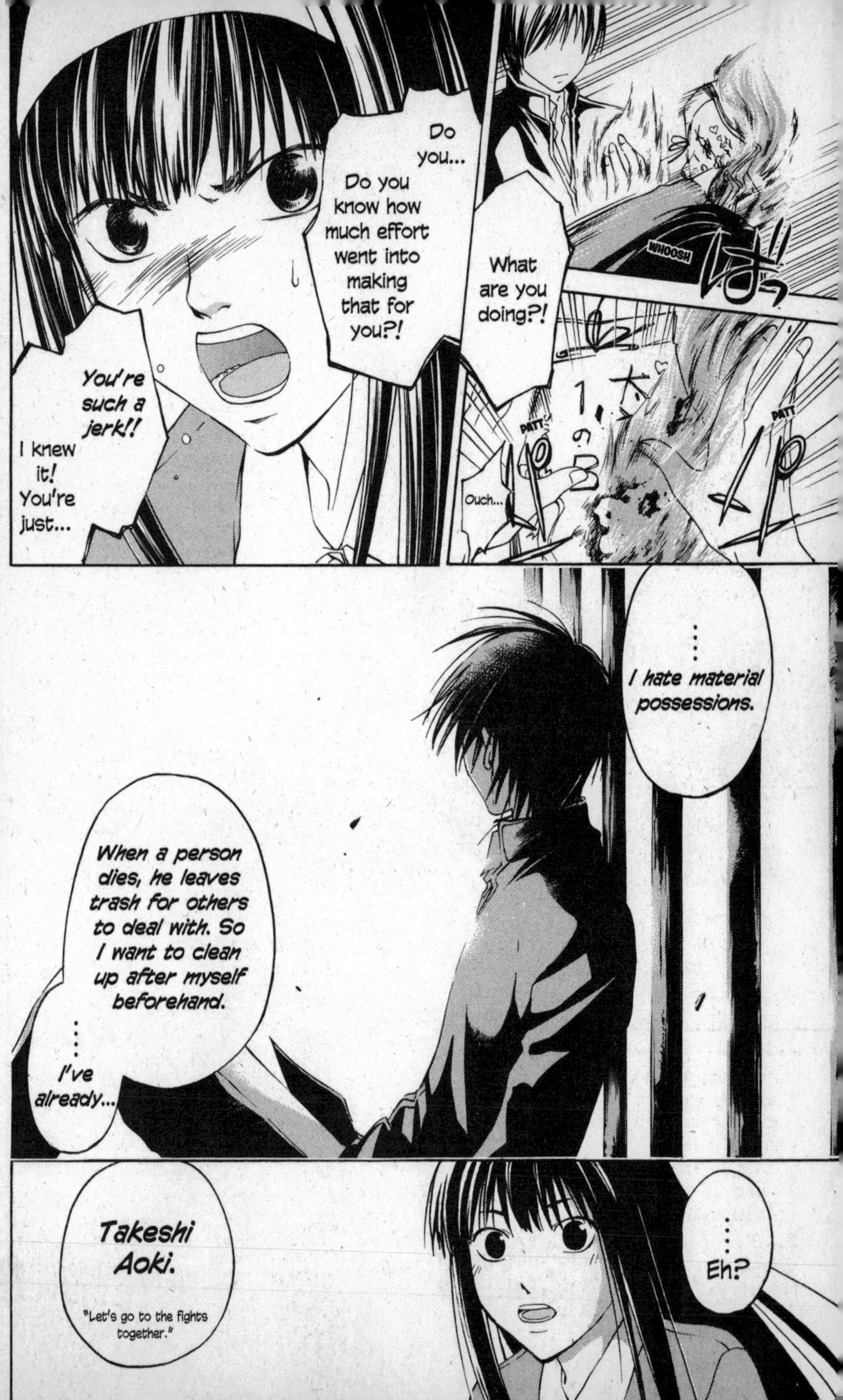
WHOOSH
What are you doing?!
PATT
PATT
Ouch...
Do you...
Do you know how much effort went into making that for you?!
You're such a jerk!!
I knew it! You're just...
... I hate material possessions.
When a person dies, he leaves trash for others to deal with. So I want to clean up after myself beforehand.
... I've already...
... Eh?
Takeshi Aoki.
"Let's go to the fights together."

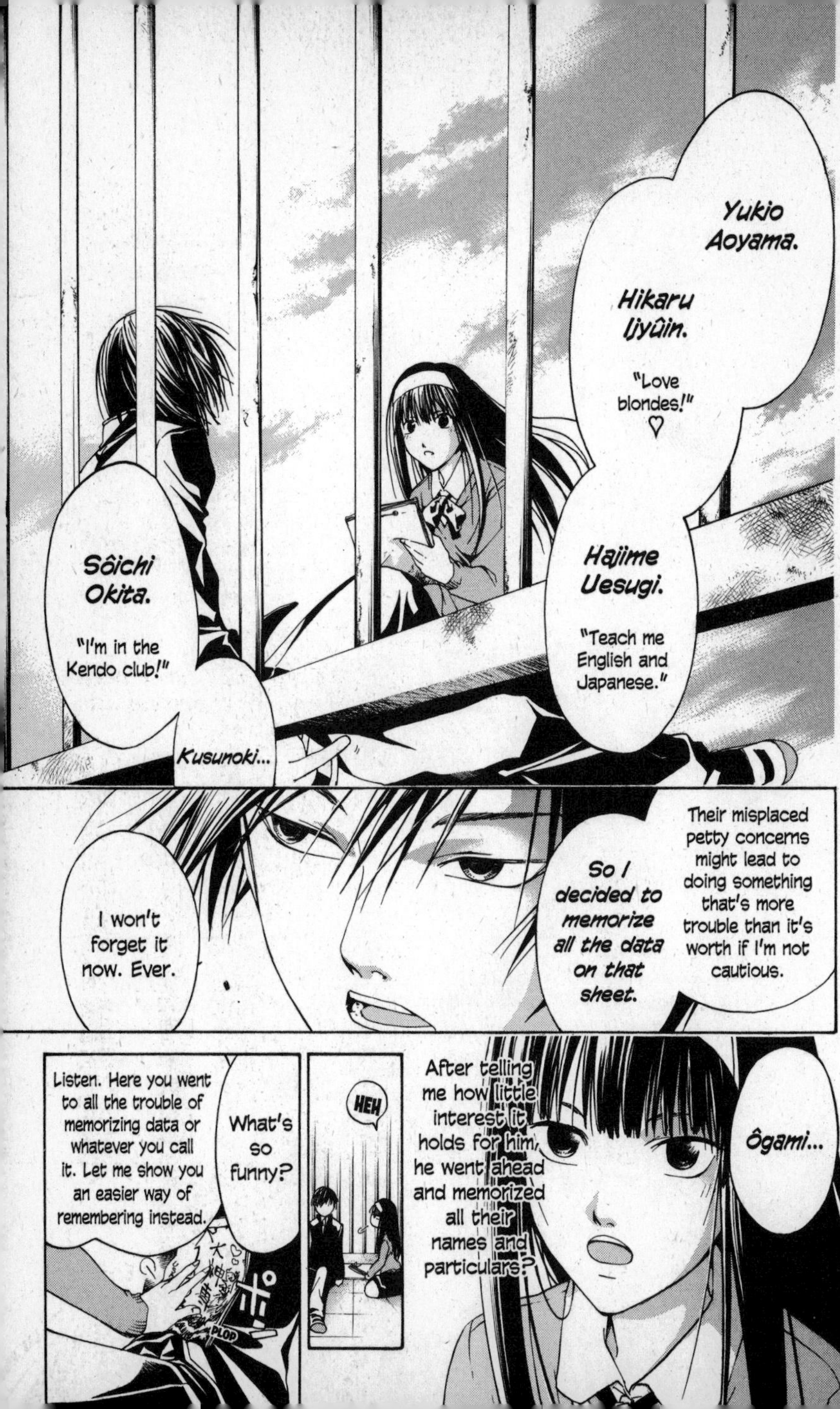
Yukio Aoyama.
Hikaru Ijyûin.
"Love blondes!" ♡
Hajime Uesugi.
"Teach me English and Japanese."
Sôichi Okita.
"I'm in the Kendo club!"
Kusunoki...
Their misplaced petty concerns might lead to doing something that's more trouble than it's worth if I'm not cautious.
So I decided to memorize all the data on that sheet.
I won't forget it now. Ever.
Ôgami...
After telling me how little interest it holds for him, he went ahead and memorized all their names and particulars?
HEH
What's so funny?
Listen. Here you went to all the trouble of memorizing data or whatever you call it. Let me show you an easier way of remembering instead.
PLOP

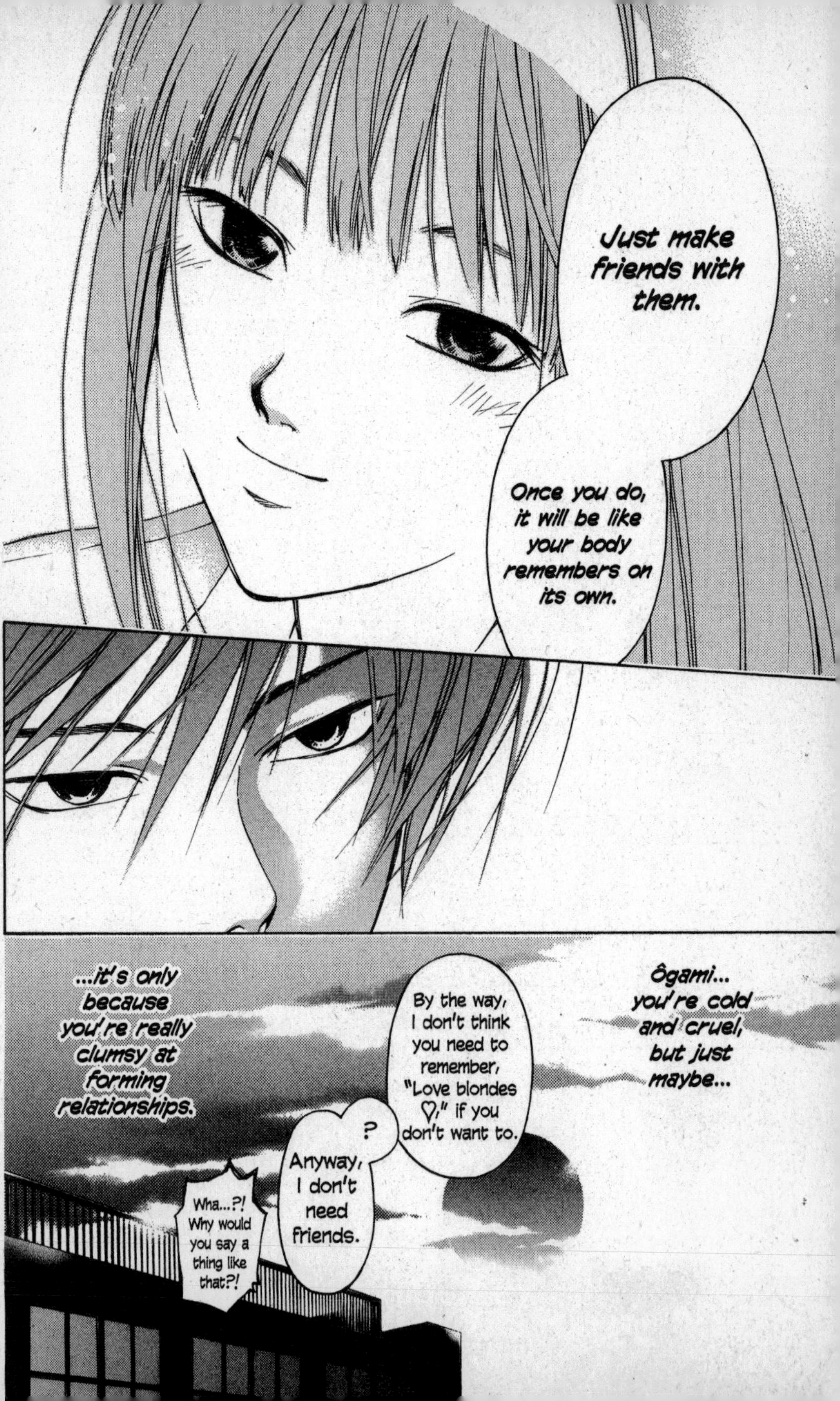
Just make friends with them.
Once you do, it will be like your body remembers on its own.
Ôgami... you're cold and cruel, but just maybe...
...it's only because you're really clumsy at forming relationships.
By the way, I don't think you need to remember, "Love blondes ♡," if you don't want to.
?
Anyway, I don't need friends.
Wha...?! Why would you say a thing like that?!

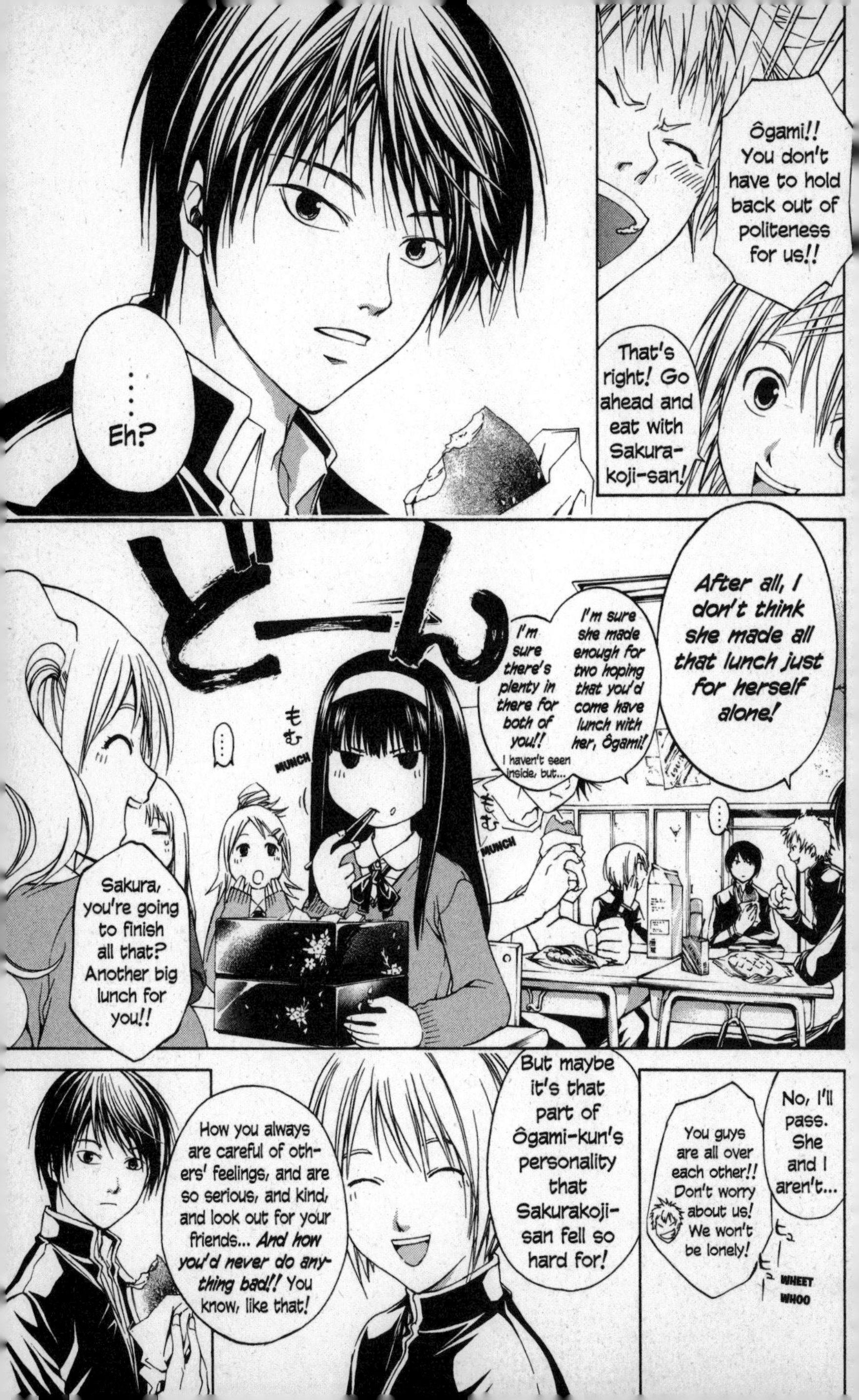
Ôgami!! You don't have to hold back out of politeness for us!!
That's right! Go ahead and eat with Sakura-koji-san!
... Eh?
After all, I don't think she made all that lunch just for herself alone!
I'm sure she made enough for two hoping that you'd come have lunch with her, Ôgami!
I'm sure there's plenty in there for both of you!!
I haven't seen inside, but...
...
どーん
もむ
MUNCH
MUNCH
...
Sakura, you're going to finish all that? Another big lunch for you!!
No, I'll pass. She and I aren't...
You guys are all over each other!! Don't worry about us! We won't be lonely!
WHEET
WHOO
But maybe it's that part of Ôgami-kun's personality that Sakurakoji-san fell so hard for!
How you always are careful of others' feelings, and are so serious, and kind, and look out for your friends... And how you'd never do anything bad!! You know, like that!

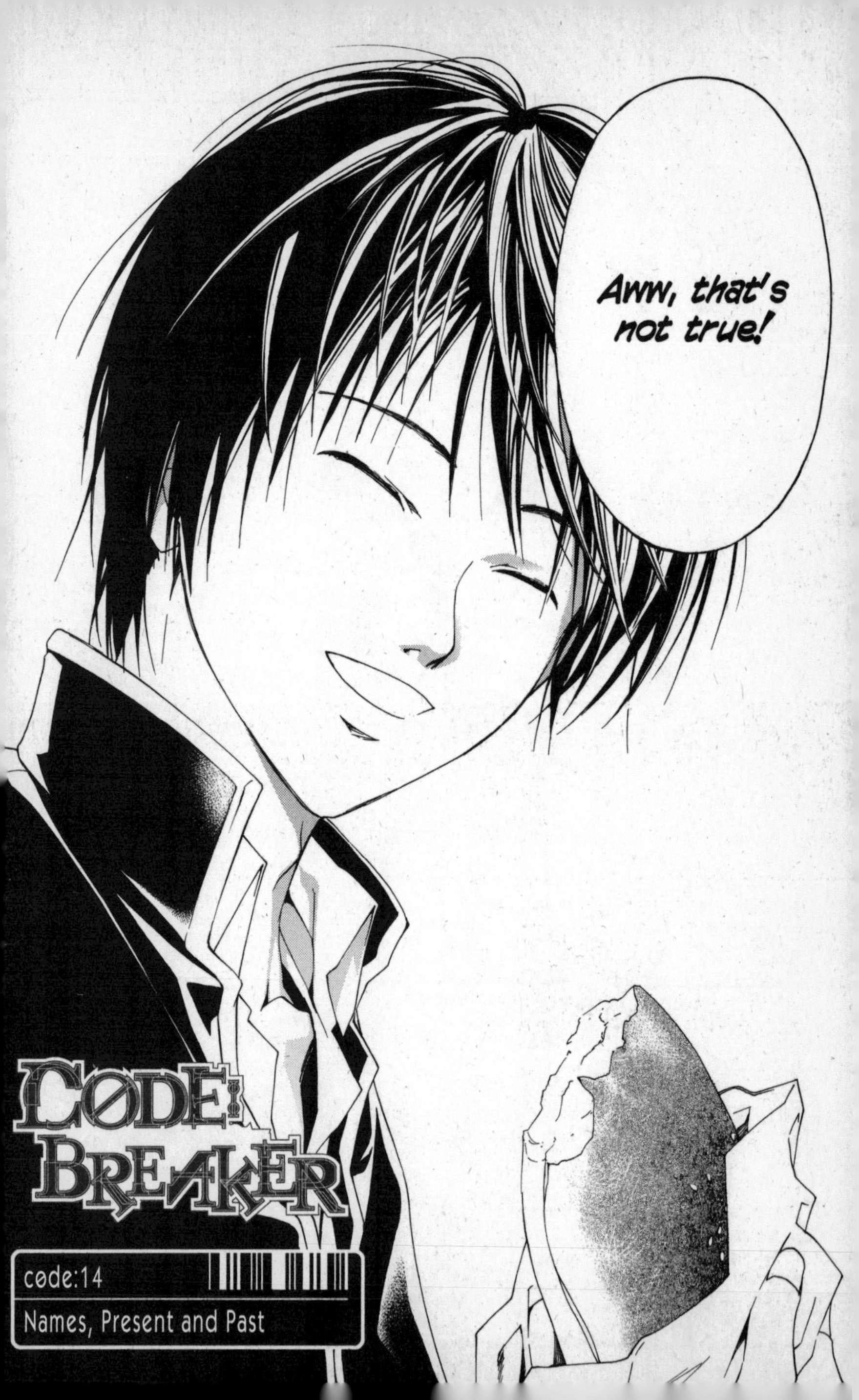
Aww, that's not true!
CODE:BREAKER
code:14
Names, Present and Past

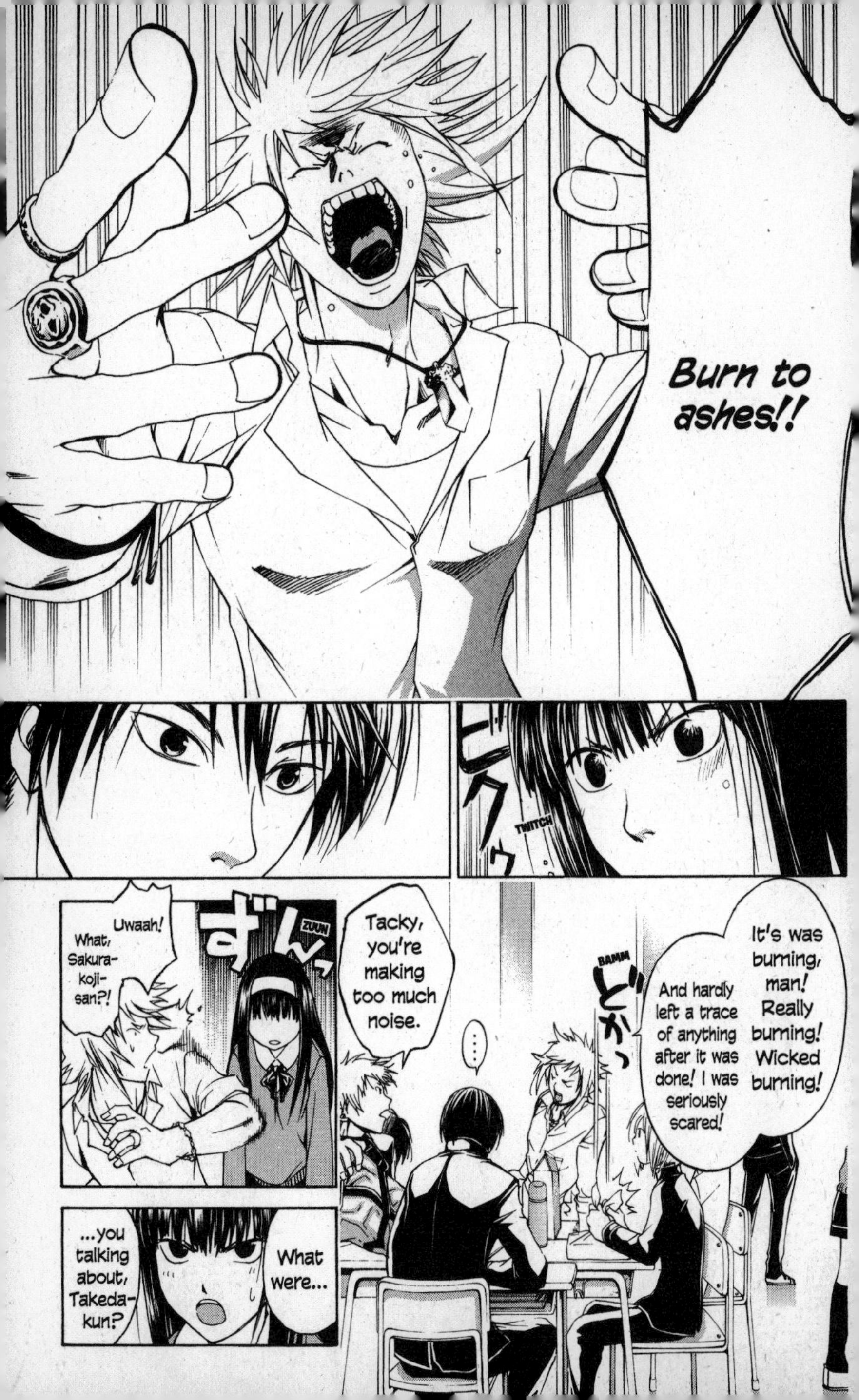

Burn to ashes!!
ビクゥ
TWITCH
It's was burning, man! Really burning! Wicked burning!
And hardly left a trace of anything after it was done! I was seriously scared!
BAMM
どかっ
...
Tacky, you're making too much noise.
ずん
ZUUN
Uwaah! What, Sakura-koji-san?!
What were...
...you talking about, Takeda-kun?

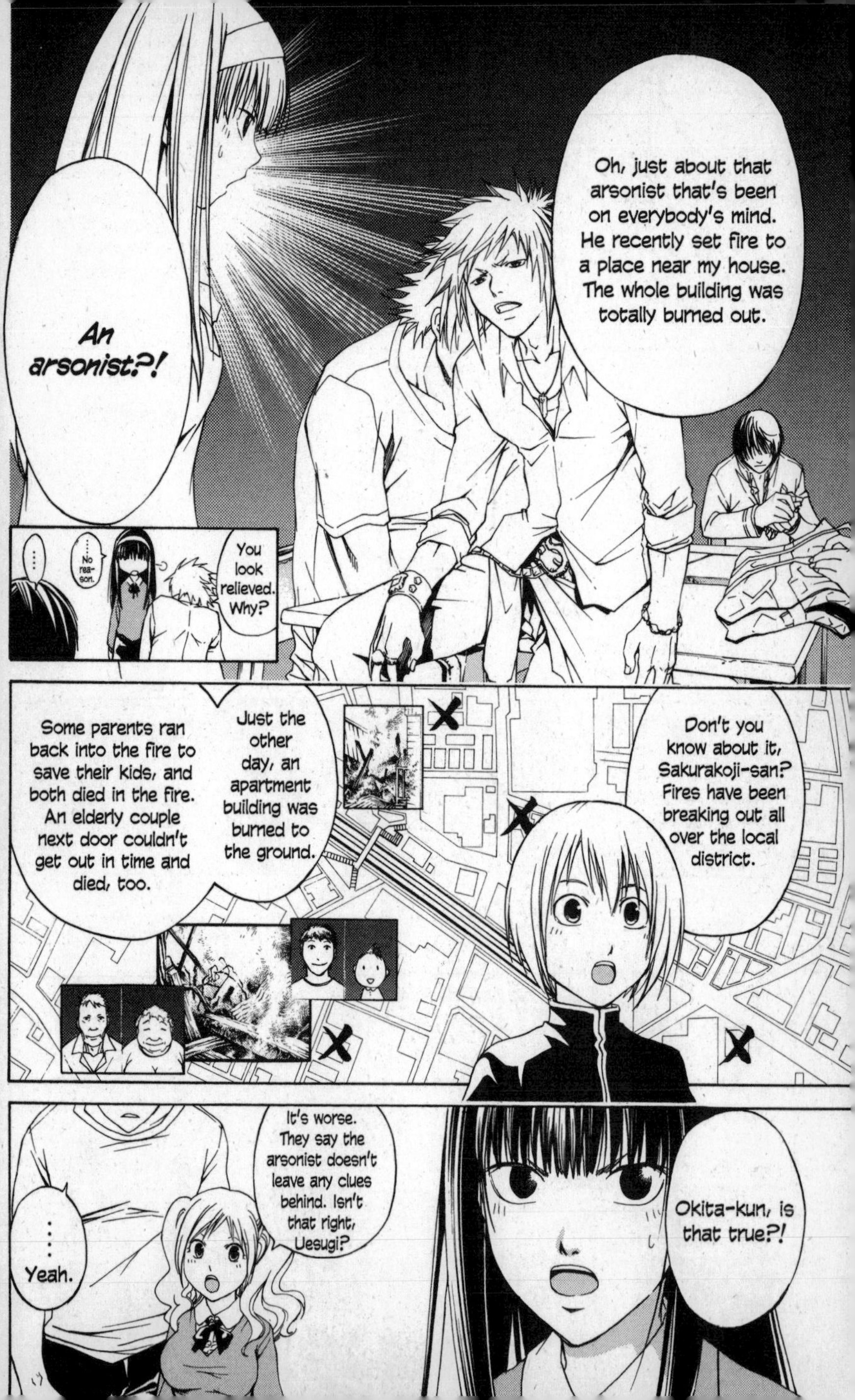
Oh, just about that arsonist that's been on everybody's mind. He recently set fire to a place near my house. The whole building was totally burned out.
An arsonist?!
You look relieved. Why?
... No reason.
...
Don't you know about it, Sakurakoji-san? Fires have been breaking out all over the local district.
Just the other day, an apartment building was burned to the ground.
Some parents ran back into the fire to save their kids, and both died in the fire. An elderly couple next door couldn't get out in time and died, too.
Okita-kun, is that true?!
It's worse. They say the arsonist doesn't leave any clues behind. Isn't that right, Uesugi?
... Yeah.

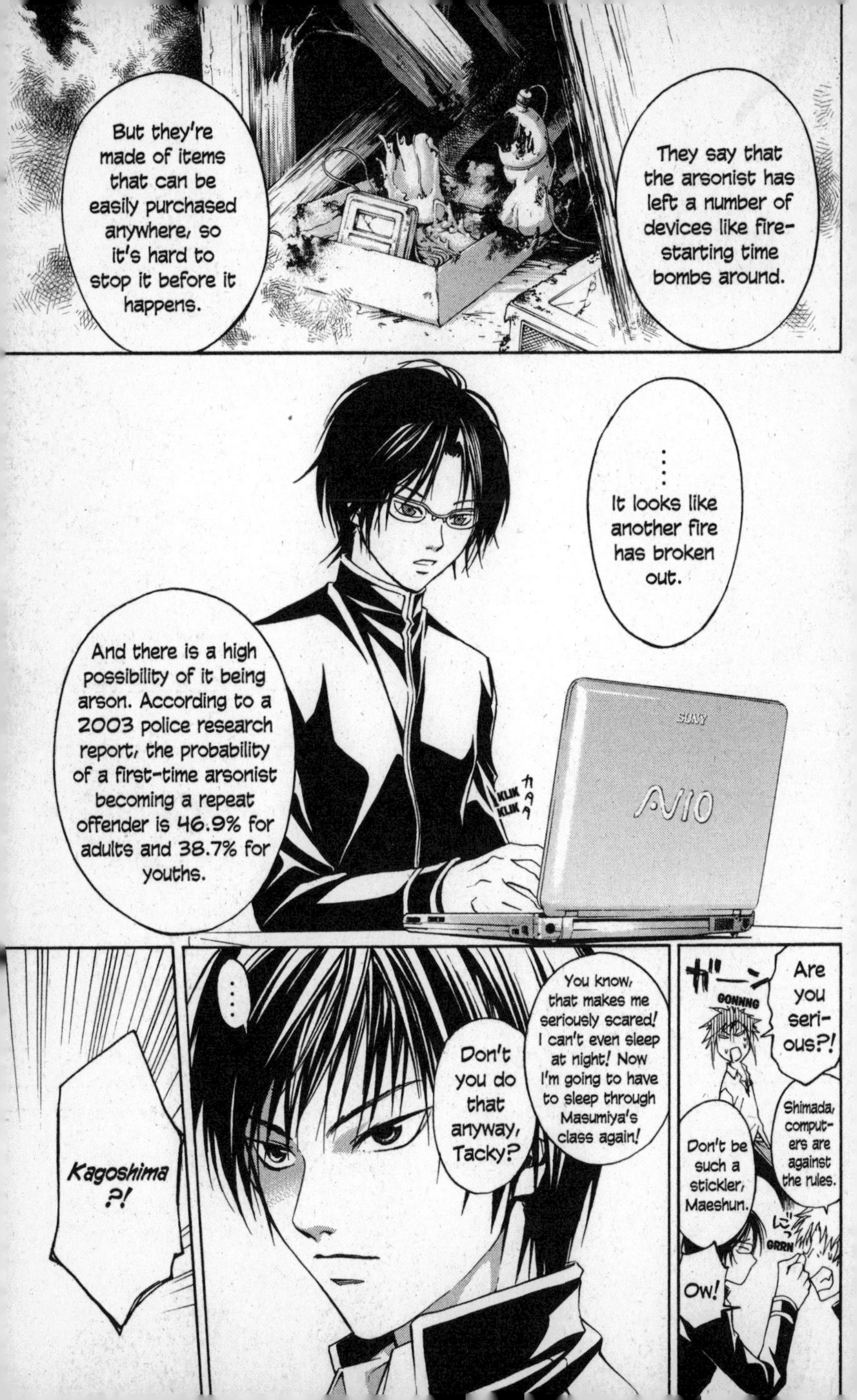
They say that the arsonist has left a number of devices like fire-starting time bombs around.
But they're made of items that can be easily purchased anywhere, so it's hard to stop it before it happens.
...
It looks like another fire has broken out.
And there is a high possibility of it being arson. According to a 2003 police research report, the probability of a first-time arsonist becoming a repeat offender is 46.9% for adults and 38.7% for youths.
KLIK KLIK
SONY
VAIO
Are you seri-ous?!
GONNNG
Shimada, computers are against the rules.
Don't be such a stickler, Maeshun.
GRRN
Ow!
You know, that makes me seriously scared! I can't even sleep at night! Now I'm going to have to sleep through Masumiya's class again!
Don't you do that anyway, Tacky?
....
Kagoshima?!

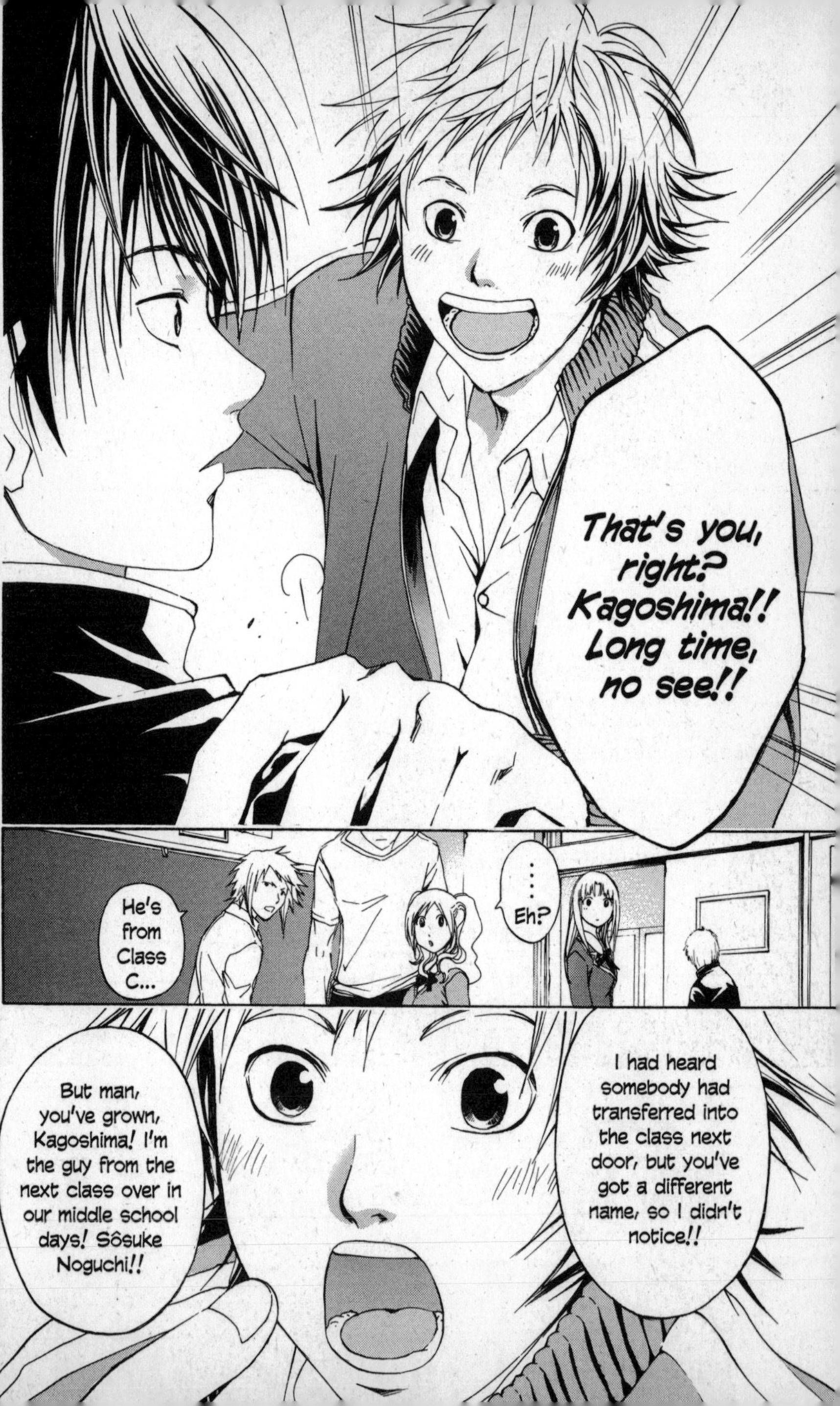
That's you, right? Kagoshima!! Long time, no see!!
...Eh?
He's from Class C...
I had heard somebody had transferred into the class next door, but you've got a different name, so I didn't notice!!
But man, you've grown, Kagoshima! I'm the guy from the next class over in our middle school days! Sôsuke Noguchi!!

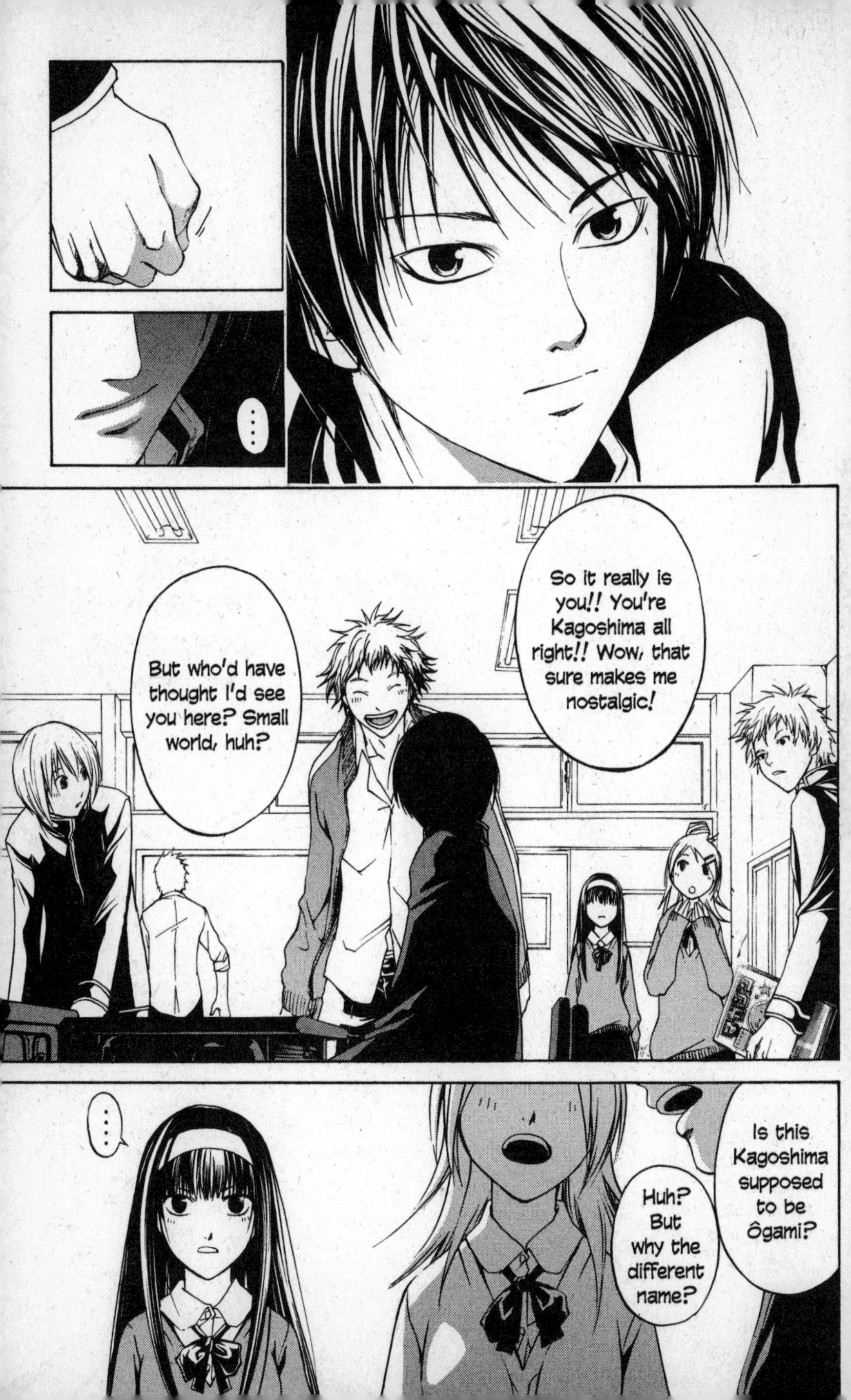
....
So it really is you!! You're Kagoshima all right!! Wow, that sure makes me nostalgic!
But who'd have thought I'd see you here? Small world, huh?
Is this Kagoshima supposed to be Ôgami?
Huh? But why the different name?
....

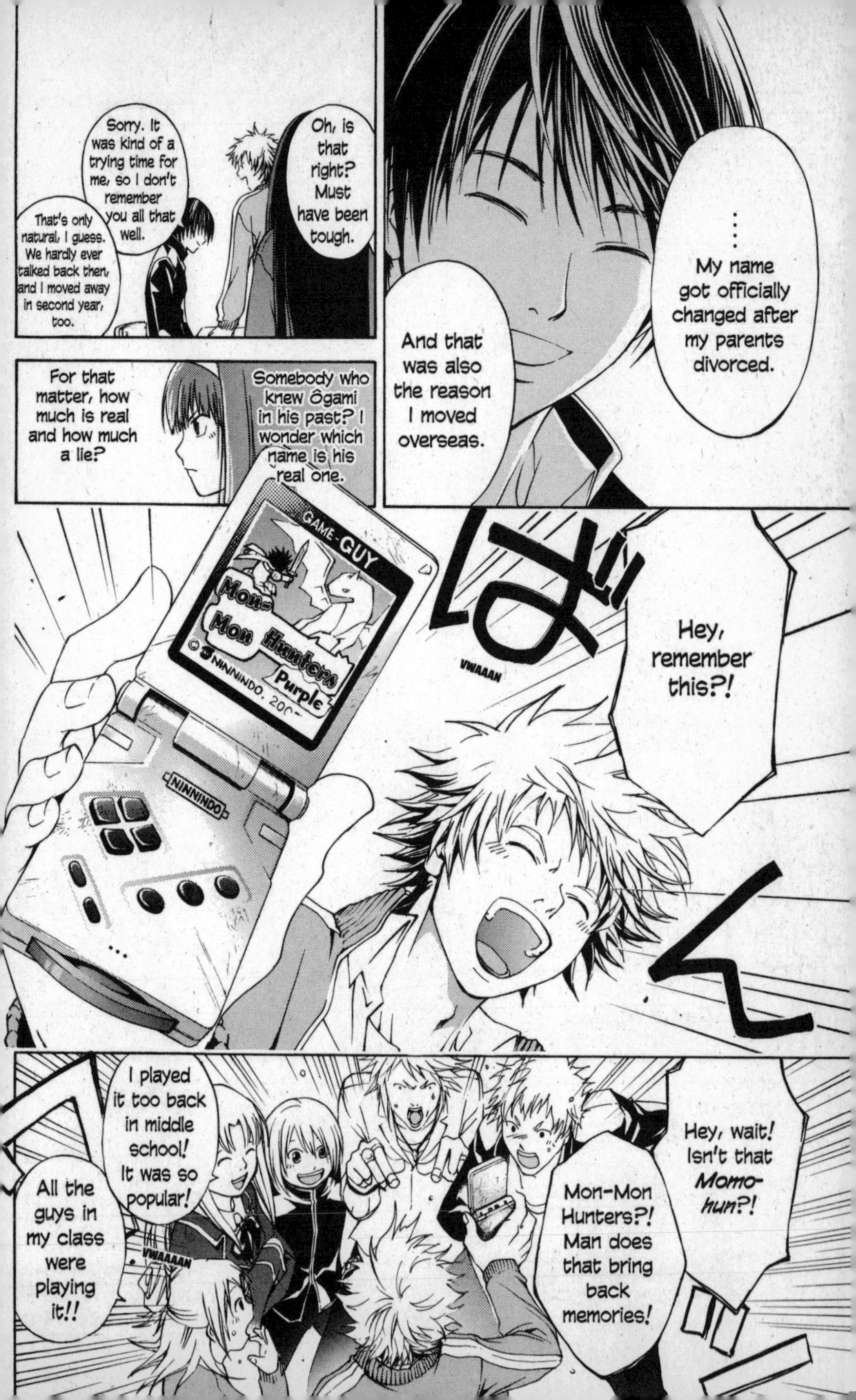

...
My name got officially changed after my parents divorced.
And that was also the reason I moved overseas.
Oh, is that right? Must have been tough.
Sorry. It was kind of a trying time for me, so I don't remember you all that well.
That's only natural, I guess. We hardly ever talked back then, and I moved away in second year, too.
Somebody who knew Ôgami in his past? I wonder which name is his real one.
For that matter, how much is real and how much a lie?
Hey, remember this?!
VWAAAN
GAME-GUY
Mon-Mon Hunters Purple
© NINNINDO. 200-
NINNINDO
...
Hey, wait! Isn't that *Momo-hun*?!
Mon-Mon Hunters?! Man does that bring back memories!
I played it too back in middle school! It was so popular!
VWAAAAN
All the guys in my class were playing it!!

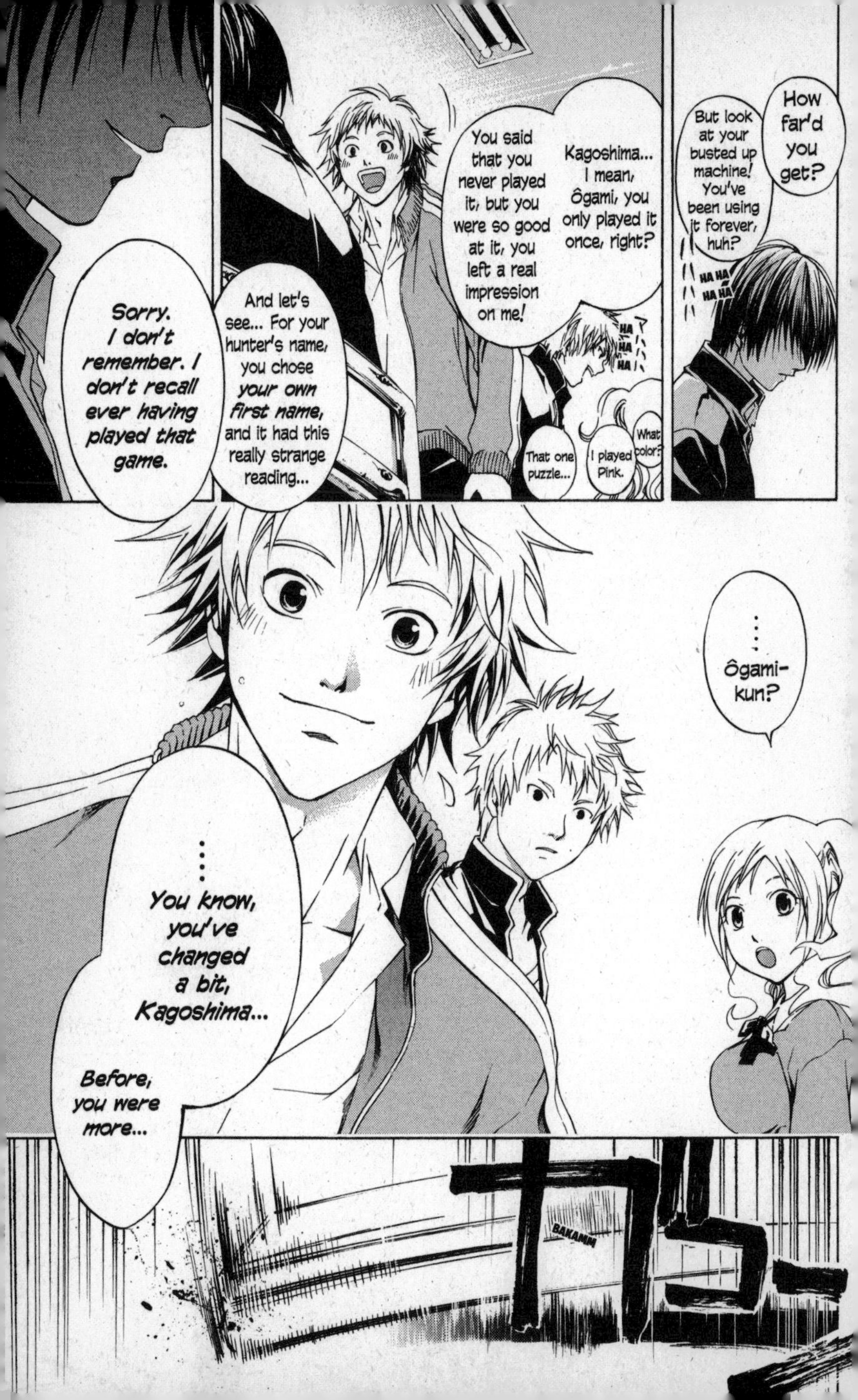
How far'd you get?
But look at your busted up machine! You've been using it forever, huh?
HA HA HA HA
Kagoshima... I mean, Ôgami, you only played it once, right?
You said that you never played it, but you were so good at it, you left a real impression on me!
HA HA HA
What color?
I played Pink.
That one puzzle...
And let's see... For your hunter's name, you chose *your own first name*, and it had this really strange reading...
Sorry. I don't remember. I don't recall ever having played that game.
... Ôgami-kun?
... You know, you've changed a bit, Kagoshima...
Before, you were more...
BAKAMM

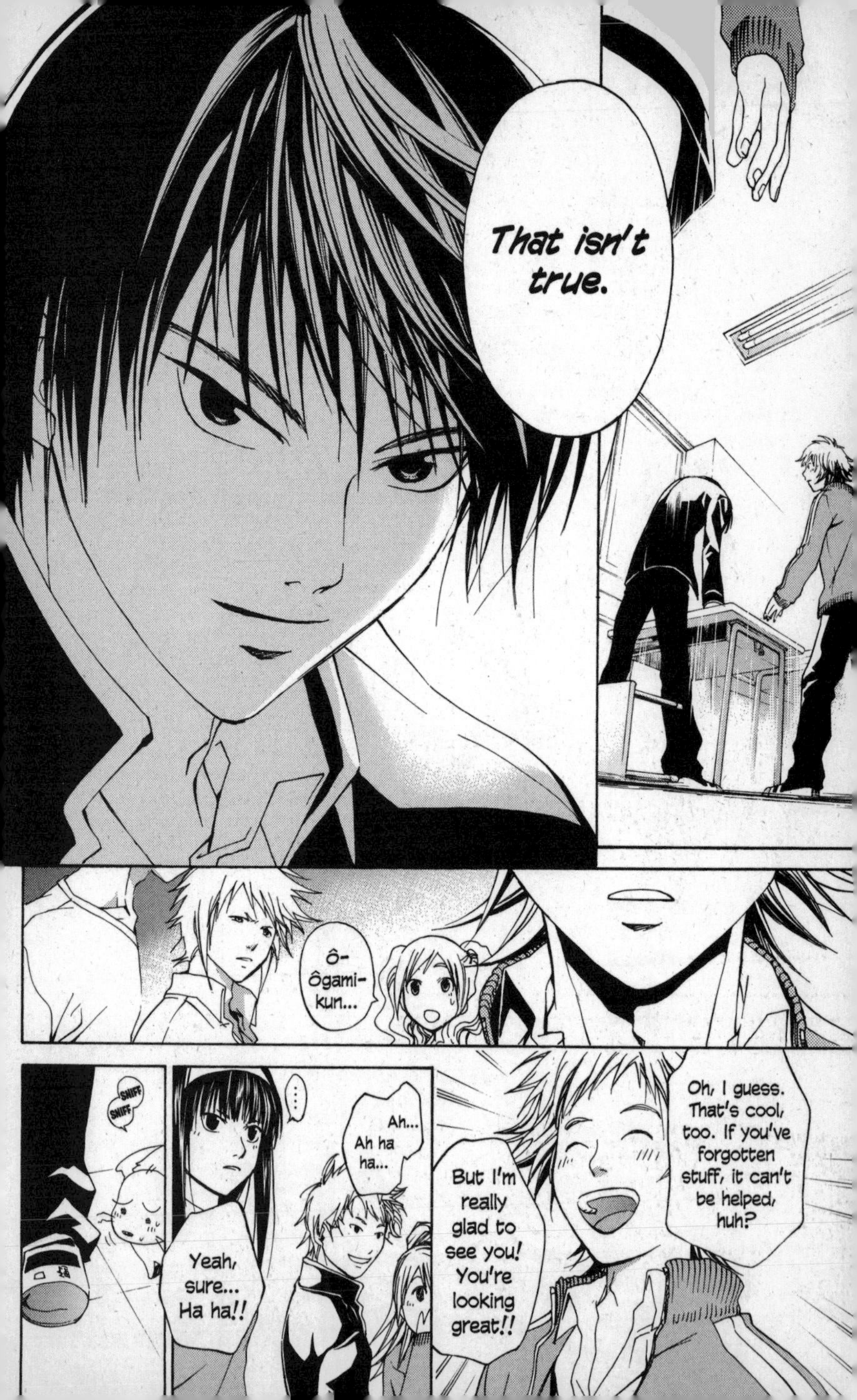
That isn't true.
Ô-Ôgami-kun...
Oh, I guess. That's cool, too. If you've forgotten stuff, it can't be helped, huh?
But I'm really glad to see you! You're looking great!!
Ah... Ah ha ha...
...
Yeah, sure... Ha ha!!
SNIFF SNIFF

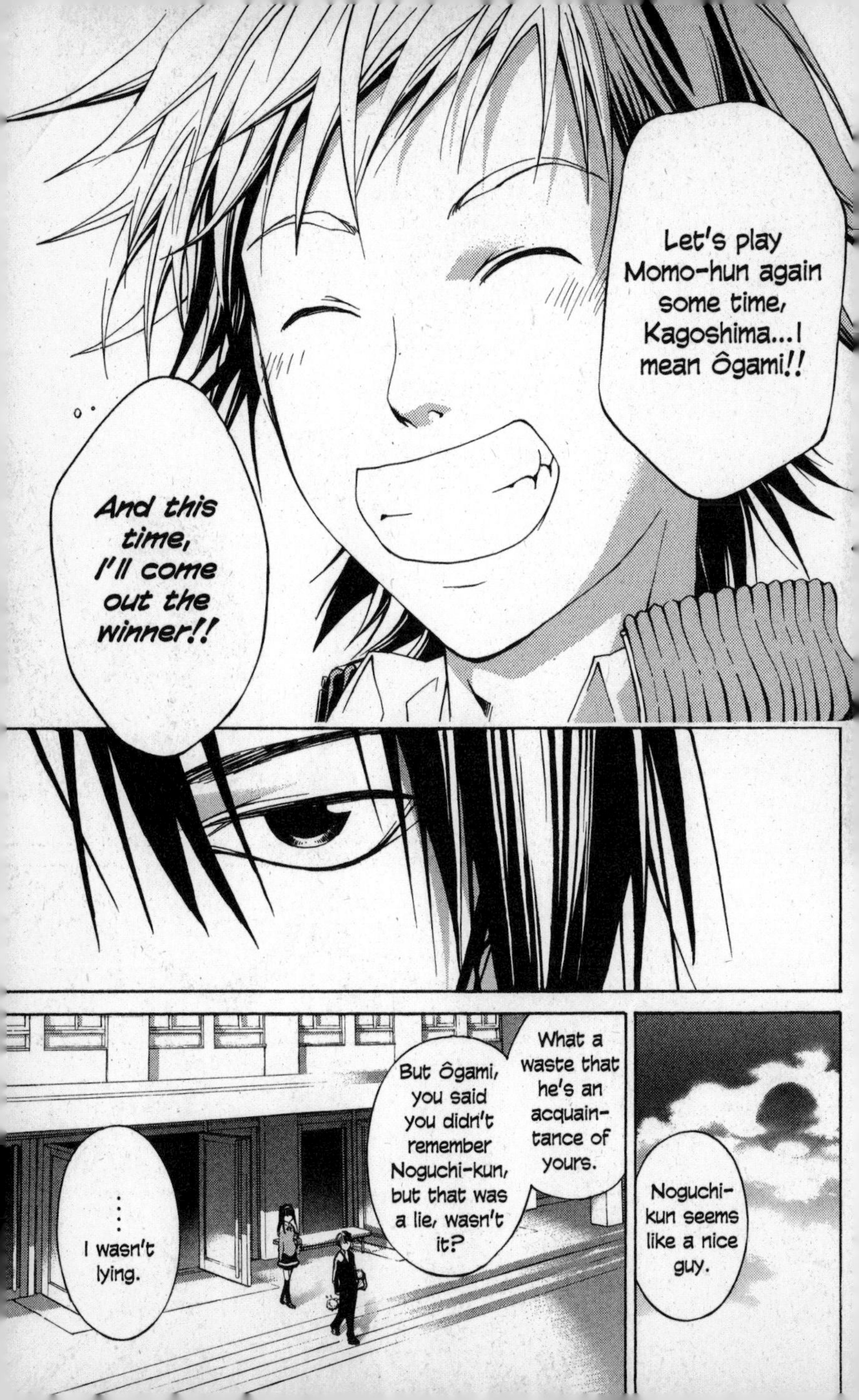
Let's play Momo-hun again some time, Kagoshima...I mean Ôgami!!
And this time, I'll come out the winner!!
Noguchi-kun seems like a nice guy.
What a waste that he's an acquaintance of yours.
But Ôgami, you said you didn't remember Noguchi-kun, but that was a lie, wasn't it?
.... I wasn't lying.

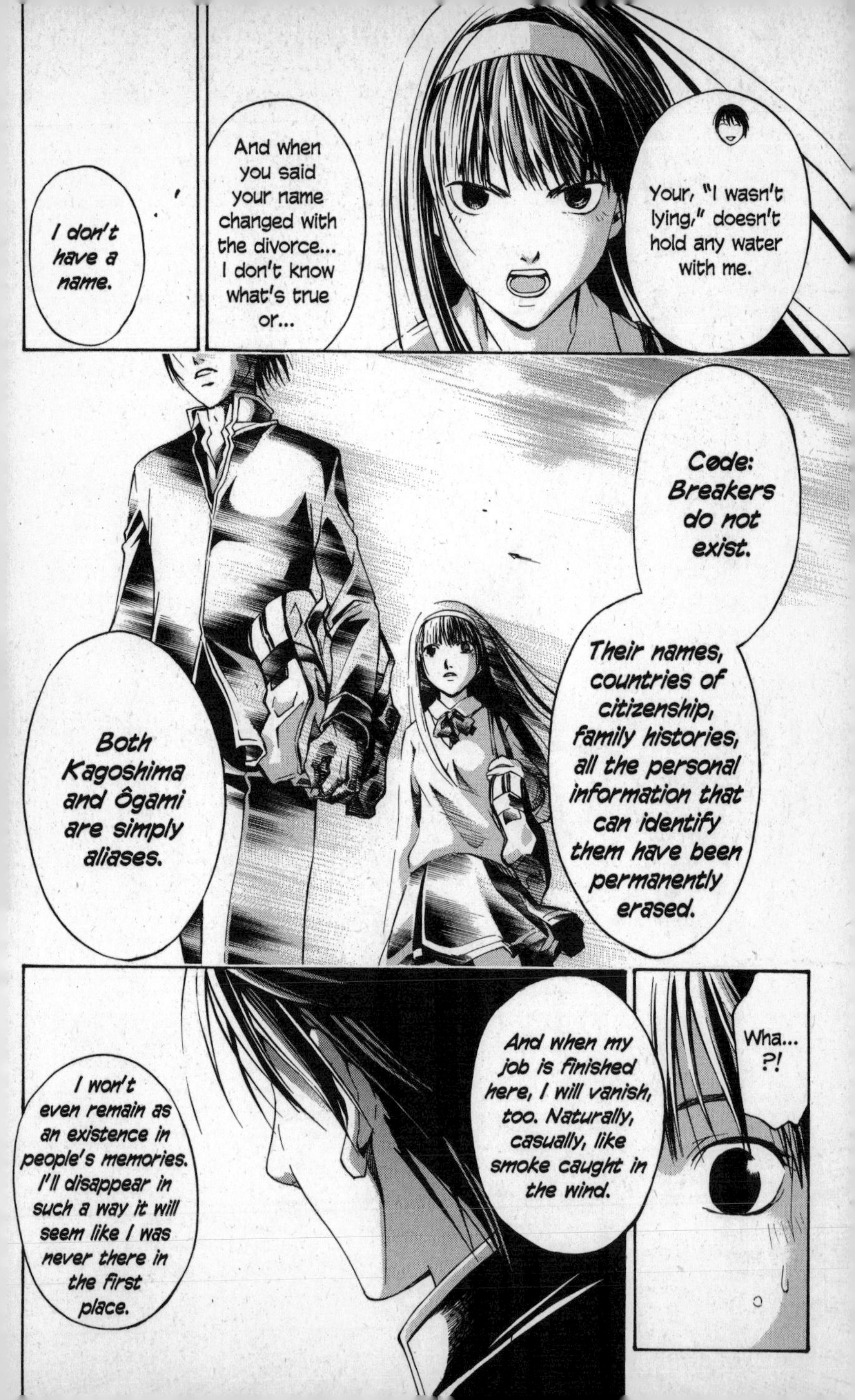
Your, "I wasn't lying," doesn't hold any water with me.
And when you said your name changed with the divorce... I don't know what's true or...
I don't have a name.
Code: Breakers do not exist.
Their names, countries of citizenship, family histories, all the personal information that can identify them have been permanently erased.
Both Kagoshima and Ôgami are simply aliases.
Wha...?!
And when my job is finished here, I will vanish, too. Naturally, casually, like smoke caught in the wind.
I won't even remain as an existence in people's memories. I'll disappear in such a way it will seem like I was never there in the first place.

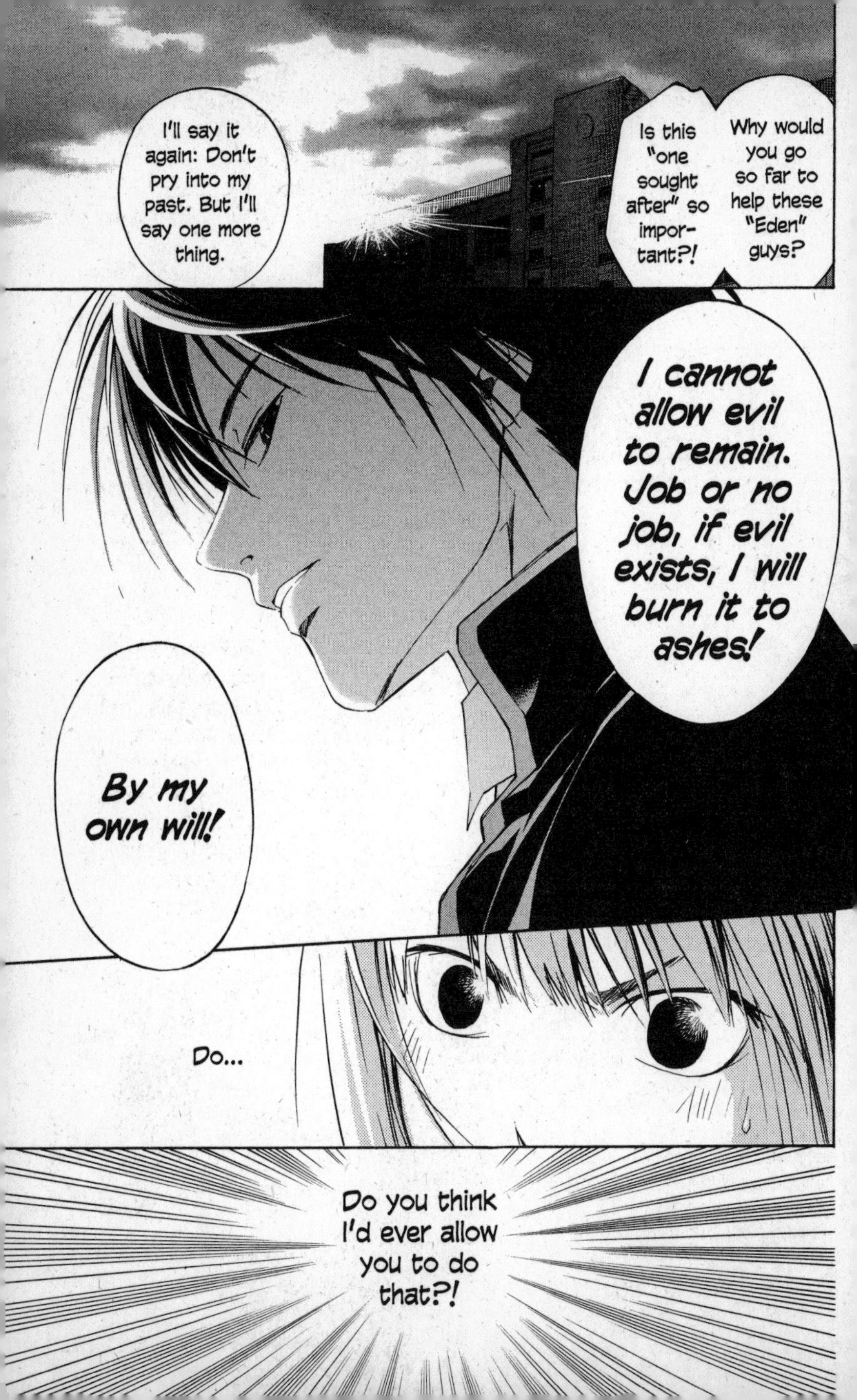
Why would you go so far to help these "Eden" guys?
Is this "one sought after" so important?!
I'll say it again: Don't pry into my past. But I'll say one more thing.
I cannot allow evil to remain. Job or no job, if evil exists, I will burn it to ashes!
By my own will!
Do...
Do you think I'd ever allow you to do that?!

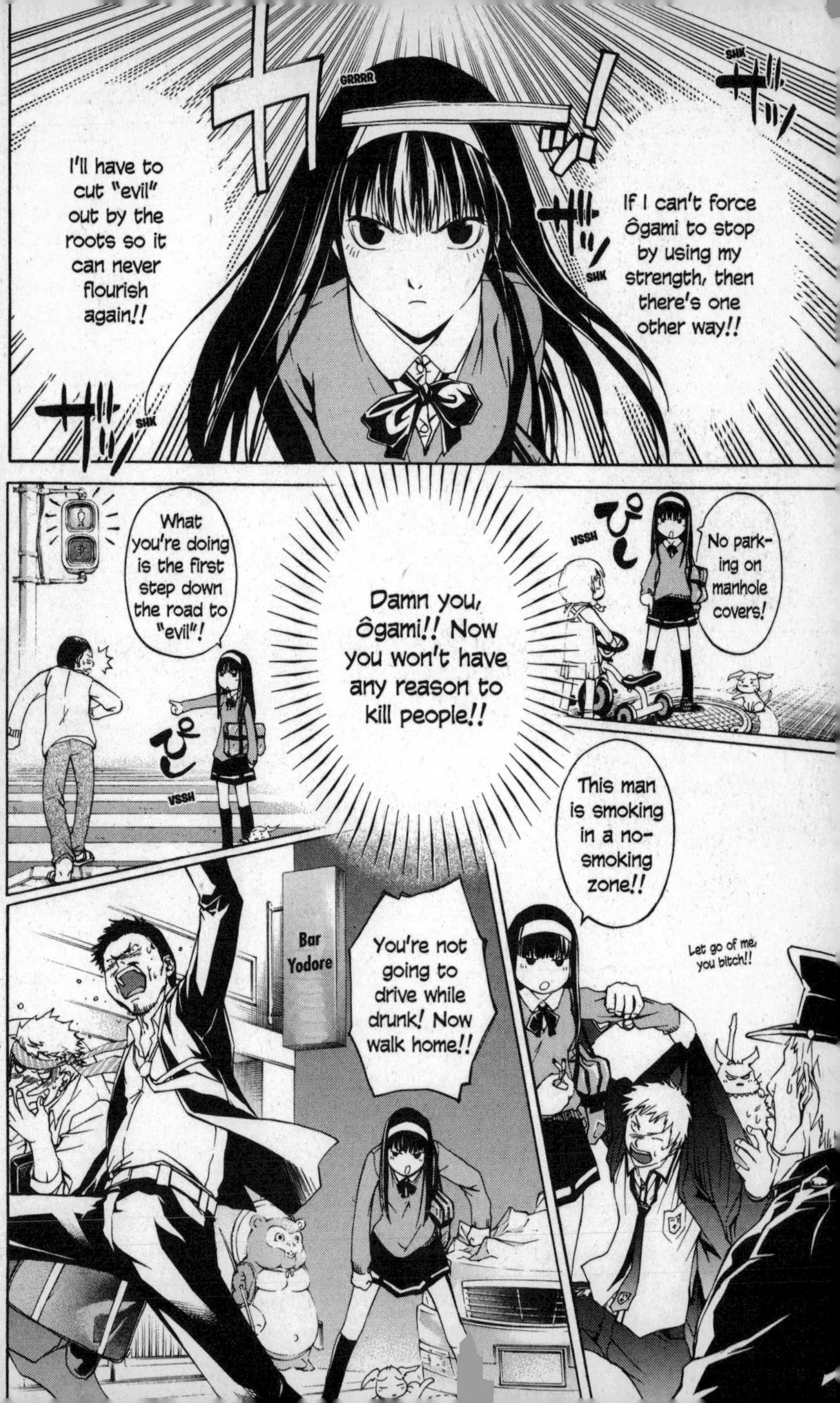
SHK
GRRRR
If I can't force Ôgami to stop by using my strength, then there's one other way!!
SHK
I'll have to cut "evil" out by the roots so it can never flourish again!!
SHK
VSSH
No parking-ing on manhole covers!
Damn you, Ôgami!! Now you won't have any reason to kill people!!
What you're doing is the first step down the road to "evil"!
VSSH
This man is smoking in a no-smoking zone!!
Let go of me, you bitch!!
Bar Yodore
You're not going to drive while drunk! Now walk home!!

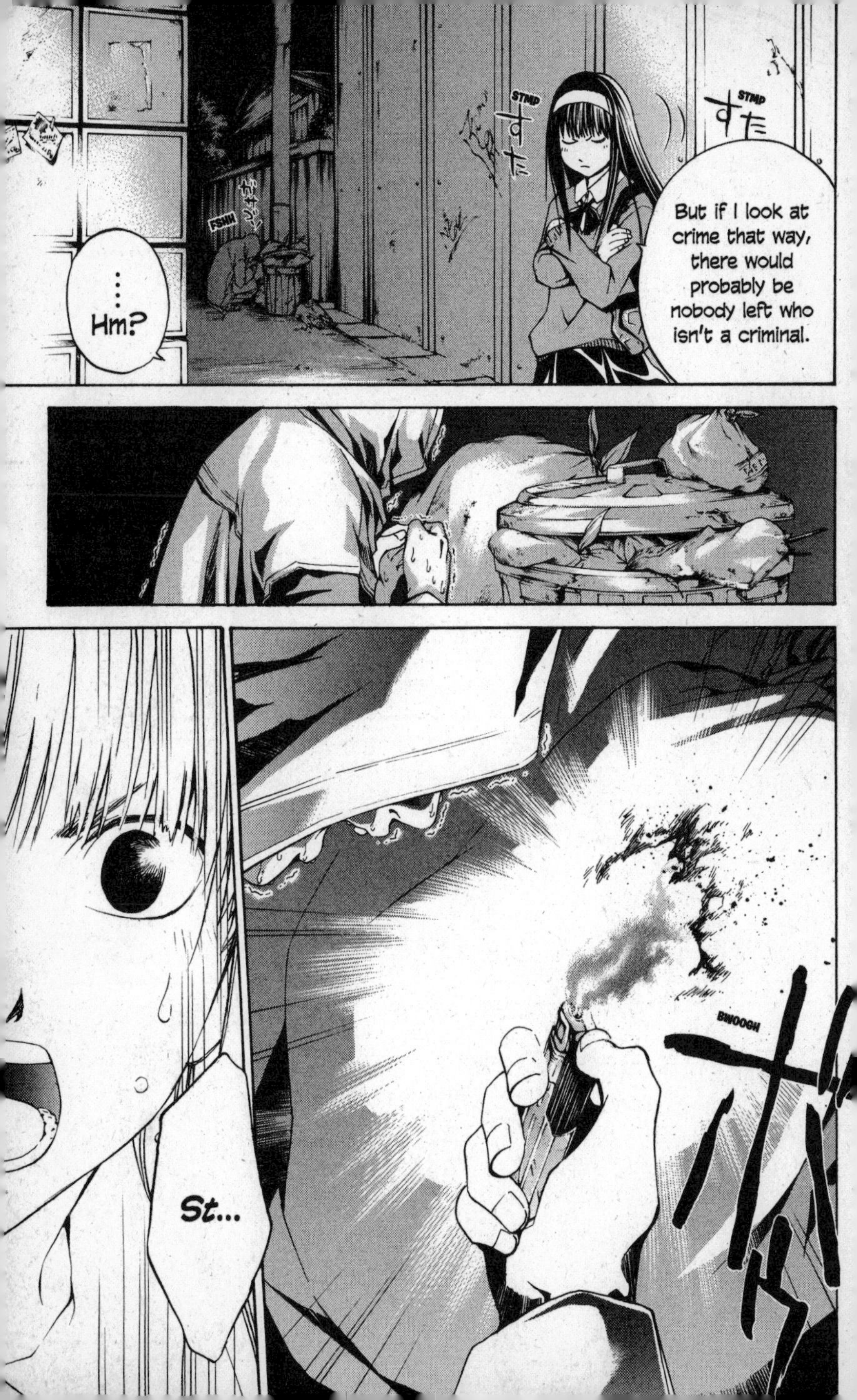
STMP
すた
But if I look at crime that way, there would probably be nobody left who isn't a criminal.
STMP
すた
FSHH
...
Hm?
BWOOGH
St...

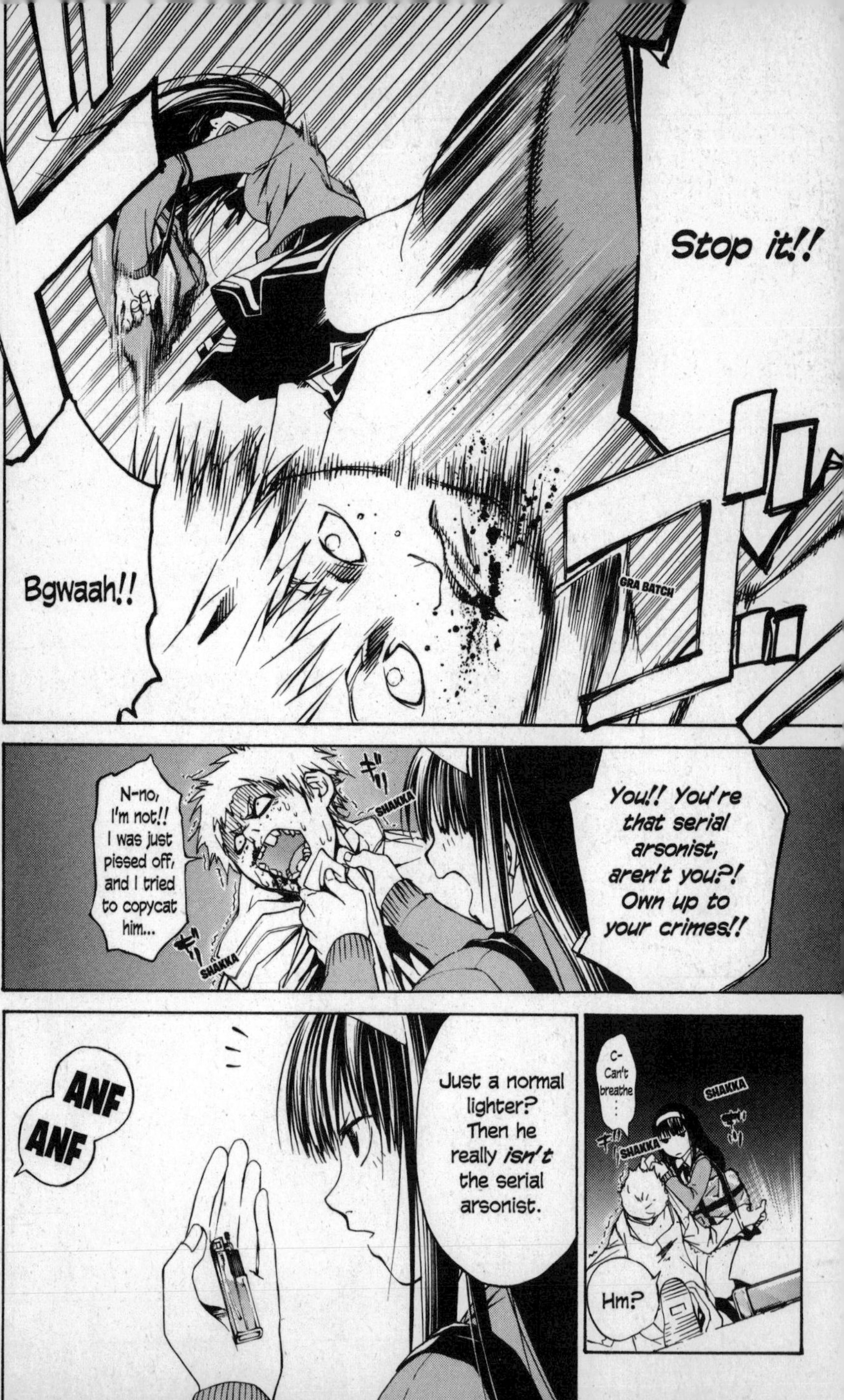
Stop it!!
GRA BATCH
Bgwaah!!
You!! You're that serial arsonist, aren't you?! Own up to your crimes!!
SHAKKA
N-no, I'm not!! I was just pissed off, and I tried to copycat him...
SHAKKA
C- Can't breathe...
SHAKKA
SHAKKA
Hm?
Just a normal lighter? Then he really *isn't* the serial arsonist.
ANF ANF

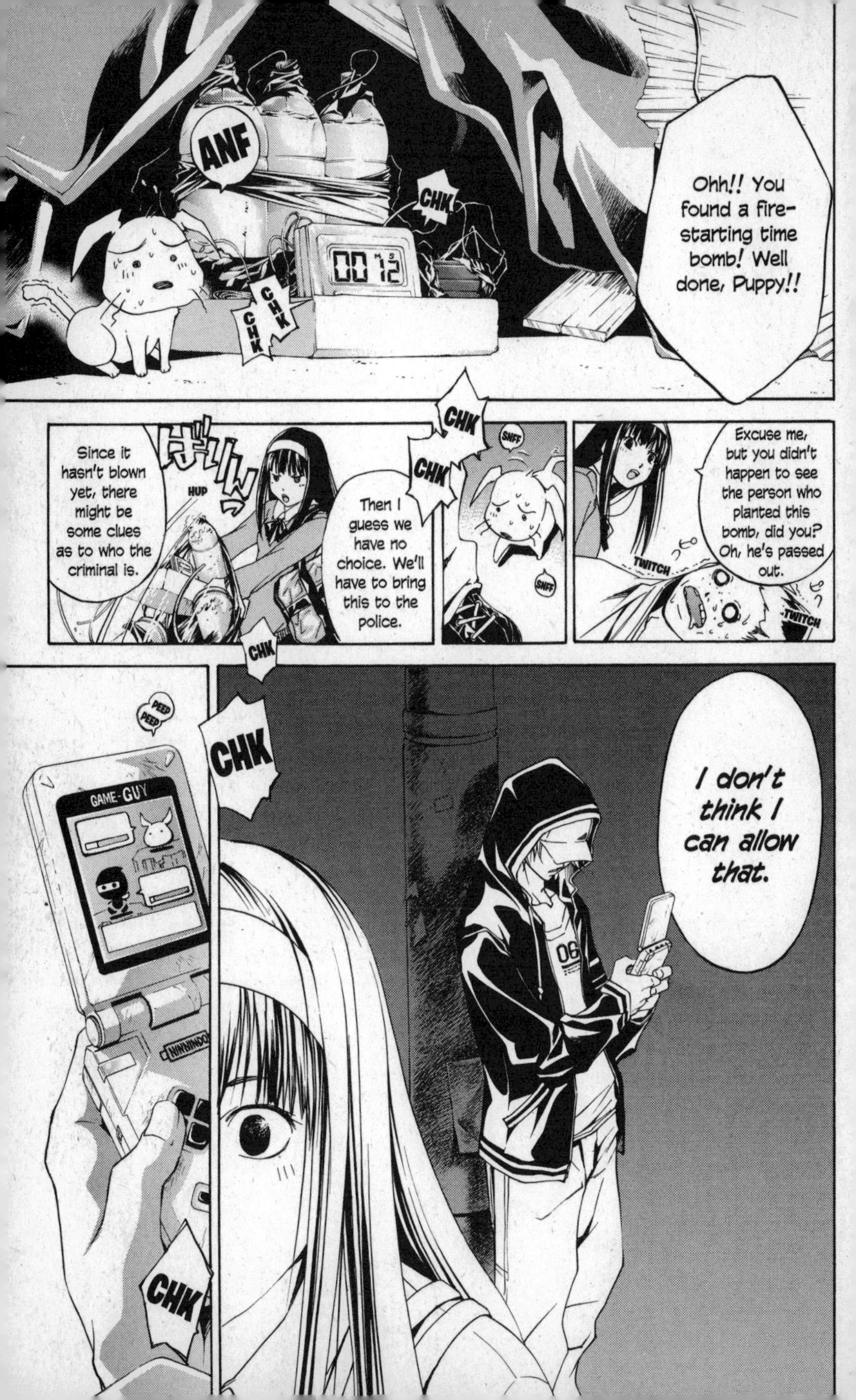
Ohh!! You found a fire-starting time bomb! Well done, Puppy!!
ANF
CHK
CHK
CHK
Excuse me, but you didn't happen to see the person who planted this bomb, did you? Oh, he's passed out.
TWITCH
TWITCH
SNFF
SNFF
CHK
CHK
Since it hasn't blown yet, there might be some clues as to who the criminal is.
HUP
Then I guess we have no choice. We'll have to bring this to the police.
CHK
I don't think I can allow that.
CHK
PEEP PEEP
GAME-GUY
CHK

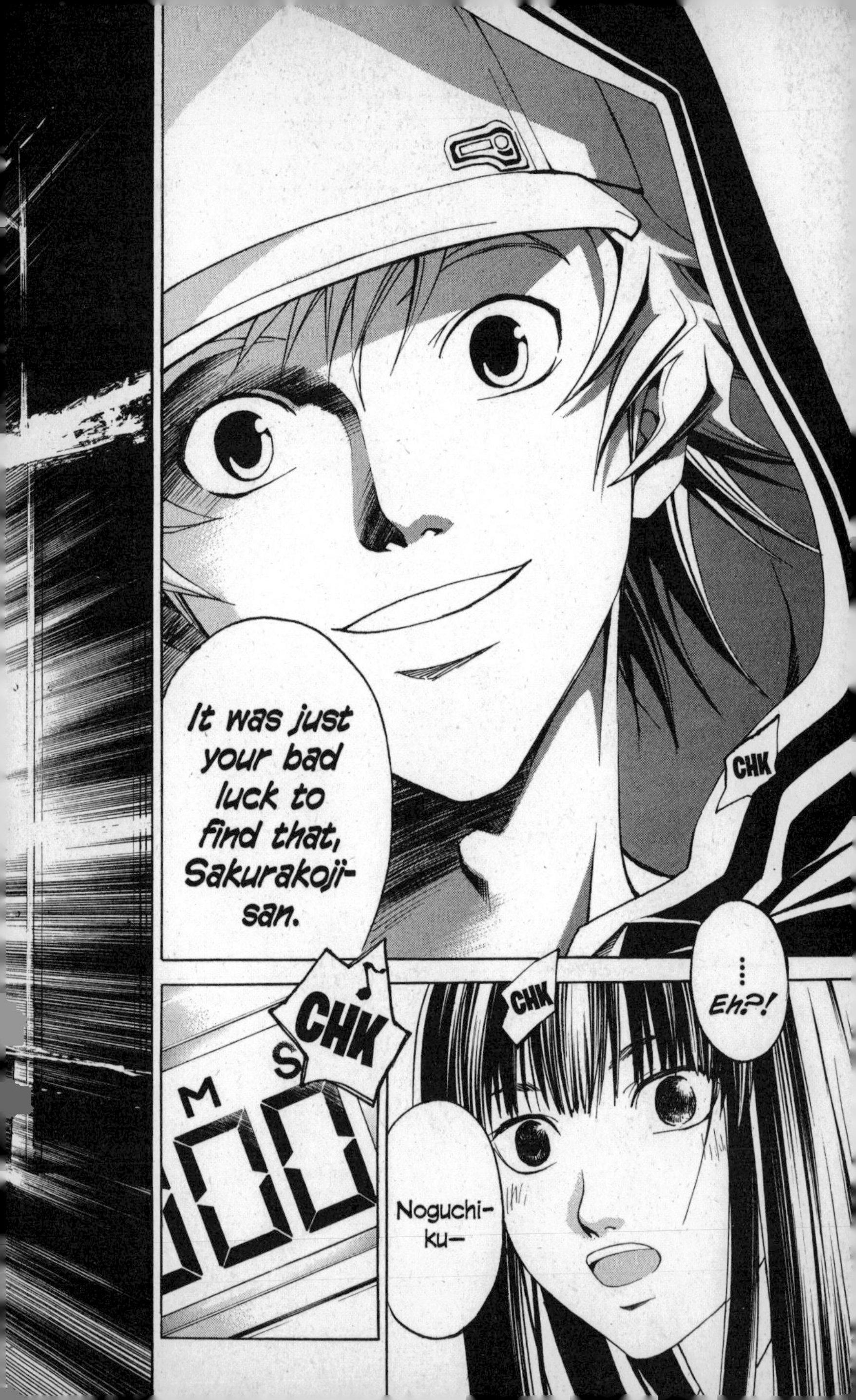
It was just your bad luck to find that, Sakurakoji-san.
CHK
...Eh?!
CHK
Noguchi-ku—
CHK
M
S

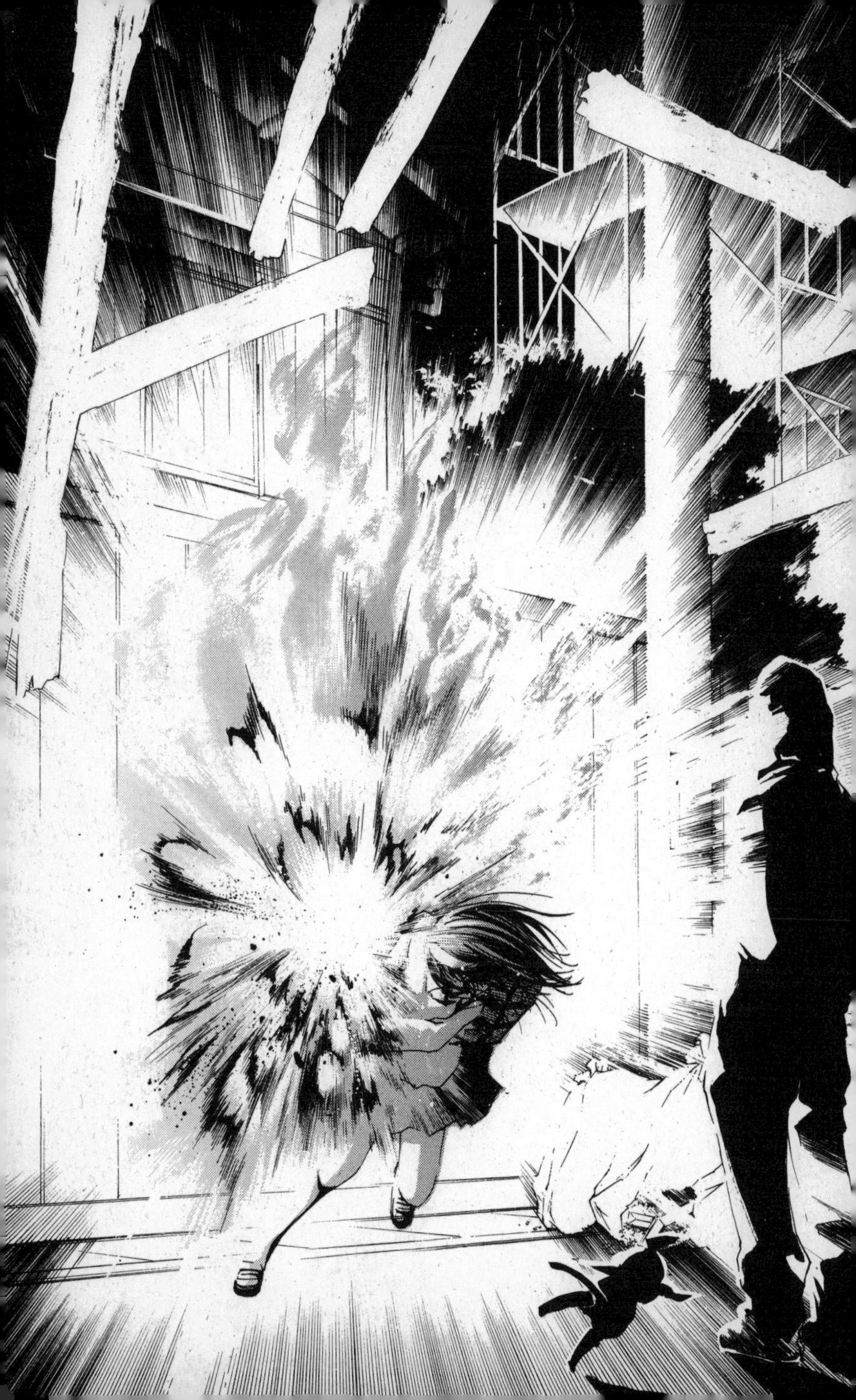

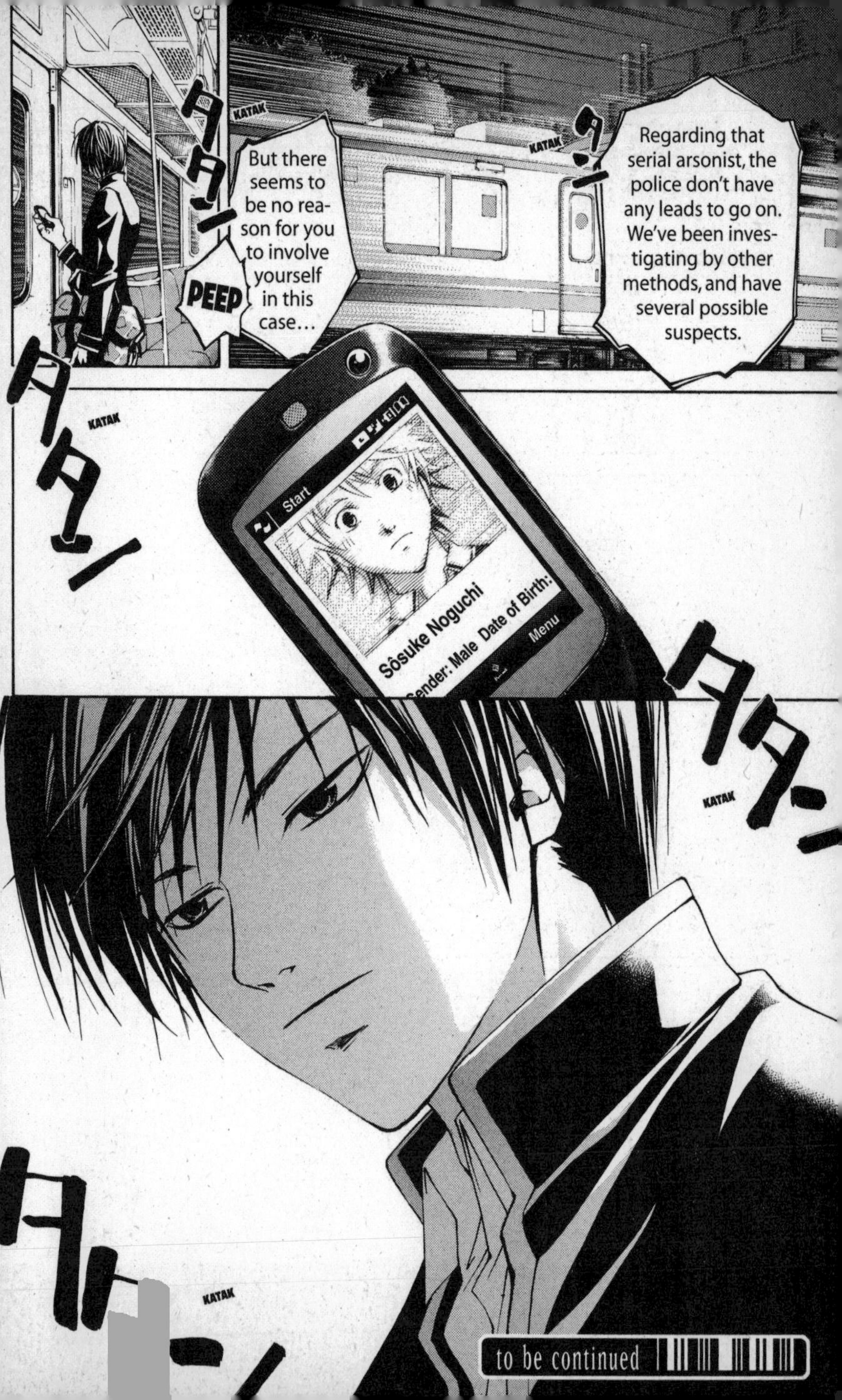
KATAK
Regarding that serial arsonist, the police don't have any leads to go on. We've been investigating by other methods, and have several possible suspects.
KATAK
But there seems to be no reason for you to involve yourself in this case…
PEEP
Start
Sôsuke Noguchi
Gender: Male Date of Birth:
Menu
KATAK
KATAK
KATAK
to be continued

Kamijyo Info

Sakura's Blue Flame

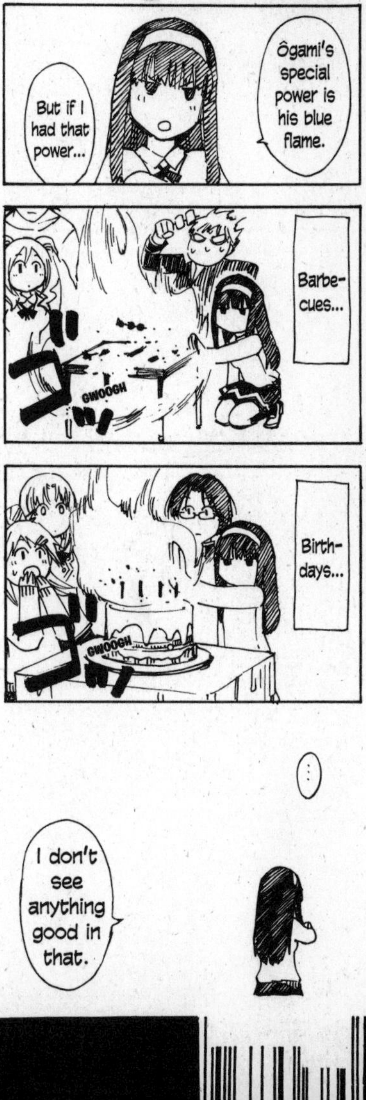
Ôgami's special power is his blue flame.
But if I had that power...
Barbe-cues...
GWOOGH
Birth-days...
GWOOGH
...
I don't see anything good in that.

Sakura's Magnetic Abilities

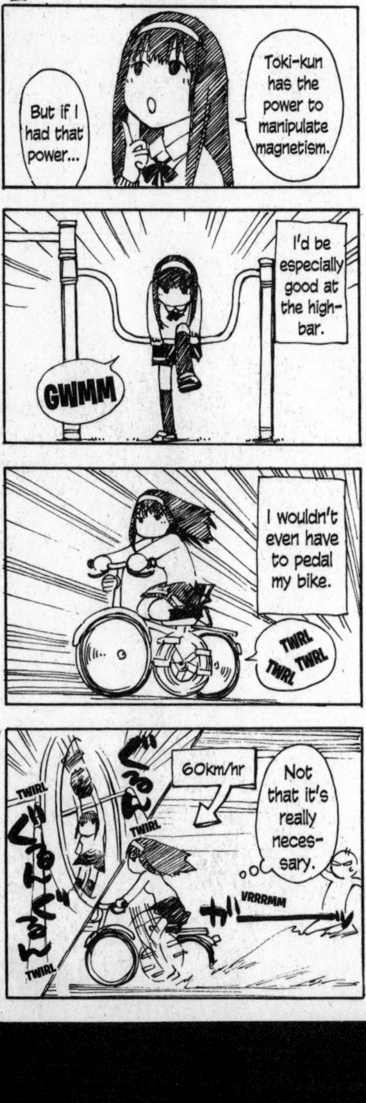
Toki-kun has the power to manipulate magnetism.
But if I had that power...
I'd be especially good at the high-bar.
GWMM
I wouldn't even have to pedal my bike.
TWRL TWRL TWRL
60km/hr
Not that it's really neces-sary.
TWIRL
TWIRL
TWIRL
VRRRMM

Kamijyo Info

The Greatest Battle in History

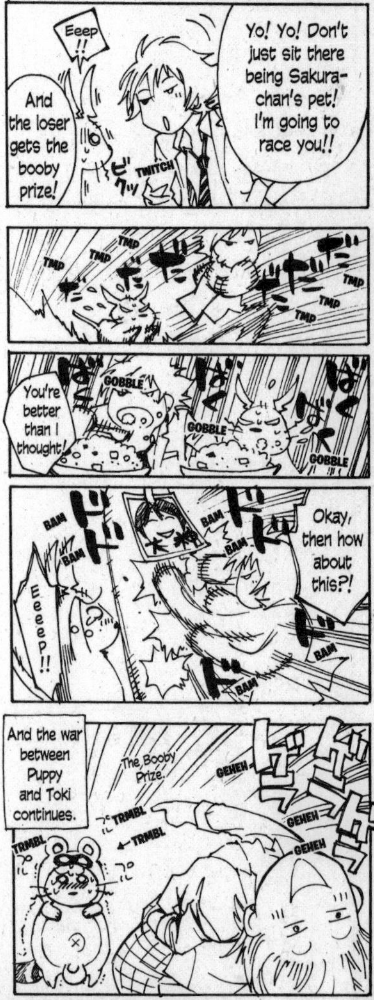

Yo! Yo! Don't just sit there being Sakura-chan's pet! I'm going to race you!!
Eeep!!
And the loser gets the booby prize!
TWITCH
TMP
TMP
TMP
TMP
TMP
TMP
GOBBLE
GOBBLE
GOBBLE
You're better than I thought!
Okay, then how about this?!
BAM
BAM
BAM
BAM
BAM
BAM
Eeeep!!
GEHEH
GEHEH
GEHEH
The Booby Prize.
TRMBL
TRMBL
TRMBL
And the war between Puppy and Toki continues.

The Road Home

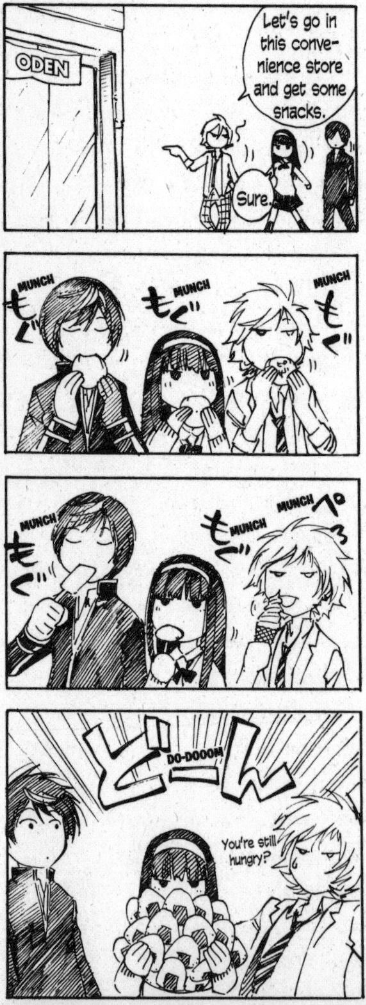

Let's go in this convenience store and get some snacks.
ODEN
Sure.
MUNCH
MUNCH
MUNCH
MUNCH
MUNCH
MUNCH
DO-DOOOM
You're still hungry?

Kamijyo Info

Start reading here!

Yo there! It's Kamijyo! Thanks for picking up *Code:Breaker 2*!! Every time I try to draw manga, I always write that I'm trying to make the most interesting manga I've ever drawn. And in that statement is truly an unabashed desire to make, what is to me, an unforgettable story. I feel that fortunately, *C:B 2* came out to have a large number of those types of stories. I hope that you all experience a wide range of feelings when you read it.

When I first started *C:B*, I had a lot of chances to reminisce about my high-school days, but to tell you the truth, all my memories of middle school, high school and college are so mixed up, I don't know which is which!! I almost wonder what kind of half-baked school life I actually had... °°

On the other hand, the time I'd go back to if I could, would be my high-school days! I feel that it would have been okay for high school to last ten years! That way, we could have had ten cultural fairs! But that's only if tests were cut back to about once a year...

Now, let's talk about the fun things that are coming up in volume 3! Guess what?! We're going to enter the Sakurakoji household! Sakura's secrets... And will we find out more about Ôgami and Toki?! And look for the entrance of a third *C:B*!

So let's meet again! See you!

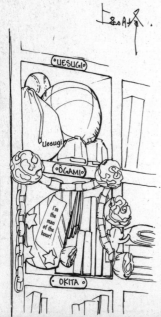

UESUGI

Uesugi

ÔGAMI

I'm the man of the hour!

OKITA

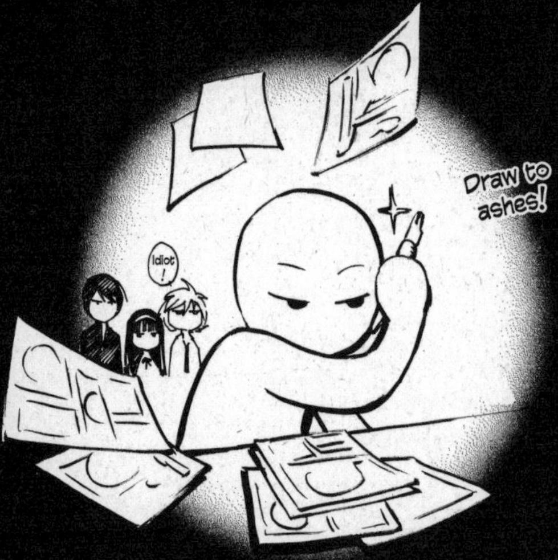
Draw to ashes!
Idiot!

■ **STAFF** ■

Shiba Tateoka, Shô Yashioka,
Kazuki Hirako, Joriimanma,
Takehiko Yamashita,
A. Taniguchi

Noguchi's "Momo-Hun" and "Ninnin" were Yashioka's, and Puppy-mon was Jorii's design!!

■ **COMICS DESIGN** ■

Masashi Hisamochi

Thanks to the editorial department and to all the other people who help support *Code:Breaker!* Thank you so much!!

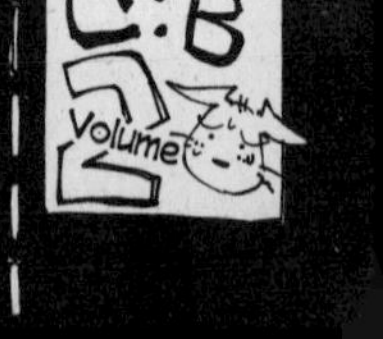
C:B
5
Volume

The Akimine Kamijyo Challenge!!

CODE:
Behind his smile is...
BREAKER
...live evil.

Gunma Prefecture/Miki Ogawa

Very well done Award

"One image that really brought out the darkness in Ôgami!!"

"Ohh, that was deep, Sakura-chan!"

"Thank you very much for drawing me as a good-looking guy."

"Toki must be so happy you drew him so handsome."

The world's Metal-Bending Champion
Code:Breaker Toki

Yamanashi Prefecture/ Kyôhei Kuribayashi

"If I was in Shibuya at the time and that happened, I'd point and laugh!"

Actually, he...
...got impaled by glass.
If that really happened...
Kamijyo-sensei, hang in there!
Ô-Ôgami-?
Sakura
From page 136, the Flame Woman.

Tokyo/Haruna Isogai

"The balance between black and white makes this very cool!"

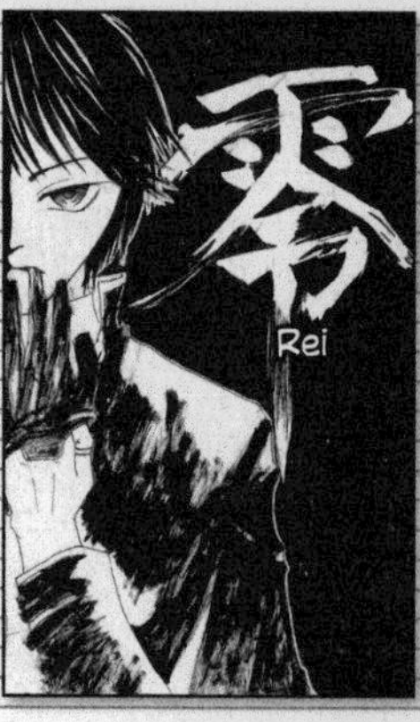
零
Rei

Gunma Prefecture/
Ritsu Tōdō

"Anf!"
("Thanks for the bone!")

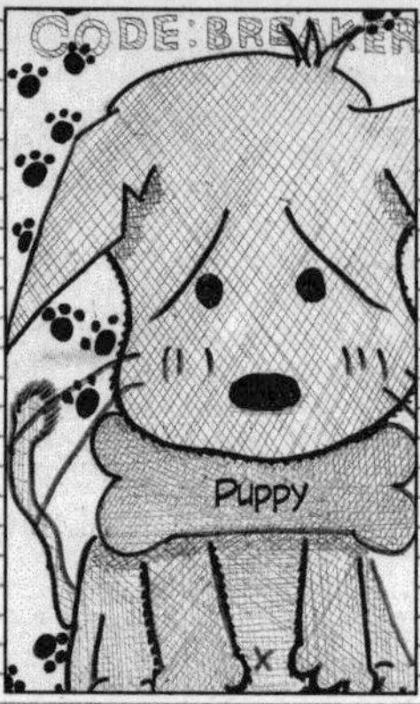
CODE:BREAKER
Puppy

Fukuoka Prefecture/
Tohsimitsu Aramaki

"This one has strong, sparkling eyes!"

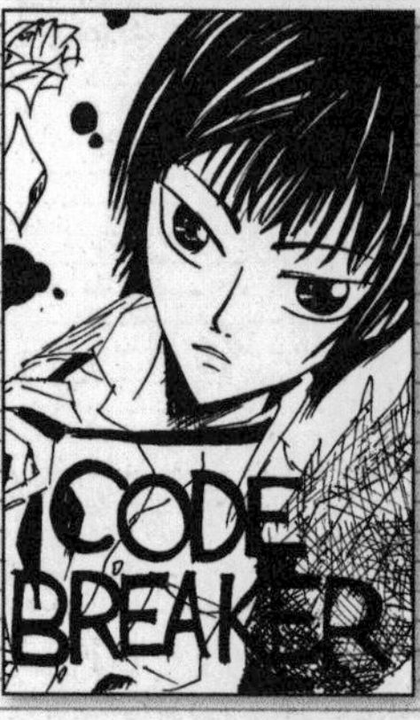
CODE
BREAKER

Kanagawa Prefecture/
Karin Hosaka

"I really like the contrast between the delicateness of his expression and the raging flames."

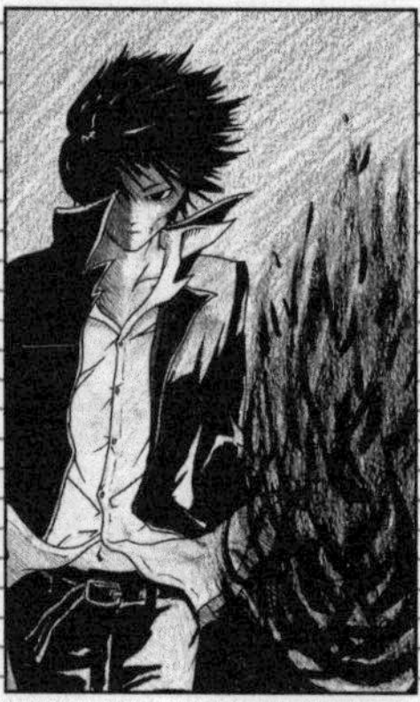

Tokyo/Yasuharu Kojima

"This 'sweet' Sakura-chan is really nice!"

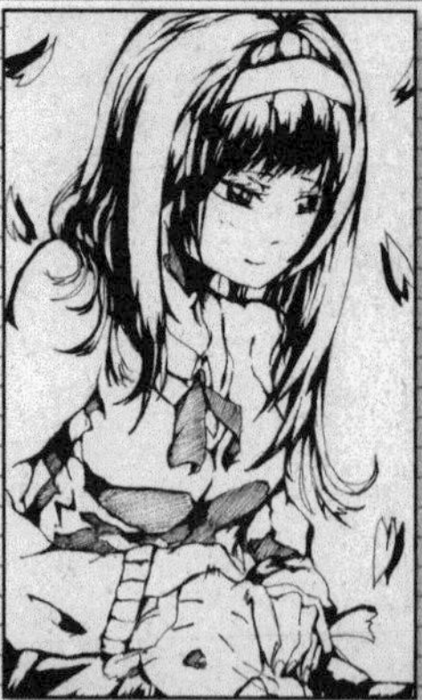

Osaka/Tōya Iwasaka

"Ohh! We just found another Jersey Lover!"

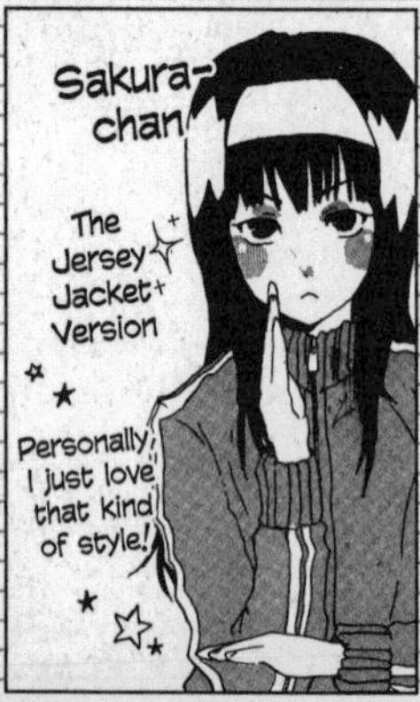
Sakura-chan
The Jersey Jacket Version
Personally, I just love that kind of style!

Aomori Prefecture/
Ramen-maru

CODE:BREAKE

Aichi Prefecture/
Shishuda

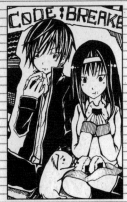

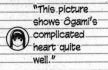

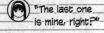

"The last one is mine, right?"

"This picture shows Ôgami's complicated heart quite well."

Okayama Prefecture/
Eri Shimpo

Rei
Dog
Keep up the fight!
Sakura
Toki

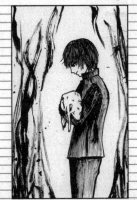

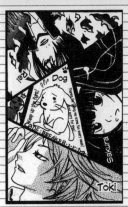

Hokkaido/Zakuro

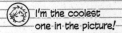

I'm the coolest one in the picture!

□ Looking for Submissions

We're looking for submissions!
We're open to your illustrations of Cøde:Breaker! The best ones we receive will be included in the graphic novels for Cøde:Breaker!

>Send to:
Del Rey Manga
1745 Broadway, 24-2
New York, NY 10019

Any letters and postcards you send means that your personal information such as your name, address, postal code, and other information you include will be handed over, as is, to the author. When you send mail, please keep that in mind.

* We also send Kamijyo your questions and words of encouragement!!

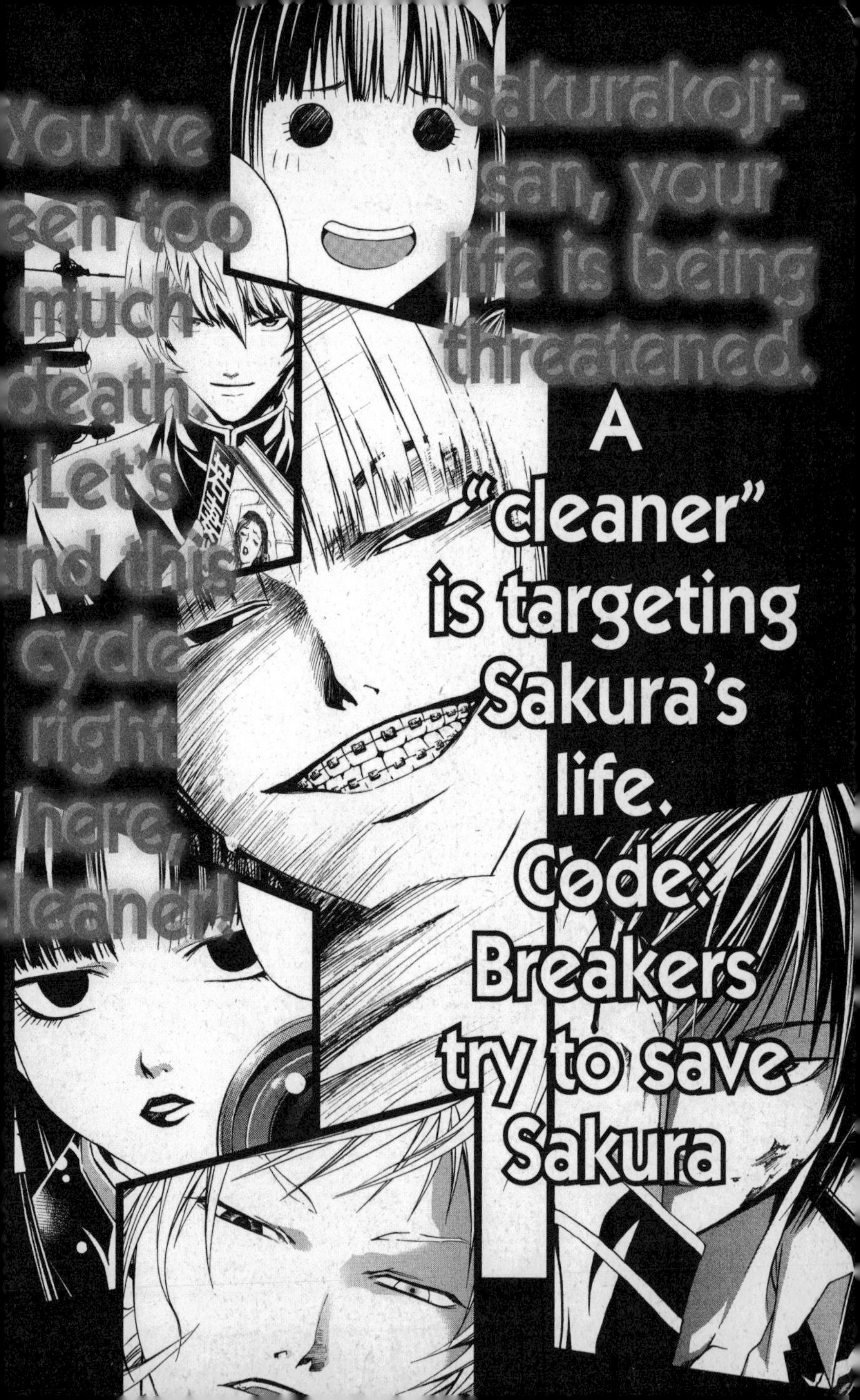
Sakurakoji-san, your life is being threatened.
You've een too much death. Let's nd this cycle right here, leaner!
A "cleaner" is targeting Sakura's life. Code: Breakers try to save Sakura

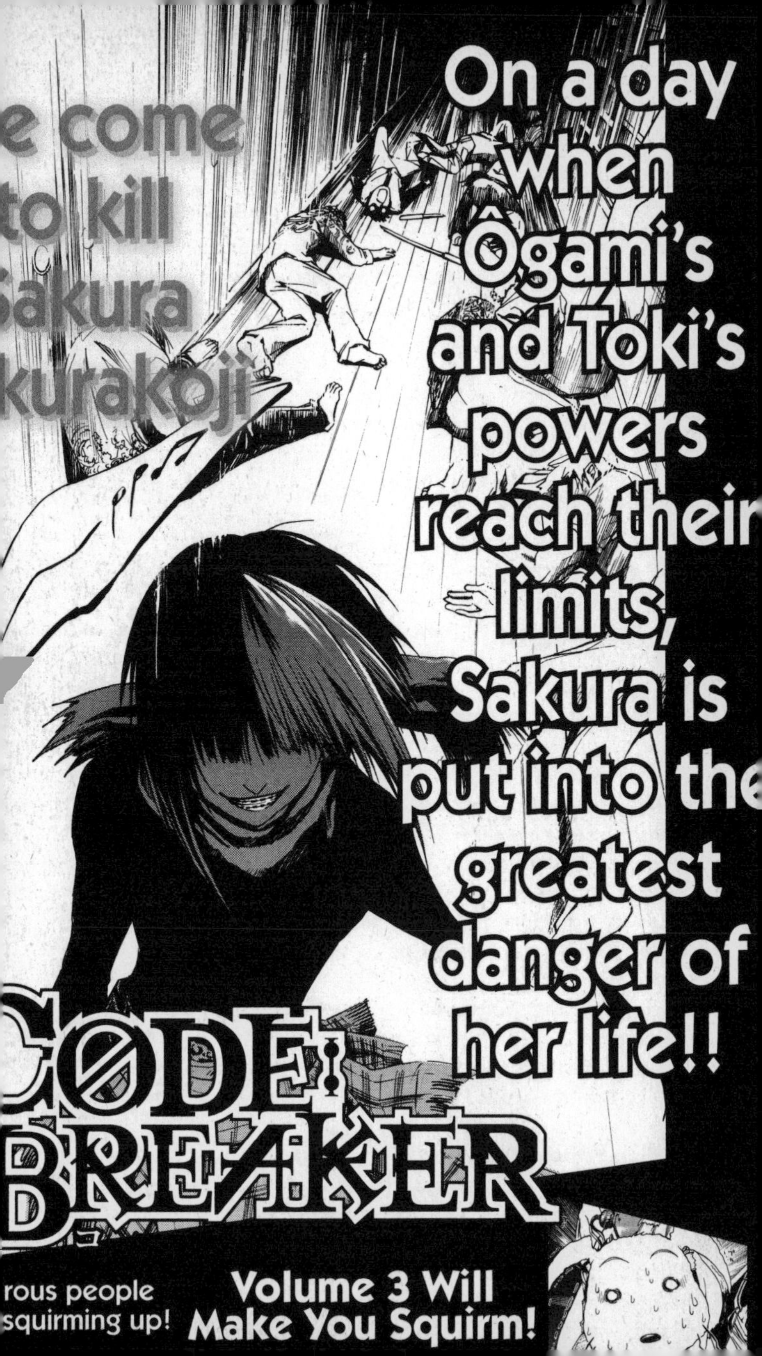

e come
to kill
akura
kurakoji
On a day when Ôgami's and Toki's powers reach their limits, Sakura is put into the greatest danger of her life!!
CODE:BREAKER
rous people
squirming up!
Volume 3 Will
Make You Squirm!

Translation Notes

Japanese is a tricky language for most Westerners, and translation is often more art than science. For your edification and reading pleasure, here are notes on some of the places where we could have gone in a different direction with our translation of the work, or where a Japanese cultural reference is used.

Yakuza, page 3
For those who don't watch Japanese gangster movies, the *Yakuza* is the Japanese word for their home-grown organized crime. Like the mafia, they are split into gangs who make their money on the despair of others—extortion, drugs, loan sharking, etc.

Mii-tan, Hii-tan, page 36
"Right" in Japanese is *migi*, and "left" in Japanese is *hidari*. It's from these two words that Mii-tan and Hii-tan come. The extra vowel comes out like a squeal of delight, and the *-tan* honorific is a cute variation of the diminutive *-chan* honorific.

Why does Sakura put up with it?, page 37
As you may have noticed, as a martial artist and with her strict sense of morality, Sakura takes rank seriously. Nenene is both an upperclassman (requiring respectful language), but also a member of the student-body leadership. Sakura is a lowly first-year student who neither wants to offend the higher-ranked Nenene, nor does she want to make waves. However, Nenene's actions are nowhere near normal—this is a scene played for laughs—and readers shouldn't come away thinking this is something that happens in Japanese high schools.

The Diet Building, page 48
The Japanese Diet (with a capital D) is the word for the Japanese congress. The Diet building is the Japanese equivalent of Capital Hill in the United States or the Houses of Parliament in the United Kingdom.

Deviation Value, Todai Admission, page 68
A high deviation value means that the students of a particular school are more likely to pass their entrance exams to get into the top-ranked universities. And the highest-ranked university in all of Japan is Tokyo University (*Tokyo Daigaku*), which is shortened to Todai. Most Japanese high schools don't even try to teach the high level of education required to enter Todai, so if one wants a chance at the prestigious university, the best way to learn

is to pass the rigorous tests to get into one of the best, exclusive preparatory high schools.

Tabata-sensei, page 85
In Japan, it is not just teachers, artisans, and doctors who are called *sensei*, but also politicians receive that honorific.

Bombay Blood Group, page 101
The Bombay Blood Group is an extremely rare variation of the ABO blood-type system that is said to appear in only one out of 250,000 people. It is slightly more common in India (1 out of 7,600), and it is named after Mumbai (formerly known as Bombay) where it was first discovered. In the Bombay group, the blood actually has antibodies that attack other blood types, so it is very important for people with Bombay Blood Group blood to receive transfusions only from other people with Bombay Group blood.

Hi-no-Taman, page 108
This is a Japanese pun of sorts. *Hi-no-tama* is the Japanese word for spark, and Japanese *sentai*-style entertainment (those groups of heroes that have about five or six members, each of whom are assigned a color) usually use the word "Man" somewhere in the title of the show's name. So in this case, they simply added an "n" to *hi-no-tama* to make the name of a fire-wielding hero.

Spetsnaz, page 110
An elite division of the GRU, Russian special forces, that specialize in behind-the-lines tactics, hand-to-hand combat, survivalism, anti-insurgency, and other tough military tasks. They are known as some of the best and most brutal military forces on the planet.

Combustible Trash, page 156
Japan separates its trash into combustible trash and noncombustible trash for nonrecyclable items. Each group, combustible, noncombustible, and recyclable items are picked up on different days of the week.

Live Evil, page 195
The original line in this piece of fan art was *aku aru,* which is a cute, alliterative way to say, "there is evil." I decided that the best way to represent this Japanese play on words in English is to use the palindrome, "live evil."

TOMARE!

[STOP!]

You're going the wrong way!

Manga is a completely different type of reading experience.

To start at the *beginning*, go to the *end*!

That's right! Authentic manga is read the traditional Japanese way—from right to left. Exactly the *opposite* of how American books are read. It's easy to follow: Just go to the other end of the book, and read each page—and each panel—from the right side to the left side, starting at the top right. Now you're experiencing manga as it was meant to be!